REFUGE

A TRUE STORY OF STEADFAST FAITH AMIDST THE HORROR OF RUSSIAN OCCUPATION

LIANE I. BROWN

REFUGE

A TRUE STORY OF STEADFAST FAITH AMIDST THE HORROR OF RUSSIAN OCCUPATION

REDEMPTION
PRESS

ABOUT THE AUTHOR

As a ten-year-old girl, Liane Guddat watched Hitler's motorcade pass by their home in Insterburg, East Prussia. Within a few short months, Insterburg was smoldering in ruins when Mutti (Liane's mother) and her four children scrambled over bricks, broken glass, and scorched beams as they tried to escape the ravages of WWII. Although not a Nazi, Liane's father had been drafted into the German army and became a prisoner of war.

Hitler's Third Reich of Germany, in its corruption and despotism, subjected many of its own people to terrible abuse before it began to crumble, abandoning them to a new kind of holocaust. Despite brutal treatment, harsh conditions, near starvation, and bodies riddled with boils, and when others around them languished in despair, the Guddats lived as faithful servants of God, and He brought great glory to Himself through them. Liane tells the true story of her East German family's steadfast faith and struggle for survival amidst the horror of Russian occupation in her autobiographies *Refuge* and *From Fear to Freedom*.

In her award-winning books, Liane Guddat Brown proclaims God's sustaining grace proven through a family torn apart by war. "We still thank the Lord for bringing us to America," she says. "For it was only by His grace that we survived at all, and, even more, that we would be allowed to live among the most privileged people in the world."

DEDICATION

To the Lord, who never fails us.
In memory of my parents
whose steadfastness in their Christian walk
is a constant inspiration to me.
To Dieter, Marlies, and Udo
who were too young to remember.
To countless Germans
whose stories have never been told.

He that dwelleth in the secret place of the most High
Shall abide under the shadow of the Almighty.
I will say of the LORD, He is my refuge and my fortress:
My God; in him will I trust.
(Psalm 91:1–2)

CONTENTS

PREFACE

I have been asked hundreds of times what I appreciate most about being a citizen of the United States. My answer to that question is always the same—freedom. I have lived under an oppressive regime. Consequently, I now have a great love for my country.

This book is a "thank You" to the Lord for leading us to America, the land in which my family has found true freedom. It is also a "thank you" to many of our American friends who encouraged us to write about some of our experiences. May we never take our freedom for granted, and may we do everything to preserve it.

This book is based on my mother's written personal accounts, extensive interviews with Kätchen, who lived in West Germany, and my own experiences. *Refuge* was published as a surprise gift for Emmy's eighty-third birthday. Every incident is true, and the names are real.

Division of the Third Reich

■■■ The border of Germany prior to August 1939.

The territory that became West Germany (Federal Republic of Germany) after the war.

The territory that became East Germany (German Democratic Republic) after the war.

The territories that became parts of Poland and the USSR when the Third Reich fell.

DENMARK

Copenhagen

NORTH SEA

Hamburg

NETHERLANDS

GERMANY

BELGIUM

Bochum

LUX.

Frankfurt

FRANCE

Munich

Zurich

BALTIC SEA

Memel

USSR

Heydekrug

Insterburg

Konigsberg

Danzig

EAST PRUSSIA

Lippehne

Berlin

POLAND

Warsaw

Kuestrin

Prague

CZECHOSLOVAKIA

Vienna

AUSTRIA

HUNGARY

GERMAN WORDS AND EXPRESSIONS

Vati – Daddy

Mutti – Mommy

Opi – Grandpa

Omi – Grandma

Onkel – Uncle

Tante – Aunt

Schäfle – little sheep

Pittimaus – Marlies's nickname

Herr – Mr.

Frau – Mrs.

Guten Tag! – Good day!

Auf Wiedersehen – goodbye

danke schön – thank you

kaputt – broken, smashed

komm – come

nicht gut – not good

Dummkopf – dumbbell, blockhead

Russian words and expressions

rabota – work

daway rabotay – get to work

1

THE BEGINNING OF THE END

"Frau Guddat!" A familiar deep voice called into our dimly lit bomb shelter. "Are you down there?"

Mutti called back an answer, barely loud enough to be heard. I saw a tall silhouette moving down the spiral stone steps, coming slowly toward us.

"Pastor Walter! What are you doing here?" Mutti sounded more weary than surprised.

"I had to come and see if you and your children survived through the night. Praise the Lord! He has been gracious in protecting you again."

"Yes," Mutti replied, "the Lord has been good to us. We are all safe."

One of the pastor's hands dropped almost unconsciously onto my little brother's head. His voice was hesitant when he finally spoke. "Four children and their mother are no longer on earth today. Last night they joined the angels in heaven." A long pause followed before he gave us more information. "They were the newest members of our church. In place of their house, I found a large bomb crater that has also become their grave. When I saw their geese still alive, standing on the rim of the crater, honking, it was rather difficult for me to understand God's ways."

"The baby was only fourteen days old!" Mutti said sadly as she drew Udo, my youngest brother, closer to her. "Why must the innocent suffer? Four children! What did they do to start this war? Why do we as civilians have to spend night after night in a cold bomb shelter while a war is being fought above us, and the enemy is successful in destroying our very existence?"

Raising his bushy eyebrows, Pastor Walter was about to speak, but Mutti hastened on. "Please—wait!" she whispered. "Our air raid guard is just entering the cellar. He is a Nazi, and everyone fears him. I don't want him to report you!"

"Thank you for the warning, but I have learned to be careful about what I say." A shadow of a smile touched the pastor's face. "Seeing spies in the congregation during every service has taught me not to jeopardize my life or that of anyone else. I have had to learn to bridle my tongue without becoming a compromiser. Let's just have a word of prayer before I leave to check on others of our congregation."

"Pray for me too!" a stranger pleaded. "Please pray for me! Both of my children were killed last night, my husband was shot at the front line four weeks ago. I have nothing to live for now! Nothing! Why didn't the bombs take me too?"

The stranger's weeping and sobbing rent my young heart. Carefully stepping over sleeping children, bundles, and suitcases, Pastor Walter slowly made his way to the lady. He took her hand and besought the Lord to comfort and strengthen her now and in the coming days. The lady wept bitterly as he talked quietly to her.

When the guard turned on the lights, we realized that our shelter was packed with people. Some of them sat motionless on their suitcases, others lay on the cold cement floor. Those who had stumbled into our shelter during the night with burning clothes and bleeding hands and faces were writhing in pain. No one had time to find cover. The bombs had fallen before the sirens were sounded. I thought back to the endless night before. Even though my ears had seemed to explode every time a bomb burst, I felt something miraculous had happened when I realized that we were still alive.

"We will go to my uncle's farm in the country today, Schäfle," Mutti told me. "For weeks we have spent every night in this damp cellar. It is becoming too unhealthy and difficult for all of us. We used to have time to rush down here before the bombs fell, but during the past few nights, the enemies have become more skilled in their surprise attacks. I have prayed again and again for guidance, and I believe that this is what the Lord wants us to do. We'll walk to Omi's house—I trust the Lord has kept her safe last night also—and see if one of her friends can take us by wagon to the country. Even if the Nazis had not confiscated our car, it seems we would not be able to drive through town this morning. All the reports are rather grim in regard to what our beautiful city looks like today."

Insterburg was smoldering as Mutti and we four children scrambled over bricks, broken glass, and scorched beams to my grandparents' house. Many homes were still burning as people stood in shock in the streets and watched the final flaming destruction of their businesses and belongings. A few firemen were aiming their water hoses at the tallest flames. But what could a fire department accomplish in a catastrophe of this magnitude? It seemed as if the whole town was an inferno. Devastation was everywhere! The huge Lutherkirche on the Marktplatz, however, showed no scars from the worst attack ever on Insterburg. The radio told us that both British and Russian planes had bombarded our city last night. Fortunately, we found Omi to be all right, but very frightened and worn out.

We made it safely to my uncle's farm and, for a short while, life was very peaceful for us even though we could still hear the explosions in our hometown. In the distance we saw the "Christmas tree" flares the enemy placed in the sky at night to light up targets. I knew it was impossible for me to hear the sirens of Insterburg, but my ears were constantly filled with that eerie sound, and my body still anticipated being jolted by the impact of the bombs.

The day we arrived back in Insterburg, Mutti's friend Kätchen came for a brief visit. She had just wanted to know if we were still alive. "We just returned home after seven days in the country," Mutti told her. "We could no longer endure living in the bomb shelter. Is everything still all right with you and the boys at the parsonage?"

"Yes, praise be to the Lord! Our small village has not been hit. I just came to Insterburg today to get my travel permit and to check on you and the children. I plan to move to my father's house in Lippehne until it is safe to return to East Prussia. I am sure the enemy will never seize a town that close to Berlin. Our armed forces won't let that happen. But right here, we are living too close to the Russian border and might be overrun any day should our front lines weaken."

"Do you really think that could happen? We are being told every day that an enemy will 'never set foot on East Prussian soil.'"

"I used to believe that, Emmy, but I no longer do. Things are becoming too critical at the border. Why don't you and your children come with me to Lippehne?"

"Kätchen, do you really mean it? I have been asking the Lord for guidance for days now. I know we have to leave here, but I had no idea where we could go. We just can't take the nightly bombings anymore. All my relatives live in the northern part of East Prussia, as you know. Some of them live in Berlin, but neither of those places are safe right now. Are you really serious about your offer, Kätchen?"

"Of course."

"Thank you, thank you, Kätchen! Your offer is an answer to prayer!" Mutti went to her friend and hugged her. "But will your dad have room for all of us? I am planning to take my mother-in-law with us wherever we go—I can't leave her here alone in this burning city."

"My dad's farm is small, and he has lived there alone since my mother's death. His house is not very big either, but his heart is. I am sure he'll take us all in. I'll write to him today and tell him that you are coming. In the meantime, God be with you till we meet again! We have a great God! He will protect all of us. And He will watch over our husbands, too, wherever they might be defending our country right now."

"See you in Lippehne!" Mutti called as Kätchen walked out of the house.

Several days later, on a cool night in August, Mutti, my grandmother, my two brothers, my sister, and I packed into a crowded train. Our papers had been checked during the daylight hours, and we had been told in which car to ride. Many crying mothers and children were turned away because they did not have travel permits. Hoping to jump a train and escape to the West, some of them had been camping at the railroad station for days.

At midnight the train finally began to move slowly out of the station. It was an unusual night for our town. There were no "Christmas trees" in the sky above. No bombs were whizzing through the air. No sirens were causing our hearts to jump from fear as the train engine pulled us along in utter darkness.

Beautiful Insterburg! Vati's hometown! Trakehner horses had made it almost as world famous as the nearby city of Königsberg where all the Prussian Kaiser were crowned. The many lovely parks and man-made lakes gave recreation to its fifty thousand inhabitants. My brothers, my sister, and I were born there, but as our train crawled out of the city that night, everything was in turmoil. Thousands had lost their lives during the past few weeks. In the darkness of the night, one could still see yellow flames briefly shooting into the air to light up chaotic ruins before vanishing again.

It was raining in torrents the next afternoon as our train, bulging with homeless and hungry people, pulled into Lippehne. War had not yet reached this town near Berlin. It seemed strange to see all the buildings intact. The rain and damp air were refreshing after the stuffy train ride, and our hearts became peaceful. But how would we ever make any progress if the wheels of the wartime baby carriage continued to fall off and roll into the gutter? The carriage appeared to be made of cardboard. With everyone's help, however, our drenched group of refugees arrived at the old pastor's house.

"Shall I knock on the door?" Mutti asked us with hesitation in her voice. Her natural curls were even curlier now that they were wet. "I don't know the man! What will we do if he does not take us in? Where will we go? We are homeless! You children don't have a father, I don't have a husband, and we have no home!" She paused for a moment and took a deep breath. "But we have a God in heaven who watches over us."

With her right hand, Mutti wiped some of the rain off her face, then knocked on the green door. Omi stood next to me with her head bowed. She must have been praying. After the longest moments in our lives, the farm door opened. The elderly gentleman inside looked bewildered by our drenched group and my crying little brother.

"Guten Tag, Herr Lehmann! I am Emmy Guddat, a friend of your daughter, Kätchen. We are the ones Kätchen wrote you about—she told you we would be coming."

The kind-looking man scrambled for words. "I have not heard from my daughter in several weeks. Her letter must have been lost. But come on in! Get out of the rain!"

After brushing some of the water out of our soaked clothes, we entered the long hallway. Mutti told Mr. Lehmann why we had left Insterburg and asked if it would be possible for us to stay with him until our hometown became safe again.

"Of course! You are welcome in my home—you may stay here as long as you like! And please call me Onkel Lehmann," the elderly preacher told us with a smile and twinkling eyes.

Mutti was visibly touched by the stranger's selfless response. With tears welling up in her eyes and a choking voice she said, "Thank you! Thank you, Onkel Lehmann! I don't know what else I can say."

Mutti then shared with Kätchen's father that she and his daughter had met in the hospital in Insterburg when their oldest sons were born. She told him about the bombing attacks and that Kätchen and his two grandsons were still living safely in their parsonage in the country. They were presently awaiting permission from the government to move to Lippehne. His son-in-law, the preacher, was still somewhere serving his country, and Kätchen had not heard from him in some time. When she finished, Onkel Lehmann showed us the part of the house where we would stay.

"I will let you make yourselves at home in the two rooms on the second floor," he said as he motioned for us to follow him upstairs. "Here we are. These are your rooms. They are rather small, but I think you will be able to manage."

"We will, and thank you so very much!"

"Mutti, look! Beds! Real beds!" Dieter burst out. "Can I go to bed now? No more bunks in the air raid shelter! Look, Mutti! Look!"

"Yes, you may take a nap, Dieter. But first you must take off your wet clothes! Open your rucksack and take out dry clothes—at least I hope they are still dry."

"I will! I will, Mutti!"

In his excitement, he could hardly open the buckle of his rucksack and didn't seem to mind at all when Omi came to his rescue.

"Does Onkel Lehmann have animals on his farm, Mutti?"

"I don't know, son. You can ask him later."

This home was so peaceful! *Thank You, Lord!* No sirens pierced our ears. We didn't hear airplanes above us. There seemed to be nothing to fear. Our rooms in our Insterburg home had been huge, but right then I was glad to trade them and the shelter for these tiny ones.

Just as we finished changing into dry clothes, the preacher invited us downstairs for cake, coffee, and goat's milk. Some of his church friends had dropped in, and we learned that it was Onkel Lehmann's birthday. He received gifts of flowers, homemade cakes, and all types of food.

We hadn't seen real joy in anyone with whom we had been in contact recently, and I felt totally overwhelmed by seeing these people bubbling over with the joy of the Lord. They sang hymns and talked for hours about the blessings of the Lord.

My soul was in turmoil. How could it be so peaceful here when my hometown in East Prussia was lying in almost total ruin? Insterburg was a German city, just like Lippehne. It didn't make sense to me. Was Hitler really the cause of all these problems as some adults said? I wondered why our leader wasn't protecting our country and us. In the Hitler Youth, I learned that our Führer loved us, and we should return his love with all our hearts. Only by following him would we bring true happiness and fulfillment to our lives. How I had enjoyed all the marching and the sports programs! Being fit to follow our leader was every young person's goal.

But why was I so confused? Why did I have to leave my home and my friends? Onkel Lehmann was a very kind man, and I liked his little farm, but I'd rather be home and have things the way they used to be.

"Liane," Mutti asked, "what are you dreaming about? Would you like another piece of Onkel Lehmann's birthday cake?"

"Yes, please, Mutti."

Within a few days, we began to grow acquainted with Lippehne. It was a picture-postcard town, almost completely surrounded by three big lakes. Private gardens and promenades hugged the shorelines. Onkel Lehmann had gardens located at two of the lakes, one of which had a small cottage nestled under big apple trees near the water. A short boardwalk led through the reeds to his tied-up boat and the open water.

Dieter loved to catch crabs with his hands in the shallow, sandy lake bottom.

Since Mutti had never prepared crabs, Onkel Lehmann taught her how to cook the delicacy. During the week, Mutti and Omi helped the preacher with the garden work and the canning while Dieter and I attended school. After church on Sundays, when the weather was favorable, we all rowed the boat around the lakes. Our new friends joined us with their boats, and in parade-like fashion, we paddled from one lake to another, singing hymns and folk songs and enjoying God's creation. It was great for us children to dangle our feet over the side of the boat and have them pulled through the cool water.

Onkel Lehmann was a wonderful teacher, and Dieter quickly learned how to feed and milk the goats. The two friends had such good times when working in the barn. I often sat on the hay and watched them. Does Onkel Lehmann miss his wife as much as Mutti misses Vati? I wondered.

"Tante Lehmann went to heaven two years ago," he told me when I asked him. "I miss her very much. But now the Lord has sent you to help me here, and I am so thankful for that. I don't know how I ever managed before all of you came."

One bright morning, Mutti told us that it was Udo's birthday. "Happy birthday, my little son!" Mutti said to her youngest child. "You are getting to be a big boy. You are one year old today. Let's see if you can take your first steps all by yourself. Oops! Down he goes!" Mutti helped Udo stand up and he tried again, but he couldn't take more than two steps at a time.

In the afternoon we all celebrated Udo's birthday at a park along the lake. It was a warm day, and instead of sitting on the blanket that was spread out on the lawn, we children preferred to sit on the grass. Udo looked so cute on his special day in short brown pants and an orange pullover. His hair was blond and straight like mine, and he was always happy and playful.

"Omi, your carrot cake is so-o-o good! May I have another piece?" Dieter begged.

"Of course, you may." As she cut a piece for him, my hand reached for another one also.

"I wonder where Emil is on this twenty-fifth day of August," Mutti said to her mother-in-law. "I wish he could see his son today, and his other three children too. Four months is a long time for children not to see their father."

"Yes, Emmy, I was just thinking about him. I can't stop praying for him and his safety. The Lord has been so good to all of us and has protected us from the bombs in Insterburg. I know He will reunite all of you. I just pray that it will be soon. You and Emil have been faithful and true to the Lord, and our God has promised to honor and bless those who really love Him and live for Him. I know that He will do that."

"Mutti, look! Quick, quick, look! Udo is walking!" Dieter called excitedly. "He is walking all by himself!" Indeed he was. We all sat and watched. My little brother looked so proud as he waddled through the grass without assistance.

At times Mutti looked rather discouraged, and she seldom smiled. She continued to write to Vati but never received a letter from him. Hearing bombs explode in the distance caused her and all of us to become more solemn again. The earth would shake and our windows would rattle. We began to wonder if bombs would hit Lippehne too. "We must pray much for Vati," Mutti told us.

The months passed slowly. Then, on a cold, windy day in November, Kätchen and her two sons arrived in our new hometown. Onkel Lehmann was thrilled to welcome his daughter and grandsons. For hours we celebrated their homecoming, even though they were very tired from the long train ride. Mutti became more cheerful again now that she could talk to her friend.

"Schäfle," Mutti said one day, "Kätchen has offered to help take care of you children while I make a quick trip back to Insterburg. I want to see if I can bring some of our belongings to Lippehne. I especially need my sewing machine. It will be a little extra work for you, but I know you will be able to manage for a few days. What do you think?"

"That will be fine with me as long as you promise to come back. If a bomb hits your train or you are captured by the Russians, what are we going to do then?"

"Trust in the Lord, my daughter! Trust in the Lord! He will take care of you and me and Vati. Do you believe that?"

"I'll try, but it is hard not to worry about you."

After Mutti returned from Insterburg, she was not the same Mutti who had left. She seemed different somehow. Her face looked sad and tired. "One side of our house has been ripped away by bombs, but I was still able to get my sewing machine and a few other things. Those possessions don't mean anything though, Kätchen. It is all earthly stuff. What does it matter whether we have it or not?"

"What happened, Emmy? Why are you so depressed?"

"I can't get out of my mind what I heard about the small village of Nemmersdorf in East Prussia."

"Nemmersdorf! That is not far from Insterburg. What happened there?"

"Well, the atrocities that occurred in that village are beyond description. Everybody in Insterburg is talking about it, and I haven't been able to sleep well since I heard those reports."

"Perhaps, Emmy, we shouldn't talk about something that troubles you so."

"Oh no, Kätchen, I believe we have to talk about it. We have to pray that these things will not happen to us."

"All right. I leave it up to you then."

"Well, when the Russian front broke into Germany for the first time along the border of East Prussia, the troops stormed into the village and started massacring civilians. All the women and young girls, down to the age of eight, were first raped and then either shot or dismembered. Several were raped and nailed to barn doors, naked. When the Germans regained control of that part of East Prussia, forty-eight hours later, they did not find one civilian alive. All the men, women, and children had been murdered. One of the villagers was found later in another town. She was the only one who managed to escape."

"That is just horrible, Emmy. Now I see why you are so worried. This can happen to anybody who is still in East Prussia." Kätchen's face was grave. "Aren't you glad we came to Lippehne? But think of our friends and your relatives back there! How we must pray for them."

"Yes, we must. We must pray without ceasing."

"Tell me though, Emmy. Couldn't these stories be just rumors?"

"Oh no, they aren't. A nurse who lives in Insterburg is from Nemmersdorf. When she heard about the massacre, she went to her village to check on her parents. She found her seventy-four-year-old father and seventy-two-year-old mother among the bodies of the villagers. There are many other witnesses too."

"How can Hitler let this happen to his people? This is inconceivable!" Mutti and Kätchen continued to talk, but I no longer heard what they said. My mind was on the gruesome war account. Would the Russians do that to us if they overran us? Everybody said they would never come as far as Lippehne. But what would happen if they did? Would we all be murdered? Why was there always so much talk about death when I had barely begun to live?

The refugees continued to flood into Lippehne, providing me with plenty of food for thought. My aunt, the wife of Vati's twin brother, came among them one day. Eventually she and Omi moved into a house with some kind people directly across the street from Onkel Lehmann's farmhouse, which was beginning to get very crowded. December brought us another friend from Insterburg, Emil Schmidtke, the choir director of our old church. Last summer he and his wife had both made plans to meet in Lippehne if the war should separate them. He took up residence in the attic of Onkel Lehmann's house. My parents had been friends with "Onkel Emil" for a long time. With so many of our own people and old friends around, Lippehne seemed even more like home. I still couldn't keep my thoughts off the terrible stories we'd heard though. I spent much of my time thinking about it, and one day my preoccupied mind got me in trouble at school.

Dieter's and my school was located right across the street from us, and we could dash to class in seconds. My classmates, however, had built strong relationships with their friends throughout their lives and didn't want to associate with me. I had been assigned a seat in the very last row of the classroom. Our hands had to be placed on the desk, one on top of the other, at all times; only when we raised them to participate in answering or asking questions, or when we were writing, were we permitted to change their position. The teachers were as strict as those in Insterburg, and they demanded total obedience. Each one had to be greeted with an outstretched, raised arm and the words "Heil, Hitler." It didn't matter where one met them—in town or somewhere on the school grounds. Upon the teacher's entrance into the classroom, all the students jumped to their feet, stood at attention, and greeted him.

It was difficult for me to adjust to the new school, especially with so many new and troubling events to think about. My grades were satisfactory, I suppose, but I didn't have a sense of belonging. One day I found myself not raising my arm to say "Heil, Hitler" with the rest of the class. The teacher noticed that immediately and called me to the front. Forty students turned to stare at me as I made my way out of my seat toward him.

"You didn't say 'Heil, Hitler'!" he yelled, his face bright red with anger. "You disobeyed this teacher! You showed defiance for our country's leader! Why? Why? Why-y-y?" With his shouts echoing from the walls, he slapped my face so hard that I almost lost my balance. My head pounded and ached with pain, and the teacher's red finger marks still burned my face when I returned home from school that afternoon. The incident took place twelve days after my eleventh birthday.

Throughout the following day, thunder-like sounds could be heard in the distance while homeless people continued to pour through our town. They were not well-liked, although some people were kind to them. The original residents of Lippehne wished the refugees would just go back where they came from. The displaced, bewildered people were met with much suspicion from many townspeople. Why had they come? Couldn't they have stayed at home? Where would they live? Were they going to eat our food? Did they have money? Why did they all look so poor, dirty, and tattered? Few had any answers to these questions, but *we* knew why they had come! We continually heard of clashes between residents of Lippehne and the refugees, however. School was canceled, and the unwelcome visitors moved into the school buildings and gym by the hundreds. That change of events pleased me. At least I didn't have to face that cruel teacher for a while.

2

CROSS FIRE!

The rumblings of war seemed to be following the refugee treks toward our town. In the distance, exploding bombs once again caused the sky to light up at night as airplanes rumbled and whined through the sky. Roars from the approaching battles set all of Lippehne to trembling. "It feels like an earthquake," people said. "Is this going to be the beginning of the end?"

Broadcasting over the radio throughout the day, the mayor assured us, "We will alert our citizenry of danger and announce the safety measures the town has taken to protect the public should anything unforeseen happen."

"Schäfle, please take care of your brothers and sister for an hour or so. I want to go to city hall and see what kind of emergency preparations our town has made for us," Mutti told me.

"You have to bundle up, Mutti," I suggested. "It is bitter cold outside today."

We had barely settled down in the warm living room to play school when Mutti returned, frozen through and through and rather upset.

"What is the matter, Emmy?" Kätchen asked. "What happened? What did they say to you?"

"Do you really want to know what Herr Schwarz, the Nazi official, said to me? While sitting smugly behind his polished desk, he glanced at me over his gold-rimmed glasses, leaned forward, and said without feeling, 'My dear Frau Guddat, as the brave wife of a German soldier, surely you are not going to panic! Those refugees from the East who have flooded our town should be chased back where they came from. They are here just to upset the people! Your fear of falling into the hands of the Russians is totally unnecessary.

"'Everything is in readiness in case of danger. Special trains and buses are at the railroad station to transport mothers and children to safety. These precautions have been taken just in case the enemy should advance as far as Lippehne, but we don't foresee that at all. So don't worry! Just go home to your children and remain calm. There is absolutely no danger!'"

That conversation took place on January 29, 1945, at 12:00 p.m. By 2:00 p.m. the news was racing like brush fire through the streets that everyone must evacuate the city within two hours. "Let's try to be ready to leave in fifteen minutes, Kätchen." Mutti was already flying about the house. "The train will be too crowded if we get there any later."

"Yes, I agree. We have to get there early."

After putting on several layers of winter clothing, I dressed my sister while Mutti bundled up Udo. We quickly grabbed our green rucksacks that had been packed for days and dashed downstairs. Onkel Lehmann said a brief prayer before we left.

Outside the house, we put my seventeen-month-old brother and four-year-old sister in a wooden box that was placed on top of the sled. The railroad station was only two miles away. Mutti pulled the sled with one hand, struggling with two bundles in the other. Dieter and I helped steady the load as best we could, but again and again the sled tipped over in the ten inches of freshly fallen snow. The little ones were crying by the time we finally fought our way to the end of our street.

But why were these people coming toward us? I wondered. The railroad station was located in the direction we were going.

"No trains! No trains at the station!" sobbed one woman. She was almost bent to the ground, struggling to pull a handcart in which her old mother was seated. The older lady looked lifeless from the cold.

"They lied! They lied! The Nazis lied to us!" yelled someone else. "They all took off by train at one o'clock! Liars! Liars! We'll all die, and they are safe."

As these reports registered in the shocked minds of people all around, many decided to return to their homes. Others like us, in disbelief, continued to battle the snow toward the railroad station. My little brother and sister were crying constantly. They continued to topple off the sled and their faces were red from the stinging snow.

"Mutti, I want to go home. I am cold," pleaded my oldest brother. The struggle was too much even for a seven-year-old. In the distance we heard bombs exploding and rumblings that sounded like thunder.

"Frau Guddat!" called a neighbor, who with her two children was stomping through the snow against the stream of people. "My children and I are just coming back from the station. There is not one train on the tracks. Thousands of people are at the station. They are freezing and crying and still waiting for a train. We have decided to go back home." She reached us and we all halted. "Hitler will come and hold the enemy back. I don't believe that our leader will forsake us. He will help us. You'll see. He'll come with his secret weapons and push the enemy back. In the meantime we'll be safe at home."

Kätchen and her sons were also suffering from the cold. "Let's all return home," she suggested. "We can't get very far in this snow, and where will we spend the night if we do continue in this trek? It will be dark in a short time."

"I agree." Mutti's weariness could be heard in her voice. "Let's all go home, get a good night's rest, and start out early in the morning."

Silently, except for the little ones crying, our group began to struggle back to the small farm. We noticed that all our neighbors were returning home also.

Moments before we reached the farm, shocking news began traveling from person to person—we must surrender! Only surrender will save us and our town! White flags have to be hung out of the windows!

"Surrender?" Onkel Emil shouted. "Where is Hitler with his army and secret weapons? Can't he defend our country?" Everyone was stunned by the news that we must surrender.

After shaking the snow off our clothes and shoes, we went into the living room, where I tried to calm my little sister and brother. Both had wet, icy faces, and their fingers and toes were red and puffy. In their suffering they sobbed so hard that their little bodies trembled. While Onkel Lehmann rekindled the fire in the tile stove, Mutti and Kätchen hurriedly ripped flags of surrender from white sheets.

"Surrender? What does that really mean?" Mutti asked everyone. "Are we just handing ourselves over to the enemy? That is the most terrible act possible for any human being. Are we handing ourselves over to the Russians? We can't do that! We have to get away from here! Will Lippehne become another Nemmersdorf? The thought is simply unbearable!"

"We tried to get away, Emmy, and you saw how far we got." Kätchen's face was drawn and white.

I was lost in my own horrible thoughts while Mutti and Kätchen silently hung the flags of surrender out of the windows on the two sides of the corner house that faced the streets. Suddenly a great explosion caused the whole house to shake. Fear brought everyone scrambling to the living room. As we all tried to get seated near the stove, someone knocked rapidly on the front door. Onkel Lehmann went to open it.

"May we stay with you tonight, Herr Lehmann? My children and I are afraid!" we heard an anxious voice pleading.

"Of course! Come on in!"

Everyone in the room extended a warm welcome to the neighbors. In our unlit room, they appeared as shadows because, just as in Insterburg, there was blackout at night so that enemy bombers could not find our city. Not long after the neighbors' arrival, Omi and my aunt arrived to stay with us until we all knew for sure what was going to happen. We all settled down as best we could, no one saying a word, but just listening to the thundering explosions moving closer and closer to Lippehne.

Mutti and the four of us were huddled on the couch. At one point I heard part of her whispered prayers, "Lord, please take all of us! Don't let one of my children stay behind alone!"

I hoped Mutti didn't mean what she was praying! As another bomb whistled through the air, I knew I should hide my tears, but hearing Mutti's prayer brought new fear to my heart. I didn't want to die. I was scared to die. How would I die? Would I be shot? Would a bomb fall on us? Suddenly I just couldn't feel my body anymore. Yes, I thought a bomb would be best.

More rapid knocking on the door caused everyone to become restless. More neighbors were seeking refuge at the old preacher's house. It didn't bother him that they had always mocked him. They had called him a religious fanatic, a religious nut, and a strange man, but in his heart he had forgiven them long ago and welcomed everyone in. Our living room was really becoming crowded now. There were twenty-nine people crowded into the small space.

"Please pray for me," requested an unfamiliar voice. "I don't know how to pray."

The earth was trembling, the house vibrating, and the windows rattling. The enemy was approaching our town.

"O Lord! Creator of us all!" prayed Onkel Lehmann. "You see us and know our fearful hearts. We're utterly helpless without You. We are in Your presence even now. We don't know what the next hours will bring, but please make this house an ark of safety for all of us. Fill us with Your peace!"

Sobbing could be heard in every corner of our room, yet Mutti was peaceful. I could sense her peace. My aunt was probably crying too. Her husband, Vati's twin, had been killed just a short time ago while defending Pillau. Now, we had only two men in the house—Onkel Lehmann and Onkel Emil, who was an invalid from World War I. He had an artificial leg.

Even though the rumbling increased with the lengthening of the night, the younger children were sleeping. We sat silently for hours and listened to the war advance. The Russians were nearing our town rapidly. Then our ears detected a new, unfamiliar sound.

"Those are cannons," Onkel Emil informed us. "They are beginning to shoot at Lippehne."

One huge explosion followed another. Suddenly light flooded the house through the bedroom window and spilled into the living room. A neighbor went to look out of the window.

"The sky is aglow!" she called. "All the buildings on the other side of the lake are on fire!"

I rushed out of my seat to take a quick look. The bright, yellow flames that appeared to touch the sky gave me the most horrible feeling. The frames of the homes resembled black skeletons. My heart raced when I realized that no one could escape those sweeping sheets of fire. I tried to snuggle back on the couch next to Mutti, but my body trembled and my mind was in turmoil. How many people were perishing in those flames? I wished my mind would just fall asleep, but it was wide awake.

"O God! O God, save us!" someone prayed out loud.

"Yes, save us! Save us!" voices muttered throughout the room.

Some of those who had never trusted in the Lord before were trying to strike bargains with Him now. "If you get me out of this, God, I will become a better person. Help, God! Help! Don't kill us, God!"

"Why doesn't Hitler come with his secret weapons?" others wondered.

Still others showed their bitterness. "I thought You were supposed to be a loving God! Why then are You doing this to us?"

Another voice pleaded, "I don't know how to pray. Please pray for us, Herr Lehmann!"

The tracks of tanks were beginning to clank on the cobblestone pavement of Main Street. Since our home was only one block away, it vibrated continuously. Long had been the nights in the bomb shelter, and scary, but this night was never-ending. It dragged on as my fear of the Russians increased. If only it were morning! Things would not be so frightening and hopeless then. Somehow, I knew, we would be rescued by our leader.

I must have fallen asleep from sheer exhaustion because suddenly loud noises awakened me. It sounded as if the house door was being broken down. All at once we heard hollering and yelling in the hallway. An angry mob of men kicked the door to the living room open, burst in, and aimed their flashlights at our eyes. I saw nothing but guns and bayonets pointing at us. Soldiers! Russian soldiers were in our house! Their eyes flew from person to person. No German soldiers here—only two old men.

"Watch! Watch! If not watch, everything kaputt!" The demand was clear. Everyone took off his watch and handed it to the enemy. Dropping them into their pants' pockets, they stormed out of the room, through the hallway, and out of the house. Onkel Emil told us that these were Mongolian soldiers because their skin was tan-colored and their eyes somewhat slanted.

There was a hush over the whole room. Our men closed the front door and jammed it with a heavy log, but almost immediately another group of soldiers kicked it open again, and ran shouting through the house in search of German men. "Watch! Watch!" they screamed when they found us all cowering in the living room. No one moved to give them a watch. That infuriated them. "Watch! Watch!" they hollered even louder. One of them then tried to explain to us what he was after by pushing up his sleeve and exposing about ten watches on his hairy lower and upper arm.

"We don't have watches. Your comrades already took our watches," Onkel Lehmann tried to tell them, but they did not understand. As they became even more enraged, Kätchen slipped into the kitchen, which was right next to the living room, and in seconds returned with a plate of cookies. She offered them to the soldiers. That move really startled them. They made her eat some first before they devoured the rest. Then, surprisingly enough, they left the house.

For hours tanks rumbled through town and Russians searched our little farm. Occasionally shots rang out in the streets. After the first few hours under Russian occupation, the soldiers' demands changed. "Woman, come!" they began commanding. But none of our ladies ever moved. They all hid their faces. No one wanted to look beautiful. One of the neighbor ladies sat with folded hands and moving lips when a Russian aimed his flashlight at her face. She must have learned to pray. Shooting outside, however, suddenly distracted the troops. They turned on their heels and stumbled out of the house.

While our two men were busy securing the front door, the women tried to make themselves ugly. They dug ashes from the kitchen stove to smear on their faces, and they messed up their hair. Mutti dashed upstairs, put on black pants, and covered her head with a black scarf. Everybody was huddling back in the living room again when the next band of soldiers broke through the front door barricade and crashed into the hallway. Of course, all the children were awake by then, and the women were pretending to busy themselves with their little ones when the warriors stomped into the room.

"Woman, come!" one soldier yelled at Mutti, but she remained seated on the chair with Udo on her lap.

"Woman, come!" he commanded even louder.

She didn't move. Then the Russian placed his pistol at Onkel Emil's forehead. No one in the room seemed to be breathing. Even the little ones were silent. Suddenly my four-year-old sister pulled away from me and ran to the Russian. She stretched her little arms toward him and wanted him to pick her up. He was so shocked that he almost dropped his pistol. Furiously he pushed Marlies back. She fell down, and he stumbled out of the room.

"Thank You, Lord," Onkel Lehmann prayed out loud, "for sending Your angel to watch over us. Continue to keep us safe!"

In the dim light of dawn, we made plans to protect ourselves. Onkel Lehmann showed the young girls a trapdoor in the bedroom floor. "That door leads to a small room in the basement," he said. "The oval braided rug shall cover that door at all times. It will be Dieter and Liane's job to pull the rug over the escape the second you have slipped into the cellar. The front door will be locked and bolted and opened only by Onkel Emil. Since he can't walk very fast with his prosthesis, the ladies will have enough time to hide."

It was almost daylight by then, and the tanks were still rattling through town. The house vibrated continuously. We didn't hear any troops outside and used the time for a quick dress rehearsal. The teenage girls learned that it was rather difficult to slide into the basement speedily and not fall off the steep steps.

Right in the middle of our practice session, gun butts were slamming against the front door. Onkel Emil hobbled through the long hallway to see about the ruckus. While we heard all the abuse the Russians hurled at him for moving so slowly, Dieter and I quickly pulled the rug over the trapdoor. With lightning speed, we zipped to the living room and helped care for the little ones. The troops, dressed in olive green uniforms and fur hats, raced from room to room and out into the barnyard in search of German men. Omi and Kätchen were busy with the children, while most of the young mothers had hidden somewhere. Kätchen was only five feet tall and pretended not to be very bright. She always smiled at the Russians and offered them something to eat. This tactic never failed to shock them.

The first day under Russian occupation seemed utterly hopeless and endless. Onkel Emil informed us that we were now dealing with White Russians. Their searching techniques were the same as the others though: running, shouting, kicking furniture and walls, hollering and screaming, and scaring us by pointing their rifles or pistols at us. They managed to be successful in frightening even the smallest child. All the children cried almost continuously.

Throughout the next few days, the stream of enemies flooding our house was endless. At one time the girls were in the basement for several hours. There was no heat in the cellar, and it was rather difficult for them to be in that musty room for so long, but considering the alternative, no one complained. The days and nights dragged on without rest for anyone. Fear of the soldiers' demands for women still gripped everyone's heart. Miraculously, however, the Lord had provided protection for each lady and girl.

One morning, finally, it looked as if we would have a few hours of peace. Most of our group were completely exhausted and asleep on the living room floor. The children were awake and had gathered in the kitchen for lunch. Onkel Lehmann was just beginning to give thanks for the meal when the front door was almost beaten down. Everyone scrambled toward their hiding places. Dieter and I ran to our assigned post. The girls were slower than usual in letting themselves into the cellar because they were still half asleep. My brother and I were still straightening out the rug when three soldiers rushed in. One of them pulled me off the floor by my arm, lifted up the rug, and opened the wooden lid. The girls were cowering in one corner as guns pointed at them and a flashlight shone into their eyes.

"You spy! You spy! You not kill us! We kill you!" one of the soldiers shouted, cocking his rifle and aiming it at the trembling girls.

"We are not spies!" the girls cried. "We are not spies!"

Kätchen sensed danger and rushed into the bedroom. She tried to tell the soldiers that the girls were hiding because they were afraid. "Afraid! Afraid!" she repeated. But they didn't understand. Another soldier brought his rifle up, imitating his companion's actions.

"Lord, help them understand," Kätchen whispered under her breath. As she spoke, the soldiers suddenly, as if on command, withdrew their rifles, turned, and left. White as sheets, sobbing, and almost fainting, the girls emerged from their dungeon. I sat where I had fallen, rubbing my arm and watching in amazement as I realized that we had again been spared.

3

NEW TROUBLES

Our house was still filled with people, and the food supply dwindled rapidly. It was decided that we would eat only two meals a day, the last one at 2:30 p.m. Church services were held in the living room at the onset of darkness, about 4:00 p.m. Since the whole town was without electric power, Onkel Lehmann read from the Bible by candlelight. After his reading, one of the children blew out the candle. This small task was always the highlight of the service for the little ones. As for myself, I loved hearing the adults tell of God's leading in their lives and the many blessings they had received during their wanderings here on earth.

"Onkel Lehmann," Mutti said softly during one service, "the Lord has been so good to us. He has put it in your heart to take us all in, and we've already seen how safe we are here. I know that your years of faith in the Lord are benefiting us now. Thank you for taking me and my family into your home. We would be homeless without you and the Lord." Her voice was beginning to break as she continued. "When I accepted Jesus as my Savior as a young teenager, I never imagined what brothers and sisters in the Lord could mean to each other, in times of joy and in times of trouble. It always amazes me how the Lord chooses just the right person for a particular job—and no one could have filled your place better during the last few months.

"Sometimes I am ashamed, though, when I think how long I struggled against the Lord because I did not consider myself a sinner. I rebelled whenever I heard that the Bible says we are all sinners. I thought I was a good person—surely I would get to heaven. But one Easter Sunday, I learned that Christ suffered and died for me personally. Then I knew that I could no longer bypass this Jesus. I, a sinner, prayed for the Lord to forgive me and come into my heart. I am so thankful that Jesus has been so faithful to me. That I am alive and speaking to you all is proof of His goodness. I hope and pray that all of you here will invite Jesus into your lives, if you have not already done so."

We spent the rest of our "service" in prayer. Everyone participated and we all felt so close to God, having reason every day to thank Him for His protection. We asked Him to keep us safe during the night and the next day. Whenever I heard Onkel Lehmann pray, I thought he must be standing in the very throne room of God.

"Talking to God is like talking to your earthly father," Onkel Lehmann would tell us, "even though He is the Creator of the universe."

Another exciting part of our devotional time for me was the hymn singing. No one sang out loud, of course. It was just a whispering choir because we didn't want to be heard by the Russians who were prowling outside. Everyone sang songs from memory. Many of the hymns were repeated daily, and after a short time, we all learned new verses from each other.

One of the neighbor ladies who, with her four children, had been staying at our little farm since the day of our surrender, had been growing increasingly concerned about her father. He had been at work when she left with the children, but she had left a note. She slipped into her home several times daily but discovered no trace of him. One day just as darkness set in, while we were assembling for the mini-service, she returned in hysterics. "He is gone! He is dead! Why, God? Why? He is dead!"

Onkel Lehmann tried to comfort her and make some sense from her words, but she could only cry uncontrollably. Finally, we were able to understand what she was saying.

"My father hanged himself in the attic! He is dead!"

Everyone was silent and stunned. Our wonderful neighbor committed suicide? I had so many unanswered questions, and I think the others did too.

Our service that night was more like a funeral. For the first time since we lost our freedom, everyone was weeping freely.

"Lord, we pray for this dear neighbor," Onkel Lehmann started, "and her young children. We are so saddened by the news concerning her father. Give this family the fortitude to stand alone now, and this lady wisdom until her husband is able to return to them. Comfort and guide them as only You can.

"And, Lord, I also pray for the other women here who don't know where their husbands are. The Bible says You are concerned about every sparrow that falls, and You know where the men, the fathers of these children, are. Guard and protect them, we ask, and draw us all close to You."

Seldom could we enjoy our services without interruptions by groups of Russians who searched the house and, with guns pointing at us, tried to intimidate us. That night's soldiers smelled filthy and could have been trailed through pitch darkness by the smell of liquor on their breath. We knew God was answering our prayers because they did us no harm.

For weeks the school across the road from us had been a home to some of the refugees from Eastern Germany. They had arrived there on foot, carrying a few bundles and pulling their children and old relatives on sleds and handcarts. One day we noticed they were filing past our windows in long, sad lines. We learned that they had been told to leave

Lippehne. None of them knew where to go, but with tears and sadness, the homeless Germans trekked toward an unknown destination.

"Mommy, I want to sit in the wagon with Grandma," we heard a little girl beg.

"No, my dear! You are four years old and a big girl. This wagon is too heavy for me already. You must walk!"

"But where are we going, Mommy?"

"I don't know yet, child. We'll go to the end of this street and then we'll see."

When the last person from the school had passed our house, everything was quiet on the street. All the adults in our home were quiet too. Onkel Lehmann broke the silence by saying, "Will we be next?"

Demanding knocks on the front door the next morning brought everyone to their feet with a jump. The knocking persisted, and Onkel Emil went to open the door. Two Russian officers told all our friends and neighbors to leave. Only those who lived here could stay. With the enemies watching, the families gathered their belongings and began their rounds of teary goodbyes. There was no time for a prayer, but I was sure that all those who remained behind whispered one for those who had to leave our place of safety.

Our service was very different that evening. No one felt like singing. The candle was lit, and Onkel Lehmann began to read Psalm 91:

"He that dwelleth in the secret place of the most High
Shall abide under the shadow of the Almighty.
I will say of the LORD, He is my refuge and my fortress:
My God; in him will I trust.
Surely he shall deliver thee from the snare of the fowler,
And from the noisome pestilence.
He shall cover thee with his feathers,
And under his wings shalt thou trust:
His truth shall be thy shield and buckler.

Thou shalt not be afraid for the terror by night;
Nor for the arrow that flieth by day;
Nor for the pestilence that walketh in darkness;
Nor for the destruction that wasteth at noonday."

"Then we skip down to verse fourteen," Onkel Lehmann continued.

"Because he hath set his love upon me, therefore will I deliver him:
I will set him on high, because he hath known my name.
He shall call upon me, and I will answer him:
I will be with him in trouble;
I will deliver him, and honour him.
With long life will I satisfy him,
And shew him my salvation."

After Udo blew out the candle, Onkel Emil, who had been the choir leader in Insterburg, couldn't resist the urge to sing. "God be with you till we meet again," he sang softly. No one else joined him.

Onkel Emil requested special prayer for his wife. She was supposed to meet him in Lippehne should the war separate them, but she had not arrived. He also requested prayer for his two grown daughters whose whereabouts were not known. His only son had been killed a year earlier when his submarine was destroyed.

The next day Mutti drew Dieter and me away from the other children. "You have no idea how difficult it is for me to ask this of you," Mutti said to us. "I have prayed much about it and have received no other answer. You know that food has become very scarce for us. Onkel Lehmann still has a few potatoes left, but our bread flour is used up and I know you haven't had enough to eat in some time. I would like both of you to go to town to see if any of the stores are open. If they are, you can buy something to eat. Go to the grocery store and the bakery to see what you can find." Mutti then prayed with us and helped us get ready to leave.

Did Mutti notice that my heart felt as though it was about to escape my body from fear? We were supposed to go out on the street? That was where our enemies were! We hadn't left the house since the day we started out for the railroad station. Now we were to leave everyone here and go out alone? Dieter didn't seem to have any questions or doubts. In minutes he was bundled up to face the cold world.

On our way to the stores on Main Street, we noticed that most of the neighbors' houses were empty. Many windows were broken and the doors ajar. Furniture, clothes, and household items were scattered throughout the rooms. Upholstered chairs were slashed and the stuffing scattered everywhere. Family pictures were ripped up, slashed, and lying on the floor. Most of the abandoned, plundered homes resembled dark caves. Their owners' treasures and lives were ruined.

On Main Street, entrances to all the stores were wide open. Refugees and elderly townspeople were searching through every box in the grocery store for food, but there was nothing edible left under the counters, in the side rooms, or anywhere else.

"No, I hadn't heard about the butcher's wife," the old lady told someone.

"Well, first she hanged her son in the smokehouse, and then she hanged herself."

It made me shudder as I heard these two women talk. A mother hanged her son? I couldn't fathom that! Would Mutti ever be capable of doing such a horrible thing? Absolutely not! Her faith in the Lord would keep her from committing such a crime. Her faith was too strong for her to become that despondent, wasn't it? But the women's chatter was going on.

"You already know that the train, which took off from the station with the Nazis before the Russians came, was completely wiped out by bombs, right?"

The train was bombed? O Lord, thank You! I found myself praying silently. You have watched over us more than we realized. All those people were killed? We could have been on that train!

Finding no food to take home to Mutti, Dieter and I left the grocery store and continued on down the street. Passing the shoe store, we noticed boxes and shoes scattered outside on the sidewalk. Inside, people were shoving and grabbing and helping themselves to the footwear they needed. There was no clerk—just boxes of merchandise strewn everywhere. I decided to hunt for a pair of knee-high boots because my shoes had been pinching my toes for some time. Dieter and I searched for a long time and finally found two matching pairs, one for each of us. My excitement about having such wonderful boots made all my fears vanish. Suddenly, it didn't matter that we were walking among our enemies. It saddened me, though, to see the bakery boarded up and to realize the disappointment it would be for Mutti when we returned without food.

On the way home, I wondered if I, for the first time in my life, had stolen something. But there had been no clerk in the store, I reasoned, and the old ladies had said that German currency was no longer valid. The store was wide open, and I needed boots in the winter weather.

Still, everyone at home was shocked to see us return with merchandise for which we had not paid. The issue of our boots was debated back and forth among the adults. "You, Liane and Dieter, already know the Ten Commandments, right?" Mutti asked.

"Yes, Mutti," we said in unison.

"Then you also know that one of those commandments of the Lord says, 'Thou shalt not steal,' right?"

"I realize that, Mutti," I answered, "but I needed boots so badly and Dieter has no winter shoes either. It took us a long time to find matching pairs. People were just throwing the boxes and shoes around. There were no clerks at the store either."

"I know what you are trying to tell me, Schäfle! But nevertheless, you were taking property that belonged to someone else. That is called stealing. We are in a war situation, but that does not change the Word of God. His commands always remain the same."

"But the shopkeeper was probably a Nazi."

"He must have been, Schäfle, because he had his business until the Russians moved in. Vati and I were forced to close our store in Insterburg when we refused to join the party. But that still doesn't give you the right to take his merchandise."

"Maybe Jesus wanted us to have these shoes and boots. There would not be any left by tomorrow," Dieter suggested with a serious look on his face.

Mutti was silent for a long time. We stood and waited for judgment to be passed. It seemed like an eternity before she finally spoke.

"If there were anyone for you to return those boots to, you had better believe that you would be doing so." Mutti paused and sighed, pulling us both to her for a hug and a kiss. "Dieter and Liane, you are not to enter those stores again. Do you understand?"

"Yes, Mutti." Our answers blended. We were sad, but I was on top of the world for the rest of the day because of my wonderful new boots. I couldn't believe I had never really looked at Mutti before today. I couldn't fathom how beautiful she was. Her dark brown, naturally curly hair and her dreamy eyes must have been the reason Vati married her. He had always said he married her because she loved the Lord and music, and because she had a sense of humor. But I thought he also married her for her great beauty. When, at times, I saw the sadness in her eyes, I was heartbroken that she and Vati hadn't seen each other in such a long time.

The following day, Mutti sent Dieter and me out to search for food. At the town square, Russian soldiers were draped over their tanks and trucks while they were eating and drinking. My mouth began to water when we saw them chewing on dark bread and sausage. We hadn't had bread in days.

Dieter slowly moved closer to a group of soldiers. He was the cutest seven-year-old with his light blond hair resembling a dandelion gone to seed. The soldiers liked him immediately and motioned for him to come closer. One Russian, with a broad grin on his face, gave him the heel of his black, hard bread. His friendliness made me bolder. I stretched my cold hand toward them, but they simply ignored me. I thought it was because I was not pretty. We stayed around the group a little longer, hoping to get more bread, but none of them looked at us again.

Half frozen, we dashed home through the snow. Being away from our family wasn't as scary as on the first day, and it made me feel good to see Mutti so excited about that piece of bread. She used it to cook bread soup. Our potato supply in the basement dwindled quickly. Mutti and Kätchen boiled them one day and fried them the next. Without salt, however, they no longer tasted as wonderful as they used to. The day Dieter and I found a block of red cattle salt at an abandoned farm was a day of rejoicing for us. Mutti and Kätchen invented a new way to cook the potatoes—they fried them in salt.

After Onkel Lehmann had given thanks for our first meal of salt-fried potatoes, he said, "Just think how wonderful our God is! I don't know if I told you this, Kätchen, but when my farmer friend brought potatoes last fall, he rolled them from his wagon right into the basement through the chute, as he usually does. When he came into the house to present me with the bill, I was absolutely shocked. He had delivered double the amount I ordered. Since there was no way for me to carry all those potatoes out of the cellar by hand, I decided to keep them. Now, of course, we see God's wonderful provision in my friend's mistake, don't we?"

One sunny, spring-like day in March, the front door was almost smashed in. Onkel Emil slowly limped to remove the barricade and open it the rest of the way. This gave the women time to hide.

"Woman! Woman! Where woman?" Three young soldiers hollered as they came running into the house. Mutti and her sister-in-law were just dashing across the courtyard to hide in the outhouse. Seeing them, the soldiers chased after them and, in their haste, flung open the door to the coal storage room instead of the one the ladies had entered. With the door being open, the outhouse door was completely covered.

"Woman! Where woman?" they yelled at Onkel Lehmann, who was repairing his handcart in the yard.

"I haven't seen the women," he told them. "I don't know."

From the kitchen window, Kätchen and I watched him trying to explain to the soldiers that he really had not seen the women because his back had been turned, but they didn't understand. One of the soldiers, in his rage, drew his sword and held it above the kneeling preacher. Instinctively, I closed my eyes.

"Where woman? Where woman?" he continued yelling.

I looked again. Suddenly, as if turned away by an unseen hand, the soldier put the sword back in its sheath, turned around, and all three quietly left the property. With our hearts racing from fear, Kätchen and I embraced.

"Thank You, Lord," she said, "for sparing my dad and protecting the women."

Mutti and her sister-in-law came trembling out of their hiding place, their faces white and tear-stained.

"Onkel Lehmann, we thank you," Mutti said while squeezing his hand. "You almost had to give your life for us. From the outhouse, we saw everything through a knothole in the door. I am so glad you did not know where we were hiding. The Lord must have struck both you and our enemies with blindness to show Himself mighty. Thank you,

Onkel Lehmann, but I wish you wouldn't have had to endure so much because of us."

In the days that followed, Dieter and I continued to go on our begging trips. My heart still raced when Mutti let us out of the door, but I was less fearful of our enemies now. There were other things, however, that troubled me. Every time we walked along the peaceful lakes, I began to tremble because I thought about the mother of whom we'd heard pushed each of her four children—oldest to the youngest—into the icy lake and then took her own life by drowning. We saw bodies washed ashore. Some of them were men; some of them you couldn't tell anymore who they'd been, but there was no one to bury any of them. The water and the elements were their grave. Why was God so good to us? I always asked myself.

"Kätchen! Kätchen!" Mutti said excitedly and joyfully one morning with her eyes sparkling. "Emil is alive! I know he is alive! The Lord has given me assurance of that during the night. The father of my four children is alive! I can't tell you how thankful and happy I am. There is no doubt in my mind! We do have a wonderful Lord!"

"Yes," Kätchen rejoiced, "we have a wonderful Lord. I am so happy for you, Emmy." She turned her head and began to weep, and I knew she was thinking of her own husband.

"Children! Liane, Dieter, Marlies, and Udo come here!" Mutti quickly gathered us around her. "We have a wonderful God! He never disappoints us! Even when everything around us looks hopeless, we can trust in Him. You all know that we have not heard from Vati in almost a year. We didn't know if he was alive. This morning, however, I can tell you that Vati is alive! He is alive and well! Our Lord Jesus told me that last night. He told me that someday we are all going to see Vati again. I don't know when that will be, but I know that God will keep His promise, and we'll be reunited. Isn't that wonderful?

"Vati will be so proud of you children, and he will be so surprised to see how you have grown. I know you don't get enough to eat anymore and your little tummies are empty so much of the time, but the Lord Jesus can overrule all those problems and still let you grow big and strong. We must believe that. I think we should thank the Lord right now for His goodness to us and for telling us about Vati."

On the evening of this happy day, Mutti handed me a poem which she had written. "Schäfle, I'd like you to memorize this. It is for Vati's homecoming celebration."

Dieter and I spent a large part of each day scavenging for food, and as a result, we were becoming well acquainted with Lippehne. We cut through this farm yard and that garden. We knew all the abandoned homes and farms. We knew where to find troops and where to gather wood and sticks for our fire. We knew where the ruins were, and we learned about the two sides of our enemies—we knew how they treated both children and adults. But one day Dieter and I learned something new.

In our haste to reach the troops camping outside of town, we cut across the cemetery for the first time. With its large trees, it had always seemed to be quite a dark place. On this warm, sunny winter day, however, the cemetery looked almost inviting.

"Why are the doors to these house-graves open?" Dieter asked.

"You mean the catacombs?"

"Yes, those houses there."

"I don't know."

"Look! The caskets are open too. There are bones on the ground and two skulls there in the corner."

For a while, we just stood there gazing in disbelief.

"These are parts of people who were alive at one time, Dieter." When I thought about my statement, my body started going into a succession of chills. Bones of people all round us? We checked further and realized that all the catacombs were open and the bones scattered. Instead of going begging, we suddenly found ourselves running home as fast as our legs could carry us.

"Why are we running, Dieter?" I panted when I regained some control of my thoughts.

"I don't know why you are running, but I am scared!"

When we related what we had just seen to the family at home, Onkel Lehmann said sadly, "Yes, at work the other day, I heard about the vandalism at the cemetery. It proved that our enemies have no respect for the dead either. The catacombs and caskets are torn open because it is there that the Russians find treasures such as jewelry, gold watches, and gold teeth."

Everyone was shocked by this explanation. Mutti gave Dieter and me a hug and a kiss and tried to comfort our troubled minds. The next day, of course, we were out begging again.

A great number of soldiers had been camping outside the city gate for several days. As we approached them slowly, they immediately began paying attention to my cute brother. They were barbecuing piglets over a huge fire built with chopped-up German furniture. One group was already eating, and they were calling Dieter over to where they were. He took off like lightning as I tried to follow. It couldn't be true! Were they giving my brother a piglet's head? What would we do with that? When Dieter turned around, I knew that this was exactly what had happened. There was no way I could keep up with my brother now. He was running toward home with his treasure, faster than I had ever seen him run. In a few moments, he had slipped into a side street and was out of my sight.

As I continued trying to catch up to Dieter, a Russian stepped into my way and told me to stop. He motioned for me to sit on a stone wall and take off my new boots. He then began to unlace his beat-up combat boots and pulled out his feet. As he began to unwrap the filthy rags which covered his bare feet, a nauseating stench filled the late winter air around us.

He then made me put my feet in his boots while he tried and tried again to squeeze his big feet into my beautiful boots. But no matter how hard he tried, they just wouldn't fit. My heart was racing, but at the same time I was rejoicing. I would never be able to walk home in his huge canoes. Shouting something I didn't understand, he angrily threw my boots toward me. In no time at all, my feet were back where they belonged. I wanted to start running away, but he grabbed me by the arm and took away my mittens that Omi had knitted for me. When he finally let me go, I wasted no time in leaving. Mutti was very glad to see me and gave me a bear hug when I finally reached home. The piglet's head was already boiling in a pot of water on the stove. It turned out to be the most delicious soup we had eaten in a long time.

"Thank You, Lord," Onkel Lehmann prayed, "for again supplying our needs."

The most important question now, however, was how would we survive without regular means of getting food? Dieter and I continued to scrounge around town for anything edible. In our search, we sometimes spent all day away from home. Our only hope was our enemies. They were vicious but had always been kind to us children.

When the Russian hospital, which had been housed in our school, was evacuated, Dieter and I found many bread crusts under the beds and among the bloody bandages. We brought them home. Mutti scraped and washed off some of the dirt and cooked bread soup. The hospital yielded enough bread for several days of food for our family.

4

ENEMY IN THE CAMP

Not a day went by without a visit from our fur-hatted enemies whose demands never changed. All the ladies at our house continued to dress like scarecrows. The influx of the Cossacks always increased after 9:00 p.m., when the curfew for the Germans began. Then one day, in the middle of the afternoon, three clean-looking soldiers informed us that the ground floor of our little house had to be vacated. It was needed for officers immediately, and those living downstairs would have to join Mutti and the rest of us in our tiny quarters on the second floor.

"Your father soldier?" a tall officer with a grin on his face asked me in broken German.

"Yes," I answered. The Russian tilted his head, seeming to wait for a more specific answer.

"He is in France."

The same officer then followed me into the kitchen and inquired of my aunt if everyone in our house was healthy.

"Yes," she told him without hesitation.

Just before darkness fell, we were all trying to find a place to sleep in our small room. As usual, no one undressed. We had gone to bed fully dressed for weeks now. Sometimes I was too warm sleeping all bundled up under the down covers, but Mutti always insisted that we had to be prepared in case of an emergency. We'd freeze to death outside if we had to leave the house suddenly.

My aunt, Dieter, and I crowded onto the couch near the window. Some of the others settled down on the bed and the rest on the floor. No one in our group was sleeping, except the little ones. Fear kept everyone else awake and quiet. Our enemies were in our house tonight.

Not a word was said, but tension was building in our room as if we were all in a pressure cooker. I could feel my aunt's heart pound even though I slept at her feet. Why did everything seem so frightening? Usually I felt safer when we were all together. I was listening into the darkness, but I didn't know what I expected to hear. Why had they forced all of us into one room? I couldn't find the answers.

My imagination, however, continued to show me all kinds of horrible pictures. I wanted to sleep, but I couldn't stop thinking. The moon was filtering its cool beams through the lace curtains and casting designs on Vilmar's face. He was sleeping so peacefully. Why couldn't I sleep like that? I was so tired.

Suddenly I heard thunder-like steps on the wooden staircase. The steps were moving upward, closer and closer, and then our door was kicked and pushed open. In the moonlight, I saw a tall shadow.

"You sleep?" the voice asked harshly in German. Nobody answered. Two more footsteps, and the door was being closed from the inside. In a very calm voice, the man informed us in broken German that he was an officer. He had studied in St. Petersburg, Russia. His parents owned a business, and he had three beautiful sisters. All three of them had been raped by men of the German SS. He questioned us about our relationships to one another. Now I realized something. This was the same voice that had asked me where Vati was. I quietly let out a sigh of relief. This Russian had been nice to me. I liked his blue eyes and neat appearance. He seemed so different from the other Russians we had encountered. I knew he wouldn't harm us. I was sure.

All of a sudden, though, he started yelling at Onkel Emil. "Why not speak right, Father? You not father of children here. Why not speak right, Father? Why?" Had Onkel Emil told him that he was our father? Why would he have done that?

"You not speak right. Why? Why?" And the officer raised his arm and shot into the ceiling with his pistol. Immediately all the little ones awakened and began to scream. He shot again and again. "You not speak right, Father. You not father!"

My ears were about to explode as he continued to shoot. In the middle of his spree of madness, the door flew open, and someone else burst into the room.

"Me do it alone!" he shouted and pushed the officer out the door. Yelling and hollering in Russian, the first visitor clumped downstairs.

The little ones continued to scream, and in the moonlight, I saw Kätchen and her two sons cowering in one corner of the room. The Russian moved over to her and ran both hands down her skinny body. "Nicht gut! Nicht gut!" he grunted, and in the same manner began to size up Mutti. Marlies and Udo feverishly clung to her. That made him furious, and he turned away from her also. Mutti's beautiful sister-in-law quickly reached over the foot of the bed for Udo and used his little body to shield her face. The Russian now moved over to our couch. "You mother?" he asked my aunt.

"Yes," she answered, trembling.

"You, Dummkopf," he shouted. "You not mother. Mother not holding child in face. Mother holding child close to heart." He grabbed Udo and shoved him back at Mutti. "You, Father," he yelled at Onkel Emil, "on floor! All on floor!" He commanded. Onkel Emil struggled to move quickly, but the wooden leg slowed the process. The invalid moved too slowly for the beast that had found its prey. "On floor," the Russian hollered again and planted his pistol on Onkel Emil's forehead.

"Shoot us all!" Mutti intervened, placing her hand between Onkel Emil's head and the pistol. "Shoot us all! Just shoot us all!"

"No, no," he scoffed. "German woman go-o-o-o-d woman." The Russian, withdrawing his pistol, stumbled to the couch. I was still at my aunt's feet because there was no room left on the floor. With one hand he seized my aunt by the hair and stretched out next to us, pistol still in his other hand.

When daylight broke and I awakened, the rapist had left. I found myself on the floor near the couch. White billowy clouds, edged in light red, were moving slowly above the school building. My aunt was crying softly. Just a few months earlier, her husband, my uncle, had been killed while defending Pillau in East Prussia. He had loved his beautiful, God-fearing wife dearly. The nightmare was over for the rest of us, but I felt it would never be over for her. As I lay quietly on the floor, I was counting the bullet holes in the ceiling. There were twenty-one.

We had no access to our kitchen that morning and everyone was hungry. How would we prepare our potato breakfast? The smell of fried bacon, which our enemies seemed to be enjoying, was trailing upstairs to our room, making us even hungrier. Were they matter-of-factly eating without realizing our plight? "One of us will have to go downstairs and request some food for the children," Mutti said boldly. But who would it be? That question was debated for some time. There was much to be considered, as no one was able to predict our enemies' dispositions. They could harm the petitioner or kill him or harm the rest of us for even making such a request. We were completely at their mercy. Finally, Kätchen could no longer bear the suffering of her two-year-old.

"I will go," she said in her gentle voice, sighing deeply. "But you must all pray for me. God will have to perform another miracle today. We all know that we have a wonderful God. He can do anything to help His children, right?" She rose from the floor, straightened her black dress and smoothed her hair, which was twisted into a bun on the back of her head.

"Before you go, Kätchen," Onkel Emil began, "I have to apologize to all of you for the problems I caused. I have already asked the Lord to forgive me for lying and telling the Russian that I was the father of Emmy's children. I lied, thinking that I might be able to protect them. But as I considered everything this morning, I realized that I just limited the Lord that way. He could have protected us without my sin of lying. All these experiences are new to us, and I would never have imagined that I'd lie under pressure. This shows me that I have to move much closer to our Lord so it won't happen again. From now on, I will be truthful with our enemies. Will you all please forgive me?"

"I forgive you," Kätchen answered.

"I forgive you too," more voices joined in.

"I have to ask for forgiveness too," my aunt said between sobs. "I am so sorry that I used a little child in trying to protect myself. Please forgive me."

"We will."

Kätchen quietly opened the door, slipped out, and closed it. The farther downstairs she walked, the bolder and more determined her steps sounded. A prayer meeting started immediately and seemed to last for a long time. Everyone was listening for her footsteps, but none could be heard. Why was she staying away so long? What was happening in the kitchen? Was she being molested? Would she ever come back? My mind was turning somersaults as it considered all these questions. Who would take care of Hanno and Vilmar should something happen to Kätchen? Why? Why was it taking her so long? It was very difficult to continue listening for her footsteps because of the little ones' cries. All of a sudden, Kätchen bounced into the room.

"This is a day of sadness but also of rejoicing," the young preacher's wife announced to everyone in her bubbly way, with a sparkle in her brown eyes. "The Lord does not forget His own. All the children are invited to feast at the table of our enemies. Let's go, children," she said, clapping her hands. That included even me, but I couldn't believe it. I was supposed to go to our enemies after what happened last night?

"Let's not waste time," Kätchen fussed at us. Quickly we all got up and started downstairs. One of the officers ran his hand through Dieter's curly hair as we filed past the men into the kitchen. He said something we didn't understand. Other Russians were standing with folded arms, watching us. One picked up Marlies, played with her blond curls and talked to her. She just smiled back at him.

Kätchen made herself right at home in her kitchen. She reached for the dishcloth and wiped the table, took dishes out of the cupboard, silverware out of the drawer, and seated the six of us, three at each side of the table. The chubby Russian chef placed a large bowl of noodles on the table.

"Now, children," Kätchen said, "let us all pray and thank our wonderful Lord for His bountiful blessings." Every pair of hands, even Udo's, were folded, our eyes were shut, and our heads were bowed. Kätchen did the same.

"Come, Lord Jesus, be our guest and bless what You have given us. Amen," we all prayed in unison. When I raised my head, I realized that all the officers, about ten of them, and the cook were watching us. Was this really true? Did I see tears in the eyes of several of the Russians?

What a feast! Noodles! Even as they were sliding down my throat, I still couldn't believe it. This must be a dream. As I felt my stomach filling up, I reasoned that it wasn't a dream. For the first time in I didn't know how long, my stomach seemed satisfied.

All the officers were standing near the table watching us silently devour the meal they had provided. When we were almost finished, one of them stepped closer to the table and handed each of us a chocolate bar. This had to be a dream. Noodles and a chocolate bar? Marlies was so excited that she went from one Russian to another to shake hands with each and say, "Danke schön. Danke schön. Danke schön." One of them picked her up again and played with her while Kätchen and I did the dishes. After we all thanked everyone, we scrambled upstairs with full tummies and chocolate bars in our hands.

"Mutti, Mutti," Dieter called and pushed the door open. "We ate noodles, real noodles."

"My tummy is full of noodles too," Marlies added. "I like the Russians downstairs. Can I go down and play with them?"

"No, my little daughter. You just stay here now with the rest of us."

It was difficult for everyone in our room to believe what had just transpired in the kitchen. "God's Word never fails," Mutti remarked with tears in her eyes, realizing that our hunger pains had been stilled for the first time in several months. "We have experienced today what Psalm 23 really means, 'Thou preparest a table before me in the presence of mine enemies.' I just can't fathom how God's Word becomes more wonderful in these difficult days."

Around noontime the rapist returned to our house. Half-drunk and red faced, he stumbled into our room, approached my aunt, and handed her a loaf of bread and a chocolate bar. With tears cascading down her rosy cheeks, she took both gifts and threw them at him. She turned away from him and continued to weep bitterly. He tried to put his arm around her, but she pushed him away. Her anger seemed to surprise him. He picked up the bread and chocolate and staggered out of the house, holding on to the walls.

Kätchen was going downstairs again to ask for some drinking water. We were impatiently waiting for her. Finally, she entered the room, totally out of breath. "When I knocked on the kitchen door to ask for water, the cook slowly opened it and asked me in. Then he said slyly, 'Me do you favor, now you do me favor.' I knew immediately what he meant, took my bucket, and raced out of the kitchen. That man expected to be rewarded for his earlier translating efforts. He seemed like such a nice man. Of all the men in the kitchen, I felt he was the one who could be trusted. But we can't trust man. No wonder the Bible says, 'Trust in the LORD with all thine heart.'"

Later in the afternoon, we heard trucks driving up to our house. Men yelled, hollered, and appeared to be joking downstairs and in the hallway. After the vehicles drove off, everything was quiet below us and remained so until Onkel Emil decided to go down to check on things. He found the front door wide open. The only traces of our "guests" were a dirty kitchen and a disorderly house. A search for food they might have left behind yielded nothing. Happy that we were alone again, Kätchen and the others reoccupied the ground floor. But while everyone felt like celebrating, my aunt wept bitterly. Her beautiful face looked drawn, and her eyes were red and without a sparkle. Mutti and Kätchen spent a considerable amount of time trying to comfort her, but their efforts were in vain.

Darkness found both mothers still cleaning the house, changing the linens, and scrubbing the greasy stove. Our small supply of firewood had dwindled remarkably while we had visitors.

"Schäfle, please bundle up your brothers and sister a little more," said Mutti. "Our firewood is almost gone and none of us have sufficient body fuel to keep warm."

"I will, Mutti. And don't worry, Dieter and I will go and gather sticks again tomorrow."

5

SCAVENGERS

Dieter and I combed through houses and farms more diligently than ever. We had overcome all fear. We even searched garden cottages for edibles now but found that all of them had already been ransacked. How beautiful the outer shells of the cottages were! Each one had its own personality, no doubt that of the former owner. Some of them were large with elaborate wooden trims, others were plain and unassuming. All of them had one feature in common, a wooden dock stretching into the open lake. A boat was usually tucked into the reeds next to the dock. Onkel Lehmann's big garden was located just a short distance from the former public beach and the large beach restaurant. His smaller garden was closer to his home at another lake.

Our potato supply was gone the week before. Ever since, everyone had besought the Lord for another miracle. Once again, He did not fail us.

"Dieter! Dieter! Look at this! Potatoes! We have found potatoes!"

"Are they still good? They look soft and mushy."

"Let's check and see. Yes, some of them are rotten, but most of them are still firm and good. We just have to sort them out."

"All right, sister. You can sort them out. I don't like to touch the soft ones. What made you look here behind this barn anyway?"

"I think that you should ask—'Who made you look here?'"

"Well, then, who?"

"It must have been the Lord. He wanted us to find this cache. I would never have scrounged around back here on my own. So this is our miracle day—the day we have been waiting for! Let's look in the barn to see if we can find a bucket or something so that we can carry some of these potatoes home."

"The Lord be praised! Another miracle!" These were the expressions with which we were greeted at home. For days Dieter and I carried bucket after bucket of potatoes home, and the rejoicing didn't cease. Mutti, especially, was glad because she felt that the potatoes would help with some of the ill-effects we had been experiencing recently because of our poor diet.

"Perhaps the vitamins from these potatoes will start the healing of your legs, Dieter," Mutti said to him. "Are any of the boils opening yet?"

"Yes, they are. White stuff is coming out of them."

"Push up your pants legs and let me see. Oh no, my son! I didn't realize they have worsened so much in the past few days. We'll have to cut some bandages and start wrapping your legs."

"Can't we do that later? I want to get some more potatoes with Liane."

"No, we had better do it right now. Let's wash your boils in salt water first. I think the red cattle salt will probably work as well as the table salt that we don't have. Are your boils hurting yet, Dieter?"

"Yes, Mutti, they are, but I am strong, you know. I want to be like Vati. And he wouldn't complain."

"That is wonderful, my son. But I know they hurt because I have quite a few on my own arms and legs. Our bodies need vitamins from good food to help heal our festering skin. But you know, our Lord Jesus can heal this skin. And we'll trust Him that He will. In the meantime, though, we have to do everything we can to keep the sores clean. I will heat some water for you, and then we'll get started."

Mutti taught my poor brother how to bandage his legs, tie the bandages, and take off the soiled ones.

"Tomorrow," she said, "I will show you how to wash your bandages and roll them."

The next morning, soldiers again beat on the front door but for some reason seemed to wait patiently until Onkel Emil hobbled to open it. Through a German interpreter, they told us that they needed laborers. Walking down the long hallway, they turned into the kitchen where the rest of our group were busying themselves. Their first choice was Kätchen. "You come," one said, pointing to her. "You rabota. We will give bread."

Didn't they see how frail she was? I wondered. She weighed only about ninety pounds. They continued to insist that she go with them.

"My daughter has to stay here with her two young sons," Onkel Lehmann said boldly. "They need their mother. I will come and work for you."

"No, we need woman."

"Please take me instead," he begged.

Kätchen's two sons clung to her. "Stay here, please, Mutti!" Five-year-old Hanno looked at the soldiers and continued his pleas. "Do not take our Mutti away." They were visibly surprised.

"You come, man," the leader motioned and began to pull Onkel Lehmann by the arm. "And you, too, woman," another said to my aunt as he started dragging her out of the house. Mutti quickly reached for my aunt's coat and tossed it to her.

"We'll pray," she called over the shoulder of one Russian.

Both workers returned home in the evening totally exhausted. "They have no respect for their own dead," Mutti's sister-in-law grumbled. "No respect. First, they buried their comrades in the town square, and then we had to dig them up and move them to another place. The stench was unbearable. Some Germans passed out. Because the sick ones failed to meet their work quota, the rest of us had to work extra hard. I didn't get the promised bread either. I wish that Russian would have shot me the other night. How much more do we have to endure? Is God forsaking us?"

There was total silence in the room. Did my aunt really mean what she said?

"I had to bury cadavers all day long," Onkel Lehmann reported. "Apparently, when the soldiers are hungry, they shoot domestic animals at random. They cut out a piece of meat to roast and let the rest of it spoil. Cadavers are scattered all around town. Two other old men and I had to dig holes and bury those stinking, rotting animals. They kept their word to me, though, and gave me a piece of bread. It is black and hard, see? But if you soak it, Kätchen, I think you can probably make some good soup from it. I also have another surprise for everybody," he continued joyfully. "I have the inner organs of a calf—one shot probably just this morning—here in my shirt. I had no other way to bring my treasure home. Can you imagine what wonderful soup we can make from this?"

Onkel Lehmann was right. The soup was delicious. The inner organs of an animal that none of us had ever eaten before really eased our hunger pangs.

"The small farmhouse is simply too crowded for all of us," my aunt announced one day. "Omi and I have decided to move back across the street now that things have become somewhat calmer. If we move, the rest of you will have a little more room here."

"But will you be all right over there all by yourselves?" Mutti asked. "The people you were staying with are gone now, you know."

"Yes, I know, but we'll be just fine."

The thought of my aunt and Omi leaving depressed me. I was going to miss both of them, but especially Omi. She was such a sweet and wonderful little lady. She always wore a long, black dress and a dark apron, which covered most of the front of her dress. Her gray hair was pulled back into a bun, and the smile seldom left her face. I loved her dearly, and I knew she loved us children very much.

In Insterburg she and Opi always did special things for us grandchildren. They even planted a fruit tree in their garden for each of us. I could hardly wait until the end of summer when I could harvest the egg-sized yellow plums from my own tree. Because most of the trees in their garden were uncommon, friends, neighbors, and even strangers came to admire them. One of their apple trees bore apples the size of a child's head.

Whenever we went to my grandparents' house, Opi would sit in his workshop on the cobbler's bench, repairing saddles and tack for the farmers. In the summer Omi kept busy in the large garden, picking fruit and vegetables and preserving them. But the thing Omi liked best was to beat fresh eggs with sugar and serve us a bowl of it every time we visited. Dieter and I took that two-mile walk to our grandparents' at least twice a week. It was always such an exciting place to be.

Many evenings we would go to their house, especially when Vati was home from the service. Sitting in the living room, we would sing hymns, read the Bible, and pray. Opi's long white beard and snow-white hair always made me visualize how the old Bible patriarchs must have looked. Opi and Vati used to take turns playing the pump organ. How I missed Opi! I was glad, though, that he had gone to heaven just three months before we all had to leave Insterburg and thus was spared being a witness to the destruction of his beloved city.

It sometimes broke my heart now to see Omi getting frailer. Dieter and I visited her often and usually found her sitting at the window reading her Bible. When we took some potatoes to her, she was always thrilled. Sometimes she grated them for pancakes, but before the pancakes were baked, she let the grated mixture stand in a bowl for several hours in order for the starch to settle on the bottom. When she poured off the batter and the sediment, starch was left in the bowl. The starch was dried in the sun to be used as flour for baking or for making pudding.

"Look at this, Liane! Look! Look what I found!" Dieter exclaimed one day while we were out hunting for food. He began bubbling with joy as we turned a street corner. "Look! There's something I have always wanted. A bike! What would a bike be doing here in the middle of the street, except waiting for me?" My happy brother reached down to raise it up.

"But Dieter! This bike has only metal rims! It has no rubber tires! You can't ride that on the cobblestones!"

"I can on the sidewalks. Just watch me!" And suddenly the empty street was filled with the noise of a tireless bike clanking down the sidewalk. Every seam in the large stone blocks accentuated the clatter as the metal rims rambled down the Luisenstraße. Dieter was too short to sit on his new treasure. He had to ride it standing up.

Should I go begging alone? I wondered. *Or should I wait for my brother, who apparently has no hunger pangs at all today?* I decided to wait, hoping he would tire of his new toy soon, but instead, he continued to ride up and down our street. Then suddenly his world crashed. A Russian approached him and told him to stop, just as he was trying to zip past me. Mumbling something we didn't understand, the soldier grabbed Dieter's bike with his right hand. But why did the soldier need this old bike when he held on to a brand-new one with his left hand? He mumbled again and shoved the new bike toward Dieter. My brother took it, jumped on, and in total silence started peddling to the next street and around the block.

The Russian made many attempts to ride the old piece of junk but was unsuccessful. Weaving back and forth as if he were drunk, he fell off again and again. It was so funny to watch this clumsy man. His snow-white teeth sparkled as he talked to himself, but I noticed he was becoming increasingly angry. I decided it was best for me to leave, yet I watched him out of the corner of my eye. Furiously he kicked the bike several times with his filthy boots before he started to push it up the street. I hoped Dieter wouldn't appear around the corner. He would definitely lose his bike. This man had changed into a mad dog.

"Can you imagine, Sister, that I have a bike?" When Dieter rejoined me, he couldn't be quieted. "My own bike! I can't believe that he is so stupid. It is so easy to ride a bike—and nobody is going to get this new bike from me either! I stopped before turning the street corners and checked for soldiers. Do you know that I watched the Russian fall off this bike, too, when I was riding past him on the old piece of metal?" Both of us were now standing in the middle of the street laughing so hard that I thought my cheeks would burst.

When we showed Dieter's treasure to everyone at home, no one seemed to be able to believe the story. I noticed Mutti, however, looking up as if she was thanking the Lord for making her son's dream come true.

"I am so happy for you, my son. You go and ride your bike for a while. You can go begging later," Mutti suggested.

"Thanks, Mutti," he said hurriedly. Dieter rushed outside, and we all watched him zip around the corner of the house with lightning speed.

I had a good time for a while, entertaining Marlies and Udo. I hadn't been able to spend much time with them lately, and it was difficult to realize how quickly they were growing up. Udo got along beautifully with his sister, and she in turn with him.

"Dieter! Dieter!" Udo suddenly interrupted our game.

"Dieter isn't here, Udo. He is riding his bike."

Then I saw Dieter myself.

"He took my new bike. My brand-new bike," he sobbed, rushing up the stairs, his dusty face tear-stained and his eyes red. "He just came out of a house when I was riding by and told me to get off. And then the Russian took it. He just took my new bike and chased me away. I want my bike back, Mutti, my new bike," he cried bitterly.

"A Russian surprised you and took your bike?"

"Yes, he did."

"I am so sorry, my son. I wish you could have kept that bike forever, but at least you had it for a little while. The Lord can give you a new bike again someday, Dieter. You know that He can do anything, right? He has proven that today, hasn't He?"

"But why couldn't He let me keep my bike, Mutti?"

"I don't know the answer to that question, Son. But I know for certain that someday you will have a bike that you can keep. I have been praying for that, and I will continue to do so. I know you are hurting terribly now, but that hurt will leave and you will feel better soon. Why don't we thank the Lord Jesus for the wonderful time you did have today with a brand-new bike and ask Him right now for another one."

"Yes, Mutti, let's do that. I know that Jesus can do anything."

Mutti and Kätchen spent much of their time caring for the children, scrubbing the laundry on the washboard, and keeping the house in order. Whenever I was at home, I helped them. I did the darning, and it took up a lot of my time since the wartime socks seemed to fall apart after every wash.

"Pull the sock nice and taut over the darning mushroom," Mutti instructed me. "Stitch the darning yarn across the hole in a nice square or rectangle. Don't pull it too tightly. When you start weaving the needle up and down over the cross threads, make sure you weave a nice, flat patch. If anything puckers, it will hurt the foot when you wear shoes."

As soon as I had mastered the first few darning lessons, I spent many hours a week on my assignment. I had to darn socks for eleven feet. Since Onkel Emil had elevated himself as guardian and protector of our family and had no one but us to care for him, I had to darn his socks too. His were the ones I really dreaded darning because they always had the largest holes. I presumed that must have been due to the fact that his whole body weight rested on one leg. Darning his socks was almost as bad as having to wash my youngest brother's soaked pants every day. Because rubber pants were no longer available, he had to wear woolen pants, which Omi knitted for him, and they had become like felt from their constant use.

I considered my lot easy, though, when I compared it to Mutti's work. She was now stitching fur coats for the Russians by hand. Several officers saw her sewing one day, and a short time later returned with furs to make long coats for their wives. Mutti sat all day now and sewed; at night she stitched by candlelight. Her fingers were often bleeding from the difficult work, but how she rejoiced when she received an occasional payment—a loaf of black bread.

New troops moved into Lippehne every few days, and it was always during the night hours that our visitors stomped through the house and yard in search of German soldiers. The hay, which they continually pierced with their swords or bayonets, was strewn all over the barn. No one would be able to survive under that hay, should he choose to hide there. In spite of the constant danger that still lurked about us, especially at night, Kätchen and Mutti became happier and more confident.

"Emmy," Kätchen remarked one day while she was upstairs visiting us. "Wouldn't our lives be barren without all these experiences the Lord sends our way? Miracle upon miracle every day! The greatest one is that we are still alive. I just marvel at the grace of God every day when I hear the shooting outside and see the wooden hearses being pulled past our house."

"We don't deserve it," Mutti replied. "God is so faithful in answering our prayers. If we knew what the future held, we might despair. But we know He is in control. He has the answers to all our questions. He knows how we will feed our six children. He knows where our husbands are.

He also knows if we will pass the tests He gives us. We must continue to plant our faith firmly in Him!"

"Mutti, my head hurts," Marlies interrupted the conversation.

"Did you bump your head somewhere, Pittimaus?"

"I don't know, but it hurts all over. I want to scratch all the time. Will my hair fall out if I do that?"

"Oh no, Pittimaus. Your hair will not fall out if you do that. Let's go to the window where we have more light, and I'll look at your head." With the sun beaming through the small roof window, Mutti immediately detected the problem.

"Lice! I have never seen any before! But from what I have heard, this fits the description. Where could Marlies get lice?" Mutti asked Kätchen. "The house is clean. The linens are scrubbed and boiled. Do you think someone else has them? The children play together all the time. Have your sons complained about anything?"

"No, they haven't. But I will check immediately," Kätchen answered with concern in her voice.

"Kätchen, I think I have the answer," Mutti whispered, leaning over the banister. "Marlies got the lice from the Russians. You know how fearless she is, climbing on their laps when any one of them sits down; and they always pick her up, too, and play with her blond curls. I think that is our explanation."

"You may be right, Emmy."

A thorough check of the house revealed no lice anywhere, except on Marlies' pillow. Mutti immediately began to delouse the little wiggle worm who sat on her lap playing with wooden beads. The sunlight was a blessing that day, especially with this painstaking task.

Fortunately, not too many of the small visitors had invaded yet. With a lot of patience, searching, washing, and scrubbing, Mutti was able to win the battle against the lice within just a few days.

"The neighbor across the street knows how to swim with the tide," Mutti remarked to Kätchen one dreary morning in March. "There is a steady stream of Russians going in and out at her place. It must be because she can converse with them in Russian. There must be some reason, though, for her lacking nothing. Don't you think so, Kätchen? Why is she so friendly with the enemy? Could she possibly be an informer?"

Mutti and Kätchen strained their minds trying to analyze the actions of the lady. The other day when she had come across the street for the first time since the invasion, she had seemed as kind as ever. She'd even brought us a bunch of carrots. How could she be a friend of both the enemies and the Germans? Both Mutti and Kätchen really wrestled with that question.

One day, shortly thereafter, the soldiers were looking for workers again. "You come! You come!" one of them shouted at Kätchen and pulled her away from the scrubbing board. Hanno and Vilmar tried to hold on to their mother, but the soldier pushed them aside and dragged her by the arm along the hallway. Kätchen was too physically weak to resist and had no choice but to go along. She was not dressed warmly either but was not permitted to get a coat.

"We will pray for you," Mutti called as Kätchen was pushed out the front door. Sadness gripped my heart, and I realized that my concern for Kätchen was growing. Mutti called a prayer meeting, and after we had finished pleading for protection for her, my soul rested in the knowledge that Kätchen was truly safe in the arms of Jesus.

"Schäfle, can you imagine that the Lord prepared me for this time many years ago?" Mutti asked as I watched her begin her fur sewing. She was carefully folding back the little animal hairs with her needle. "You see, if I had not learned this when I took tailoring lessons as a teenager, I wouldn't know how to sew fur seams invisibly. It just amazes me," she continued, "how wonderfully our heavenly Father cares for us, even while we are young, teaching us lessons that we can draw on later in life.

"My mother always used to say to my sister and me, 'A girl has to be able to do everything.' And I am so glad she made that a slogan. I did learn so much when I was young. Besides the fact that many of the skills I gained are pleasurable, they have helped me so much in life. How barren my life would be if I didn't know how to cook, bake, sew, knit, crochet, embroider, and do garden and farm work. As I think of these things, I wish I had more time to fulfill my obligation to the new generation, you and Marlies. You have had to learn many things fast, my Schäfle, during the past few months. I just wish I had the time to teach you more. Perhaps someday I won't be so busy. I am really pleased, though, with the excellent job you are doing in darning the socks."

"Thank you, Mutti. But I don't like to darn. Knitting and crocheting are more exciting to me. Do you know that I have been crocheting for six years already?"

"Yes, I am aware of that. That field is inexhaustible, however. You need to become more proficient in knitting too. That green and yellow pleated skirt you knitted for the large doll, should have, I think, a yoked popcorn-stitch ski sweater to match, don't you think so? When the days lengthen, and I have finished my orders, I will teach you that knitting technique, all right? I should have some time in another week."

"I can't wait, Mutti. I can't wait."

Several hours after Kätchen had left with the soldiers, someone knocked on the downstairs bedroom window. Hanno rushed to the front door and called, "Mutti! Mutti! Liane, please open the door. Mutti is outside!"

"Please calm down, Hanno. How do you know that?"

"I saw her through the window."

After assuring myself that it was indeed Kätchen, I opened the door. Mutti had left her sewing to check on all the commotion in the hallway.

"Kätchen, what happened to you? You are as white as a sheet," Mutti remarked. "Why are you out of breath? Are you all right?" Kätchen leaned against the hallway wall as tears uncontrollably rushed down her face and onto the heads of her sons. Both of them had their arms slung around her tiny waist. Her dark dress was wet in the knee area, and her hair untidy. She was incapable of talking as she continued to sob and tremble. All of us stood in total silence.

"Our very lives are at stake." Kätchen finally broke the silence with a quivering voice. "Our nation cannot survive this tyranny. The Russians want us dead. They are going to kill us all, one way or another." She faded into a breathless pause.

"They herded about sixty women into the school across the street. They had to clean up the mess the hospital left behind, scrubbing walls and floors, while the soldiers beat them with their guns if they didn't work fast enough. Many of the women have bleeding hands and are exhausted. I worked with them for a while. During some of this time, we could hear screaming from somewhere nearby. There was no time to wonder about that though, because soon I was marched to another building and pushed into a long, very narrow room.

"'Daway rabotay, woman!' the young Russian commanded as he shoved me with his gun. 'You scrub walls!' Then he left.

"After my eyes got used to the dim light, I was about to begin. But suddenly, I began to shudder. 'Can this be true?' I was thinking. 'Are these walls splattered with fresh blood? Is this the blood of those we heard screaming? Where are they now? Are they alive or dead?' My body began to tremble at these thoughts, and I knew I had to get out. But how could I escape without getting shot? The huge school yard was filled with Russians guarding the workers. 'Please, Lord, help,' I whispered and immediately felt strength surging through my body. Leaving the room, I started walking across the school yard with all the Russians watching me, including the one who had pushed me into that bloody room. Nobody stopped me. They all stared straight at me—through me—as I walked past them and out through the gate. And here I am!" Her dark eyes were moist and sparkling as she continued, "Our God is real! He is real! He is the same God who delivered Daniel out of the lion's den. He must have blinded my enemies so that they could not see me walk across the school yard. If they had seen me, they would definitely have shot me. Oh, children! What would we do without the Lord?"

With that question lingering in the hallway, the little ones began to play again, and Mutti and Kätchen talked quietly until Onkel Lehmann returned home from work.

6

THE EYE OF THE STORM

Early the next morning, someone beat violently on the front door. When Onkel Emil opened it, a Russian said in broken German, "You all out! All out of house! Officers need house. Out right now!"

"Do you mean you want us to vacate the house? For how long?"

"Not know. Need house right now," he repeated rather impatiently. "All out! Out now!"

"We need a little time," Onkel Emil pleaded. "Need place to go. You give us thirty minutes to move?"

"No! You out fifteen minutes!" and the spokesman and his two buddies planted themselves in the hallway and waited.

"I'll quickly go to the home of two of our elderly church ladies to see if we can move in with them," Onkel Lehmann suggested. He was on his way out as he spoke.

"Schäfle, check your rucksack quickly and add a few more clothes, your most important clothes. Then please dress Marlies and Udo warmly while I gather some of the other things we need," Mutti told me, words tumbling out of her mouth as quickly as water rushes through rapids.

Completely out of breath, Onkel Lehmann returned with good news. "We are welcome at the home of the two seamstresses. These two Christians didn't even hesitate to invite the ten of us into their home. Praise the Lord."

The rest of us raced here and there, grabbing this and reaching for that.

"The handwagon is ready," Onkel Emil called. "Bring your bundles."

Dieter and Onkel Lehmann squeezed past the Russians with our luggage and rushed into the yard. Hurriedly we threw things into the wagon while Onkel Lehmann worked feverishly to organize them so that no space would be lost.

"Out! Out! Fast!" the spokesman shouted, becoming very impatient. "We not take things. You come back. Officers good to Germans." One of the men stomped up the curved staircase to our living quarters. He saw Mutti's Bible on the table of our room.

"You read Bible?" he asked Mutti with a twinkle in his eyes.

"Yes, I do."

"Me too," he told us. "You not worry. Not take things. Not worry." He clogged downstairs again.

Udo and Vilmar were seated on top of the bundles as Onkel Lehmann opened the little shed door that led to the street. The handwagon rumbled across the cobblestones as he and Mutti pulled it. It wasn't easy for Kätchen and me to help steady the little ones while carrying bundles and fighting the cold wind that whipped our faces on this sad March morning. As we struggled uphill on the next street, we could already see the white stucco house of the two sisters.

They were lovely ladies, and I was excited about seeing them again. After our boat rides last year, they often invited us to their house for cake and coffee. Their yeast cakes, topped with fruit and streusel, were always delicious, and we children were served plenty of milk. As we trudged up the hill, I thought, *Why, why, why do I always think about food when*

I know that my caved in and empty stomach hurts even more then? When will I finally learn not to dwell on thoughts of food?

It was a miracle—the two little ones weren't crying. They actually seemed to be enjoying the cold, fresh air and their ride on top of the bundles. They were taking an interest in everything: houses, clouds chasing each other, and two Russians walking down the other side of the street.

After arriving at the sisters' home, we opened the huge door and entered into a passageway that ran under their house and into a small backyard. Quietly we all stood there while Kätchen went up the staircase to their living quarters. Dieter immediately set out to explore. He would have loved to spend more time in the yard and investigate the many doors there, but with danger lurking everywhere, Mutti called him back.

"Look at this, Mutti," he said excitedly. "When this huge passage door is open, it completely covers the little red door up there. That's neat, isn't it?"

Mutti looked at the small door at the top of another shorter set of steps and nodded her head. It seemed to me as though she was acting mechanically, as though her mind and thoughts were far from us.

"I wonder what is behind it." Dieter's curiosity was unsubdued. "Can I walk up those few steps and see?"

"Yes, Dieter." We hadn't heard one of the sisters coming down the stairs until she spoke. "That is where you and your family will live. There will not be room for all of you in there, so Kätchen and her family will have to come upstairs with us. Here is the key to the door. Go and see how you like your new home."

I followed close behind as Dieter climbed up the wooden steps. He pushed the long metal key into the keyhole, turned it, and pulled down the large door handle. The door fell open and Dieter shouted with excitement, "Mutti, come and see this cozy little place!"

Mutti carried Udo up the steps into our new home.

"This is so small," Dieter continued. "Where will we all sleep?"

"We'll all sleep there in the bedroom," she answered and began to check the kitchen.

"I'll sleep here in the kitchen," Onkel Emil's voice thundered. None of us had heard him coming and we all jumped. "I will not leave you here alone. That is too dangerous, especially at night. I will protect my family. Onkel Lehmann will take care of Kätchen, and I will take care of all of you now that we have to split up."

I liked Onkel Emil, often feeling sorry for him when he talked about his wife and two daughters, but I resented it when he called us "his" family. I had to admit that he had protected us many times in the past few months, but when he spanked Dieter for practically no reason, I hurt too. Mutti always interceded for us, telling him that we were not his children, therefore he had no right to discipline us. He seemed to feel, though, that he had to help Mutti in Vati's absence.

Kätchen and Onkel Lehmann lifted their bundles off the wagon, took the boys, and moved upstairs with the sisters. After our belongings were taken off, we pulled the wagon into the courtyard. I didn't remember ever having seen handwagons in Insterburg. They resembled miniature hay wagons with four closed sides, five to six feet long and two feet deep. The rims of the four wooden, spoked wheels were covered with a metal band. The axle and the handle bar were also made of wood. It seemed that everyone in Lippehne had such a wagon to transport hundreds of different items.

Our small furnished apartment was cold even though we were bundled up. Only a few pieces of firewood were left at the stove. "Dieter and I will go and gather some firewood, Mutti, all right?" I asked. "It was quite windy last night, and there should be some sticks at the promenade."

"Thank you, Schäfle. You are thoughtful and helpful. Before you leave though," Mutti told us, "We have to make some plans for our safety. You see, our new home is located only a few buildings from the main road that leads to Berlin. That means many troops are constantly passing through Lippehne, just a few houses from us. That makes it far less safe here for us. We also live only a short distance from the town square, and you have told me that the square is always crowded with Russians. Living here is much more dangerous than it was at Onkel Lehmann's farm. So we have to take certain precautions. If nobody finds us here, we can be as safe as Noah was in the ark. But if we are careless, it could be the end for us."

"Your mother is absolutely right, children," Onkel Emil added. "This location is terribly dangerous. We are really at the mercy of the enemy here if they find us. We have no basement to hide in, no barn, no outhouse, and no shed. We are an open target for the Russians. The Lord can protect us here, too, as He has so miraculously done at the farm, but we have to do our utmost not to give away our hideout."

"We all have to be very quiet from now on," Mutti continued, "so we will not be detected. When you two leave the house to go begging, we will first check the street for soldiers without touching the curtains. We will also open the door very quietly, a crack at first, and listen for sounds in the passageway. Then we will peek, and if no one is in sight, you two will tiptoe down the steps. Should someone watch you when you return, don't come toward our home. Don't make any moves toward our door if a Russian is nearby."

"We understand, Mutti," Dieter said very somberly. "We'll be careful."

Onkel Emil went to the window that overlooked the street. "Coast is clear," he whispered.

Mutti cracked the apartment door, listened, and then opened it a little more. She kissed Dieter and me and said, "The Lord keep you," as we carefully moved down the steps.

Our walk to the lake was considerably longer from our new home. We were thrilled to see that a lot of dead wood had fallen out of the trees during the past windy night, and nobody had beaten us to it this morning. We had no problem filling our arms, but it was much more difficult to carry our loads home because of the distance. After delivering the wood, we went on a begging tour. The only place we found Russians eating was at the town square.

"Look at that, Liane," Dieter said with a big grin on his round face. "A motorcycle! Every man's dream."

"You are not a man yet, little brother."

"But I'm dreaming! I wonder what it is like to ride a motorcycle," Dieter mused.

"I wouldn't know. I have never been on one, but did you know that Vati had a motorcycle when he was courting Mutti? He always traveled from Insterburg to Memel on it to see her."

"No, I didn't know that. I just know about our Olympia car, the one with the colored rings on the front that the SS took from our garage. Do you think they would have taken it if Vati had been home?"

"Yes, they would have. They had orders to take our car whether Vati was there or not. They told Mutti not to be upset about losing the car. We would lose a lot more, they said. And they were right about that."

While we stood on the sidewalk and talked, the motorcyclist suddenly stopped in front of us. The smiling Russian pointed to Dieter and the back seat and motioned for him to jump on. In a split second, my brother had hopped on and slung his short arms around the Russian's waist. Then the pair took off, riding in huge circles in the square. The Russian hollered at his buddies and grinned constantly. Dieter's smile was almost touching his ears. He was so happy. His dream had come true. After many dizzying loops around the square, his friend stopped and they both got off. Then the soldier motioned for Dieter to wait while he climbed onto the tank and vanished inside. A few moments later, he reappeared, and I couldn't believe what I saw. He ran his fingers through Dieter's curls, smiled at him, and gave him a whole loaf of black bread. Dieter shook hands with his friend and dashed toward me. "This is heavy," he exclaimed proudly. "Here! Lift it!"

"It certainly is. It seems to be heavier than a five-pound loaf of German bread."

"What do you think Mutti will say when she sees this?"

"She'll be happy, Dieter."

I was glad for the food, but just once I would have liked the joy of being the one to surprise Mutti with some bread.

In just a few minutes, we reached our home. When all our safety checks were made and we felt nobody was watching us, we opened the huge, heavy door, dashed up the steps, and slipped into our little apartment. Mutti and Onkel Emil couldn't believe their eyes. A whole loaf of bread? Dieter, with his face aglow, proudly told the fairy tale he had just experienced. A trip on a motorcycle and bread? That was almost too much for anyone to believe.

When we were all set for our devotions, Mutti was heartbroken to realize that her Bible had remained behind on the table at Onkel Lehmann's house. Onkel Emil had not had his Bible for some time. It was lost with his luggage on the trip to Lippehne.

"We will now have to search our hearts and see how much Scripture we have memorized." Mutti opened our spiritual time. "Let's see, children, how much of God's Word we have hidden in our hearts. But first we'll start with a song. Let's sing.

"Because I am Jesus's little sheep
I am glad forevermore
My good shepherd knows me and cares for me
He loves me and calls me by my name."
(Hayn, "Weil ich Jesu Schäflein bin")

"Yes, Mutti," Marlies said excitedly, "He loves me, too." Her curls bounced around her head when she moved and talked. She was so cute. "I like to sing that song all the time," she continued. Suddenly she began to sing a solo of "Jesus Loves Me." When our little soloist was finished, we all sang in whispering tones, "God Is Love, He Came to Redeem Me" and many other beautiful songs. Onkel Emil started quoting Scripture. When my turn came, I quoted John 3:16, "For God so loved the world, that he gave his only begotten Son, that whosoever believeth in him should not perish, but have everlasting life."

"Does that mean He loves the Russians too, Mutti?" My brother looked puzzled.

"Of course, Jesus does, Dieter. God sent His Son for the whole world, for every human being. You see, the Lord does not care whether you are Russian or German. Neither does He care if you are rich or poor. He is concerned, however, whether you are going to heaven or hell. He is concerned about each one making the right decision. He wants everybody to be forgiven of his sins and to live in heaven with Him."

"I see."

"Now here are my verses," Mutti said.

"He that dwelleth in the secret place of the most High
    Shall abide under the shadow of the Almighty.
I will say of the LORD, He is my refuge and my fortress:
    My God; in him will I trust." (Ps. 91:1–2)

Then Onkel Emil joined Mutti,

"Surely he shall deliver thee from the snare of the fowler,
    And from the noisome pestilence" (Ps. 91:3).

Alone he continued,

"Thou shalt not be afraid for the terror by night;
  Nor for the arrow that flieth by day" (Psalm 91:5).

"How comforting," Mutti added.

"Let's all pray now," Onkel Emil continued. "We thank You, Lord, for using our enemies to sustain us. We belong to You, Lord, and we thank You that we can always depend on You to help us.

"You know the whereabouts of our loved ones. Please keep my wife safe and strong. Watch over my daughters. Keep Emmy's husband and the father of these children from harm. We pray for Kätchen and all the others upstairs, even those we don't know; please keep them safe.

"Forgive us where we have displeased You and sinned against You. Cover all our sins with Your blood. It is too difficult for me to understand why You, the Almighty, even show concern for us and love us, but we thank You for everything. I pray this in Jesus's name. Amen."

During the night, the passageway was filled with noisy and drunken soldiers. We heard them stomping up the longer wooden stairs which led to the apartments of the sisters and several other young ladies. The next morning silence had set in again, and we noticed that the huge passage door was wide open, completely covering our small door.

In the following days, our begging trips often yielded nothing edible, but we were usually successful in finding firewood. Mutti was busy all day caring for Marlies and Udo. Both of them were crying more every day because of hunger, and Mutti's biggest problem was keeping them quiet. I felt so sad every time I saw her cupping her hand over Udo's mouth so his crying couldn't be heard. There was nothing to eat besides a few potatoes that Dieter and I had found at the cache several days ago.

The next morning, Onkel Emil could no longer endure the little ones' suffering, and he decided to risk his life by going out in search of food or a job.

"Surely the Russians will not harm a one-legged old invalid of World War I," he whispered jokingly as he prepared to leave.

"We can't predict what they may or may not do, Emil. So please be careful," Mutti advised.

We all helped check the street and passage before we gave Onkel Emil the signal that it was safe to step outside. He didn't return until late in the afternoon, but his face was aglow. Onkel Emil handed Mutti a can that contained about one pint of watery soup, and one slice of dark bread. "This is my wage for the day," he announced proudly. "I am the tailor for the Russian commander, and he wanted me to find other Germans who are capable of doing tailoring and organize a tailor shop. We are to sew uniforms for the Russians. The pay will be one can of soup and one slice of bread per day."

"This is cabbage soup. Thank you, Emil!" Mutti said in a voice filled with emotion. "You are a wonderful help to me and my children. Congratulations on your new job too. You'll have to tell me later how you expect to go about setting up your tailor shop and how you plan to find your personnel. But right now, I'll heat up the soup and feed my starving children."

Each day from then on, we gave thanks for the soup Onkel Emil brought home for us. He needed nourishment, too, but was kind and selfless. Even though his ration put some food into our stomachs, we still continued to suffer from hunger pangs.

One day after returning from work, Onkel Emil paid Kätchen and the others a visit. He learned that they were barely surviving on the few supplies the sisters still had and Onkel Lehmann's wage for the work he continued to do for the Russians, one slice of bread per day. Every night, the noisy and drunken Russians visited the two young women in the next apartment, but none of the others had been molested. Onkel Emil called our attention to the fact that we had already been away from the farm for two months.

"It is a miracle, a real miracle," he said, "that we have lived in complete safety throughout all that time. During the hours of greatest danger, the night hours when the open season on women begins, the Lord always keeps us hidden behind the passage door."

Dieter and I continued our hunts for food, day after long, cold day. Often we found things for which we were not looking. "Why are they taking the skin off the man's head, Liane?" Dieter asked nonchalantly as we walked past the window of a home.

"What are you saying? Taking off skin?"

"Yes, look in that window."

We doubled back, and I was truly scared when I saw the gruesome sight. Dieter was right. An autopsy was being performed right in front of the low window of a home. The sight of it made me shiver. Both of us suddenly found ourselves running along the streets of Lippehne. We were running without knowing why, and we arrived at home totally out of breath, with just a few pieces of firewood under our arms. I think we forgot to return to the lake for more wood.

Days later, we found a much more pleasant surprise. "Close your eyes and open your hands, Mutti," we whispered after our return home.

Mutti squeezed her eyes shut and stretched both hands out in front of her.

"Pussy willows and a birch branch?" Mutti said totally surprised, "Is it spring?" She began to weep.

"We don't want you to cry, Mutti. We want you to be happy."

"It is spring, and I didn't even know it here in our little ark. You children are like the dove that told Noah that the waters had receded and that there was life outside the ark." Then she hugged us. "Thank you, children! Thank You, Lord, for showing Your love to me! Thank You for showing me that Your love is as fresh as spring every day!"

In the midst of our excitement, a timid tap on our door told us that a friend must be visiting us. How thrilled we were to see Onkel Lehmann. He had decided, at great risk, to return to the farm to check on things there, and he had come to tell us about his experiences.

"I knocked on the door and was amazed that the officer invited me in. I informed him that I just wanted to get a few things and look around. He was very friendly and gave me permission to do so. I noticed immediately that several pieces of furniture were missing and decided to go upstairs to check on the two sewing machines. What I saw there proved to me again that we have a God who cares about His children. You remember, Emmy, that the two machines were standing in the attic side by side—your new cabinet-type Singer machine and my wife's old treadle machine. Well, my wife's machine is gone, but, believe it or not, yours is still standing in the same spot."

"You mean they took the old machine and left my new one? The Lord must have struck them with blindness! Maybe they didn't consider the small table to be a machine. I have had the feeling for some time that it will be my sewing that will keep my children alive, and now I know that for certain. Thank you, Onkel Lehmann, for the wonderful news! I just have to pray now that the machine will remain there until we return to your little farm. Did they say anything about when we'll be able to return?"

"I asked them, but they didn't answer me."

A few days later, just as Dieter and I were in the process of dragging firewood into the passage, we noticed that Kätchen was knocking gently on our door.

"Emmy," she said excitedly when Mutti opened the door. But the smile quickly vanished from her face when she saw Mutti reaching for Udo's mouth and holding it shut. "Emmychen, I am sorry—how long can our children endure this?"

"He is crying all the time now. I can't let him cry out loud. We can't let them find us here."

"Our poor children. How sad I feel. Here is a little piece of bread for you and a little flour."

"Thank you, Kätchen, thank you so much! Where did you get this?"

"I went to our little farm. Since the officers there were kind enough to my dad, I decided to walk home myself and ask for some food. One of them inquired as to what we need. I told him that we have nothing to eat and would really appreciate some fat, a little sugar, and some potatoes. He said he would place food for me in the courtyard under the old cover of my mother's first sewing machine, so that no one else would see it. It seems they have to be very careful even among themselves. After looking around a little, I went outside and was surprised that the officer had indeed kept his promise. He really had placed some food under the cover. It was another miracle. Without our Lord caring for us so miraculously, we definitely would not have survived this long. So take these few things, Emmy, and feed your starving son."

The two mothers encouraged each other for a few moments before Kätchen quietly slipped back upstairs.

Kätchen's visit had refreshed Mutti, and she even sang while Udo and Marlies were munching on a piece of bread.

Mutti began preparing our dinner. "We will have Klunkersuppe tonight," she told us joyfully.

"Klunkersuppe? We haven't had that in half a year."

"Yes, I think you are right. It has been a long time. Why don't you cook it for us tonight, Schäfle?"

"I hope I still remember how to prepare it." I thought hard. "Let me see. You bring the water to a boiling point, add a pinch of cattle salt, and then drop the little moistened lumps of flour into the boiling water, right? Then you let it boil for a few minutes and what do you have? The most wonderful soup ever for our empty stomachs."

"Perfect, Schäfle. Just perfect."

That night, even though I had been busy all day, it was very difficult for me to fall asleep. The ruckus from the drunken soldiers in the passageway was louder than ever. Suddenly screams pierced through the courtyard.

"Help! Help! Lord, help me!" Voices of young women rent the air, and men's voices answered with cruel laughter. I buried my head in the featherbed, hoping for silence, but the drunken brawling continued to be mingled with the screams of women. Was there no one to help them? The cries of pain and agony absolutely horrified me. How I wished there was something I could do. There I was, safe in bed—what was happening to them? I tried to envision things and wondered if Kätchen was one of them. Heavy boots constantly stomped upstairs to the apartments. Throughout the night, screams of girls and women filtered into our little home.

"God, why are You so good to us?" I asked. "So many are suffering right now and we are safe here in Your ark. Why, Lord? Why?" There was really no way for me to answer my own questions, except that I thought God must have a special purpose for keeping us alive and safe. If so, I reasoned, then nothing would be able to harm us until the Lord allowed it. With that comforting thought, I was finally able to get some sleep.

When I awakened in the morning, the sun was shining brightly. Everything was quiet and peaceful, and I was certain that the horrible screams of the previous night were probably just a bad dream. Before I was able to set my thoughts in order, Kätchen walked into our room. Was I relieved to see her that day!

"Praise the Lord for protecting us all through another night, Emmychen!" she said, bubbling with excitement. "We were safe again under the shadow of the Almighty. Did I mention to you before how we always bolt our door and secure it with a heavy log? Well, last night someone was beating on the door during all that screaming, and before we could open it, a Russian, a messenger of God, broke through the door."

"What did you say? A Russian, a messenger of God?"

"Yes, Emmy! My dad was on his knees, crying before the Lord and interceding for all of those whose screams we heard. The Russian recognized my dad as one who had worked for him and said, motioning at all the frightened ladies in our room, 'You are father here? No afraid. Me back.' And with those remarks he left. A short time later, he returned with bacon and bread. Can you imagine that? Bacon and bread?"

Mutti was speechless.

"We have a gracious God, Emmy, don't we? You or I could have been one of those who were tortured and raped last night by those drunken beasts." Both women embraced and wept uncontrollably.

Several days later, in early May, the streets were filled with jubilant Russians. "Hitler kaputt!" they hollered. "Hitler kaputt!" What did this mean? Could this mean the war had ended? Everyone was guessing, but no one seemed to have an answer. On his way home from work, Onkel Emil heard the same expressions of joy from Russians in the streets—"Hitler kaputt! Hitler kaputt!" Onkel Emil also shared another story he heard at work. His coworkers told him of a lineup of Germans who were to be shot because one of the Russian comrades was found dead.

"You Germans kill comrade. You kill friend," Russians yelled to those in the lineup. In order to prove the Germans guilty, an autopsy was performed publicly in the town square. To the embarrassment of all those watching, the autopsy showed that the soldier died of nothing other than an overconsumption of alcohol. Instead of being shot, the frightened Germans were set free.

All through the night, drunken Russians celebrated by yelling, hollering, and shooting in the streets. "Hitler kaputt! Germany kaputt!" These phrases filtered into our little home continuously, along with screams and sobs from women and girls. Bottles or dishes were smashed against the passage walls, and none of us were able to sleep.

"What will happen if the war is really over?" Mutti asked Onkel Emil the next morning. "What will we do? Will we stay here? Where else can we go? How can we find our loved ones?"

These questions and many more went back and forth like ping-pong balls.

"How can we make any plans if we don't know for certain that the war has ended?" Onkel Emil said. "Perhaps these are just rumors. I can't believe that the Germans gave up so easily. Hitler would fight, fight, fight for us. How can you even consider that the war is over, Emmy?"

"Do you really believe, Emil, that God would not punish Germany for the way Hitler moved with destruction into foreign lands and uprooted people? Even more, Hitler degraded God's chosen people by taking away their businesses and burning their synagogues. Had they harmed anybody? No! They lived peacefully among us. Then he decided to mark every Jewish person by having him wear the yellow Star of David on his clothing. Look how much we have suffered—and we were supposedly Hitler's people. That same man hated Jews. So we probably have no idea how much more they have suffered! I believe, as I think you do, too, that any crime committed against God's people is a crime committed against God. Do you think God can quietly overlook all this? He wouldn't be a righteous God if He did."

"Yes, I agree. But the problem is that those who did not support Hitler now also have to suffer. Look at the predicament in which we find ourselves. Our families are ripped apart. We are barely surviving. All this because of one man who set out to conquer the world. If we couldn't cling to our Father right now, things would be utterly hopeless for us. What would we do without our faith and without the anticipation of our heavenly home? How could we even exist without the knowledge that He is still in control of the universe?"

"I don't know," Mutti replied sadly as she turned to Udo and Marlies who were crying bitterly, but softly. "I really don't know. I just don't see how you can still believe in Hitler and his miracle weapons and his miracle powers. Hasn't that man put us through enough yet? Are you by any chance a Nazi yourself?"

"What do you think, Emmy? Can a born-again Christian be a Nazi?" Onkel Emil seemed insulted that she had asked such a question.

At midmorning Onkel Lehmann came to our door with the exciting news that the Russians had vacated his little farm.

"Let's all return home as quickly as possible," he suggested, "before anyone else moves into the house."

Hurriedly Mutti and I packed our few belongings and put coats on the little ones. Dieter and I brought the handwagon from the courtyard and began placing our bundles in it. Kätchen, Onkel Lehmann, and his two grandsons were just scrambling down the stairs. They added their bundles to the wagon. With Udo perched in the middle of everything, we took off over the bumpy, centuries-old cobblestones. We encountered no soldiers on the streets as our small parade moved to the end of the block and turned left toward the little farm. Dieter and his friend, Hanno, were happy to see each other after so many weeks.

"This warm spring air is so refreshing, Emmychen, isn't it?" Kätchen bubbled.

"Oh yes! I think Noah and his family must have felt this way when they left the ark."

"Will you tell us that story tonight, Mutti?" Dieter pleaded. "You tell the story, and when you come to the animals, I'll name them."

"We'll do that, my son."

"Bow-wow, bow-wow!" Udo tried to bark when he heard the word *animals*.

7

HOME AGAIN

The green front door of our little farmhouse was wide open when we arrived, and the boys were so excited about being home again that they could hardly be restrained. Eagerly they tried to run into the house, but Onkel Lehmann held them back.

"I'll go in first and check things out. I don't want you fellows to encounter danger. You may come as far as the hallway and wait there."

"The house stinks," Hanno said to those of us still standing outside as he held his nose. "It stinks terribly."

"Horribly! Terribly!" Dieter chimed in. "Phew! Phew!"

"I guess it is safe," Onkel Lehmann reported. "I can't see anyone anywhere."

We started bringing the bundles into our home, and soon everyone agreed that the house stank terribly. Mutti carried bundles upstairs, and I followed her with Udo. Suddenly I heard her cough and gag. When I reached her, I realized that she was vomiting.

"What is the matter, Mutti?" I asked, but found the answer myself. The laundry tub, right next to our room, was filled to overflowing with human waste. Kätchen rushed upstairs to check on all the commotion, and when she saw the tub, she also got sick.

Mutti had left a note for Onkel Emil, so before too long he arrived at the farmhouse, knocking on the door in Morse code. Onkel Lehmann let him in, but Onkel Emil's joy was short-lived as well when he smelled and saw what Russian culture had done to our home.

"How will we ever get rid of this mess?" he wondered aloud. "I believe Onkel Lehmann and I will have to be in charge of emptying the kettle, since the stomachs of both of you women are so weak. We'll have to carry the waste to a field bucket by bucket."

"Have you seen the outhouse yet, Emil?" Mutti asked.

"No, I haven't."

That, too, looked beyond description. Feces were piled high all around the seat, in the corners, and on the floor.

When darkness set in, Mutti and I had accomplished quite a bit in setting our room in order.

"We'll have to clean the rest of it tomorrow," Mutti told me. "We accomplished quite a bit today in cleaning and discarding filthy rags. What I can't understand, though, is that after all that work, the house still stinks. We'll probably have to clean for weeks to get this place back in order."

What a joyful time of devotions we had that night. We were reunited again, and we were all back home.

"Thank You, Lord." Onkel Lehmann prayed, "for being so good to us. You are the great Creator, and You have shown us over and over that You do not forsake those who trust in You. You have kept us safe while we were apart, and You graciously returned our home to us. Lord, we thank You. Every day You become more precious to us. Earthly possessions mean less now than they did a few short months ago. Lord, may we not cling to anything or desire anything but You.

"Lord, I pray for our enemies. Let us somehow be a blessing to them. Let them see that we love You. O Lord, don't forget all the people of this town, those who are still at home, and those who are wandering about somewhere. Please don't let our neighbors forget the promises they made to You in this very room. Forgive us where we have sinned today. O Lord, place all our shortcomings under Your blood. Lord, we love You, and we praise You, and we thank You. In the name of Your precious Son, Jesus. Amen."

When we awakened the next morning, our room still stank.

"I'll help you clean for a while, Mutti, before Dieter and I go begging. I'll scrub the floor for you."

"That's good, Schäfle, thank you. I'll scrub some more of the filth in the attic while you finish this room."

With a hand broom and dustpan, I started sweeping under the bed and became excited.

"Mutti, come see what I found. Why didn't we look under the bed sooner? Our curtains are back there."

Stretching out on the floor on my stomach, I slid under the bed, reached for the curtains, and slid back out.

"How disgusting! Mutti, come and see. The curtains have been torn into pieces and guess what's wrapped inside?"

"Sick! Sick! Sick!" Mutti said, and her whole body seemed to go into convulsions. "That is Russian culture! Dung wrapped in curtains!"

With the broom, I shoved the lace curtains onto the dustpan and dumped them into the garbage. Mutti helped me move the heavy bed, and I continued scrubbing the floor. Suddenly I heard Mutti making strange noises in the attic. "What is the matter, Mutti?" I called, rushing to her. She just stood there, with her right hand pointing at her discovery—our canning jars, lined up near the sewing machine, were filled with human waste.

After days of vomiting, gagging, scrubbing, and discarding, Mutti and Kätchen finally turned our sickening situation around.

Onkel Emil enjoyed his work at the tailor shop and was thrilled to hand Mutti his soup and piece of bread every night. Along with other Germans whom he had recruited and trained, he was a valuable tailor for the Russians. Onkel Lehmann had been recruited by the Russians from his digging work to guard the pianos and sewing machines that they had taken out of homes. The valuable items stood at the railroad station for months, covered with snow or soaked from rain. Not one piece had been shipped to Russia because of the destruction of the railroad tracks.

Shocking and disgusting were the ways of many Russian guards at the school across the street. Dieter and I eventually had to quit taking our shortcut by way of the promenades because of one character who stood, always against the same tree at the entrance, making obscene gestures and keeping his privy part exposed. The searching of homes and raping of women continued as new troops regularly moved into Lippehne.

Since the war had ended, we were able to have more contact with other Germans. Being less isolated, however, also brought more sorrows. We learned of all kinds of atrocities that had ruined the lives of Germans in various ways. The mind of a neighbor's beautiful fifteen-year-old daughter snapped after continual public rapes by the Russians. She acted and talked like a baby.

The twenty-five-year-old mayor's daughter was forced to help clear the town of rubbish and cadavers. As guards stood over her with their rifles, her spade hit a body. It was that of her father. He had been missing for several months. Two of Onkel Lehmann's young female church members were suffering great physical pain because of the many rapes they had to endure. The wounded hands of those whose fingers had been chopped off by the Russians, so they could take the gold wedding bands, were healing very poorly without medical attention.

One day another order reached the few Germans left in Lippehne. From the Russian commander it came—all Germans must leave. Only those considered valuable to the Russian labor force—Onkel Emil, the tailor, and Mutti, who assisted him by working at home—were to stay. Since we lived with Onkel Lehmann and Kätchen, they were also allowed to stay. Some of the Germans rounded up two weak and undernourished horses to pull a hay wagon laden with sick and old people. For us, the worst meaning of the order was that Omi and my aunt would have to go also, since they were no longer living in Onkel Lehmann's house.

"Mutti, I don't want them to leave! Omi can't leave us!" Even to myself, I was beginning to sound frantic.

"Oh, Schäfle, how I wish we could do something to keep her and my sister-in-law with us longer, but we can't. Only the Lord can comfort us now. Only the Lord knows if we will ever see them again."

"God be with you till we meet again," Mutti said with tears streaming down her face as she kissed her mother-in-law. Silently weeping, she gave her sister-in-law a hug. I just wanted to hold on to Omi and not let her go. Her face was so etched in sorrow that I could hardly bear to look at her. We only embraced and cried—our sweet Omi—Vati's wonderful mother. Why did she have to leave us? And my aunt, why? Why? I didn't think I would ever get over it—not as long as I lived. Omi sat on the wagon while my aunt followed on foot. Brokenhearted, we stood and watched our loved ones slowly turn the next street corner. *War! War! I hate it,* I thought. *It kills! It separates!*

After that, the languages Dieter and I heard on our begging trips were no longer German and Russian, but Polish and Russian. The Polish people were being brought to Lippehne by the Russians to help them claim the conquered land. The Poles were very angry people because the communists had forced them out of their homes. In Lippehne they were given the privilege to move into any home they chose. Those arriving first continued, as had the conquerors, to loot and steal from the few

Germans who were still in town. They rushed from one vacated house to another, helping themselves to whatever they needed and wanted. They burglarized and harassed the Germans, after the 9:00 p.m. curfew especially. They, and everyone else, were aware of the fact that to go and report a crime during the curfew hours called for immediate arrest. This law made the Germans and their belongings open prey for anyone.

One day while searching through a farm for something edible, my brother and I climbed into the attic and found a pile of small seeds.

"Wheat! Wheat! We have found wheat!" Dieter called excitedly.

"No, that is not wheat, and it isn't rye either. I remember what grain looks like. Opi had fields of it on his farm. But this is not wheat. Don't you remember how we used to play hide and seek among the sheaves in the field? We used to call the eight or ten sheaves, which were leaning against one another to dry, our houses; and we always sat inside, munching on kernels of wheat or rye. Those kernels didn't look like these."

"I remember the playing part, but I don't remember what the seeds looked like. I also remember the storks always walking between our houses and gobbling up the frogs. Do you remember the racket they made when they stood on their huge wagon wheel nest and clapped their beaks? Every morning when I wanted to sleep, they woke me up with their beaks."

"Did Opi ever tell you, Dieter, that the same stork couple had come back to the same nest every spring for fifteen years?"

"They must have liked that huge wheel Opi put in the tree for them to build their nest on. But how did we get on the stork subject?"

"It all started with the seeds."

"Anyway, I don't know what kind of seeds these are. Let's take some home and see if Mutti can use them. I think I saw a small bucket downstairs. We can scoop them into that, and if they are edible we'll come back for more."

"You children," Mutti greeted us. "You scavengers—where did you find millet?"

"In the attic, on a farm," Dieter answered proudly. "We can get more. Would you like more?"

"What can you do with millet?" I still wasn't sure about those strange-looking seeds.

"We can grind it and make flour. We'll grind it in the coffee grinder, a little bit at a time."

Kätchen came and joined the excited group. "It will take a long time to turn this into flour, but with everybody helping we will be done in no time."

"And think of the nutritious millet soup and millet pancakes we'll enjoy," Mutti added.

Dieter, the little provider, seemed so proud to help. "Let's go, Liane, and get the rest of the millet seeds."

Later that day, after the rest of the millet had been safely cached, Mutti gathered us four together. "Today, children," Mutti announced, "I want to hear you recite your poems. We haven't done that in several days, and we must make sure that we are ready for Vati's homecoming. You start, my little son. Can you say your lines?"

Udo stood up straight and tall, hands at his sides and intermingled with some baby talk said,

"Vati, dear Vati, I greet you today.
I pray that you never again go away."

When he had finished, he dashed into Mutti's arms for his reward, a hug.

Then Marlies, the little charmer, placed herself in front of us and curtsied:

"Vati, O Vati, I love you today.
Will you stay home so that we can play?
I waited so-o-o-o long to see your face
And know that it is only God's grace
That we can all be together again
And with you love Jesus and not be afraid.
I am so glad you are at our house.
I love you, Vati. Your little Pittimaus."

Another quick curtsy and with two leaps she was in Mutti's lap. Dieter's and my poems were considerably longer, and Mutti took in every word. Our performance seemed to please her because her face was glowing with pride and joy. "Vati will be so proud of you and so happy to see you all. We must pray more that our reunion will be soon."

"We must pray for Hanno and Vilmar's Vati too," Marlies added. "Vilmar cried yesterday. He misses his Vati," she recounted with a sad face.

"Yes, we will pray for him too."

As we sat on the couch in our room, we all prayed for a long time for everyone we knew, especially for Omi, my aunt, and Vati. We had no idea where any of them might be, or what they might be suffering.

Our water situation was becoming serious. We had learned to live with only two hours of running city water daily. For the past few days, however, we had no water at all. Hauling water from a large well in the town square had become another new assignment for Dieter and me. We pumped our buckets only half full so that they were not too heavy for us to carry home. For several days we helped supply water for our needs. When the city again returned to the two hours of running water, we filled every pot, tub, and bottle in the house, just in case the supply would be turned off again. During bath time that week, we would really have to conserve.

"There is no other way but for all of us to use the same bathwater," Kätchen announced after dinner. "Of course, we can't use much soap either since our supply is almost exhausted. Lathering will not be allowed. A few hand-turns around the soap per person is it. I suggest, Emmychen, we go by age. What do you think?"

"That is a splendid idea."

"I don't plan to participate in the 'bathathon,'" Onkel Lehmann said. "I must disagree with the concept that it is a splendid idea. You'll have one less, then."

"Well, we start with Udo. He is the only one who gets clean water," Mutti told everyone and started to get him ready. The scum was scooped off the top of the water after each person. I was glad I was number six in line and not the last one like Onkel Emil. No one complained, though, and everyone was thankful for the bath and for being able to greet the Lord's day with a clean feeling.

"God, Creator of the universe," Onkel Lehmann prayed during our Sunday service, "we praise You for Your goodness to us. We thank You for Your love to us, for sending Your only Son for us, and for the countless blessings You have given us.

"Thank You for Your daily protection and the miracle of sustaining us on so little food. Lord, You know our bodies continue to weaken, and some of us struggle with boils. Heal us if it is Your will.

"We commit all our loved ones to You and our neighbors who have had to leave, wherever they are today, and our enemies."

As Onkel Lehmann's voice went on, I realized the prayer must have been too long for Udo. He had fallen asleep.

One day at the old bakery, Dieter and I noticed people standing in line. The smell of fresh bread filled the street and made us hungry. We walked to the end of the line and stood there along with everyone else, waiting to get into the store. When I took a closer look at the Polish ladies, I realized that they all looked rather sad. All of them were wearing scarves to cover their hair, and few of them talked. They just stared and appeared oblivious to everything going on around them. When, after about an hour and a half of waiting, we stepped up to the counter to ask for bread, we were told that we could not buy bread without Polish money. Polish money? Where could we get Polish zlotys? Dieter broke down and cried. "Where can we get zlotys?"

A few days later, a Polish lady came to our house carrying a bag of fur pieces. She had heard about Mutti's sewing ability and asked her to sew a fur coat. She would pay Mutti in zlotys when the coat was finished. For a whole week, Mutti worked every day and by candlelight throughout the greater part of the night. The promise of getting Polish currency for her sewing gave Mutti the added energy to finish the sewing project. How delighted she was when her customer gave her five hundred zlotys for the work.

"I'll go to town today," she said joyfully, "to the new grocery store. I wonder what I can buy with all this money. What our bodies need most right now is fat. That is one item I definitely plan to purchase." She disguised herself as an old grandmother. She put on a long black dress, covered her beautiful curls with a black scarf, and hobbled up the street with a cane.

When Mutti returned, Kätchen opened the door to let her in. Mutti scuffed into the hallway, pushing one foot in front of the other, back bent low, breathing heavily.

"Emmychen, you look very uninviting." Kätchen jested. "Is that how you moved through town?"

"You better believe it!"

The two friends laughed so hard that they had to hold their stomachs.

"Now let me see you move to the end of the hallway again, Great-grandmother! You are a wonderful actress! How I wish I had a camera to take a picture of you," Kätchen giggled. "Tell me now, what did you purchase with all that money? I've been so caught up in the drama and excitement of your acting, I almost forgot to ask what you were able to buy with your riches."

"Well, Kätchen, here it is. My week's wage yielded one pound of butter and nothing else."

"That is all you got for five hundred zlotys?"

"That is all."

"Is the butter fresh?"

"Funny, Kätchen, you should ask that. I never thought of checking. I was just so happy to get it." As Mutti and Kätchen unwrapped the butter, they didn't even have to hold it close to their noses. The butter was rancid.

However great our disappointment, the news that Mutti was an excellent seamstress quickly spread through the Polish community. Several women brought their fabrics and ordered dresses. Mutti no longer accepted money as payment but requested food. Dieter and I were also becoming more deeply involved in Mutti's new sewing business. We took our buckets and walked to the other side of the lake to the homes that had been destroyed on the night of the invasion of Lippehne. There we searched through the ruins for charcoal, which Mutti used in her flatiron.

As Mutti's business increased, our trips to the ruins also became more frequent. Occasionally we found Russian soldiers and asked them for bread. Our Russian vocabulary continued to grow, and we were now able to approach them in their own language. The smell of garlic on their breath seemed stronger during the summer days and their uniforms now consisted of olive-green pants, blouse-like shirts, and leather belts. Without their hats they seemed funny to us because they were all shorn. "No lice that way," one of them told us when Dieter asked.

Late in the spring, a day of celebration came to us. One of Mutti's customers, a farmer's wife, came to pick up her dress and insisted that Dieter and I return to her farm with her. We couldn't understand why, but Mutti trusted her and let us go. It was a warm, sunny day. Walking through town, we followed the lady across one open field after another. It seemed we would never get to the farm, but finally she pointed it out to us in the distance. She tried to converse with us in Polish, but we didn't understand one word. Upon arriving at the farm, the heavy-set lady took us to her kitchen and offered us each a cup of milk.

"Danke schön, danke schön," Dieter said as he reached for his and quickly gulped it down. How I wished I could talk to the kind lady! I would have told her that we hadn't had a drop of milk since January, and how much we appreciated her kindness.

She was dipping into her huge can again, filling a small aluminum can with milk. She handed it to me. To Dieter she gave a loaf of bread and a piece of lard wrapped in paper.

"Go home!" she said with a big grin which pulled up her rosy cheeks to look like small balloons. "Go home!" After we thanked her again, she opened the door for us, and we left.

"Do you think Udo will like the milk?" Dieter asked excitedly.

"He will, even though he doesn't know what it is. He is too small to remember milk."

"I don't think he is small. He will be two years old soon."

"That is true, but he can't remember things yet as well as you and I can."

On our way home, we tried to imagine what Mutti and Kätchen would say when they saw our treasures.

"Let's sit down here for a while, Dieter, in the soft, green grass and take a rest."

A lark, Mutti's favorite bird, was singing beautifully as I watched the clouds which hardly seemed to move. In a hedgerow nearby, I saw a sparrow preening itself. How peaceful it was here in the country. There seemed to be nothing to fear.

As we were sitting, watching the birds fly by, Dieter finally could contain himself no longer. "Do you think I could have some of that milk? I could use the lid for a cup. Then it won't be so heavy for you to carry either."

"No, Dieter. Absolutely not. We are going to carry every drop in this can home. I'm sure, though, that Mutti will give you a little more when we get back."

Both of us fought down the temptation to lighten our load by eating some of our wonderful gifts, but we did not yield and arrived home with every drop of milk and every crumb of bread.

"You brought milk and bread and lard? This is just unbelievable. A miracle!" Mutti rejoiced when we showed her.

"Praise the Lord! We can't believe it!" and more expressions of this kind sprang forth from both Mutti and Kätchen. What a feast we would have! But why was Mutti crying? Could it have been that she was so happy because her undernourished children would drink milk that day?

8

TIMES OF TESTING

A new influx of Russian soldiers made our lives become more restless and fearful again. One night all of us were huddled in one room when, at about 10:00 p.m., someone beat furiously on the front door. Onkel Emil limped to the door, but before he could open it completely, the impatient soldiers forced it open, ramming him into the hallway wall. They raced from room to room, aiming their flashlights at the faces of the sleeping children, under the beds, and anywhere they thought a German soldier, or a woman, might hide. After an unsuccessful hunt, they looked in vain for vodka and food. The farm yard, coal shed, and barn didn't yield anything either.

"German woman beautiful," one of the soldiers said as he ripped Mutti's black scarf from her head. "Not this. Why this?"

"Because German woman afraid. Afraid of Ruski," Mutti answered.

"Not be afraid, woman. Ruski wants love German woman." With that he tried to embrace her, but she pushed him away. His persistence made her angry, and she continued to fight to free herself. Suddenly the soldier realized that his comrades had left, and he dashed out of the room. Most nights brought incidents such as that. It was very unusual to have a calm night, especially since there were Polish troops now, also, who searched houses and stole whatever they desired.

Daytime had its own surprises. One morning a Polish soldier banged on the door. "Woman, come," he commanded when Kätchen answered. "Come work."

"You have to wait," she said boldly. "I have to dress my children first. I have to take them along." With that, she left him standing in the hallway and went to dress Hanno and Vilmar, who were still in their pajamas.

When she returned with her sons, the impatient soldier yanked her by the arm and repeated, "Woman, come!"

"I'm coming. I'm coming."

Mutti leaned over the banister and whispered, "We'll pray, Kätchen. Goodbye!"

"Lord, please protect them," Mutti pleaded as we all gathered around her. "Watch over them and let no evil befall them. I also place Dieter and Liane in Your care again as they go begging. You have been so good to us. Show Yourself to all of us today in a mighty way. Blessed be Your name. Amen."

I usually tried to catch up on my darning before we left to go begging, since those projects took up most of my spare time. As sock fibers weakened, everyone's holes continually became larger. There was no time left for my favorite pastime, knitting. The only socks I didn't have to darn were the woolen knee socks I had knitted for Dieter. They were still in perfect condition in spite of the fact that they had to be washed so often. His bandages sometimes slipped, and the boils would seep right into his socks.

"Why do you think the Russian is watching us, Liane?" Dieter asked later as we walked along the mirror-like lake in search of firewood.

"I didn't realize somebody was watching us."

My eyes moved toward the gardens along the promenade. I saw the Russian with a rifle slung across his back, beginning to move in our direction. He approached us with a big smile on his face and told us that he wanted to learn German. He pointed at trees, flowers, houses, and gates, and wanted to know the German word for each one of them. Then he began pointing at different articles of clothing I wore, and I continued to give him the German equivalent.

Dieter was becoming rather bored with the lessons. He raced to the water's edge to perfect his skill at skipping pebbles across the lake. As the learning session went on, the Russian touched me and wanted to know the word for underwear. My heart had been racing from the moment he began talking to us, but now it threatened to jump out of my chest. It pounded and pounded, loud and hard. I pushed back his hand.

You must get away, my mind told me. I took one step back and the Russian took one forward. Would he shoot me if I ran? I could see his smiling face turning angry.

Take a chance. Run! Run! Run! something told me. Scarcely realizing what I was doing, I whirled around and dashed away. I heard a rifle being cocked behind me. Heavy footsteps followed. I just knew this was life's end, but I still ran. I waited for a shot to ring out. *Do it fast, please!* I thought. The rifle cocked again. I couldn't try to duck or dodge the bullet—he would catch up to me then. *Run! Run! Faster!* My mind screamed at me, but I was moving as fast as I possibly could. I couldn't run faster.

As I dashed across the school yard, I realized that the sound of stomping boots was growing fainter. *Run! Run! Just a few more seconds!* I could see our house across the street. Never before had it been such a welcome sight. Totally out of breath, I stopped just short of the front door. "Thank You, Lord, for fast-moving legs," I gasped half-aloud. Glancing back for the first time, I didn't see a Russian anywhere. But was he watching from somewhere so that he could come for me later? I immediately decided not to tell Mutti about the incident. How would we survive if Dieter and I were no longer allowed to go begging?

Kätchen and her sons returned home late that afternoon. "Emmy and Lianchen, let me tell you about our great God," she said with a sparkle in her deeply sunken eyes. "When we arrived at the Polish headquarters, they told me that all buckets and scrubbing brushes were already in use. Why would they round up more women than they had buckets? That was very strange indeed and made me wonder. We were then led into the very room where we used to conduct our church services before the Nazis turned it into their headquarters. When I was confronted by five stern-looking officers, I silently prayed, 'Lord, take control and keep me strong.'

"Two of the officers spoke German rather well. They fired question after question at me about our family, our occupation, our relatives, our home, and our plans for the future. They asked if I knew where Wilhelm is and if we have a radio here in the house. They even interrogated Hanno. Did he see a radio at our house this week or did he hear one? Then they continued asking me questions. Have we made contact with anyone in the West? Do I know of German soldiers hiding somewhere? Did we ever hide soldiers? Are any Nazis at our house? How many people are living at our house? What are their names and ages and what are their occupations? What is our religion? And then they reverted to the question of the radio and repeated many others. But, Emmychen, I know that our God strengthened me. My mind did not tire even after all those hours of strain."

"Praise His name," Mutti responded joyfully. "Our God is wonderful." Then suddenly she had a puzzled look on her face. "Is it possible that our quiet neighbor from across the street was spying on us? Did she turn us in?"

One really had to wonder. Why did she have food when everyone else in town was starving? Was food her payment for spying? "But where would she get the idea that we possessed a radio?" Mutti continued. "That was taken by the first troops! Where would we get one now?"

"I don't know." Kätchen sank into a chair. "But that question came up more than any other and made me wonder too—oh, Emmy! Do you think our neighbor is tiptoeing past our window in the evening and when she hears us sing and talk to the Lord, she thinks that is a radio?" Both of the mothers exploded with laughter when they realized that it could have been possible.

The next Sunday afternoon, someone really did creep up outside our house. Tap! Tap! Someone quietly tapped on the living room window. A peek through the curtains revealed a kind-looking man with a white beard. Who could he be? When Onkel Emil opened the door just a crack, the stranger asked if this was the home of Ernst Lehmann, the preacher.

"Yes, it is," he answered.

"I am a preacher too," he said in German. "Is Ernst Lehmann at home?"

"Yes, he is. Come in," responded Onkel Emil, inviting him into the living room.

After introductions, the old preacher tearfully began to tell us about his family. "The Russians have taken my wife and my six children to Siberia. They are probably at hard labor there in the coal mines, along with many thousands of Germans and other Polish people. I was too sickly and of no use to them in the slave labor camps, so they forced me to leave my home and come here to help them occupy Germany. I know that God brought me to Lippehne for a reason, even though that reason is still unknown to me. I am sorrowful for my wife and children, and that is why my hair and beard are white. There are a few Polish believers here in town and a Russian who is a believer. We meet on Sunday mornings, just one block from here, at my house. Please come and fellowship with us. But please be careful not to give our meetings away."

We had a time of fellowship and prayer before our new friend left. The following morning he returned with two of the most wonderful gifts—a loaf of white bread and a small piece of margarine.

In spite of the unexpected blessing of food, Mutti seemed somewhat discouraged that day. Early in the afternoon she had an unusual request. "Schäfle, can you and Dieter pull me to the lake in the handwagon today?"

"Of course, Mutti, but why do you want to go to the lake?" I thought immediately of the mother who, along with her children, committed suicide by drowning in that same lake.

"I just have to find out if the cool water of the lake will give my legs some relief from pain." Mutti had been suffering much lately. Her legs were so swollen and blistered from near-starvation that it was difficult for her to walk at all.

With Mutti, Udo, and Marlies all loaded into the wagon, off we went. The July sun had us perspiring in the short time before we arrived at the lake. Tiny ripples danced across the water, and the breeze felt wonderfully refreshing. Mutti gathered her long black skirt, slowly seated herself on the small dock, and lowered her legs into the water. The rest of us quickly removed our shoes and socks and did the same. Because Udo's legs were too short, I had to hold him down over the edge of the dock to reach the water. Dieter, of course, tried to catch some crabs, but they were considerably faster than he. Udo's and Marlies's happy chatter was almost as beautiful as the songs of the birds, and I noticed signs of both joy and pain on Mutti's face as she watched her children relishing those few moments in nature.

"Do your legs feel better in the water, Dieter?" Mutti asked.

"They feel much, much better, Mutti. Can we come down here every day?"

"I wish we could, my son. The water feels soothing on my legs too. We'll try to come again if you children are able to pull such a heavy load."

Sunday morning finally came—the day we were to go to the Polish preacher's house. The church service started at 9:30 a.m. We had made plans the previous night to try to make the journey as inconspicuously as possible. Onkel Lehmann would be the first to leave our house at 8:30 a.m. Ten or fifteen minutes later, Kätchen and her sons would meander down the street. Mutti, Udo, and Marlies would remain at home. It would have been impossible for Mutti to walk that far. Onkel Emil, Dieter, and I would start our stroll ten minutes before church time.

If any of us spotted any soldiers, Russian or Polish, we were not to enter the preacher's house, but instead just walk right past. Bibles were to be hidden under coats and jackets.

Thankfully, everything moved as precisely as planned. When we arrived at "church," we were all relieved and grateful that everyone from our house had made the walk safely.

It was difficult for me to distinguish one Polish lady from another at church. They all wore babushkas and their round, wrinkled faces looked old and weather-beaten. Their eyes sparkled, though, and their mouths were drawn into smiles. The presence of a Russian soldier in the room gave me a scary feeling. When I first saw him, I looked quickly away, fighting panic. When I dared glance at him again, my fears were somewhat calmed by the kind-looking expression on his face.

The Polish preacher opened the service with a prayer of which I understood nothing but "Amen." Then he began the song service with the hymn "Amazing Grace." Everyone sang in a hushed voice and in his native language. The subdued singing continued until tears filled the eyes of everyone in the room.

"Please read Psalm 91 for us, Pastor Lehmann," the Polish preacher said in German.

After Onkel Lehmann finished reading the whole psalm, he reviewed the promises God has given us in that psalm alone: He will deliver us, He will cover us with His feathers, He will give His angels charge over us, He will answer if we call on Him. As he spoke, everyone's head nodded in agreement. Did they understand German? I wondered. Bible readings in the Russian and Polish languages followed the message. Then everybody began to sing again. It was such a strange yet warm feeling to realize that voices in three different languages could sing about the same Lord. Sometimes I had imagined what it would be like to attend a service in a foreign country. I had wondered if people would worship in the same manner as we did in Germany. Or was God really worshiped in other countries? How could He listen to prayers in so many different languages?

Suddenly a strange realization struck me. We no longer lived in Germany! We lived in a foreign country! Our government was both Polish and Russian, but no longer German. What country did that make the soil on which we stood? My thoughts had strayed while the adults in our service were taking turns praying. As they whispered their prayers, many of them were weeping. When the soldier prayed, however, I immediately felt anger welling up in me. Not until I reminded myself that he was a believer in the Lord Jesus, too, did a stillness take over my heart. All Russians must not be bad. Jesus died for him just as He did for every single human being on earth; therefore, my thoughts toward him must be kind and loving.

After a few more songs—all of them sung from memory—we closed with the hymn "Blest Be the Tie That Binds." Everyone in the small room formed a human chain by holding hands. I was sitting next to the Russian, but I couldn't make myself take his hand. He reached over and took my hand anyway, gently placing it in his as we continued singing:

"Our hearts in Christian love;
The fellowship of kindred minds
Is like to that above."
(Fawcett, "Blest Be the Tie That Binds")

The night was unusually calm. Everyone, except Onkel Lehmann, felt better after a peaceful rest. He wasn't feeling well but planned to go to work anyway. During the day most of our thoughts were still on the church service of the day before.

"What a blessing to worship with other believers," Kätchen said to Mutti as we washed the laundry in the kitchen. "One could sense the Lord's Spirit in that small room. We could hardly understand one another, but there was no doubt in my mind that we were one in the Lord. The blood of our Lord reached into Poland and Russia, 'that whosoever believeth in him should not perish, but have everlasting life.' I am so glad I asked for forgiveness of sins as a young person and invited Christ into my life. How would we cope today if He weren't our Comforter and Helper?"

"Of course, Kätchen, I feel exactly the way you do. At times, however, doubts set in. We try to live pure before Him with His help, and we love the Lord. So why do we have to go through such difficult times? Why can't we fill the stomachs of our little children? Then again, I am just overwhelmed by the fact that we are still alive. When I realize that this alone is a miracle, my fainting heart revives itself and I just love Him more."

"Emmy, I think we'll experience even greater miracles. Can you imagine today how we will be united with our husbands? I can't, but I know that we will be. We must be faithful to our Lord during our struggles and not waver. We must not turn from Him as Israel did time after time. He has bought us with a price, His precious blood. Nothing we go through today can compare to His suffering. He understands everything we are going through, and He will give us the strength to come forth as gold as Job did."

"Schäfle," Mutti interrupted the train of thought, "don't wring the underwear too much. It might tear. Instead of wringing the water out, just squeeze it out with your hands, all right?"

"I have already been doing that with the socks."

"Only the Lord knows when we will be able to purchase new clothing. In the meantime, we have to be very careful with the few things we still own."

"Aren't our little ones pure joy, Emmychen? Look how nicely they are playing in the courtyard." Kätchen motioned for Mutti to look out of the kitchen window. "The sun is so wonderful for all of them. Even Hanno's cheeks are getting a little color."

"We should be more thankful for our children," Mutti admitted. "They don't complain, even though they are always hungry. They get along so well with one another. Isn't it amazing that they never run out of things to play, even though they have so few toys? We are truly blessed women, aren't we, Kätchen?"

In the evening, Onkel Lehmann slowly entered the kitchen with his little chunk of bread.

"It is a truly ridiculous job to guard furniture at the railroad station because we know it will never be shipped to Russia. The elements have their claim on it rather than our enemies. Since it is a job I am required to do, however, I should not complain, in spite of the fact that it wore me out completely today. If you don't mind, I'll go to bed early," he said. "You can divide my morsel of bread between you."

Kätchen's eyes followed her father with a look of concern as she watched him shuffle into the living room.

"Vati must be sick," she said sadly.

The next morning, as Dieter and I prepared to go on our food hunt, Kätchen slowly climbed upstairs with the sad news that Onkel Lehmann and five-year-old Hanno were very ill. "They both have diarrhea and don't feel well. Let's pray that no one else will get sick."

Dieter and I ventured to the far side of town to visit Onkel Lehmann's big garden. We found the gate wide open and the hedge on either side of the gate scraggly and in need of pruning. The little summer house had been vandalized and several of the windows were broken. We searched through the reeds for the boat, but it had vanished. The vegetable rows, which last year had been neatly planted with carrots, beets, lettuce, beans, and cabbage, now resembled a large weed patch. The red and yellow currants, and the gooseberries, promised to be a good crop in a few weeks. A few marigold seeds had defied winter's cold and planted themselves near the long garden path. They were blooming beautifully.

"Dieter, if it would not have been so dangerous a few months ago, we could have come to put vegetable seeds into the ground. Onkel Lehmann saved his seeds, but now it is too late for this year. We'll have to come back when the berries and apples are ripe and get some. Wouldn't it be wonderful to eat fruit right now?"

"Don't talk about it, please! That is not fair to my stomach," Dieter pleaded.

"Do you hear all that noise at the public beach? There must be quite a few soldiers at the beach restaurant. Why don't we go and see? They might give us something to eat."

We decided to take the narrow path along the reeds to the swimming area. Only one garden separated Onkel Lehmann's property from the beach. When the narrow path and reeds ended and we were out in the open, we noticed that the white sand was cluttered with olive green uniforms. Nude soldiers were swimming, wrestling in the water, and jumping off the diving boards. I felt terribly embarrassed, and we quickly crossed the wide sand strip toward the restaurant.

The restaurant had always been a beautiful spot. The tables had been neatly covered with white linen tablecloths, and the wooden chairs never seemed to leave a mark on the highly polished parquet floor. The huge windows that overlooked the beach area and the hills on the other side of the lake were constantly sparkling. Folk music played softly as people enjoyed meals or just pastries and coffee.

As we went closer, Dieter pointed out all the broken windows. The main door was wide open and my heart was crushed when I saw the awful change that had taken place since the fall. The floor of the huge dining hall was littered with cigarette butts, garbage, beer bottles, and broken glass. Furniture pieces, table, and chair legs were lying here and there with the tabletops and seats nowhere in sight. It made me wonder if Lippehne would ever again be the way I remembered it.

Onkel Lehmann was not able to go to work again the next day. He had a fever accompanied by chills, and Hanno appeared to have the same problem. Since it seemed to be a contagious disease, we were no longer allowed to go downstairs to visit or play. Our small quarters became even more confining with the first floor off limits. Mutti sewed in our room, and the four of us children spent more time in the attic. Two of the walls were slanted and two small sky lights could be propped open with a notched metal bar. When we wanted to see what was transpiring on the other side of the street, we just climbed on a chair, opened the hatch, and stuck our heads out. Udo and Marlies were upset when they realized they were too small to be able to look out.

Two soldiers came to our house to inquire why Onkel Lehmann had not reported for work. "When they saw him and Hanno in bed," Kätchen told us from the base of the steps, "they quickly covered their mouths with their hands and said, 'Typhoid! Typhoid!' and almost stumbled over each other to get out of the door. That is a disease of poor sanitation and hygiene, isn't it? How can that be, Emmychen? Everything is clean here. How do they know what disease this is by just looking at the sick ones?" We didn't know the answer to that, but a whole week passed without soldiers coming to the house and harassing us. Our first peaceful week since January!

"The soldiers must have passed the word around," Mutti told me, "that there is a contagious disease at the Lehmann's house. That should explain why we haven't been molested by them." Suddenly her face lit up and her eyes twinkled as she seemed to have come upon something pleasant.

"I have an idea, a great idea. If we wish to have another peaceful week, we'll just nail a poster on the front door with the word 'TYPHOID' on it." Quickly she informed Onkel Emil and Kätchen of her brainstorm, and both of them agreed with it wholeheartedly.

A short time later, the green front door had a heavy, white piece of paper fastened to it, bearing the name of a deadly disease.

9

THE DEADLY DISEASE

Onkel Lehmann's fever rose, and so did Hanno's. It was almost a blessing that neither of them had an appetite because things seemed hopeless with Kätchen's breadwinner laid up. She was no longer bubbly and joyful. Two of her men, as she called them, were sick, and there was no doctor in town and no medicine for whatever their illness might be. We couldn't pray or sing together anymore—everything was so different. I had never thought that I would miss the sick ones so much. Gloom was settling into all our hearts, for we realized that both of them were growing steadily weaker.

"There is nothing we can do but pray," Mutti told us. "The Lord can make them well in an instant, if He so chooses. He can heal as He did in Bible times. We don't know what His plan is, and often we don't understand it, but we must trust Him to do what He deems best."

"But how can it be best for my friend Hanno to be so sick?" Dieter asked.

"I don't know, Son. I don't know. Only the Lord knows."

The Polish preacher was almost out of breath the next day when he came to the house to tell Kätchen that he just heard of the reopening of the Lippehne hospital. It was staffed by Polish doctors and nurses, and he planned to go immediately and see if Onkel Lehmann and Hanno could be admitted. Half an hour later, he returned to inform Kätchen that there was room for both of them. Kätchen quickly readied the handwagon and placed her weak father in it. He had a very high fever now.

"Please pray that Vati will be able to withstand that fifteen-minute bumpy ride in the handwagon," she pleaded with us as we waved goodbye through our tears. "He is a very sick man."

We listened to the rattle of the handwagon as the metal bands of the wheels hit the cobblestones.

Tired and worn out, Kätchen returned for the second load, her oldest son. Was it my imagination or had I detected some gray hair peeking out from under her black scarf? She hadn't had gray hair two weeks ago.

Marlies and Udo were tugging at me. They wanted me to play with them, but I just didn't feel like playing. Sadness had engulfed me too. Two of our family members were in the hospital! Who would be next? Would we all get sick? Would we all die? When we heard the noisy handwagon clanking down the street again, we knew it was Kätchen. Dieter and I rushed to push the iron bar from the small barnyard door and help her pull in the wagon.

"You take care of the children, Schäfle. I have to go and talk to Kätchen," Mutti told me.

I was trying my best to entertain my brothers and sister, while at the same time listen for Mutti's footsteps. A long time went by before she finally came upstairs again. Her eyes looked red and puffy. She must have been crying.

"Kätchen can go and visit Onkel Lehmann and Hanno at the hospital every day until they are well enough to return home," she reported.

"Can I go and see my friend Hanno too?"

"No, Dieter, children are not allowed to visit the hospital."

"With whom can I play now in my spare time? Udo and Marlies are too little. Vilmar is too little. Liane is too busy. Here I am now, all by myself."

"Come here, you little curly-head," Mutti said and opened her arms. "Let me give you a hug. So you are feeling sorry for yourself, are you?"

"I do. I have no friend. My friend is in the hospital."

"You don't have to feel lonely, Dieter. You still have all of us. Do you know what, Son? I have a marvelous idea, an idea I think you'll like."

"What is that?"

"I have an assignment that will be just perfect for you."

"What is it Mutti? What is it?"

"I think an eight-year-old young man would make an excellent teacher for the little ones. I hereby nominate you, Herr Guddat, as teacher of these students. Use the old mattress there as the classroom area and set things up the way you like. Teach your students the alphabet and teach them some of the things you learned at school. You might also want to check them on their knowledge of poetry. By that I mean," her voice dropped to a whisper, "the poems for Vati's homecoming."

"Yes, Mutti, yes! I'll start right now." A few minutes later, when Mutti and I peeked into the attic through the cracked door, the only school in Lippehne was in session and every student most attentive.

Kätchen was very discouraged the next day after she returned home from the hospital. "Emmy," she said, "we must continually pray for my men. The diagnosis was that both of them have typhoid and have to be in isolation because the disease is highly contagious. I am not permitted to even set one foot in the hospital. I have to go there daily, however, and pick up their soiled laundry, which the nurses will place at the entrance. Both of them are too weak to use the bathroom, and the hospital staff does not launder anything. The Lord will have to give me an extra measure of strength to help me do that job without getting sick myself."

The nights of continued peace helped all of us to gather physical and emotional strength. Even Kätchen was able to endure the daily stress of walking back and forth to the hospital and doing the laundry for the two sick ones.

"I saw my son today, Emmychen." She returned one day with a shadow of a smile. "I found a tall ladder near the hospital, dragged it there, and leaned it against the window on the second floor. Emmychen, I wanted to cry when I saw Hanno, but I could not let him see my tears. My poor son is just a shadow. I waved to him, but he couldn't wave back. His eyes are black-looking and sunken in. He just stared at the window. Oh, how I wanted to hold him in my arms and comfort him! I saw Vati through the window also. He is on the first floor. He is very bad, too, but he at least raised his arm a little to wave back to me."

The next day, Kätchen pushed herself into the house, bent over, sobbing, and exhausted. When we saw her in the hallway in such despair, no one said a word or asked a question. We all knew that something terrible had happened. Mutti embraced her and let her cry.

"I wish I would have never had to hear those words," she stammered, "'Frau Mecklenburg, your father will live, but your son will die.' This is what the doctor told me. Why, Lord, why?" Her frail body was wracked with pain, and there was no one who could help her. All Mutti's efforts were in vain.

Onkel Emil really struggled that night to have everybody join him in our time of devotions. Only Marlies and Udo were willing to help him with the singing. Quietly they sang:

"God is love, He set me free.
God is love, He loves ev'n me.
That's why I repeat it again,
God is love, He loves me."
(Rische, "Gott ist die Liebe")

Kätchen wept softly as Onkel Emil led in a few more songs. Then, leafing through the book of Psalms, he read to her.

"Wait on the LORD:
Be of good courage, and he shall strengthen thine heart:
Wait, I say, on the LORD. (Ps. 27:14)

"The LORD is my strength and my shield;
My heart trusted in him, and I am helped. (Ps. 28:7)

"I sought the LORD, and he heard me,
And delivered me from all my fears." (Ps. 34:4)

Then we all quoted the Twenty-third Psalm in unison.

"Kätchen," Onkel Emil continued, "we are unable to comfort you tonight. We wish we could help you, but we have no idea how. There is only One who can still your soul, and that is the Lord Jesus Christ. Rest in Him completely! I know some of what you are going through. Mally and I lost our only son in the war, as you know. We've known the sorrow, but I am still no expert on it. When I look back, I think there were really only two things that helped us in the loss of our only son—knowing that the Lord still cared and was still in control, and knowing people were praying for us. Our friends wanted to help us, too, but there was nothing more they could do to ease our pain."

As the prayers ascended that night, I found myself constantly tormented by thoughts of death and dying. Except for the little ones, everyone wept, but when we wished each other a restful and peaceful night, Kätchen once again had that lovely smile on her slender face.

Sometime later I came wide awake without knowing why. It must have been the middle of the night. Why is Udo crying? Marlies was awake and so was Mutti. Then I realized someone was relentlessly beating on the shutters of the downstairs windows.

"Woman, open up! Open up! Need suit for dancing! Your father in hospital said you give suit."

The racket continued, and the same command again came upstairs from the street. Onkel Emil hit his head on the slanted wall of the attic as he tried to scramble out of bed to get downstairs. He angrily told the two men to leave.

"It is midnight," he shouted. "Go away!"

"No, Emil," Kätchen said, "here is Vati's suit. Just give it to them." Then I heard the front door opening and someone saying, "Thank you. Thank you." Abruptly, calm and silence returned to our house.

A couple of days later, Dieter and I figured that the berries at Onkel Lehmann's farm should be ripe. Excitedly we hurried across town to Onkel Lehmann's garden. As we carried our little buckets, I envisioned how it would be to pick currants and gooseberries and take them home for everyone to enjoy. The summer weather had been gorgeous. How wonderful the warm sun felt as we meandered along the lake. Only a few puffy clouds were sailing gently across the sky. The birds chirped, diving in and out of the treetops, leaves rustling. I thought it must be nice to be a bird and have so much fun and nothing to worry about.

The tall, stately linden trees along the promenade bathed in the golden warmth of the sun. The still lake was a perfect mirror of everything we saw. It was so peaceful.

"I wish I would know the names of some of the birds, Liane. I like that beautiful song. Let's sneak up on the little one over there in the grass and see if we can catch it." Dieter began to tiptoe through the lawn of the park, but the little bird must have been watching too. It soared into the blue sky before Dieter could even approach it.

"Do the Polish people like flowers, Liane?"

"Yes, Dieter. Everybody likes flowers. Why do you ask?"

"Because I don't see any flowers in the gardens this year, only wild daisies."

"You know, I hadn't even noticed that, but I think you are right. They probably didn't have time to plant any because they are just getting settled here in Lippehne."

It hardly surprised me to find the gate to Onkel Lehmann's garden wide open again when we arrived, but Dieter was quicker than I to notice more.

"We closed the gate when we were here the last time, didn't we? Now will you just look over there!" His voice rose in disappointment as we passed through the gate. "Can you believe it?"

"Can I believe what, Dieter?"

"Look at the berry bushes over there! The berries are gone. Somebody stole them! This is Onkel Lehmann's garden. Why do they do that to us?"

My heart sank. It was true. All the bushes were picked clean.

"Dieter, I think this is no longer Onkel Lehmann's garden. It belongs to everybody now. The Germans don't seem to own anything anymore."

"Maybe we can find a few berries at the very bottom of the bushes. Let's check." But our search was in vain.

"The birds must have gotten those that may have been overlooked by the thieves." I could hear the disappointment in my own voice.

"We came too late," Dieter said with tears in his eyes. "Maybe we can beat the thieves to the apples. They are still small and hard."

"Yes, let's try that. We'll ask Kätchen when they are supposed to be ripe. But now, let's gather sticks on our way home, so we won't go back empty-handed. I think we should do some begging too."

On our way back home, we gathered sticks on the promenade. Our arms were almost full, but we were still scouting. Suddenly, out of nowhere, a huge horse appeared, charging toward us with a thunder of hooves.

"Let's duck in here, Dieter! Fast!" I dropped my sticks and pulled Dieter into the entrance of a farmyard which we were just passing. We hid behind the gate.

"That was close," Dieter whispered as the horse tore past. "We could have been killed." We were so relieved that we almost missed the new danger. Barely in time, I saw the figure moving up behind us.

"Watch out, Dieter. Run! Run!" The farmer's wife swung a broom and came running after us, yelling and screaming. Dieter dropped his sticks, and we ran as fast as we could, angry Polish words following us. When we finally reached the park, we saw nothing—no horse and no farmer's wife. The trees still basked in the sun and the birds still played hide and seek. Starved and empty-handed, we arrived at home.

The nurse at the hospital informed Kätchen that both Onkel Lehmann and Hanno were being given one slice of bread each day, but neither of them would eat.

"I told Hanno through the closed window, 'When you start eating, I'll come and take you home.' It was terrible, Emmychen, he only stared at me and didn't respond at all. He doesn't seem to care about coming home. I feel so helpless. What can I do to help my son?"

"I have no idea, Kätchen. Did you try again to get into his room?"

"Yes, I did, just today, but they still won't give me permission. Typhoid is too contagious."

"I can't help you, Kätchen. All I can do is pray, and I am doing that."

"Thank you, Emmychen, thank you. I know there is nothing anyone can do. Only our Lord can ease the pain."

"Yes, what would we do without Him?"

"Emmychen, I want to help you a bit. I'll take care of your little ones while Dieter and Liane take you to the lake to cool your sores. Would you like me to do that? I sense that you are in a lot of pain."

"Oh, thank you, Kätchen. That sounds like a marvelous idea. Thank you for your suggestion."

"But be very careful. A young Russian soldier followed me all the way to the hospital this morning. Please be careful. I'll be praying for you all."

It was very difficult for Mutti to walk now. Her legs were always swollen. We took her to the lake as often as possible, but when she slowly slid off the handwagon, we had to help her down to the dock and take off her shoes. Dieter's bandages would be off in seconds. He also got relief from the cool water. The sun bathed everything in its warm glow, even the cemetery on the other side of the lake, so that the tombstones and catacombs looked pleasant among the green trees.

"Mutti, what happened to all those who died by drowning since we lost our freedom? Did anyone bury them? And the man's body which Dieter and I saw in the lake a few months ago, what happened to it?"

"I have no idea, Schäfle. I presume that the German work crews probably buried them somewhere. Those who died in the treks from Eastern Germany were not so fortunate. They were just dragged into the ditches along the roads. Nobody had time to worry about the dead. Staying alive and escaping the enemy were everyone's main concerns. Thousands will never know the final resting place of their loved ones. Just think of all those people whom the Russians mercilessly crushed with their tanks! No one knows the miseries the German people have suffered. No one knows what they will continue to suffer.

"Hitler was shaking his fist at the face of God, and all of us are paying for that now. I read somewhere that he once said that after he had won the war, he would sit on a throne and would make all the preachers crawl under it on their knees. You see, Schäfle, God had to prevent that. No one mistreats or plans to mistreat God's people without having to pay the consequences. God is a just God, and I feel He is pouring out His judgment on Germany."

"But we have loved the Lord, Mutti! You and Vati, all our grandparents and great-grandparents have been believers in the Lord. Why then do we all have to suffer? And Onkel Lehmann? He loves the Lord with all his heart."

"I know what you are saying, and I don't have the answers to your questions. All I know is that God is still on the throne, He still loves us, and no matter what happens, we must believe that and trust Him. His Word says, 'I will never leave thee, nor forsake thee.' Isn't that a comforting promise?"

"Yes, it is."

"Help! Someone help!" Dieter called excitedly. "I caught one. I caught a crab! Where can I put it?" With his right hand on the back of the crab he splashed toward us. The little animal squirmed and the claws flopped back and forth in search of something to hold on to. "I should have brought my bucket. We could have taken it home and cooked it."

"I didn't think about that either, Dieter," Mutti said sadly. "But you are fast today to have caught this one."

"Can you hold it on your lap, Mutti, when we pull you home? I will show you how to hold it so it won't bite you."

"I guess I could do that."

We arrived at home refreshed in body and spirit. For dinner that night Dieter enjoyed one mouthful of crab meat.

10

ONKEL LEHMANN

It was the sixth day of September, and Kätchen didn't have to tell us. When she returned from the hospital, we knew that one of her men had died. We could see that her whole being was torn by grief.

"He went to be with his Lord this morning. He no longer has to suffer. Our Vati is safe in the arms of Jesus." Mutti helped Kätchen to the couch in the living room where the two friends sat down, held hands, and wept.

Onkel Lehmann died? But the doctor said that he would live! My mind whirled. Our best friend was gone. I couldn't comprehend it. Yes, I had seen a lot of death, but death took on a different meaning that day. It was Onkel Lehmann's death.

I was trying to keep the children entertained, but Dieter had to take over for me because I was no longer able to function. Sadness gripped my heart and wouldn't let go of me. We would never see Onkel Lehmann again? The kind, gentle man? He always lived close to the Lord. Whenever he prayed, I had thought that he must be standing directly before God. He had such a love for people and helped them in many ways, but his greatest concern had been for their souls. "You must be born again," he told the neighbors who sought refuge at our house. "One way leads to heaven and one way leads to hell. You alone have to decide where you want to spend eternity. Our loving God does not force anyone to accept the gift of His Son. You must reach out and take it."

What would we do now without Onkel Lehmann's prayers for us? How would Kätchen live without him? How would we all exist without him? Just to have been in Onkel Lehmann's presence when we were in difficulty had always soothed us.

"Onkel Lehmann went to heaven today, children," Kätchen said as she gathered the little ones around her. "He went to be with Jesus. Isn't that wonderful? He loved the Lord Jesus very much and couldn't wait to see Him. And now he sees Him as clearly as I see all of you and you see me. We will miss Opi terribly here on earth, but we can't be sad. Heaven is a far better place than anywhere on earth. It is much more beautiful, and there is *nothing* better than seeing Jesus every day."

"Will he see Ulli, too, Mutti?" Vilmar asked excitedly.

"Yes, Vilmar, Opi is right there with your brother."

"Oh, that's good. Then Ulli won't be so alone."

"Yes," Kätchen said. "Opi will keep him company until we get there." Then Vilmar pulled Udo by the hand and both wanted to dash off to play.

"Come here now, Vilmar," Kätchen told him and caught him by the arm. "Come, sit on my lap." I noticed that she was almost too weak to pick up her two-year-old.

"Hanno is still very sick, and I would like all of us to pray for him right now."

"Will he go to heaven too?" Marlies asked.

"I don't know, Pittimaus. We want him to stay with us here on earth, but maybe Jesus wants him to be in heaven too. We'll just have to let Jesus decide. He knows what is best."

The next morning Dieter and I went to the lake to get evergreen branches from some of the hemlock and spruce trees. After several trips our arms were scratched up, but Mutti had enough greens to make two wreaths. The funeral service was to be the next day. Two of Onkel Lehmann's old carpenter friends and coworkers came to the house to tell Kätchen that they had built a casket for him.

"We could find only a few boards and had to build it very low," they remarked.

"You have no idea what your expression of friendship means to me," Kätchen told them. "You are so kind. Nothing I could say would adequately tell how I feel about what you have done. Thank you very much—I will ask our Lord to reward you richly."

"I wonder, though," Kätchen continued, "if you know that Germans are not allowed to be buried in a casket."

"We know that. But not even in death will we permit our friend to be humiliated and embarrassed by our enemies. We will not stand for that no matter what the consequences will be for us. We will stop by tomorrow morning to pick up your handwagon and then meet you at the hospital. Auf Wiedersehen!"

"This is a true miracle, Kätchen. Our Onkel Lehmann will be taken to the cemetery in a casket," Mutti rejoiced with tears in her eyes, "and he will not be made a laughingstock. Praise the Lord. He has again showed Himself faithful to His children."

Our Polish preacher friend walked alongside us to the cemetery. Mutti's legs had improved enough for her to limp slowly with the aid of a cane. Nobody talked, not even the little ones. Did they understand the reason for this outing?

It was a warm, sunny September day, and the long walk to the outskirts of town was sad but oddly refreshing as well. No one seemed to think about the enemy possibly lurking behind a house or tree. Our thoughts were on heaven that day, and we must have been oblivious to fear.

The closed casket was placed next to the open earth in the new part of the cemetery, a green meadow. A wall of small shrubs sheltered us from the breeze. The preacher and Onkel Emil each took one of the wreaths and laid it on the roughly hewn board casket. Onkel Emil then began to lead us in singing some of Onkel Lehmann's favorite hymns.

"Safe in the arms of Jesus,
Safe on His gentle breast,
There by His love o'ershaded,
Sweetly my soul shall rest.
Hark! 'tis the voice of angels,
Borne in a song to me,
Over the fields of glory,
Over the jasper sea.

"Safe in the arms of Jesus,
Safe on His gentle breast,
There by His love o'ershaded,
Sweetly my soul shall rest."
(Crosby, "Safe in the Arms of Jesus")

Then we all continued singing softly:

"When peace, like a river, attendeth my way,
When sorrows like sea billows roll;
Whatever my lot, Thou hast taught me to say,
'It is well, it is well with my soul.'

"And, Lord, haste the day when the faith shall be sight,
The clouds be rolled back as a scroll,
The trump shall resound and the Lord shall descend,
'Even so,' it is well with my soul."
(Spafford, "It Is Well with My Soul")

The preacher sang all the songs in his native language. Onkel Emil then pulled Mutti's Bible out from under his coat, opened it to 1 Thessalonians and began reading from chapter four, verses thirteen to eighteen.

"But I would not have you to be ignorant, brethren, concerning them which are asleep, that ye sorrow not, even as others which have no hope. For if we believe that Jesus died and rose again, even so them also which sleep in Jesus will God bring with him. For this we say unto you by the word of the Lord, that we which are alive *and* remain unto the coming of the Lord shall not prevent them which are asleep. For the Lord himself shall descend from heaven with a shout, with the voice of the archangel, and with the trump of God: and the dead in Christ shall rise first: Then we which are alive *and* remain shall be caught up together with them in the clouds, to meet the Lord in the air: and so shall we ever be with the Lord. Wherefore comfort one another with these words."

While the adults listened attentively to the Bible reading, I watched Kätchen. Her face was drawn and sad, but her eyes were dry. She was constantly looking upward. Did she see her father in heaven?

Onkel Emil supported himself on his cane while the pastor read some Bible passages in Polish. Then we continued singing the hymns Onkel Lehmann had most often requested. Prayers of thanksgiving were offered for Onkel Lehmann's life, for his walk with the Lord, for his witness and example he had been to others, for the end of his suffering, for his kindness and love for others, and for his being at rest now and in the presence of his Lord.

As we stood there celebrating Onkel Lehmann's graduation, I noticed a young-looking couple walking slowly toward a casket and an open grave only about fifteen feet from us. I had wondered about that grave when we first arrived at the cemetery, for there were no flowers and no people, just a casket and the open grave. Our service was almost over when the lady opened the other casket, threw herself across it, and screamed as I have never heard anyone scream. Kneeling down in the grass, she leaned over to kiss the body, mingling her wailing with words we did not understand. When we were finished with our service, we all moved over to the couple and stood in silence with bowed heads. A young boy about my age lay in the plain casket. He looked handsome in his white suit, white shirt, and black shoes. Someone my age dead? So young? It could have been I, I knew, but as I stood there, my only thought was of whether or not he had been prepared for eternity.

The preacher reached down and placed his hand on the lady's shoulder. Her whole body was shaking. He said something to her, took the husband's right hand, enclosed it in both of his, and spoke to him. How I wished we could help this couple and tell them of God's peace, but we couldn't. The woman's hysterical screams followed us for a long time after we left the cemetery.

Surviving without being able to purchase food became an ever-greater problem. Other than Onkel Emil's watery soup, we had no means of getting provisions. Mutti still sewed, and sometimes her pay was bread and lard.

"Emmychen, on the way home from the hospital I picked these apples. I don't know if anyone owns the garden now or not, but I was just too hungry. I had to get something to eat. Here are some apples for you and the children."

Mutti's mouth was beginning to water, I could see that, and so was mine.

"Apples! Fruit! Kätchen! You, the pastor's wife, took apples, or shall we say, stole apples? I can't believe it. You really did that?" Mutti teased with a twinkle in her eyes.

Kätchen looked at the floor. "For all we know, Emmychen, the owner of that tree may not even be alive now. I do feel uncomfortable about it, though, and I've already asked the Lord to forgive me. The Lord forgave King David when he ate the showbread—He understands our hunger pangs."

"He was hungry, too, when He walked on this earth." Mutti consoled her friend. "How would He otherwise ever know and understand what we are going through?"

One day the neighbor across the street informed us that some of the railroad tracks were repaired, and trains were reaching Berlin regularly now. We could probably board one and leave for Germany. She had heard of several people who had left for the West.

"Are you planning to leave too?" Mutti asked her.

"No, I don't plan to leave Lippehne. I like it here. I have a good life."

After that conversation, it seemed that no one at home talked of anything else except escape.

We couldn't tell any outsider about our plans. We had to leave secretly. Of course, we could take along only what we were able to carry, so preparing everything in detail was of utmost importance. The adults spent much time debating about the move, but on one thing they all agreed. The timing of everything would have to depend on Hanno's recovery. There appeared to be a slight improvement in him, and Kätchen thought he might be released from the hospital in another week.

"We must pray hard for that," Mutti said. "We also must pray more diligently for food, because without food Hanno can't regain his strength. And if he is too weak to walk, we can't leave, because there is no one strong enough to carry him."

The Russians had somehow learned of our secret meetings, and our church services had been forbidden. If the group should defy headquarters' orders, the punishment for all would be most severe, the pastor had been told. Our emotional survival was again being challenged and tested—again we had to live without fellowship. We needed that warmth in Christ. We all wondered why the Lord allowed us to be so isolated.

On Sunday we all walked to the cemetery to visit Onkel Lehmann's grave. His body had such a peaceful resting place. The earth above the grave had settled since our last visit and the wreaths still looked fresh. After quietly standing there for a while, we softly began singing some of his favorite songs.

"When all my labors and trials are o'er,
And I am safe on that beautiful shore,
Just to be near the dear Lord I adore
Will through the ages be glory for me.

"O, that will be glory for me.
When by His grace I shall look on His face,
That will be glory, be glory for me."
(Gabriel, "O That Will be Glory")

Onkel Emil asked us all to bow our heads and close our eyes. He then began to praise the Lord for the beautiful, peaceful day and asked Him to protect Vati, Kätchen's husband, and his wife. Then, except for the little ones, we all prayed the Lord's prayer in whispering tones.

"Kätchen," Mutti said, "we have faith in the Lord, but what does our faith do for us? What does it matter whether I believe in the Lord or not? We have absolutely nothing to feed our children today, and look at our godless enemies. They are strong and healthy—and our children are sick and covered with boils. Our enemies don't seem to believe in anything, and we believe in the Creator of the universe. So why is God so silent? Why must we suffer so? Why is your son so ill?"

I had never heard Mutti express doubts. Was it really Mutti who was talking that way?

"Emmychen, I have never heard you talk like this before." Kätchen was concerned. "It seems to me that the devil is really pulling you down. That definitely isn't the voice of someone who loves the Lord dearly! Please don't let Satan get hold of your heart. You know that the Lord is far greater, and He will miraculously provide for our children. Emmychen, you must not talk this way! Our children need to see our strength, our true strength, and not the onslaughts of the devil. If we let our faith weaken, we have nothing to live for and will never get out of Lippehne. So, Emmychen, 'Be strong and of a good courage; be not afraid, neither be thou dismayed: for the LORD thy God is with thee whithersoever thou goest'" (Josh. 1:9).

The two friends stood in silence until Mutti began to weep.

"Oh, Kätchen, you are right. How could I permit Satan to tempt me and then succumb to it? The Lord has done so many marvelous things for us that I will never be able to forget." Then I saw her lifting up her head to the sky. "Forgive me, Lord, for doubting You. I am sorry, Lord."

On the way home, we received a scary surprise. "Russians! There are Russians! They have already seen us—let's turn back to the cemetery," Mutti exclaimed, panic-stricken.

"No," Onkel Emil said, "they have definitely seen us. We have to continue walking. Try to act as though you're not afraid."

The Russians were sitting at the edge of the woods around a large fire. Suddenly Dieter took off toward their small group at top speed.

"Lord, protect him," Mutti prayed out loud.

Onkel Emil told us to pray fervently but to keep walking. We kept an eye on Dieter and the soldiers. Before there was time to do much worrying, my brother moved away from the troops and came running back toward us.

"Look, Mutti," Marlies called out. "He is carrying something. He has something under each arm."

In no time he had caught up to us. Totally out of breath, he stuttered, "Look, Mutti! Look!"

Mutti was so touched by the sight of his treasures that she wept. Kätchen joined her, for under one arm Dieter carried a large loaf of dark bread and under the other a whole barbequed piglet. Everyone was shocked at the sight of this miracle. Mutti ran her hand through Dieter's curly hair and cried.

We were still eating from that piglet a few days later when we had another adventure. "I smell smoke," Onkel Emil said as he returned from work and entered the kitchen.

"I don't smell anything," Mutti answered, throwing a few small chips of red cattle salt into the pot. "I think what you probably smell are our boiling piglet bones. We are having bone soup tonight. When we add your soup, Emil, to this kettle, we shall have a true feast."

"Come, Emil," Kätchen said, pulling him by the arm, "come into the living room and rest your weary leg. We'll call you when dinner is ready."

"I smell something now too," Mutti said a few moments later. She opened the black metal door of the stove to check on the burning sticks, and in an instant enough smoke escaped to fill the whole kitchen. Although she stoked the fire and closed the door, smoke began to filter through the cracks in the door. "Something is definitely wrong, Kätchen."

Onkel Emil came back into the kitchen. "What is all the commotion about? Aha! Emil's nose isn't so bad after all, is it? Now the little women are having problems they can't solve, right? Why don't they let this man help them?" he asked with a big grin on his face. "Here, Liane, you hold my cane while I find the problem." He pulled the metal latch on the door to check on the fire and again thick smoke billowed into the kitchen. Most of it quickly found its way through the large open window to the courtyard. After checking the stovepipe and vents, Onkel Emil concluded that the chimney was clogged. "We are in trouble. We need a chimney sweep."

"Where can we find a chimney sweep?" Kätchen asked, laughing. "The chimney sweep is no longer in Lippehne. He was in the army, and who knows where he might be today."

When Mutti checked our bone soup, it was no longer boiling. The sticks had turned to warm ashes.

"So what does the man propose we do?" she teased.

"We have to do the job ourselves. We have to clean the chimney."

"You certainly can't do it, Emil," Mutti declared. "How will you get through the attic window, onto the roof, and to the chimney on one leg? That's impossible."

"And Kätchen is too small and skinny. The wind will blow her right off the roof," Onkel Emil added.

"So that leaves me," Mutti continued her joking, "an able-bodied, strong woman."

"We should wait a bit and make sure that the fire is out completely," Kätchen said. "In the meantime I'll go to the coal shed and get Vati's chimney brush. I think he had one in there somewhere." With those words, she dashed out of the kitchen and returned a few minutes later with a large metal coil and a brush.

"Emmy, be careful! Get on the step stool now—there! When you have braced yourself, we'll give you a push to help you out the window."

"Don't push too hard or I'll end up on the sidewalk, face down. This window is made for slender people only, that's for sure—oh no, I can't climb up there!" We could only see half of Mutti as she twisted around to stare up at the chimney. "Do you have any idea how steep this roof is?"

"You are the only one who can do it, Emmy." Kätchen encouraged her. "Just don't look down—keep your eyes on the chimney."

After Mutti was out of sight, we all listened to the steel brush scraping the walls of the chimney.

"Lippehne has a new chimney sweep—Emmy Guddat," Onkel Emil announced. "I am amazed what that woman can do."

It was to be more difficult to get Mutti back into the attic than it had been to get her out. She handed the brush in first, then slid in as best she could. When she turned around, we all began to roar. Her face was black with soot, and the whites of her eyes seemed to stand out from her face. Our laughing became so loud that the children dashed upstairs to join in.

"Well," Mutti said, trying to wipe a sooty face with sootier hands, "my mother told me that a girl has to be able to do everything, but I never thought that would include sweeping a chimney."

11

THE FIRST ATTEMPT

"My son is coming home! Hanno is coming home!" Kätchen burst into the house a few days later, singing and bubbling over with joy. "The doctor said he can come home tomorrow. He has to eat well, I am told, to regain his strength. That order will present a real problem from the human point of view, but it will be no problem for our Lord. The Almighty can help, and I know He will."

Everyone was excited about Hanno's return, Dieter especially. His friend was coming home! When Kätchen carried a little bundle of skin and bones into the house the next day, though, we realized that it would be a long time before anyone could play with Hanno. Even little Vilmar's excitement quickly vanished when he looked at his brother.

Hanno spent all his time in bed. We were allowed to visit him, but he was oblivious to our presence.

"Rejoice!" Mutti tried to encourage Kätchen. "Look what my customer just brought me—one whole loaf of white bread. One half is for you, Kätchen."

"Oh, thank you, Emmychen! Thank You, Lord!" With tears wetting her face, Kätchen quickly cut a slice of the bread and took it to Hanno.

He nibbled at it very slowly, finally finishing the whole slice. After a week of having one slice a day, he miraculously became stronger.

No one had molested us in weeks, and everyone gathered strength at night while the typhoid sign remained on the door. The leaves were beginning to prepare for the last splendor of another year, and soon the trees would be decked in yellows and golds. Eventually they would drop, helping to protect the earth beneath with all its dormant life. The little seedlings would be safe from the onslaught of winter, bursting forth with new life in the spring. The decaying leaves would also give them some of the nutrients they need to become strong plants.

The days continued to grow shorter, creating an increasing problem for Onkel Emil, who had to work on sewing orders at home in the evenings. "I am going to the Polish headquarters to see if we can be hooked into the town's electrical system," Onkel Emil told us. "The days are just getting too short, and I can no longer finish orders. I will inform the magistrate that without power at home it will be very difficult for me to meet the deadlines of the Polish and Russian government."

What a wonderful surprise we had a few days later when someone turned on the light switch, and we realized that we had electrical power. It didn't really bother us too much that blackouts occurred frequently. We knew it must have been difficult for the Polish workers to familiarize themselves with the German power system.

"I will help you get to the West," Mutti's Polish friend told her one day when she picked up a dress. "If you will sell me your silverware," she continued, "I will pay you five thousand zlotys."

"Oh no," Mutti said and looked very surprised. "That is not enough. It is real silver, and there are complete sets for twelve people and all the extra serving spoons, ladle, meat fork, and other serving pieces."

"Five thousand zlotys is what I will give you if you want to sell it," she insisted. "That is probably enough to get you to the West."

"Are you sure?"

"I think so."

"I had no choice," Mutti told Kätchen later. "Is there a choice between real silver and freedom? Here is the money—our tickets to freedom or groceries. What will we choose?"

"We don't have a choice but to leave. Do you think that is enough money to cover our tickets to Berlin?" Kätchen asked.

"I hope so. It's all we have. I'm so glad we succeeded in finding a safe hiding place for the silver and were able to sell it now when we most need the money."

During our devotions that night, we thanked the Lord for the money and asked His guidance for our trip. The moment the little ones were tucked in, everyone gathered in the living room again to finalize the plans and begin preparations to leave Lippehne in two days. The neighbor across the street had again assured us that trains were leaving, and since no one else had the connections she enjoyed, everyone always accepted what she said.

There was quite a bit of excitement at our house. The thought of someday again leading a normal, peaceful life charged everyone with extra energy to do all the packing and planning. Onkel Emil would carry an extra burden—in his leg. Birth certificates and other valuable papers were rolled into tiny bundles and packed neatly into a small cloth bag, custom made to fit into the upper cavity of his prosthesis. Everyone's wedding bands were hidden there also. For some strange reason, his leg had never been searched by the enemy, a fact that all the adults were counting on for our crossing the border.

At times the Russians had thought that Onkel Emil was reaching for a gun when he used his hand to put the artificial leg into a position that was comfortable for him. But in spite of the pain Onkel Emil had to endure in his stump, especially during a change in the weather, the prosthesis had always been a blessing to the rest of us. Many times there would not have been the opportunity for the women to hide fast enough, had it not been for Onkel Emil's slow hobbling to the door.

"I have already had a dress rehearsal with Vilmar today," Kätchen said chuckling. "I put one layer of clothing on him and then tied some of the valuable papers to his chest. When I finished putting several more layers of clothing on him, he said, 'Mutti, Mutti. I can't put my arms down. I am too fat.' And it was true—the little fellow looked like a clown. I'll really have to work on that paper problem tomorrow. I wish I had a camera to take a picture of him."

"I'll probably run into the same problem with my children, Kätchen, but we do have to wear layers of clothing just in case we should lose our suitcases and bundles. I know that I'll really have to work on that too."

The following day was crammed with preparations for our journey. While the children entertained themselves, Mutti, Kätchen, and I packed.

"Schäfle," Mutti told me, "put the embroidered tablecloths and some of the other handmade bed and table linens into the suitcase. We'll at least try to get them across the border. I spent many years doing all that work for my hope chest, and it would be nice to have a reminder of our home in Insterburg."

As I placed the white linen cloth with all that gorgeous blue and yellow embroidery work into the suitcase, my mind flashed back to our huge dining room in Insterburg. For special occasions this beautiful tablecloth had covered the large table. It matched the gold-rimmed china and sparkling silver perfectly. The huge walnut buffet of the dining room suite contained several drawers filled with linens, which Mutti had done in draw work, eyelet, and embroidery before she met Vati. Huge glass doors led from the dining room to the balcony, where we loved to play and in the winter scatter seeds and crumbs for the birds. The doors were covered by floor-length lace drapes when they were closed. The most beautiful blooming plants graced a tall stand in the cove.

The china cabinet was filled with crystal vases, silver dishes, and many gifts from friends. Next to the china cabinet was a large window that overlooked about a half mile of the Hindenburgstraße, the main street of Insterburg. It had been from the window that I waved to Adolf Hitler when his motorcade drove down the hill toward the Marktplatz. All the schools were closed the day the Führer visited our city. He looked exactly the way he did in pictures, I thought to myself. Then I loved him. Now I hated him.

"Schäfle! Liane! Stop dreaming!" Mutti called to me. "Keep at your packing. We have a lot to do today. When you are finished with that project, you can get your own clothes ready for tomorrow. I suggest you wear two pairs of socks, your boots, and two dresses, plus the outer clothing, of course."

The neighbor from across the street suddenly appeared at the house to check on us. She saw the flurry of activity and the packing and knew for certain that we planned to leave. "Well," she said, "I see that you did decide to escape."

"I wouldn't really put it that way," Mutti replied. "We have the money and plan to purchase our tickets just like everybody else. I wouldn't really call that 'escape.'"

"Well, you know what I mean. So if I don't see you again, have a safe trip, and goodbye."

The farmer's wife who stayed at our house in January offered her help in getting us to the railroad station. She told us that we could use her hay wagon and her two old horses for transportation. "Please return the team and wagon to my farm after you and your belongings are at the station."

"Of course," Mutti replied. "I will return them promptly."

"You, Frau Guddat? You are such a refined lady from the city. You don't know how to handle horses, do you?"

"Of course, I was raised on a farm. My parents owned a large farm near Heydekrug in East Prussia. I do know how to handle a team of horses and a wagon."

"That's interesting. I would never have thought that someone like you knew what it was like to have dirty hands."

When Onkel Emil returned from work, the hallway was filled with bundles and suitcases. He finished his packing in a very short time by putting all his belongings into a duffle bag. "I am finished packing," he announced. "You ladies have packed for two days now and are still going strong? How can that be?"

"No comment," Mutti said.

Our devotional time was very sad that day. This was our last evening on the little farm! Where would we live next? Where would we be by this time tomorrow night?

"Only the Lord knows," Mutti told me.

I thought it must be especially difficult for Kätchen to leave her parents' home. She had already given up her own home, and now she had to suffer the loss of another place dear to her. I felt rather depressed that night, too, but how much more difficult it must have been for Kätchen.

"Lord, we commit our way to You. We know that You will lead us and direct our paths tomorrow. We love You, and we implore You to strengthen us and protect us," Onkel Emil prayed. "Guide us with Your eyes as You have done so many times in the past. Lord, save us from this system of deprivation. Unite us with our loved ones soon. Help all the children to be in good spirits tomorrow and let everything go smoothly. We thank You for answering our prayers, and we bless Your wonderful name. Amen!"

"Let's leave the house at 6:30 a.m.," Onkel Emil suggested. "That will give us an extra hour to get to the station. It will also give Emmy sufficient time to return the horses and wagon and about half an hour or so for anything unforeseen."

"Everything sounds fine to me, Emil. Do you know what?"

"What, Kätchen?"

"It never ceases to amaze me how precise you are in figuring out time schedules for Emmy and me. We certainly wouldn't know what we'd do without you and your pocket watch."

"Sh-sh-sh, Kätchen! Not so loud! Do you want somebody to hear you and come and turn me in for having been smart enough to keep my pocket watch out of the enemy's hands?"

"Just make sure your leg doesn't start ticking when we have to go through inspection somewhere tomorrow," Mutti joined in the fun.

"That's enough, you ladies! I see you are getting tired and giddy. Let's make a quick check of everything and then go to bed. We have to be alert for our trip."

"Good idea!"

"The last night in our featherbeds," Mutti added. "Only the Lord knows where we will sleep tomorrow."

What a gorgeous morning! It promised to be a nice day. There was not a cloud in the sky, and the little ones were as chipper as the birds. After a soup breakfast, we all left. Mutti was ready with the wagon, the luggage was loaded, and Kätchen locked the house and put the key in her coat pocket. Mutti was softly humming a song.

Even though I don't know the way,
You surely know it, Lord,
That makes my soul quiet and peaceful.
(Redern, "Weiß ich den Weg auch nicht")

Mutti's humming and cheerfulness calmed me too.

We arrived at the station with plenty of time to spare. Quickly everybody helped unload the luggage so that Mutti and Dieter could return the team. While we organized the suitcases and bundles, which had just been thrown off the wagon, we noticed that we were being watched closely by some men who stood idly around the station. One of them slowly wandered past our belongings, suddenly turned, grabbed one of our bundles, and ran off. Onkel Emil tried to limp after him, shouting angrily, but the thief continued to run. From then on, we were each assigned a suitcase or bundle to sit on and one to hold on to.

Slyly the men continued to move around us. "There is no train running," one of them told us, but we pretended not to hear him. We waited and waited, several hours. We had not seen any railroad personnel. Could it be true?

"I hear something," Dieter said excitedly. "I hear the tracks humming! Come over here and listen!"

My heart began to jump.

"Our freedom train!" Mutti rejoiced. "I hear it too. Our freedom train!"

"Everybody grab some luggage, quickly!" Onkel Emil's voice grew sharp.

"I am ready!" My eyes followed the tracks into an endless stretch of meadows. "Yes, there it is! It is coming closer."

"Why isn't it slowing down, Mutti?" Dieter asked. What he said was true. The train was moving too fast. It whizzed right past us and the Lippehne station. Nobody said a word, not even when another thief took off with one of our suitcases. Onkel Emil swung his cane at him, but it was too late. He got away.

"That must not have been our train," Onkel Emil reasoned.

Utterly speechless and with our hopes dashed, we all stood in a discouraged little group with the sound of the train still ringing in our ears.

"Did we pray enough about our departure?" Mutti began to analyze our predicament. "Perhaps it was only our will to leave and not the Lord's. We were all so busy preparing for our journey that even our devotions were cut short."

"You may be right, Emmy. We have been awfully busy. Maybe our time to leave Lippehne has not yet come."

"That is all right, Mutti," Hanno said. "I like Opi's farm. It is so much better than the hospital. I would like to go back to the farm."

"I think you will go back to the farm. Dieter and I will go and borrow the horses and wagon again before it gets dark. We'll see you later."

Mutti took Dieter's hand, and a few minutes later, we watched him and his "old grandmother" slowly turn the first street corner and head toward the promenade. It was safer to walk there than through the center of town.

The little ones were very hungry and restless, and so were the adults. Those men prowling around us had to be watched every single second. Apparently, they had no intentions of letting us out of their sight. They knew, of course, that we had packed only our very best things. At last Mutti was coming with the team and wagon. Quickly we loaded what we had left back on the wagon.

"The longer we stay here," Onkel Emil told me in a very disappointed tone, "the longer we all have to wait for a reunion with our loved ones."

"I am so anxious to see Vati, and so is Mutti. Why then couldn't the Lord let us get away today?"

"It must not have been His time, Liane."

"What is going on at our little farm, Kätchen?" Dieter asked nervously, peering over the bundles on the wagon.

"What do you mean, Dieter? What do you see from up there?"

"I see people coming out of the little farm. They are carrying things."

"What are they carrying?"

"I don't know. I can't see."

Yes, suddenly we saw it too. People were marching in and out of our house, but by the time we arrived, the front door was wide open and not a soul in sight anywhere. The whole street was empty. As we looked across the street, our neighbor sat knitting in her usual chair at the window.

"Lord, we thank You for this little place which You have preserved for us." Onkel Emil began praying while we were all still seated on the wagon. "We can't thank You enough for the miracle You performed again today."

I wondered how he could even pray such a prayer. We hadn't gained our freedom; the robbers took our luggage; the house had been ransacked; our hopes of seeing our loved ones were dashed. I just didn't understand. There was absolutely nothing to be thankful for as far as I was concerned.

"Yes, there is," Mutti whispered in my ear while Onkel Emil was still praying.

How did Mutti know what I was thinking?

"We did not lose our home, Schäfle. Someone could have easily moved in here while we were gone, but no one did. That is a true miracle."

12

ADVENT

The trees were bare; the flowers had been killed by the first frost; the air was nippy. Seldom did the sun warm the earth as the days became shorter. At times my own soul seemed to get entangled in this gloomy picture. I thought about the days at my grandparents' farm and all the delicious food we used to eat. I thought of the sugar eggs at Omi's house. I thought of the good times we had when Vati was still with us. I reveled in those memories often, but hardly ever finished my dream without being jolted back into reality, realizing that all those things and the people who were dear to me were now part of the past. At times, I found myself becoming lifeless, even though my heart was still beating within me.

On our begging trip one day, something pleasant happened to reverse that trend. We noticed people on the street with handwagons loaded with sugar beets.

"Mystery! I will solve that mystery," Dieter proclaimed. "Where did people get those beets?"

It didn't take us long to trace the beets back to a large farm outside of town.

"Dieter, can you imagine thousands of pounds of sugar beets lying in those caches undiscovered all year? They are from last year's crop. Why hasn't anyone found them sooner?" No one at home was able to answer that question for us. It must have been a special surprise the Lord had reserved just for that time.

Onkel Emil and Mutti took the handwagon and, with Dieter and me leading the way, hurried back to the farm. After arriving at the cache, we quickly dug under the soil and straw cover and pulled out the huge cone-shaped beets. Even though they had lain buried for one year, they were firm and had not lost moisture. Many of them must have weighed three or four pounds each. The wagon was filled in a very short time. We managed to get the heavy load home with Mutti and Onkel Emil pulling and Dieter and I pushing. Kätchen, hearing us come, opened the passage door to the courtyard so that we could pull right in.

"What a blessing the Lord has bestowed on us today! We can give our children something sweet to eat," Mutti said to Kätchen, bubbling with joy.

"Let's all pitch in and unload these beets," Onkel Emil suggested. "With everyone's help we'll have the job done in a few minutes."

We had a busy evening. We were all very tired, but the next morning Kätchen was nowhere in sight. We knew her sons loved to sleep in, but she always rose early. Checking the courtyard, Mutti was surprised to find the handwagon missing.

"I think I have an idea where Kätchen is," she remarked, entering the kitchen. "She must have gone to get sugar beets." Mutti was right. A short time later, we heard the handwagon pulling up to the passage door.

"I had to help provide for my sons," she said, looking like a child expecting punishment for having left the house without permission.

Making syrup or molasses from sugar beets was a project in which all but the little ones were involved. The beets' skins were creamy white and somewhat rough. Soil embedded in the little crevices was scrubbed out with a stiff brush and water. In assembly-line fashion, we all worked at cleaning the beets and then peeling them.

"I'll start cutting them into pieces," Mutti said. "By the time Onkel Emil comes home from work tonight, we can build a fire under the large kettle and start boiling the beet chips. Can you imagine syrup on bread? Sweet, dark, thick syrup?"

My mouth was watering at the thought. It was that vision that immediately gave all of us a fresh surge of energy to continue the boring and strenuous chore. Mutti's and Kätchen's hands were getting blisters, and their arms were sore from cutting up the hard roots. Only with the encouraging words of hymns and telling of jokes did the job become more bearable. All day we were munching on beet chips. Our taste buds must have been surprised to encounter something sweet—something they hadn't tasted all year.

Onkel Emil pitched in at night with the syrup project. He also set everything up for a good fire the next morning.

"I think we should all get a good night's sleep and rise early in the morning to light the fire and start the boiling process. You ladies will then have to keep the fire going all day. In the evening, we will take turns tending it and stirring the beets. Is everyone in agreement?"

"No objections," Mutti said.

Eventually, after the pulp had been removed, the boiling produced half a kettle full of liquid. The mixture was boiled slowly for two more days until a dark, thick syrup remained. The processing of the second load of beets was finished by the first Sunday of Advent, and prayers of thanksgiving and praise were offered with a new joy during our devotions. One of the foremost prayers continued to be for our freedom. "Lord, help us gain our freedom, but not our will, but Yours be done. You can move heaven and earth to take us out of Lippehne. We don't know why You delay answering our request. Give us patience. Help us to rely continually on You for guidance. Don't let our own will get in

Your way. Let us be a true witness for You, even before our enemies." This and similar prayers were offered daily.

Advent! What a time of celebration! This was the first of the four Sundays before Christmas. It was a time of preparing our hearts for the birthday of our Lord. The poems Mutti had written for everyone, young and old, were almost committed to memory. Mutti was making an Advent wreath from the evergreen branches Dieter and I brought home.

"We don't have four candles to place into the greens of the wreath," she said apologetically. "So this year one candle will have to suffice. It has to last until Christmas. We can light it only for a short time during our celebrations."

The first night we lit the candle was a thought-provoking evening for me. As I watched the sparkle from the reflection of the light in everyone's eyes, I remembered what Mutti had told me. She said that our eyes had become dull because of the lack of vitamins. Now I understood what she meant. Udo looked especially cute tonight with his twinkling eyes and bleach-blond hair. Marlies, with her china doll face and almost white curls, was doing what everyone else was—enjoying the slight flickering of our Advent candle. Hanno's face still looked sallow, but both his and Vilmar's eyes sparkled in the reflected candlelight. When I studied Dieter's face, I saw joy in him also, even though he had to suffer so much with his open leg sores.

"Fellowshiping with our family is just wonderful, isn't it?" Mutti said softly, as if she had read my mind. "What would we do without our big family here? What would we do without each other? The Lord is so good to us, isn't He?"

It was often difficult for me to understand how Mutti could be so thankful and joyous. I sometimes saw her saddened and weeping, but usually she was happy. How could she be so happy tonight? Had she forgotten our beautiful Emmanuel church in Insterburg and what it was like there at this special season? A huge, decorated Advent wreath, hung from the high ceiling of the church, thrilled hundreds of our church friends. Vati would open the Advent service by playing the huge pipe organ, one of the largest in all of Germany. The whole building would vibrate when he played, and the choir sang "Lo, How a Rose" and many other songs pointing to the birth of Jesus. Bible passages would be read and praises offered to the Lord with Advent songs. In Sunday school, we children would have the final rehearsals for the Christmas pageant.

What do we have now? Memories. Nothing but memories. That was a lot to be thankful for, Mutti reminded me. As I seriously considered that, I tended to agree.

Onkel Emil opened the Christmas season for us by reading the story of the conception of Jesus from the book of Luke in the New Testament. "He shall be great, and shall be called the Son of the Highest: and the Lord God shall give unto him the throne of his father David: And he shall reign over the house of Jacob for ever; and of his kingdom there shall be no end" (Luke 1:32–33). He read most of that first chapter and then prayed.

"Why do we have to blow out the candle before we sing, Mutti?" Dieter asked. "Can't we do it after our songs?"

"No, my son, we have to do it now. We have to be able to light it for three more Sundays, and if we use it all up now, we will have nothing left."

The last look I saw on everyone's face before Vilmar blew out the candle was a sad one. During the singing of our beautiful Advent songs, however, I sensed that all the faces in the room must have been smiling again. No one could sing so joyously with a grumpy face.

In the following weeks, Onkel Emil received many requests to sew. His reputation was growing among the Polish people, but he had little extra time to do more work. He and all his assistants worked on army uniforms six days a week. In the evenings he was tired and worn out. His payment remained the same—watery soup and one slice of bread. His coworkers often shared heartbreaking stories with one another, and often Onkel Emil returned home totally depressed. Most of the stories were of struggles to survive and hopes for escape.

Dieter and I had become professional scavengers by this time, but the Lord still continued to provide for us in unexpected ways. One day we returned home just in time to hear Kätchen saying goodbye to a Polish visitor. "Goodbye, and thank you again," she said as she closed the front door. "Emmychen, you can't imagine what my friend just gave me! One bar of soap—soap! What luxury! I had to laugh when she lifted up her skirt and pulled the soap out of her bloomers. She was laughing too. I guess not even the vilest system can keep people from helping one another. Isn't that marvelous?"

Sometimes Dieter and I were sent hunting for things other than food or firewood—such as a Christmas tree. That one was a tough assignment.

"We have to walk faster, Dieter. My arm is getting numb."

"I can't walk faster. We should have cut a smaller tree. I never knew Christmas trees were so heavy."

"Don't complain. I think it will be worth it when we see it all decorated with the paper chains we made and the Scheerenschnitt snowflakes."

"Why don't we stop right here on the street and shorten the tree? Then it won't be so heavy."

"No, we can't do that! We have to drag it home like this."

Mutti and Kätchen were delighted when they saw us pulling such a beautiful tree into the house. They immediately confiscated it and told us that we would not be able to see it again until we celebrated the birth of our Lord the next day.

"If we can't help with the tree, we should go and finish memorizing the Christmas story, Liane."

Upstairs in our room, Dieter and I settled down on the couch for some serious mental exercise.

"Let's continue, Liane!" Dieter commanded, and his dark eyes looked stern. "We have to finish memorizing the Christmas story. Only three more verses to go."

"'And all they that heard it wondered at those things which were told them by the shepherds. But Mary kept all these things, and pondered them in her heart. And the shepherds returned. . . .' Sure wish I could have been one of the first people on earth to see the baby Jesus," Dieter interrupted us, "'glorifying and praising God for all the things that they had heard and seen, as it was told unto them'" (Luke 2:18–20).

"Do you smell something baking, Liane?"

"That can't be." We held our noses in the air like rabbits that had detected the scent of fresh lettuce in someone's garden. It was true. Something was baking. It was no use, though, to continue guessing what it might be. We were simply not allowed to go into the kitchen without permission on this day before Christmas Eve, and not even Dieter was able to solve the mystery of the delicious aroma that was trailing upstairs.

Christmas Eve morning! What an exciting day this was going to be! As I looked out of the window, I realized that the earth was lightly dusted with snow, our first snow. The wind took the little flakes and pushed them into little swirls that danced around on the sidewalk. Airy snow clouds were being swept off the schoolhouse roof. They were joining the flakes below. A short, old lady with a black babushka and long black skirt was shuffling along the school building. She was weighted down by a bundle of firewood. Her long skirt swept a bare path on the sidewalk, which the little flakes covered again quickly. She looked lifeless and uncaring. I wondered if she would be celebrating Christmas.

The afternoon seemed long. The sky was dark, and the clouds released a few snow flurries every now and then. Why did I have to take a nap today along with the little ones? I knew they had to be wide awake for our celebration tonight, but I could have managed without a nap. Even though this had been the rule at our house ever since I could remember,

I really thought an exception could be made for someone my age. Taking a nap on Christmas Eve afternoon was nothing but torture. I knew it freed Mutti to decorate the tree without interruption and wrap the gifts, but what I couldn't understand was why all those activities took such an awfully long time.

The bread soup seemed to taste extra good that Christmas Eve night. It must have been the beet syrup sweetening that made it so special.

"Yes, Pittimaus," Mutti was trying to answer some of Marlies's chattering questions. "We will all put on our Sunday clothes. You wouldn't go to a birthday party unless you were dressed up, right? And tonight, we are celebrating the birthday of Jesus. Even though we can't see Him, we dress up for His special day."

It was almost dark when we all filed into the living room. The beautiful tree stood in the corner, one candle perched near the top of the branches. Everyone was singing:

"O come, little children, O come one and all,
O come to the cradle in Bethlehem's stall."
(Schmid, "Ihr Kinderlein Kommet")

The singing continued after we had found our favorite seats in the living room. "O Tannenbaum," "Softly Falleth the Snow," "O Thou Glorious," and many other traditional German Christmas songs made this celebration more special than any other we'd had in the course of the year.

Hanno and Vilmar were radiant with joy as they quoted Isaiah 9:6.

"For unto us a child is born, unto us a son is given:
And the government shall be upon his shoulder:
And his name shall be called Wonderful, Counsellor, The mighty God,
The everlasting Father, The Prince of Peace."

The boys were very deserving of the applause they received.

It was almost pitch-dark outside, and I couldn't wait for that one candle to be lit. A few more songs, songs the German people have enjoyed for hundreds of years, warmed our hearts. Finally Onkel Emil got up and very deliberately limped toward the tree. Striking a wooden match, he lit the candle. He hobbled back to his chair and with both hands lifted his prosthesis into a position that was comfortable for him.

When I looked around the room, I saw sixteen eyes focused on that one candle. No one said a word. Everyone just enjoyed the candle's warm glow and the brightness it gave all of us. Suddenly Mutti broke the long silence, "The light of the world is Jesus. Today is Jesus's birthday. Let's hear the birthday story, Schäfle and Dieter."

Standing next to the tree, we gave a curtsy and a bow and began reciting Luke 2:1–20, "And it came to pass in those days, that there went out a decree from Caesar Augustus, that all the world should be taxed. . . ."

Our performance was flawless and our audience attentive. Were Mutti's eyes filled with tears? Udo sat patiently on her lap, and she gave him a few extra squeezes.

"We will all pray now," Onkel Emil continued, "and thank God for giving us His only Son on this Christmas Day."

"I know that verse, Onkel Emil," Marlies interrupted. Sliding off the couch and placing herself in front of the Christmas tree, she curtsied and said, "For God so loved the world, that he gave his only begotten Son, that whosoever believeth in him should not perish, but have everlasting life" (John 3:16). A quick curtsy, and she jumped back onto the couch with a big smile, her natural curls dancing around her head.

"That is wonderful, Pittimaus! You quoted that verse well!"

"God gave all of us a gift, a present, on this special day many, many years ago," Onkel Emil continued. "He gave it to the whole world, to every single person. And this gift is Jesus. You children all know the story of Adam and Eve, don't you? And you know that they did wrong. They sinned. Because of them, we are all sinners too. God loves people so much and wants to fellowship with them, but the people always want to go their own way. Then God told the people to offer sacrifices and confess their sins. Many animals had to die."

"Is that when little lambs had to die?" Dieter asked.

"Yes, Dieter, that is right. Innocent lambs. But one day God said, 'That is enough. I will send My own Son to earth, and He will be the last sacrifice ever. He will die on the cross. He will be buried, and I will raise Him from the dead and take Him back to heaven to live with Me. I will give everyone on earth a choice. They can believe on My Son, thank Him for dying for them, and come to live with us in heaven for eternity, or they can reject My gift and forever burn in hell.' So, you see, God really loves us a lot, doesn't He? He gives us the very best gift He has—His Son. Many people don't want to accept God's gift. They don't want to ask Jesus into their hearts. But I hope you will not reject Him. Your mommies and I have asked for forgiveness of our sins many years ago and asked Jesus to come into our lives, and He did. We talk to Him every day in prayer, and we read the road map to heaven, the Bible. Jesus gives us peace and joy. He gives us strength, and we are looking forward to spending eternity with Him. Do you know what eternity means?"

"Yes," Hanno answered. "It means forever, and ever, and ever, and ever, and ever, and ever. . . ."

"That's enough, Hanno," Vilmar broke in.

"You children know how good the Lord has been to us during these difficult days," Onkel Emil continued. "He has protected us. He has shown us so many miracles. He helps us to survive even though we don't have much to eat. He keeps our minds strong, and He will bring all our families together again."

"But why didn't God protect Opi from typhoid?" Hanno asked. "Why did he have to die?"

"That is a good question, Hanno, but I don't have the answer to it. I can, however, imagine that Jesus said to Himself, 'That Opi Lehmann is very special to Me. He has loved Me ever since I became his Savior. He has lived for Me. He has told many other people about Me. He is very special. I think I want him to come and live in heaven with Me.' And then Jesus took him to heaven to live there forever and ever."

Kätchen's eyes were filled with tears. "Emil, you said that so beautifully. Thank you!"

Our festivities continued with the singing of "Stille Nacht" and praying. The homecoming poems were recited, and we sang more songs. Mutti herself recited a poem, dealing with the Germans being to blame for all the trouble in which Germany found itself because they rejected the grace of God.

Our candle was rather short now, but continued to shed its glow on those who, with great fascination, sat and admired it.

"Children," Mutti announced, "God gave us two gifts tonight. One is the gift of His Son and another one is under the tree. We'll let Udo go and get the gift that is for everyone."

Udo slipped off Mutti's lap and reached for whatever was under the large doily. When the doily fell off, we couldn't believe our eyes. It was a plate full of cookies. Cries of excitement and surprise came from almost everyone.

"Cookies! Cookies! Cookies!"

"There are two millet cookies for each man, woman, and child," Mutti announced joyfully. "How is that for a Christmas surprise?"

"Two cookies?" Hanno exclaimed. "What a feast!"

"I will save one of my cookies for tomorrow," Marlies declared. "Tomorrow is Christmas Day, Mutti, right?"

"Yes, it is, Pittimaus."

"Emmychen, I just can't praise the Lord enough for His goodness to us," Kätchen rejoiced. "On this Christmas Day, my Polish friend came to pay us a visit. When she saw our Christmas tree, she said, 'You German people do what we Polish folks would never dare do.'

"'What is that?' I asked her, and she said 'We would never dare put up a Christmas tree.' Then she lifted up her skirt, and guess what she had under it to give us on this special day?"

"Why don't you tell me?"

"Under her skirt she carried a can of goat's milk as a Christmas gift for us. Can you believe the goodness of our Lord? A gift, straight from heaven, for our children."

"That is a true miracle, Kätchen. I just hope that when we are able to serve our children full glasses of milk every day, we will not forget the miracle the Lord performed today."

"You said that beautifully, Emmychen, and I agree. In the good days, we usually tend to forget how the Lord has shown Himself faithful to us in times of trouble."

13

CAPTURE

January 1, 1946! Would this be the year the Lord would reunite our families? Would this be the year we could leave Lippehne? While we had these and many other questions on our minds, rumors were starting that more Germans would have to leave town.

"We will not be able to go because of my job," Onkel Emil said. "They would never let me go, I was told. But we know that with God all things are possible. We can't stay here. In order to be reunited with our families, we have to leave. We must pray hard and seek God's guidance. People tell me that trains leave for Berlin daily now. This fact can be to our advantage. Two women from my tailor shop have been whispering about visiting Berlin and beginning the search for their loved ones."

Mutti's eyes lit up when Onkel Emil shared that information.

"I have relatives in Berlin," she said. "Perhaps my aunt and her husband have heard where Emil is."

"But, Mutti, you can't leave!" I objected. "You can't leave us here alone."

"You won't be alone, Liane. Onkel Emil and I would be here to help you, should your Mutti decide to go," Kätchen intervened.

"But if something happens to Mutti, who will take care of the four of us?"

"Schäfle, we belong to the Lord. He will take care of us—but I don't even know yet if I am going. I really have to pray much about this and seek the Lord's guidance."

The next day Onkel Emil returned home with more details about the trip the ladies had planned.

"The ladies have worked ahead feverishly, so that I would give them six days off. Not two but four ladies are taking the trip, Emmy. The neighbor from across the street is one of them. She is going along as their interpreter. The women told me that anyone is welcome to join them. Since the war has been over for months now, they don't foresee any problems."

"Did you find out, Emil, when they plan to leave?"

"Yes. They expect to leave on January 10 and return on January 16."

"Oh, good," Mutti said, took a deep breath, and hugged me. "If I go, I'll be home on your birthday, Schäfle. I wouldn't want to miss the birthday of my oldest child."

I couldn't bear the thought of Mutti's leaving. Even though everyone was still praying about it, I had the feeling that she would go to Berlin. I knew it had been very difficult for her without Vati, and if she could learn where he was, life would be easier for her. I determined to help even more with my brothers and sister to make Mutti's dream come true.

"If I go to Berlin, Schäfle, you will be in charge of everyone during the day while Onkel Emil is at work. Kätchen, of course, will assist you in any way she can. You have helped me so much with your brothers and sister that I know you can handle things beautifully. With the Lord giving you strength, you won't fail. Tell me now, honestly, how do you feel about my going?"

"I wish you wouldn't have to leave, Mutti, but if you can locate Vati, I'll be very happy. So I am all set to take over for you."

"Thank you, Schäfle! Thank you!"

As January 10 approached, I felt less strong, but couldn't let Mutti detect that. She had made the decision to go, and her rucksack was packed. Our time of devotions was sad for me. I would miss Mutti so much. I was glad it was dark in the room so that I could hide my tears.

Prayers and goodbyes were said hurriedly the next morning. The neighbor from across the street would walk to the station with Mutti and meet the others there. We were not to accompany her.

"I love you, children. The Lord keep you." These words lingered in the cold winter air as Mutti stepped into the street.

When I turned around, Kätchen was right there to embrace me. I needed her comforting hug.

"I have always wanted a daughter like you," she told me, "but instead of giving me a daughter, the Lord has blessed me with three wonderful sons. The oldest one, of course, is in heaven now. Is it all right with you if I consider you my daughter for the next six days?"

"That would be just wonderful, Kätchen. I think you know how much I love you."

"Now, Liane, if you need anything, I'll be right here to help you in any way I can," she added, giving me another hug. Kätchen's offer thrilled me, but I still sensed a huge burden of responsibility.

My brothers and sister were wonderful. They were obedient and helpful to me in many little ways. When Udo needed help dressing, Marlies helped him. When Marlies required help, Dieter assisted her. Dieter was also my right hand because he could entertain everyone so well. Playing mailman and post office was one of the favorite games then. Hanno and Vilmar always joined in the fun.

One day Dieter and I walked to the bakery to buy bread. The bread line shrank very slowly, but after two hours of standing in the cold, we were getting excited about reaching the warm store. There were only ten more people ahead of us. Suddenly Polish words, which we had learned to recognize, were passed to the end of the queue, "No more bread today."

Very disappointed and hungry, we trudged home. On the way we decided that we would leave at 7:00 a.m. tomorrow. Surely no one would be there that early, and we would be first in line. When we arrived, however, quite a few women were already lined up past the store and several houses. As we waited, we constantly stomped our feet to keep them from freezing. Everyone else was doing the same, but nobody managed to stay warm today. It was just too frigid. Our bodies were numb from the cold. The wait was worthwhile that day, for two hours later, we returned home with a loaf of dark bread. I spent the rest of the day cleaning and scrubbing Onkel Emil's room and the staircase. The next day was to be Mutti's homecoming day.

Finally, it was January 16—my birthday and Mutti's homecoming! Kätchen and Onkel Emil sang a choir number for me.

"With this song, we wish you the Lord's richest blessing for the coming year. May our Lord give you health and joy, and may He return your Vati to you and your family. May the Lord keep you and watch over you," Kätchen said as she cupped both of my hands in hers. She then gave me a hug and a kiss.

"Kätchen's wishes are mine too, Liane. The Lord bless you." Onkel Emil, who was about six feet and two inches tall, bent down to give me a kiss. As I was standing there in the kitchen, a line of five little well-wishers filed past. What a way to start my birthday! I was so touched by all the fuss everybody made because I was twelve years old.

While Dieter and the children entertained themselves, I started my workday by making the beds.

"I want to help, Liane," Marlies said as she suddenly appeared to assist in straightening out the featherbed. I had fluffed the feathers almost perfectly, but what were her little hands doing to it? The bed resembled a camel after she left, and I had to start "building the bed" all over again.

In typical German fashion, I worked and worked on the beds to give them a smooth, square look. The feathers had to be pushed in just the right direction to achieve that. After that job was done, I continued to work toward my goal, to have all the darning and mending done by the time Mutti returned. While I sat near the window and darned, I heard Onkel Emil's voice downstairs. What was he doing home at noon? He had never come home at this time of day.

"Liane! Dieter!" his deep voice rolled upstairs. "Come on down, you two!" In seconds, Dieter and I were reporting to him. "Let's go into the living room. I have to tell you something. You come too, Kätchen," he said as we passed through the kitchen. "Let's all sit down."

When we were seated he continued, "I heard some disturbing news today. I heard that all the Germans who returned from Berlin by train yesterday were arrested by Russian soldiers and were taken to jail. It is possible that this will happen again today. Those who were seized were walking out of the main gate of the station. Others had no problems. We cannot allow them to capture your mother. So I suggest the following safety measures: you, Liane and Dieter, go to the station to meet Mutti. Be there before the train arrives at 3:30 p.m. The moment it stops and you see your mother getting off, dash toward her—there'll be no time for hugs and kisses—and tell her to follow you quickly around the outside of the station building. You can't run. That is too conspicuous. You must walk very fast to avoid the crowd that will be filing out through the main gate. When you are away from the station, take one of the side streets home. Don't walk on Main Street! Do you understand everything? Do you know your assignment?"

"Yes, Onkel Emil," Dieter answered. "We understand."

"I think we should all pray right now about the situation," Kätchen suggested. "We have a powerful God. He can let everything go well this afternoon."

After we had prayed for protection for Mutti and the other women, Onkel Emil left for his shop.

"If I didn't have a sewing deadline to meet and could walk faster, I'd go to the station myself," he said. "But I know you two can do a better job warning Mutti than I can. So I'll see you all tonight."

My heart seemed to be skipping beats. We didn't have to wait until Mutti reached home? We could see her twenty minutes earlier? That was a lovely birthday surprise. I had missed her terribly. I wondered what news she had of Vati. Where was he living? Had she perhaps seen him? How was her visit with her aunt and uncle in Berlin? All these questions raced through my mind. Darning was no chore because of the joy that lay ahead. Even Onkel Emil's large sock holes were woven shut in no time. I was so glad I could keep busy until it was time to leave. A quick check showed me that Udo's face and hands had to be washed again. His blond, straight hair had to be combed even though I knew it would not stay that way until we returned from the station. Marlies's dress was neat and her curls beautiful for Mutti's homecoming. A further check showed that no one had pushed a little hand into the featherbeds. The washbowl was scrubbed and filled with clean water. Everything was just the way Mutti would like it.

After Kätchen had prayed with us, Dieter and I bundled up and headed for the railroad station. It was a bitterly cold, snowy day. There was almost no one on the street.

"We don't have to walk so fast, Dieter. We have plenty of time."

"Aren't you anxious to see Mutti?"

"Of course. But getting there early doesn't make the train come any sooner."

"Well, yes, I know that. I just can't wait to see her."

"I know. I know, little brother. I feel the same way you do."

We walked silently for a while. I heard only the squeaking of my boots as the snow crunched beneath them. Last year, just before the

Russian invasion, I had celebrated my eleventh birthday without Vati too. On my tenth birthday Vati had called. That was also the day the Lyceum in Insterburg, the school I was to attend after elementary school, was engulfed in flames and partially destroyed. It was a terrible sight from our living room window. The most wonderful birthday memories, though, were those of our family celebrations. Opi, Omi, and Vati's twin brother would come to our home in the afternoon, eat yeast cakes and torten with us, and bring exciting gifts. A special birthday or winter treat was always apples baked in the tile oven. Why did my thoughts always stray to food? It wasn't fair to my body. The saliva glands experienced too many disappointments.

Just a few more steps past the rotting furniture, the pianos, and the sewing machines, and we would turn to go around the depot to wait there.

"If we stay right here at the corner of the building," Dieter whispered, "we can see the train coming and overlook all the cars at the same time."

"Good thinking, Brother! Good idea!"

The tracks were beginning to hum, and we knew that we would see Mutti in a few moments. The train grew larger and larger as it approached Lippehne. The whistle gave off a deafening sound as the brakes squeaked and caused the mass of metal to come to a screeching halt. The conductor stuck his head out of the window of the engine compartment and called, "Lippehne!"

My heart was racing.

"There she is! Come, Liane! Mutti! Mutti!" Was it really Mutti? She looked so tired. Her clothes were dirty, torn, and wet.

"Come quickly this way!" I said, grabbing her by the arm. "They are arresting people. Don't go through the building!" We walked as fast as we could without running. Suddenly two Russians ran toward us with their rifles aimed at us.

"You come! You come!" they yelled and yanked Mutti by the arm.

"But I have children!"

"You come!"

"I want to say goodbye to my children." She tried to turn around to see us, but they pushed her ahead of them.

"Mutti! Mutti!" Dieter cried. One of the Russians turned around and almost hit him with his rifle.

"Daway! Daway!" they hollered and continued to try to chase us away, but we followed. Mutti made another attempt to talk to us. As she turned around, her captors became furious and pushed her ahead of them with their rifles in her back.

"We have to follow to see where they take Mutti," I told Dieter. Sobbing, he nodded his head.

"Daway! Daway!" the Russians yelled at us again when they heard us talking. One of them turned and flung his arms angrily, motioning for us to go away. That really scared me. We walked more slowly to increase the distance between them and us. Suddenly they turned left on the street which led to the KGB headquarters.

"We can't lose them, Dieter. Let's run!" Quickly we caught up to them. The Russians noticed that immediately, and one of them started chasing after us. We had no choice now. They would kill us if we persisted. We must run home.

Kätchen and all the children were standing in the hallway saying, "Willkommen!" as we knocked and the door opened. They naturally expected Mutti to walk in with us. Instead, Dieter and I just stood on the step and cried.

"Mutti was arrested by the Russians. She was taken to headquarters." Intermingled with sobs, we told Kätchen the whole story. The sad news caused her visible pain.

"Come into the kitchen and get warm," she told us, embracing Dieter and me.

Marlies could hardly be comforted. "I want to see Mutti. I want to see Mutti," she begged.

Udo joined the heartbreaking cries. I needed to pull myself together. It was my job now to cheer them up. I decided to play games with everybody. Onkel Emil, I felt certain, would know how to get Mutti released from jail.

14

NOTHING BUT TRUST

As we recounted the capture episode for Onkel Emil, a depressing and helpless feeling settled into my soul.

"I will use my connections and my reputation as head worker for the communist regime to get Mutti out of jail. You two bundle up, and we will all go to headquarters. They'll release Mutti tonight yet, you'll see."

We trudged through the empty streets in utter silence. In order to avoid inhaling the icy winter air, we covered our mouths with our mittened hands.

"Lord, I have only one birthday wish," I silently prayed. "Please let Mutti come home."

Onkel Emil pushed the few strands of hair, which the wind had blown down, to the back of his head. He knocked on the door of the massive stone building, the headquarters of the Russian KGB. No one answered. He pushed the large handle, but the door was locked. Most of the rooms in the building were lit except for the basement windows. Mutti wouldn't be in a dark basement! Several other structures were fenced in and the gates locked.

"Hello! Hello!" Onkel Emil called into the darkness, but there was no response.

"We could throw a snowball at one of the windows. No, I think we are better off not doing that. It seems we can't accomplish anything here tonight, children. If Mutti doesn't return tonight, we'll come back tomorrow morning."

The walk home in the bitter cold air seemed unbelievably long. The neighbor's house across the street was still dark. She must not be home yet either.

The throne of God was bombarded that night with petitions for Mutti's release.

"Lord, You know that these children need their mother," Onkel Emil prayed. "Protect her tonight. Let no harm come to her. Lord, You are testing us. May we not fail You, but may we remain faithful and true. Let us take everything as from Your hand. And please, keep up Emmy's spirit; with Your Spirit, lift up hers."

By the time we were all tucked into our beds, Mutti still wasn't home. Was she sleeping in a bed tonight? Was she warm? Was she all alone? All through the night, I awakened and listened in vain for her.

Each of us had one slice of bread spread thinly with beet syrup for breakfast. I cut Udo's slice in small, bite-size pieces the way Mutti always did it. This helped him to eat the sticky substance without getting too messy. Onkel Emil planned to stop at the KGB headquarters that morning and ask for Mutti's release.

"Children, be all ready for her homecoming today. You had the house clean and in beautiful order yesterday. Do it again today."

"We will, Onkel Emil," Dieter agreed quickly. "We'll be ready."

By late afternoon there was still no sign of Mutti.

"Mutti! Mutti! Come see this!" Hanno called to Kätchen. "Didn't our neighbor go to Berlin with Dieter's Mutti? She is sitting in front of her window." Running to Kätchen's bedroom window, I too saw her sitting and knitting in her favorite chair.

"Liane, you and Dieter go across the street, please, and ask our neighbor to come over for a visit," Kätchen requested quietly and quickly.

A few minutes later, the neighbor and the two of us, along with Kätchen, were sitting in the living room.

"Please tell us," Kätchen opened the conversation, "what happened to all the others in the group who went to Berlin."

"Well, we were all arrested at the railroad station and taken into headquarters for questioning."

"Where are all the other women?"

"They are still there, I presume, if Frau Guddat isn't home yet, and I gather from your questions that she has not yet returned."

"Why do you think you were arrested?"

"Well, the Russians told me that I was a spy. Everyone going to Berlin is considered a spy. Of course, I told them that this was not the case with me, and they let me go. I am glad I didn't have to stand at attention outdoors any longer. I could not have taken it. An hour was enough for me. The others were still standing under guard and shivering when I left." Throwing back her shoulders and blinking her eyes several times, she was definitely trying to impress us. Her attitude seemed more haughty than saddened by the plight of the others.

"I am glad you could get home quickly," Kätchen said, "but did you make any attempt to help your friends?"

"Well, Frau Mecklenburg, I think I did what I could. The Russians were very friendly when I addressed them in their own language. They seem to like it when a German speaks Russian. They told me I could go home. If I would have turned around then and asked for the release of the other four women, they might have reconsidered and called me a spy too. So when they told me to go home, I did not want to risk losing my freedom. I just left. And that is all I can tell you. I hope I have explained everything to you. I must really go now. My sauerkraut and pork are probably burned by now. Auf Wiedersehen!"

"Auf Wiedersehen!" Kätchen said. "Thank you for coming over."

All of a sudden, I felt something welling up inside me, and I realized that I despised this lady, who not too long ago taught me several new knitting techniques. My heart became faint when I thought about Mutti having to stand in the cold for hours. Her feet and hands were always sensitive to cold.

"That conversation didn't help us, Liane, did it?" Kätchen asked after she had locked the front door. "We must pray continually for Mutti. The Lord can perform miracles today as He did in Bible times. Do you remember the story of Peter in the book of Acts? Peter was in prison. He was chained between two soldiers, and guards were stationed at the prison door. Then an angel came, loosed the chains, and told Peter to get dressed. With the Lord's messenger leading, Peter walked through the locked iron gate into the city."

"Yes, I know that story."

"You see, Liane, Mutti is in prison, and our God is the same yesterday, today, and forever. He doesn't change. What He did then, He can do today. And that is what we will pray for, a miracle that will return Mutti to us quickly."

"I have tried everything possible to get Emmy's release," Onkel Emil explained after returning home and handing Kätchen his cabbage soup and slice of bread. "When I petitioned the Russians, they just snickered and told me to get out." Onkel Emil blew on his hands in an effort to warm them up before taking off his coat. His face was red from the cold and even his gray hair and bushy eyebrows looked frozen. "Someone said the temperature is five degrees Fahrenheit today. It would not surprise me, Kätchen, if I just handed you frozen soup."

"That is all right, Emil. Thanks to the good Lord, we still have a fire that can warm it up," said Kätchen as she poured the watery soup into the pot and added more water to it.

"We have to pray for a miracle," Onkel Emil said. "Only a miracle can bring Emmy back soon."

"Funny that you would put it that way. Liane and I have just come to the same conclusion," Kätchen added.

During our devotional time, we entreated the Lord to strengthen Mutti and keep her safe. We also asked for a miracle.

"I suggest you and Dieter go to the commander's headquarters again tomorrow," Onkel Emil said before we went to bed. "You don't have to hide your tears. Don't be afraid to cry. Try to get into the building and tell the Russians you need your mother. Seeing you children plead for your mother may carry more weight with them than my going. I, of course, plan to go to intercede for her also. I'll go later in the day."

The next day I bundled up Marlies while Dieter got ready by himself, and the three of us ventured out into the deadly cold to beg for Mutti's freedom. When we arrived at the jail, two Russians chased us away from the main door.

Marlies cried bitterly, "Mutti! Mutti! Mutti, come home!" But no one seemed to hear her.

We placed ourselves under various windows and called for Mutti, yet not a single person came to the window. The two guards had been patient with us, pretending that we did not exist. Suddenly, however, one of them ran toward us. He yelled and motioned for us to leave.

"We'll stay. Don't move!" I told Dieter and Marlies. That infuriated him. He took the rifle off his shoulder, and I immediately sensed danger. "Let's run!" I commanded, and we started running home. Marlies's little feet could hardly keep up with us. She ran and sobbed as we tried to drag her along.

Onkel Emil gave a similar report in the evening—unsuccessful. Our prayers for a miracle, however, continued.

"We'll use the same tactics again today," Onkel Emil told us the next day. "You children go to the prison and cry for your mother. I will make another attempt to see the commander. Why should they want to hold these women so long? The two workers from my tailor shop must still be there also. I have had no word from them."

By evening it was plain that we had accomplished nothing. As we compared notes, we found that we all had again received the same treatment from the Russians. We were first ignored, and then we were chased away. There was not one ray of hope.

"Tomorrow we'll walk to headquarters together, and I will try another angle." Onkel Emil informed us. "I plan to tell the Russians, hopefully the commander himself, that I, as tailor, will no longer oversee the work in the shop for him. I will tell him that I refuse to head up the work crew if Emmy is not released immediately. Perhaps that will give him something to think about."

Our plans were carried out on a cold and dreary Sunday afternoon. Would this be our miracle day? Onkel Emil even gained admission into the headquarters building along with the four of us.

"You Emil Schmidtke? You see commander? Commander out of town. You back tomorrow. Commander here then."

Apparently, the pressure was accomplishing something because Onkel Emil's name had filtered down to even the guards. Heavy hearted, but clinging to a new spark of hope, we slowly walked home. I knew Udo would love to stop to make some snowballs, but we had to obey Onkel Emil, and he had told us to go straight home.

Most of the houses on our street were occupied again. Instead of curtains, there were sheets, rags, and paper covering the windows of most of the homes. This led me to believe that the new residents must be poor. The Polish folks we met on the street were all elderly. Thus far we had not seen any young people or children.

Onkel Emil and I sang for Kätchen's birthday.

"On the wings of the eagle we are carried
Across the turbulent ocean of time."
(Wethern-Viebahn, "Auf Adlers Flügeln getragen")

We had no birthday cake or gift to give her, but with our hugs and kisses we gave her all our love. It was Monday, January 21.

"Kätchen's birth was quite a miracle," Onkel Emil stated. "What would we do without her? Where would we all be without her? It is because of her and the Lord that we are here at her dad's house. We might not have had a place to live without Kätchen. My birthday wish and prayer for you is that you will be reunited with your husband this year."

"Mine too," I chimed in.

"We'll celebrate more tonight," he continued, as he put on his coat, ready to leave. "And don't forget to pray for a miracle today!" The hallway echoed his voice.

"Thank you, Emil, thank you for the wonderful birthday wishes and the song. You are all so dear to me. And, Lord, for today I have only one request—please set Emmy free. Please return the mother to these children. They need her. Please make this a miracle birthday, Lord."

Again Dieter and I set our rooms in order, and everything was immaculate for Mutti's homecoming. Since any day could be our miracle day, we always had to be expectant. Kätchen watched Udo while the three of us went to the jail again. Dressed in her white fur hat and cute coat that Mutti had made, Marlies looked like a doll. She was the one who cried the loudest when we attempted to make our presence known. If only we could get a glimpse of Mutti! Then we would at least know that she was all right, I thought. Unfortunately, we didn't see anyone but the guards. The snow glistened beautifully on the lake behind the headquarters. Chunks of ice were scattered around in various areas. Ice fishermen must have chopped the holes.

"I want to go home. My feet are frozen," my little sister complained. "Please let's go home."

"I am frozen too," Dieter added.

"But we can't go home. We have to see the commander. Let's see if we can walk right past the guards into the building. We'll all hold hands and walk really fast."

"Mutti! Mutti!" Marlies called when we approached the huge door, but that was as far as we got. The Russians seemed to know what we had in mind and planted themselves, with their legs spread, between the door posts.

"Daway, daway!" they hollered at us and almost pushed us down the steps backward. "Daway!"

We had no choice now. We had to leave again—quickly. One of the guards chased us to make sure we left. When we no longer heard the snow squeak under his heavy boots, we knew that we were not being pursued and stopped to catch our breath.

Kätchen tried to comfort us as she did every day, but the longer Mutti was absent, the more fruitless Kätchen's efforts became.

"Come and warm your hands and feet here at the fire. Hanno! Vilmar! You boys come here too. We have to have a prayer meeting. I feel we should pray right now for your Mutti's release. You come and sit next to Kätchen, Udo.

"O Lord," she began. "You see our disappointed and humble little group here. Please answer our prayers. You have performed many wonderful things in the past. You have guided us, helped us, and protected us many times. Please give Emmy the strength to withstand everything that is put in her way today. Don't let the spirit within her weaken. Give her the assurance that her children are safe in Your care. Give her an extra measure of faith to endure all the testing. Just place

Your loving arms around her and comfort her. Let her experience Your love for her in a mighty way. Keep discouragements from all of us. Forgive us for our shortcomings. We love You. In Your strength, we want to live for You daily. We thank You for answering our prayers. Blessed be Your holy name. Amen."

15

MIRACLE FOR MUTTI

Because we were not able to get warm, Dieter, Marlies, and I huddled near the stove for a long time. My little sister's feet still felt like chunks of ice. I just hoped her feet hadn't been frost-damaged during the latest attempt to free Mutti. The white ring on her cheeks was finally fading, and she no longer complained about her face hurting.

"Someone is knocking on the front door," Dieter said. We all sat in shock and began to listen. The knocking grew louder, but nobody moved. What should we do? Hide? Jump into the trap basement? Then the knocking turned into banging. We knew we had to open the door, but fear kept us from moving.

"Let's all go," Kätchen said in a weak voice. The pounding became fierce, and we all tiptoed into the hallway. "Who is it?" Kätchen asked bravely. There was no answer. The banging continued. We stood in silence and the house vibrated from the pounding. "Who is it?" she called again.

"It's Mutti!" Dieter said. "I know it."

"How do you know?"

"We just prayed for her, didn't we?"

Reaching for the latch, Kätchen cautiously pulled back the heavy door.

"Mutti! Mutti! Emmy! Tante Emmy! Mutti!" We were all shouting at once. "A miracle! We just prayed for you." Everybody reached out to hug Mutti and welcome her, but she quickly stepped back.

"I am sorry, please stay back. Please don't touch me. I am infested with lice. I must get rid of these pests first. Then I will hug and kiss all of you," she said with tear-filled eyes. Mutti looked so drawn and haggard. Even her wide cheekbones seemed to be sunken.

"Mutti! Mutti!" Udo cried.

"I'll hug you in a little while, my son. You all go and play, and I will be done with the cleanup in no time."

A short time later, we saw Mutti's fur-lined coat lying on a pile of snow in the courtyard.

"Hopefully the cold will kill the lice," Kätchen said.

I couldn't believe Mutti was home. Even though we had prayed earnestly for her return, I couldn't comprehend it. A quick check upstairs showed me that everything was still clean and in order. I thought Mutti would be pleased.

Once Mutti considered herself presentable and safe, there was no end to all the embracing, loving, and kissing. Udo and Marlies clung to Mutti like burdock to a piece of clothing.

"Children, our God is wonderful. Do you know that I am the only one who was released from prison, the only one of more than twenty people? That is a real miracle of God—except our neighbor, of course, was set free immediately."

"Emmy! Emmy! Thank God you are back!" Onkel Emil walked in to join the general confusion of the homecoming celebration. "Come here! Let this old man give you a hug!" Mutti freed herself of her two youngest, and he embraced her.

"You must have put a word in for me. Did you?"

"Yes, I did, but why do you ask?"

"Well, this afternoon, just before my release, I was again questioned about my trip to Berlin. Today, however, the questioning session started out differently. 'You know Emil Schmidtke?' they asked me. That question made me think that you must have been in touch with them. I have a lot to tell you. That I am alive and here at home, though, is something I still can't comprehend. There are still more than twenty Germans in the jail. We can't forget them. We have to pray for them. You have no idea how they are suffering. Day and night the Russians showed us that they were the conquerors. They were using many tactics to demean us and avenge themselves. I'll tell you some things later. Right now I have to share the most exciting news ever with all of you. All the hardships I had to endure since I left here are overshadowed by the joyous news I got in Berlin."

"What news, Mutti?" Dieter asked quickly.

"I found out, Dieter, that your Vati is alive and well. He is in a prisoner of war camp in Africa. He was captured by the Americans in southern France and taken to a camp in Algeria. He is in the town of Gerryville, right at the edge of the Sahara Desert."

"How did you find that out, Emmy?" Kätchen inquired.

"Well, that is a miracle too. On the lampstand, at my aunt's house, I saw a small leaflet written by, of all people, our Pastor Walter from Insterburg. He has started organizing a search for his church members and calls for everyone from his congregation to get in touch with him. Since most families have been torn apart, he then helps reunite them. I immediately got in touch with him, and that is how I learned about Emil. Pastor Walter also informed me that Emil's best friend, Kurt, from the Insterburg choir, was in the same camp. It is strictly an officers' camp, and the French commander treats all the prisoners very well. Because the commander himself was once a prisoner in a German camp and was treated well, he is now repaying the Germans for their kindness to him. The prisoners are not allowed to work, so they just wile away their time. Vati apparently plays in a band and is organist at the camp church. The camp food is reported to be excellent. This exciting news and my experiences of the past few weeks make me even more determined to do everything possible to leave Lippehne. Our families have to be reunited. Our children have to have an education. This can never happen as long as we remain here. Before any more restrictions are put on us by this regime, we have to leave. We have to work hard for our freedom. There is no doubt about that, and we have to start immediately. The Lord has ways to get us out of here, and I know He is just waiting to show us His greatness again."

"You want us to leave Lippehne?" Dieter asked with a long face. "I like it here. I like this little farm. Where will we live when we leave here?"

"I don't know, my son, but I am positive that the Lord has a place for us somewhere."

"Will we eat potatoes there and drink milk?" my little sister wondered.

"We will have more to eat there than we have here, Pittimaus, and someday perhaps all your tummies will again be filled. The Berliners have ration cards. They get a little bread and a few grams of fat every day. Children are allotted some milk. It is still not enough to satisfy hungry stomachs, but it is quite an improvement over our situation."

"When will we leave the farm, Mutti?"

"I don't know, Dieter. Only the Lord has the answer to that question. We must pray diligently for His guidance and ask Him to show us very clearly when we shall make our move."

"What are the conditions like in the West, Emmy?" Onkel Emil asked.

"Because I had been there for only a few days, I can't tell you very much. I learned, however, that Germany has been divided into zones. Each zone is governed by a different nation. There is the American zone, the British zone, the French zone, and the Russian zone. The city of Berlin is also divided into four sectors. All the victors wanted a piece of that once glamorous city. Unfortunately, the war has stripped the city of all its glamor. From what I have seen, there is very little left except rubble. For three hours I climbed over ruins, broken glass, charred bricks, metal beams, and craters. It was quite rare to see a building that was still intact."

"How did you find your aunt's house, Emmy, in the midst of all that destruction?" Onkel Emil wondered.

"That was the most difficult part of my visit to Berlin. I asked people for directions to my aunt's street and usually they said, 'That street was totally destroyed' or 'I don't know.' People were just wandering aimlessly among the ruins, stooping occasionally to pick up a charred piece of wood that they would use for firewood, or looking in the ruins for something that might have escaped the flames. I saw only discouragement in those I met and talked to and soon found myself overcome by the same hopeless feeling. People live in holes to escape the elements. I saw one determined group of people though. In spite of the terribly cold weather, they were working for a better future. They were cleaning bricks by using stones to beat the mortar off, then stacking them neatly into piles. That picture really touched my heart and exemplified the spirit of the German people. We can't sit by idly and do nothing about our destiny. We have to rise and help shape it ourselves and rebuild our country for us and our children.

"But I must get back to my story. When it began to get dark, I prayed really hard. 'Lord,' I said, 'please let me find my aunt's house. You lead the way. I am exhausted and at the end of my strength.' I stopped in my tracks, stood still, and began to scrutinize the area around me. I saw ruins, ruins, nothing but ruins. Then I looked behind me and saw part of one house. I even saw curtains in some of the windows. I braced myself, climbed over rubble to that partial building, and rang the doorbell. And what do you think? Only our Lord can perform such a feat. My aunt opened the door! The remnants of her house resembled a small fortress in the midst of the ruins of Berlin. The sweet lady was shocked yet glad to see me. We embraced and cried. She has suffered a lot during the bombing attacks. Her husband was killed *one* day before Germany capitulated. When the Russians invaded Berlin, they fell upon the surviving women, young and old, and disgraced everyone they could find.

"My aunt was brutally raped by a Russian youngster. Then the young soldier tried to wash himself in the toilet bowl, but the water continued to run out, so he then stuffed a towel in the hole to keep the water in. The Berliners have really endured much and have a difficult road ahead of them. Farther west, life is not much better because of the refugee problem. More than twelve million people from the East are supposed to have fled to the West. By leaving their homes and farms, many tried to escape the deportations to Siberia; others were chased out of their homes by the Russians and the Poles. Those traveling people had been favorite targets of the enemies, however, as the Allies are now learning. Hundreds of thousands lost their lives on the open roads. Starvation, suicide, and sickness are continuing to kill thousands of those who survived. My aunt met a young refugee mother from Silesia combing through the ruins one day. She was scrounging around for food for her young daughter. Two days later, she met her again, and the two-year-old had died. In certain areas of the western and southern parts of Germany, some reconstruction is beginning, and the children have even returned to school."

"Does that mean that we have to go back to school when we go to the West?" Dieter broke in.

"Yes, my son. You see, if you want to make something of yourself, you have to have an education, and to get a good education, you have to return to school. I know you'd rather do all kinds of other exciting things instead of attending school, but to be properly prepared for life and get a good job when you are older, you have to acquire all the tools you can. You are a smart young man already, and because of it, I think you will find learning in a new school interesting and challenging."

"I hope you are right, Mutti."

Our devotional time was filled with praise and thanksgiving for Mutti's release. When the little ones were tucked into bed and the rest of us gathered in the living room, we learned more about life outside of our little farm. In a few days, we would have spent one year under the Communist regime. We had not read one newspaper or heard one radio broadcast. We had not talked to one person who had been in the West, except Mutti. We had no idea where all our relatives were. In the course of the year, we had not had any mail—not from Vati or Tante Martha in America. All our friends knew that we had moved to Lippehne. Why had we had no letters from any of them? Why were we forced, for so long, to be isolated from the rest of the world?

Mutti was right. We had to leave. We had no freedom at all.

"When we first left," Mutti continued, "we all felt that it would be safer to board the train from the next town, so we walked to the next railroad station. I wish that we had gotten off there on our return trip as well. But before I tell you what occurred in Lippehne, I'll start with our experiences after we left Berlin.

"As planned, the five of us met at the railroad station in Berlin at noon. We boarded the train to Küstrin and moved slowly through destroyed towns and villages. Many times the train had to be rerouted because of broken tracks. Again, in a small village, among a field of rubble, people were cleaning bricks. This made me realize that Germany will someday rise above the ruins. In Küstrin we had to change trains. We had all planned to jump the train before it came to a halt and quickly board the connecting one. But when we were ready to open the car door, we noticed Russians running along both sides of the train. 'Get down!

Down on the floor!' our neighbor commanded, and we all dropped to the floor. All the other passengers did the same. When the train stopped, we remained on the floor.

"Suddenly the doors were forced open and Russians stomped into the car. They told us to get up and pushed us out of the door. Screaming and hollering, they herded all of us to their headquarters. No one was allowed to talk. All our papers and tickets were taken away. 'You spies! You spies!' they yelled and shoved about twenty of us into a small room, which was furnished with only a few chairs and a table. I don't know what I would have done had I not felt the Lord's closeness at that moment. I thought about Emil and the children, and the seriousness of my situation began to overwhelm me. But then that still, sweet voice said, 'I will guide thee. Don't be afraid. Don't fear for your family. They are in My loving care. Lean on Me, My child.' How sweetly He talked to me and gave me His peace.

"When it was dark, some of us placed our heads on the table and tried to sleep. But our neighbor began to whisper, 'We must escape. I have checked things out. There are only two Russians guarding us, and they are busy with their vodka bottles. They will be drunk shortly. Then we will sneak past them and start running.' About ten minutes later, she and I were the first to escape. We slowly opened the door and tiptoed past the sleeping guards out of the building. Just as we had reached a hedgerow, we heard the soldiers yelling and knew our escape attempt had been unsuccessful. The moonlight and the freshly fallen snow made it very easy for them to track us. Our neighbor told them in Russian that we had to go to the bathroom, and that was true, too, but they chased us back into that room. I put my head on the table and fell asleep. Then something jolted me out of my deep sleep. It was our neighbor again. 'Let's go,' she said. 'The guards are stone drunk and sleeping.' She and I left the room and started running toward the ruins of Küstrin. We zigzagged like rabbits for a while to confuse the Russians in case they pursued us."

"Excuse me, Emmychen," Kätchen interrupted, "the guards were so drunk that they never noticed you were leaving?"

"Yes, they were so inebriated that they never opened their eyes as we were sneaking past them. Three other women of our group, and others from our room had also escaped and stumbled through the ruins as fast as possible. All of a sudden, though, we heard soldiers yelling and knew immediately they had detected our escape. We continued to run and then threw ourselves into a ditch near the railroad tracks. In our fright, we did not realize that we had thrown ourselves into a ditch of water and ice. We thought it was just snow. For about seven miles we crawled along the ditch parallel to the tracks. We were wet and frozen through and through. When we came to a railroad station, we all decided to drop our earlier plans of walking to Lippehne and instead take a train. Fortunately, we didn't have to wait long before one arrived. As we jumped on, I was praying that the conductor would somehow forget to ask for our tickets because we didn't have any, and the Lord again answered my prayer. I suggested to the others to leave the train one stop before Lippehne and walk home. Somehow I sensed that things would not go well there, but I was outvoted by my companions. Because they were all cold and anxious to get home, they wanted to stay on the train. I submitted to their wishes, and we were all captured in Lippehne. Tomorrow I'll tell you about my jail experience. Now I really have to go to bed and get some sleep."

"I don't blame you, Emmy," Kätchen agreed. "You have gone through a lot."

"And all this because of one man! Hitler!" Onkel Emil added. "Germans are chased, herded, raped, molested, and killed, long after the war has ended! We just had no idea what life is like outside of Lippehne. I had thought, however, that it was better than your description of it.

You are right, Emmy! We will not sit here in isolation and hope for an improvement. That may never come. We have to leave here, and we have to leave soon."

As we went upstairs, Mutti placed her arm around my shoulders. How wonderful it was to be near her! I was so thankful tonight. Mutti was at home! Vati was well! But when I thought of what she had gone through—crawling in a ditch, being wet and cold and hungry—I wanted to cry.

"Good night, Schäfle! Thank you for taking my place while I was gone. You did a wonderful job." Mutti kissed me.

My brothers and sister were exuberant throughout the next day. Mutti was home! They were constantly hugging her.

"Schäfle, would you and Dieter please grind some millet for me? I need to cook some soup," Mutti told us.

When I watched Mutti prepare the soup and sweeten it with a little of our syrup, I sensed an urgency in the way she did it. I also noticed that later, when she sewed, she did it differently somehow. The needle seemed to fly faster than ever.

"I am starting to sew for our freedom, Schäfle," she told me when I asked her why there was such a difference in her actions. "With the Lord's help, we will leave soon. I have to make up for lost time and finish some of these projects so that we can get money to buy bread."

Would I have time for some knitting today? I hadn't touched the socks I was working on for a long time. I wished I could spend one whole day just knitting, but it didn't seem likely that I would any time soon. I kept dreaming about it, though, and whenever I knitted, I thought of Omi. She taught me so much. She had taught me how to shape the heel of a sock and how to knit double with one thread. "This gives the sock extra warmth and strength," she explained. I also thought of the wonderful time we always had in her garden in

Insterburg. We played in the gazebo and almost touched the sky on the swing Opi had built especially for us children.

One day when I was on the swing, Opi had killed some chickens and roosters in the backyard. Suddenly a beheaded rooster began flying straight toward me. I screamed and ducked, almost falling off the swing. Opi recaptured his dinner and began plucking the beautiful feathers. Yes, I liked all the memories. But what had become of my sweet Omi? Where was Mutti's sister-in-law? Had Omi survived the trip out of Lippehne on that cold day? As days slipped into the past, all our questions remained unanswered.

Mutti's heart was often broken when we talked about her parents on the farm in Schilleningken, East Prussia, and her ninety-three-year-old grandfather. Were they still alive? Would we ever see them again? "We'll see them in heaven, if not here on earth," Mutti said. "They are all believers in the Lord Jesus."

At times, I couldn't bear the thought of possibly not ever seeing them here on earth, and I felt especially sorry for my youngest brother. Would he miss out on so much? Would Udo never know how much fun it was to build sandcastles on the sandy riverbank, right next to their farm? Would he never swim there and take boat trips? Would he never ride high atop the hay wagons or drive to church in the black and yellow horse-drawn carriage? Would he never be bundled up and cozy under blankets and sit next to the Schiller Omi on the sleigh when she goes to town? Would he never hear the ringing of bells that were fastened to the horses' harnesses and see the beautiful horses move into a trot, pulling the sleigh to church? Would Udo never smell the freshly rendered honey from Opi's hives? Would he never play in the hayloft? Would he never sit at the long table in the living room and hear Opi read the Bible and Omi play the guitar? Would he never sit on his great-grandfather's lap, look at his smile, twinkling eyes, and curly gray hair? Would he never take a walk with him across the meadows and watch the storks in the fields?

As I dug into the files of my memory, I considered myself unbelievably rich, and I hoped that Udo would someday have the same wonderful memories of his grandparents and the rich ways in which they shared their lives with him. Was it possible that someday everything would again be as I knew it? Or would our memories be the only link to the past of which the war could not deprive us?

16

THE RUSSIAN JAIL

It was quiet on our little farm. The children were sleeping, and darkness had drawn the rest of us into the living room to learn more about Mutti's experiences.

"Liane and Dieter told you how our capture at the railroad station was carried out. They also must have told you how they followed us until the Russians became angry and chased them away. You have no idea how difficult it was for me to see my children cry and not be able to touch or comfort them. Well, after Dieter and Liane left, all those taken captive that afternoon had to line up outside. Under guard, we had to stand at attention some distance from one another and were not allowed to talk. Frozen through and through, my clothes and shoes still wet, we stood in the cold for hours. The first one to be called in for questioning was our neighbor. When she passed me, she mumbled through her teeth, 'I'll get you all out.' She must have thought she would be able to accomplish that with her knowledge of the Russian language. The cold began to numb my legs and hands, and I wanted to stomp my feet to get the circulation back, but that was not permitted. We were standing there suffering from the winter's chills when I suddenly noticed our neighbor strutting out of the building. She held her head high and didn't even glance at us. She had gained her freedom. I was the last one to be called into headquarters. Four officers with stern faces were firing questions at me. 'Why did you go to Berlin? What did you do there? How long were you there? Where do your relatives live?' Dozens of other questions were hurled at me. Many were nothing but traps, but the Lord gave me wisdom to recognize them and not fall into them."

"Did they speak through an interpreter?" Onkel Emil wondered.

"No, one of the officers spoke German fluently. Over and over, I told them that I had visited my aunt to see if she had any idea where my husband was. My four children need their father. We have been separated during the war, I told them. Constantly they yelled, 'You spy! You spy!' Nothing I said convinced them otherwise. Finally, they confiscated my handbag and rucksack and motioned for two guards to take me away. They led me through several dark corridors, opened a door, and pushed me down the steps into a dark cellar.

"When I got to the bottom of the steps, a clammy, strange odor reached my nose. I stood still, listened into the darkness, and realized immediately that I was not alone. The air was cold and damp, but I could hear several women sobbing. I asked who else was present. Quite a few names were called out, including the names of my travel companions—our neighbor, of course, was not there. Then I asked them why they were crying. That question made the sobbing increase. 'Well,' I said, 'I see the captors have accomplished what they set out to do. I, for one, will not give them the satisfaction of seeing me cry. Crying does not help our situation at all. There is only One who can ease our pain right now, and that is the Lord Jesus Christ.' Then I explained to them how they can get peace and comfort through Him."

"I am glad you could be a witness for the Lord right there in the jail cell, Emmy," Onkel Emil rejoiced.

"Yes, Emil. I had quite a few opportunities to speak of the Lord. We began to feel our way around the dark room and found rough boards nailed to the wall near the window, which consisted of iron bars rather than glass. That explained why it was so cold in the room. We climbed on top of the high wooden planks, and huddled close to each other to get some warmth, but even in that position, we shivered when the icy winds from the lake blew over our bodies. No matter what we tried, it was impossible to get warm without blankets. We attempted to sleep. Some of us had almost succeeded but were suddenly awakened when the door above the steps was kicked open. Boisterous guards ordered us to get out of the cellar. Quickly we slid off our boards and felt our way up the steps.

"We were herded outdoors—there were about twenty-five of us—and forced to line up, standing at attention. To keep us alert, the guards constantly cracked their whips. Their attempt to frighten us that way was successful, I suppose. I shivered so hard that I believe you could actually see my body shaking. One row to my right, I noticed someone bending back and forth like a tree in a storm. The crack of a whip brought that poor prisoner back to reality again, and she managed to stand still for a short time. Several of the prisoners from the other cells were men. After about two hours of standing in the snow and being whipped by icy winds, we were chased back into the cold cellar. In our cell we again climbed on top of the scaffolding, longing for warmth and sleep. We had hardly settled down when we were driven outside once more to stand in the cold for two hours to be 'counted.' By the time we returned from our second lineup, none of us were capable of remaining awake for another minute. Most of us were just beginning to fall asleep when gun butts were again beating against our door. It was still pitch-dark and we, along with the other prisoners, had to go to the dining hall for breakfast, which consisted of one slice of dark bread and one cup of malt coffee. The coffee was only lukewarm and didn't do much to give us warmth.

"As soon as we had finished eating, the guards hollered, 'Daway rabotay! Daway rabotay!' The men were given the task of felling the trees around the headquarters compound, and we women had to saw them into firewood. The saws were terribly dull, but that didn't matter to our captors. With the Russians standing over us, we had to struggle. If we didn't work fast enough to suit them, they pushed the end of their rifle barrels into our bodies to remind us that they were the ones who held our lives in their hands. Finally, it was dinner time. The exhausting work had warmed us up and made us hungry too. We were led to the dining hall for a bowl of watery soup. The Russians told us Germans to go to the end of the line. Their friends, the Polish prisoners, would eat first. But they did more than eat! When they had finished ladling their soup, they all took turns spitting into the soup. 'Now you eat, you German pigs,' they sneered. None of us touched that soup. We all turned around and left the hall hungry."

"So you all worked hard all day and ate nothing?" I asked.

"That's right. Could any of you have eaten that soup? Schäfle, I normally would not tell this next experience in your presence, but you have seen so much in the past one and a half years that I know the next story will probably not shock or surprise you. So I'll let you stay up a little longer to hear this too. Or would you like to go to bed now?"

"No, Mutti. I'd like to stay. I probably can't sleep tonight anyway when I think of all the suffering you went through."

"All right then, Schäfle. Well, the Russians were absolutely furious with us Germans for daring to refuse the soup they had provided and came up with an idea to further humiliate and punish us. Ten of us women had to stand in a circle in the dining hall. Then they pushed a nude Polish man into the center of the circle. 'He many lice,' one of the guards shouted. 'You woman pick lice.' Nobody moved. The guard repeated the command. Again, nobody moved. Then he stared at each of us. When he fastened his eyes on me, I prayed, 'Lord, help!' Instantly

I sensed a calm flooding my soul. I stepped forward and said, 'We are German women. We refuse to do anything that dirty.' He must have understood me very well, and that defiance caused him to blow up. 'You woman pick lice,' he repeated. I again told him we would not do that. His face turned bright red. He stepped forward and aimed his rifle at me. I expected him to shoot me. Instead, he suddenly stepped back, became silent, and made us stand in that circle for what seemed like an eternity. None of us looked at the poor shivering Polish man. When the guards deemed our punishment sufficient, they chased us outside again to saw and chop wood. After sawing wood until evening, we were herded inside again. On the way in, we grabbed some snow, when the guards were not watching, and did what was strictly forbidden—we washed ourselves. I guess I didn't mention yet that our bathroom facility consisted of only one bucket in our cell.

"In the building, they took us to the dining hall and gave us one slice of dark bread and one cup of lukewarm malt coffee. At night everybody in our cell was exhausted physically, and I suggested that we sing to keep up our spirits. So we softly sang hymns and folk songs. But as soon as the guards heard the singing, they ordered us to be quiet. By that time even the slow followers had noticed the calming effect of the singing, and they continued with the rest of us in a whisper tone. When we were almost settled on our boards and ready to doze off, the first night's procedure was repeated. We were chased out of the cellar and lined up outside. The whips were cracked, and we were not allowed to move. This night, however, was much colder than the previous night. A fierce wind was whipping across the lake. Even the guards in their long, heavy coats and fur hats seemed to be freezing. They just let us stand there while they went into the building. The minute they left, I was confronted with a new problem—escape. This was a perfect time to escape. The guards were inside. The night was clear and bright. The lake was frozen and just a few feet away, and I still had strength to run. If the guards remained inside for a while, I thought I could make it. But then suddenly something suppressed my wonderful escape thoughts—the snow. Tracking me would have been too easy, and flying bullets have no obstacles on the lake. They would not have any trouble hitting me. And what would my four children do without me? My heartbeat slowed down and I said, 'Lord, You brought me here for a reason, and I trust You to get me out of this situation. Please help me. Amen.' Instead of running, I continued to pray and work my feet into a stomping rhythm that revitalized my whole body. Even though I was still chilled, I felt an extra surge of strength—supernatural strength. About two hours later, we were chased back into our cells, where we again groped for sleep and warmth."

"Emmychen, I just can't fathom what you have gone through," Kätchen admitted, "but I still want to hear more of your story."

"The next morning after breakfast, I was given a very special assignment. A guard led me alone to the Russians' personal restroom. 'Rabotay! Rabotay!' he yelled with a mean look on his face as he pointed at the feces piled all around the toilet seats. The sight of it made me gag. 'Rabotay! Rabotay!' he continued hollering. I looked around for a bucket or brush but found none. I wanted to search in other rooms for a bucket, but he did not let me. Then I went outside to get snow, and with my bare hands and the snow, I cleaned that human dung. The Lord was good to me by keeping me strong and not permitting me to faint from that horrible sight and the stench. After I had finished, I walked past the guard, went outside, and did the forbidden thing again—I washed my hands with snow. He didn't say anything but chased me back to saw and split logs.

"Our noon meal was again mixed with Polish spittle, and we all refused to eat the soup. While standing in the soup line, I saw the most horrible sight—a male German skeleton with a buttonless shirt, light pants, and blue bare feet in wooden sandals. He was trying to balance himself while waiting for his meal. One of his friends whispered to me, 'His feet are blue up to his ankles because they are frost-damaged. He also has dysentery. He is in a single cell right next to ours, without a bed or blanket. Every morning guards take him to the lake where he has to chop a hole in the ice, take off his soiled pants, wash them, and put them back on.'"

"That poor man," I interrupted. "Dieter and I thought all those holes were made by ice fishermen."

"No, Schäfle. There is one hole in the ice for every day of that man's suffering. But he is no longer chopping ice. He died."

For a while we sat in utter silence. My thoughts were on that man. Did he have a family and children? Might something terrible be happening to Vati right now? Was life really worth living? How could everyone here still talk about a loving God?

"Emmychen," Kätchen said, "why is all this happening to our people? What have we done to deserve this? What was that man's crime?"

"The righteous Judge knows," Onkel Emil answered. "He will let justice prevail someday. We don't have to worry about that. I am glad He knows about our future too. If we didn't have that assurance, life would be utterly hopeless. Your story, Emmy, is incredible. You poor woman! What you have gone through! Even though it is late and we are all tired, I would still like to hear the rest of your jail experiences."

"I am rather tired, too, but I'll finish. Well, those first three days as a prisoner seemed like an eternity, the nights especially. On the morning of the fourth day, the lady cook went around the jail to look for two women to help her in the kitchen. You can't imagine how overjoyed I was when she selected me as one of the two. The thought of working in the warm kitchen and perhaps getting more to eat was absolutely thrilling. Escaping the guards was even more exciting. Our first assignment on the kitchen crew was to scrub the dining hall, several adjacent rooms, and the kitchen. We were all getting rather weak from working so hard and eating only two slices of bread per day. Scrubbing and scraping the thick filth on the floors took a lot of strength and patience, but the Lord graciously provided those. We laughed out loud when we discovered an inlaid floor underneath all that dirt."

"You were not punished for laughing?" I asked.

"No, they must not have heard us. After the kitchen was scrubbed and polished, the cook, a kindhearted Polish lady, decided to keep me on as her permanent helper. When we were alone with no guards in sight, she always handed me something to eat. She, of course, was not allowed to do that, but she risked getting caught to help me. It was absolutely wonderful to be in a warm kitchen from morning till evening. At night I had to return to the cell to try to keep warm. Again, we had to line up outside at least twice for several hours during the night, but I could then return to the kitchen the next morning. All my cellmates envied me. How they wished they, too, could work in a warm place and get more to eat. The Lord has been good to me. But with the life of ease I now enjoyed, a new problem arose. It was lice. Since we had to eat, sleep, and work in the same clothes without personal hygiene, those little troublemakers spread like wildfire and infested all of us. Scratching was useless and required too much energy. So we all just suffered while they multiplied.

"As I was rolling out pastries in the kitchen, a Russian officer entered. He came toward me and asked, 'You know Emil Schmidtke? You live in Luisenstraße? You mother have four children?' When I answered yes to all those questions, he growled, 'Woman, come.' Fear overcame me. I became almost paralyzed, my mind racing. How could I escape? I was not going to let them rape me. 'Lord, help!' He raised his voice and repeated his command, 'Woman come.' I still didn't move until he added, 'You go home.'

"Had I heard him correctly? Go home? The cook got the message before I did. She threw her arms around me and said, 'No! No! No!'

but the officer waited for me to follow him for more questioning. Three officers again bombarded me with more questions, but they must have realized that there were no deviations from my earlier answers. Then they winked at one another, returned my purse and rucksack, and without a word gestured for me to leave. I didn't look behind me and almost floated down the street. Thank You, Lord! That was all I could think of at the time. And here I am! The bedtime story is over.

"Before we retire, though, I want to thank you again, Emil, for working so diligently for my release. The Russians really must have high regard for you and your work. They would not have freed me otherwise. And, Kätchen, thank you again for watching over my children so beautifully. To you, Schäfle, a bouquet of roses, but since I don't have roses, I'll give you a big hug and a kiss with all my love."

17

IMPROVEMENTS

"Kätchen," Mutti said one morning, several weeks later, "Liane told me that we have a small grocery store in town now. I think I'll take my silver dishes and linens and see if I can trade them in for food. I am so glad the Lord allowed me that one trip back to Insterburg right after we moved here to salvage some of our belongings. It is a miracle, too, that the Russians have never found the dark, wet basement here under the kitchen floor. I have the feeling that those things down there will be the means of our future survival."

While Kätchen and I finished the laundry, Mutti went to the grocery store to barter her wedding gifts and hand-embroidered linens for food. Our scrubbing boards were barely put away when she returned with a whole bag of groceries.

"The owner of the store, a Polish lady, was so excited about all my treasures," Mutti announced. "She gave me ten thousand zlotys. Come and see all the things I bought! Here are two loaves of bread, half a pound of butter, half a pound of sugar, some salt, one potato for each person, and a little black tea for you, Kätchen. Tomorrow the children can go and buy some milk."

"Emmychen, I know all the things you took are worth much more and can't ever be paid for in food or money. But in times of starvation, there is absolutely nothing worth more than food."

"You are right, Kätchen. If I think about all the years it took me to do all that handwork, I get sick about it. But how could I hold on to things of the past while my children are starving?"

"The barber shop will be open in a few moments," Mutti informed all the members of our household after dinner. "Everyone in need of a professional haircut, please meet in the kitchen. We cut hair on even the smallest heads as you well know, and we start with the youngest and cut our way up to the oldest." And with that remark she gave Onkel Emil a funny look.

"You know I don't like to be last."

"And that is exactly why I said that," she chuckled. "It is too difficult to work on little boys while they are half asleep. So you'll just have to be last."

Finally, Onkel Emil's turn came, and while he was sitting under Mutti's scissors, he told those of us who were watching about the latest happenings at the tailor shop.

"The two women who went to Berlin with you, Emmy, were released from jail last night. I hardly recognized them when they reported for work this morning. They look so old and haggard. The six weeks of hard labor and little food have really taken a toll on them. They don't look as if they can live very long. They are just skin and bones. I continually thank the Lord for having set you free so quickly. Where would I go for my haircut if you were too weak to give me one?"

"Is that all you can think about, Emil?" Mutti said with a little bite in her words.

"Now, Emmy, you mustn't be so touchy. Can't you take a bit of humor anymore? We have to keep up our spirits. We have to be able to have a sense of humor—if we don't, we are emotionally defeated."

"You are right, Emil. I'm sorry. It's just that my thoughts were on those two women you described. I could have been one of them who had to suffer so long. Why is the Lord so good to me?" There were no answers to those questions. I often wondered myself why we were still alive and relatively healthy when according to statistics and human reasoning, we should all have been dead long ago.

"You children really play well together," Kätchen remarked as Mutti was cleaning up the barbershop. "It is a joy for me to see that. What are you playing today?"

"We are playing post office, Mutti," Hanno said. "Dieter is the clerk behind the window, Marlies is the cleaning lady, I am sorting the mail, Vilmar is the mailman, and Liane is watching."

"Well, that is really nice. You are well organized, everyone has an exciting job to do, and no one is left out. It must bring joy to the heart of our Lord to see you getting along so well. Now, since I am here, does my little mailman have a letter for me?"

"Yes, Mutti," Vilmar said excitedly. "I have two letters for you. One, two," he counted as he handed them to Kätchen.

"I have seen that one letter many times before. It is one of those old letters that always shows up during post office play time. But this one is new to me. Where did you children get this? Where did it come from?"

"I don't know, Mutti. It was just lying on the floor in the hallway this morning."

No one knew anything about this mysterious piece of mail.

"The writing is unfamiliar," Kätchen continued, "and so is the sender. But it is addressed to me. That means I can open it." She turned the letter over and again read the address. Finally, she pushed her small finger in the flap and ripped it open.

"The first page seems to be written in Polish. Why would anyone write to me in Polish?" Baffled by this question, she rushed to Mutti. "Look at this letter, Emmy! The children were playing with it."

"Is the second page written in Polish too?" Mutti asked. Kätchen glanced at the backside of the page.

"Oh no! Look at this! It says Wilhelm Mecklenburg, Bochum, Germany. What does all this mean? Does it mean that Wilhelm lives in Bochum? Just where did this letter come from? I'm going over to the Polish preacher to let him translate it for me." In seconds Kätchen was ready to leave for the preacher's house.

A short while later, she returned, feet hardly touching the ground as she flew into the house. "Listen, everybody! Listen! Another miracle! Wilhelm is well! He is pastor of a church in Bochum. Can you believe it? Thank You, Lord! Thank You, Lord!" Kätchen was nearly beside herself with joy. "He met the man who wrote this letter in his church. He was someone's guest there and played the violin for one of the services. When Wilhelm found out that this Christian had connections in Poland, he asked him to send his address to his friends and from there on to us. It simply boggles my mind to think that we received it. Only the Lord knows how it got here. We have a great God! Wilhelm is alive! Hanno! Vilmar! Your daddy is alive and well! Praise be to His wonderful name! My husband is alive!"

The rejoicing continued long after Onkel Emil had returned from work.

"Thank you all for your prayers!" Kätchen was still overflowing with joy.

Deep in thought and sad-looking, Onkel Emil quietly limped into the living room. He was the only one who had not yet heard from his life's partner.

It was only a few days later that his sadness increased even more. "The final purging is occurring," he reported sadly after returning from work.

"What do you mean by that, Emil?"

"A Russian officer came to the tailor shop today to announce that all of my seamstresses and their families have to leave Lippehne tomorrow.

They must leave. No one is given a choice. Our neighbor is also among them. 'Don't ask any questions—just leave or we will make you wish you had left,' they were told. 'You and your family stay,' the officer told me sternly. 'You are not allowed to go. We need you.' I told him that I can't do the job alone. 'We send Polish women. You train Polish women,' and with that he left the shop."

"What an opportunity that would have been for us to get across the border," Mutti said. "Our time to leave must not have come yet. The Lord must have a better way for us than 'walking' toward freedom."

"Do you know what this new development means for us?" Onkel Emil asked. "It means that we are the only Germans left in the town of Lippehne. We are the only ones of a population of five thousand. What is the Lord trying to tell us? Why is He keeping us here? Again, we have to look to the future for our answers. Some things we will not understand until we get to eternity. It was just heartrending to see my coworkers get that terrible news. Most of them are mothers with children, and some still have their elderly parents living with them. None of them have Polish money to purchase train tickets. We have to pray hard for all of them."

"Yes," Kätchen said. "And we have to pray that it will not be too cold for those poor folks tomorrow. Physically, I know I could not survive such a trip. I just don't feel strong enough anymore."

"Now, Kätchen!" Mutti said as if to scold her. "We will not let discouragement grip our hearts, will we? Discouragement is not of the Lord! You know that! Our Lord always says, 'Be of a good courage! Be not dismayed! Be strong! Be not afraid!' We can't be faint-hearted. We have to keep our minds stayed on Him continually. We can't look at our frail bodies and waning strength. The Lord is our strength! He is our Rock! He will help us, right? We have to be emotionally strong for our children, for each other, for the sake of our mates. We can't permit discouragement to take hold of us. We have not suffered nearly as much as some. The Lord's desire is for us to worship Him and not complain as did the children of Israel in the Bible."

"You are right, Emmy! Thank you for setting me straight! I don't know what I'd do without you and your friendship."

"I consider you my dear friend too, Kätchen. And that is why it troubles me to see you downcast."

With her optimistic spirit, Mutti then proceeded by drilling us on Vati's homecoming poems. Did she really think we'd forget if we didn't recite them every single day? Or did she want us to be reminded of Vati through our recital sessions? It became boring for me to recite so often, but when I saw her gentle smile of approval and her beautiful, dreamy eyes, I realized how difficult life must have been for her without her husband. Then I became ashamed of my feelings of rebellion. *Thank You, Lord, for such a wonderful and courageous mother,* I thought to myself, and then I recited my poem.

"Honey! We have a jar of honey!" Mutti announced. "What a delicacy! A customer gave me honey instead of money today."

We hadn't tasted honey in more than a year. It always used to be our favorite spread. One of Mutti's friends, her Polish customer, brought us a jar. Oh, how I had always enjoyed honey! My love for honey started at my grandparents' farm. Dieter and I would always watch Mutti's father gather the honey from his hives. Then he would put the honeycombs in the separator, and Dieter and I were allowed to crank the wooden handle. Opi was seldom stung by his bees because they knew him. But Mutti's brother was once attacked by a swarm. Covered with them from head to toe, he raced down to the river, screaming in agony, and dived into the water. When he came back to the surface, he watched hundreds of bees struggling for their lives, but his own life was saved.

"Everybody, please line up," Mutti instructed. "The Lord has given us a very special gift today. We have one jar of honey. Each man—we have only one—woman, and child will today be able to enjoy one teaspoonful of honey. In three days, each one will be given another spoonful."

My mouth was beginning to water as I saw Mutti dipping the spoon into the thick, golden mass. Honey! What a treat! I used to take the enjoyment of eating honey for granted. I used to take many things for granted, now that I thought of it. I never considered food anything special. We always had plenty of it. Udo pulled up his nose when he tasted the sticky substance. He acted as if he was eating something sour.

"It is so sweet!" Marlies exclaimed.

"Did bees make this honey?" little Vilmar asked with his eyes widening.

"Yes, my son. They did."

"How, Mutti? How do they do it?"

While everyone was still smacking and licking their lips, Kätchen gathered the children around her and tried to explain how bees manufacture honey.

"Honeybees collect honey from trees, flowers, bushes, and blooming weeds. They fly into the fields, woods, gardens, and just about anywhere they can find nectar. They especially like clover, heather, and linden blossoms. They collect the honey from the plants and take it to their hives so that they have food for the queen bee and the thousands of bees in the hive during the long winter months."

"Do bees eat honey too?"

"Yes, Vilmar, they do. But they usually have much more than they need. So the beekeeper takes the extra honey out of the hive and uses it himself or sells it. That is how we got this honey. It was bought, and then Tante Emmy's customer gave it to her. Each little bee makes only about one teaspoonful of honey in its life. Can you imagine how many bees the Lord needed to make one whole jar full of honey?"

"Very, very many," Hanno answered.

"Very, very, very many," Marlies added.

Onkel Emil went through many struggles in the next weeks to rebuild the tailor shop. The new personnel consisted of Polish women. Communicating with them was the major problem. After a few days, however, he was once again singing when he came home from work. He had been a soloist in several operas, and music was still his passion. He was always in a good mood when the house resounded with his tenor voice. Even Russian officers were fascinated by his voice. A group of them once requested that he sing part of an opera for them.

The Polish preacher told Kätchen that he planned to start the church services again. He had been meeting with just a few people at a time during the winter months. The meetings were held in different homes. No one had advance notice of the location. Keeping the get-togethers a secret from the government was of utmost importance. Now that spring was here and warmer weather began, the meetings would occasionally be held at the cemetery.

Many other things weighed on our minds during those days though. It became increasingly more difficult for Dieter and me to find firewood. After a stormy night, we would leave the house as soon as daylight broke, but we seldom found much. The old Polish ladies usually met us with large bundles of sticks that they had gathered in the middle of the night. The charcoal supply was also dwindling. There were still charred beams in the top of some of the buildings, but it was definitely too dangerous for us to climb up there. The eight sacks of coal and ashes Kätchen had sifted out of rubble near the hospital one day were also used up.

"Lord, send a big storm that will make big limbs fall out of the trees," Onkel Emil prayed one day, "or send us a warm spring early." Meanwhile, we were looking toward new ways of building up our food supply. Kätchen returned to her father's old garden plot to try to clean it up and get it ready for planting some vegetables.

"Can you imagine, Emmychen, what a Polish woman told me while I was in the garden today?"

It was one of the few times I ever saw Kätchen truly angry.

"She said 'Why are you so foolish to do all that work? You won't be allowed to stay here and harvest it anyway. You will be chased out just like the rest of the Germans.'"

"She was that brazen?"

"Yes! Who was she to tell me what I could or couldn't do in my dad's garden? That really made my blood boil. They just come here and take everything from us and then keep rubbing it in."

"Yes, Kätchen," Mutti said, "I can imagine how you must have wanted to lash out. I don't blame you for becoming angry. But at least you did not lose your life because of your anger. Do you remember the man here in Lippehne who had just finished building his house after years of work? Because he didn't want the Russians to have it, he, in his anger, destroyed it, and the Russians shot him."

"I remember."

"I think we are learning that a war doesn't bring out the best in people. I believe we really don't understand our innermost being until we are in the grip of war and hatred. How would we ever know what we are capable of doing? How would we ever know how much suffering we can endure? When we sit in nice, warm homes with our families, enjoying a life of ease, we can't fathom the real war that can be fought within one's body and soul."

"You are absolutely right, Emmychen. I never thought about that."

18

TICKETS TO FREEDOM

The weather became warmer. It brought not only promises of a warm spring, but another exciting possibility. We first sensed the change one day when Mutti came home, appearing to be floating on air. Of course, we wanted to know what had happened, but she wouldn't tell us. "I will tell you all later. All I can say is that I sense something good might come our way."

No guessing helped. Not even Kätchen could find out what the secret was. Mutti remained firm.

"I will tell all of you after dinner. Onkel Emil has to be here too."

Before we settled down for our devotional, she finally shared the cause of her excitement with us. "You all know my Polish customer and friend. And you know that she has come over regularly to check on my sewing and sometimes just to visit. She speaks German beautifully, and I am learning Polish from her. In the course of time, we have become well acquainted. One day I happened to tell her of my hopes and dreams for our future, and she promised me that she would do anything she could to help us leave Lippehne. Until today she has been completely silent on that subject, and therefore, I thought that she was not serious about her offer. I also couldn't imagine how she could be of help to us. Today, however, she made me aware of the fact that she has been working quietly on our behalf. She told me the Polish district magistrate went on vacation, and his assistant is a good friend of hers. She has talked to her friend, and he will give us authorization papers to leave Lippehne for ten thousand zlotys. After my initial shock and joy wore off, I informed her that we would really have to think about the offer. Also, we don't have that sum of money. 'I'll buy your sewing machine for ten thousand zlotys,' she said. That didn't surprise me because I knew she has had her eye on my machine for a long time. She was always fascinated by it. I told her once that she could have it for her efforts should we leave Lippehne.

"Anyway, I wasn't sure what to tell her. The thought of perhaps leaving caused my whole being to jump with joy. But the ethical question crept up—could the Lord use these means to get us out of Lippehne? What do you think?"

Both Kätchen and Onkel Emil were unusually quiet for a long time. Finally Onkel Emil broke the stillness by saying, "That is bribery."

"Yes," Kätchen added, propping her chin on her hand. "Can something wrong be used to give us the desires of our heart? Can this be of the Lord? That is a difficult question."

All through the evening, the adults tried to answer the question. Was this of the Lord?

"We all have to pray constantly and diligently until the Lord gives us an answer," Mutti suggested. "Humanly speaking, this sounds like a great opportunity to gain our freedom. But is this the Lord's will?"

The prayers that night were pleas for God's wisdom. "Please, Lord, help us to make the decision that is in accordance with Your will. Show us very clearly what You want us to do. We don't want to stray from Your guidance and Your will for our lives. Please, help us, Lord!" Each one of us spent much time in personal prayer that Thursday night.

Early Friday morning, Mutti's friend knocked excitedly on the front door. Onkel Emil had not yet left for work. "All the paperwork will be done for you," she told everybody. "Your train leaves from Lippehne at six o'clock on Sunday morning. You will have to leave here at five o'clock, while it is still somewhat dark, so that nobody will see you. My friend himself will come to your house on Saturday night and bring you the papers and tickets." She then wished us a good day and left.

"Let's pray hard," Onkel Emil said, closing the front door behind him as he left for work.

"What do you think, Emmy? Shall we start packing while we pray? This might just be another disappointment. But, I think we have learned that we should pray more."

"I agree, Kätchen. I think we should do as you suggest—pack and pray. Since our hopes have been dashed before, we can't get them up too high. Kätchen—I just had a terrible thought! What if this offer is a trap the magistrate is luring us into? If we go along with his plans, we can be accused of wrongdoing, and who knows what he'll do to us then? But on the other hand, I don't think my friend is that kind of person. I think she is sincere and really wants to help us."

"There are many instances in the Bible, Emmy, in which the Lord uses the enemies to help His people. He, of course, can do that in our case too. Maybe this is not a setup, but His divine leading." The day flew by, even though we had a lot on our minds, because we all kept very busy.

"What have you ladies been doing all day today while the man of the house was working?" Onkel Emil asked teasingly when he came in from work.

"Well," Mutti said, "we have just been twiddling our thumbs while waiting for the master of the house to return. And now that he is here, we shall continue to do so while he sits down and tells us what he has accomplished today."

"This man has kept a lot of Polish women busy—quite a feat in itself. Only a few speak a little German, and the Polish words I have acquired don't seem to help much. So we all just muddle through the day and try to achieve our common goal of making uniforms for the Russians. Most of the women despise the Russians because they forced them out of their homeland to come to Lippehne. Right now, I can't imagine how those two peoples will ever live harmoniously.

"A few of the women have sewing experience, but the rest are novices. So far, it is difficult to get much productivity out of them. I have tried to work ahead on some cutting and several other jobs, so that they can continue without me for a while—in other words, I have begun to prepare in case we should decide to leave on Sunday. But now I want to know, all jesting aside, what you ladies did today aside from praying."

"We packed," Kätchen replied.

"Does that mean you think it is the Lord's will for us to leave?"

"We don't know, but Emmy and I decided to pack and pray. We have placed the situation completely in the Lord's hands. If the assistant magistrate really comes with the departure permits tomorrow night, I think we can consider it His will. And in that case, we are ready. If he does not come, we have had a dress rehearsal in packing and will be more efficient stuffers for our real trip someday."

"You ladies are wonderful. You combine faith with reason, hope with reality, and the results are preparedness for a dream that just might come true. I like that. And since you have almost finished packing for our journey to freedom, I will pack a few clothes in my bag tonight too."

Prayers of praise and thanksgiving ascended to the throne of God during our devotional time. Again everybody meditated on the beautiful words of Psalm 91.

Because he hath set his love upon me, therefore will I deliver him:
I will set him on high, because he hath known my name.

He shall call upon me, and I will answer him:
> I will be with him in trouble;
> I will deliver him, and honour him. (Ps. 91:14–15)

"Give us wisdom to discern Your will, Lord." I heard these words, but it was rather difficult for me to concentrate that night. My mind was being abused by my thoughts. Gnawing questions continued to torment me. Where would we live if we left Lippehne? In some of the ruins Mutti told us about? It was only April and still cold outside at night. Here we at least had cozy beds. Would we have to sleep on the floor in some overcrowded building as the refugees in our school had to? Would we be overrun by tanks as many of them were?

When Mutti came to give me a good night kiss, I tried not to let her sense my concerns. "I love you too, Mutti," I responded to her good night wishes, but pulling the warm feather coverlet over my head, I continued to think.

On Saturday afternoon Mutti's Polish friend brought the ten thousand zlotys and asked for the sewing machine. Mutti told her the machine was hers after we left and gave her a key to the house. "If we don't leave, I'll return your money to you."

Her friend agreed. She wished us a safe trip, gave Mutti a hug, and left.

Saturday night approached at a snail's pace, but finally the bundles and suitcases stood in the hall, packed for the next morning, and the clothes were neatly laid out—one little pile for everyone. Our food for the journey consisted of bread and two small milk cans, the bottom half filled with lard, and the top half with beet syrup. It was 9:00 p.m. now and pitch-dark outside. All the little ones were sleeping. No one had delivered papers.

"It looks as if we have been misled again," Mutti said sadly. "What does all this mean?" She was really talking to herself because nobody voiced an opinion. Were all of our hopes and dreams for the future dashed again? I detected sadness in the room. Nobody seemed to be breathing. Were they praying? What were they all waiting for so late at night? A miracle? How could anything happen now? I was beginning to feel sorry for all the adults. Was this really just a trap or a hoax? For two days we had been rushing around and for what? Just to sit and wait for nothing? Why didn't somebody say something? What are they thinking? This silence was torture to my mind. It felt as if everyone was waiting for death to knock on the door.

"Please say something!" I found myself bursting out.

"We don't know what to say," Mutti said very calmly. "We don't know what to say."

Suddenly, a knock on the front door. My heart crushed against my throat. I knew I couldn't speak now even if I wanted to.

"Was that a knock?" Onkel Emil asked.

"Yes, it was," Kätchen answered.

Onkel Emil got up and hobbled to the door, the rest of us following behind. We stood in the hallway and listened, but there was no more knocking.

"We must have been mistaken," Onkel Emil said, but decided to open the door anyway. I became scared when I saw a short, stocky person quickly glancing both ways on the dark street before entering.

"You have money?" he asked. "I have papers."

Mutti went to get the ten thousand zlotys and handed them to Onkel Emil.

"I count money first." He counted out the bundle of money in the dim hallway light. "No, you not get papers. Papers cost fifteen thousand zlotys." Onkel Emil told him that the deal was ten thousand zlotys and we didn't have any more money. The stranger turned around to leave.

"Give fifteen thousand zlotys, then papers."

"We don't have more money. Good night," Onkel Emil said and walked the man to the door. Just before opening the door, the stranger angrily yanked the money out of Onkel Emil's hand, shoved the papers at him, and slipped out of the house into the dark night. After the door closed, everyone stood in the hallway in total shock, staring at the papers in Onkel Emil's hand. He flipped through them exclaiming, "These are our tickets to freedom! This is the sign we have been waiting for! Rejoice!" Everyone was speechless. "Why aren't you happy?"

"I am just numb," Mutti answered, sighing deeply. "I can't believe it! Freedom is awaiting us! We will see our life's partners!"

Kätchen stood in the hallway sobbing. "I can't believe it either, and I am so happy. But I am also sad. I must say goodbye to another place on earth that is so dear to me—the home of my parents."

After a short prayer meeting in the hallway, we carried the bundles and suitcases into the courtyard, placing them in the handwagon. Then Mutti and I double-checked on everyone's clothes for the next morning. I was going to wear two pairs of stockings, my boots, two dresses, a sweater, and a coat.

"Yes, I know you are going to be warm, Schäfle," Mutti said. "But we have to wear extra clothing just in case our bundles somehow get lost. You go to bed now. I'll wake you up at 3:30 a.m. so you can help me. Good night, Schäfle," and she kissed me.

I felt very strange that night. Sleep usually came quickly, but for a long time, I lay wide awake. I thought of Kätchen and her last night in her parents' house. She had spent her childhood here. Would she ever be able to return to Lippehne? Would I ever see the beautiful lakes again? Were we really going to leave tomorrow? I knew everyone was glad that the Lord controls our future, so I knew I should be too. After all, it was only by the Lord's protection that we were still alive and well in Lippehne! No other Germans were. With that thought reassuring me, I drifted off to sleep at last.

19

ESCAPE

It was Sunday morning, April 26, 1946. The darkness still hung about us, thick and heavy, as we left for the railroad station at 4:30 a.m. There was no way to muffle the noise of the handwagon as it rattled along the seamed sidewalk, but we encountered nothing out of the ordinary and arrived at our destination before 5:00 a.m. As we approached the station house, we noticed a group of nuns standing nearby with their arms raised while Polish men took their luggage and threw it on a pile of suitcases. I stood next to our luggage, wondering if the same might happen to us, when a controller came over to us to check our papers. He took our tickets and papers and vanished into one of the back rooms. Time stood still while we were awaiting his return.

"Why isn't he returning with our papers?" Kätchen asked Mutti after we had waited quite a long time. The train was almost due to arrive. Suddenly he reappeared to tell us that specialists were not permitted to leave. He was yelling louder and louder to overpower the noise of the oncoming train.

"You can't leave. You are specialists."

"But we have permission to leave, don't you see that? And besides that, I have worked ahead so that the work will continue without me."

"Are you sure?"

"Yes, of course."

When the train came to a halt, he finally shoved the papers into Onkel Emil's hand and said, "Go!"

Mutti quickly lifted Udo and Marlies into the car and then helped Dieter. When she turned around, a man was running away with two of our suitcases. I saw him throw them on the luggage pile. Onkel Emil quickly retrieved them while the thief was busy stealing from other passengers, and flung them into the train. Mutti somehow managed to help Onkel Emil up the steps while the train was beginning to move. He stumbled and fell into the entrance of the compartment but quickly pulled himself up. "Thank You, Lord! Thank You, Lord! Thank You, Lord!" he rejoiced with the rest of our family.

Kätchen and Mutti hugged each other, their faces wet with tears of joy as the train blew its whistle and pulled out of Lippehne.

All the children were excited about traveling by train.

"Mutti, I see the whole world going by real fast," Hanno bubbled. "All the trees are moving!"

"Why are the houses all fallen down?" Marlies questioned. None of the little ones waited for answers but, instead, fired question after question.

Happiness had taken hold of our group as never before. Everybody was joyous. Why then did I have to be plagued by fear? My heart was torn apart by fear. What would happen when the magistrate returned from his vacation today and discovered that we had left Lippehne? It would be no problem for him to come after us with an army jeep, catch up to us at one of the railroad stops, and take us back. What would our punishment be then? All of us, young and old, would probably have to go to that terrible jail Mutti was in. These thoughts took all the joy out of the trip for me. Wasn't it strange that none of the adults had mentioned this possibility? Was my fear unfounded? Why hadn't they thought about it? Yes, I knew the verses, "Trust in the Lord with all thine heart;" (Prov. 3:5) and "be not afraid." I had heard these verses many times. That day, however, they offered no comfort to me at all.

"We are approaching Küstrin," Mutti told us, "the town where I was captured and from which I escaped by running. What will befall us here today?"

"The Lord knows, Emmy. It won't be anything we can't bear," Kätchen replied.

"I just wish we wouldn't have this long layover in Küstrin. What are we going to do here until tomorrow morning?"

"If there is nothing for us to do, we'll have to wait and learn to be patient."

The train was slowing down, blowing its whistle, and screeching to a halt. Fortunately, our car stopped at the station building, and we didn't have to carry our belongings too far. After pulling, pushing, and dragging all our baggage, we at last reached the waiting room. We walked in and found the room completely empty. There were no tables, benches, or chairs.

"We'll just have to settle on the floor," Onkel Emil said bluntly. "Why don't we all settle over there in that corner while Kätchen and the boys stay in this corner. Let's all eat a little bread, and in the evening the children can stretch out on the bundles to sleep."

When dusk set in, men began to move about inside and outside the station building. One walked over to Kätchen and offered to put all her luggage in safekeeping. He told her that Poles would come at night and steal things from her. He could help save her belongings by locking them into one of the station buildings and returning them the next morning before the train came.

"Don't do it, Kätchen! No!" Onkel Emil intervened when he noticed that she seemed to be about to agree with the man. The man continued to talk to her and the children, and she finally gave him some of her things.

As the night lengthened, more creatures stalked in the darkness.

"Don't move—breathe quietly!" Onkel Emil whispered when the waiting room door opened again.

I had not yet slept a wink, and I didn't expect to because the door swung open constantly and shadows walked back and forth. We truly must have been under the Lord's wings because no one noticed us crouched in the dark corner. Nine of us were there, and all of us were safe.

Suddenly we heard rifle bolts clicking outside, and when the door opened, my heart jumped. We were going to be shot. The magistrate had found us. I was right. These were Russians! I could see the outlines of their fur hats! They knew we escaped and planned to cross the border. This would be the end for all of us. They were calling something into the room, but none of us moved. My whole body seemed to be paralyzed. The guns were clicking again, then there was silence for what seemed like an eternity. Suddenly they turned around and left.

The night seemed endless. We must have sat there on the floor for at least twelve hours, and it was still black outside. Oh, how we longed for morning! I couldn't stand the scuffling around of these creatures of the night.

A rough voice awakened me. "Frau, komm! Komm!"

Then Hanno screamed as if he was hurt.

"Frau, komm!" No, this was not a dream. A Russian wanted to rape Kätchen. Hanno screamed again at the top of his lungs, and the soldier left abruptly.

"I told Hanno to scream," Kätchen whispered. "My son saved me, with the Lord's help."

Finally light was beginning to encroach upon the darkness of the night.

"Thank You, Lord, for the morning light," I heard myself whispering.

We continued to cower in the waiting room until daylight flooded the filthy building.

"Our train is due soon," Onkel Emil said. "I suggest we all go outside and find the platform from which our train is leaving."

"Where is my friend from last night?" Kätchen asked. "I think I told him when our train would leave, didn't I?"

And now we were all on the lookout for the Polish man, but he was nowhere in sight. Several men came and offered their assistance again. One helped Kätchen to the platform while she was carrying Vilmar. Another one wanted to help Mutti, but she refused his help. More and more men were encircling us, moving back and forth like vultures. I was in charge of one bundle and of Udo, who was carrying his potty in his rucksack.

At last our freedom train slowly pulled into the station. Mutti again helped us children in first. As she prepared to lift a suitcase into the train, a man jerked it out of her hand and ran off with it. As another one said, "I'll help," he reached for two of our bundles and disappeared with them between the railroad cars.

Finally, all of us boarded the train, and the steam engine pulled us out of Küstrin.

"I have nothing left," Kätchen said, "absolutely nothing. They took every single piece of my luggage. But praise the Lord! I have my two sons!

"The Lord gave, and the Lord hath taken away;
Blessed be the name of the Lord" (Job 1:21).

Holding her sons tightly, she began to weep.

The train moved slowly toward Berlin. At times it almost stopped.

"We must be changing tracks often," Onkel Emil reasoned. "We are making so little progress. Did you notice that we have passed some of the ruins twice?"

"Yes, I did," Mutti answered. "We seem to be zigzagging like a rabbit, except at the speed of a snail."

"What destruction! It was difficult for me to imagine such a horrible picture, Emmy," Onkel Emil continued. "Will Germany ever recover from all this devastation? How many thousands of people are buried under that rubble?"

"No one will ever know," Mutti concluded sadly. "And no one will ever know how many families have been torn apart by this war. No one knows how many children have been orphaned and how many parents have lost their children. I just marvel at the love God has shown to us."

"Yes, Emmy, you are truly blessed," and tears began to well up in his eyes.

"I am sorry, Emil. You will find your wife and daughters too. We will continue to pray that you'll hear from your loved ones soon. You have done so much for Kätchen and me in protecting us, and you have been such a friend and comfort to us. We just know that the Lord will reward you because He knows we can't. He will bring your family together."

"Mutti, look! Look up there! A bathtub is hanging there on the side of the wall. It is ready to fall. And I see half a bedroom with a dresser still standing there high up in that tall ruin. Where is the other half?"

"The other half, Dieter, is probably under the rubble. That must have been a beautiful home at one time. Look at the beautiful wallpaper and the pictures on the wall. I wonder where the residents of that home are today."

For miles, we viewed nothing but the ruins of Berlin. This was the capital of Germany, one of its most beautiful cities. It had been founded in the year 1244. Gorgeous churches dating back to the year 1250, museums, opera houses, bridges, and monuments made it world-famous. The elevated and underground railway systems provided excellent transportation for its almost four and a half million people. Today we saw none of the old splendor. An occasional intact building here and there among the rubble was a rarity. Only a skeleton of the proud German city was left.

"End station! Everyone please leave the train!" We heard over the loudspeaker after the train came to a halt. Kätchen and her sons left the train first, then the rest of us followed.

"We are free! We are free! We are free!" Kätchen called and passersby gave our group either a strange or a pitying look. "Where do we go now? We are free to go anywhere, but now we don't know where to go. That's funny, isn't it?"

"Yes," Mutti answered, "but we have prayed that the Lord would lead us to the right person, Kätchen, and we believe that He will, right? But first I think we should thank the Lord for the air of freedom we are breathing right now. Do you realize it? We are free! Free! Free! Free of a system that daily caused us to live in fear and hunger. Free of a system that denied us all God-given human rights."

"Thank You, Lord, for our freedom!" Onkel Emil prayed, while leaning on his cane with both hands. "Continue to lead us this day. We praise Your holy name. Amen."

We were still standing on the platform. There was no one else, only piles of rubble and debris. We didn't seem to be able to get our bearing. One thing, however, we *knew*—we were free!

Outside the station we noticed a lady wearing an armband with a red cross, walking toward us. She informed us that we could find temporary lodging at one of the refugee camps about four miles away. She gave us directions, and we started the long, tiring walk to the camp. After our arrival there, we were questioned thoroughly at the camp office about our home, relatives, plans for the future, and much more. All the information was meticulously recorded. A young man then took us to the soup kitchen and offered us a bowl of soup and a slice of yellow bread.

"You are probably not familiar with this type of bread," he said, "are you? It is cornbread. The bread is baked right here by German people and the meals are also prepared here. The supplies are a gift from the Americans."

After our meal the young man showed us to our new home—a long wooden building with a flat roof.

"I am very sorry that we don't have nine beds close to each other. You will have to divide your group. Four of you can sleep in these two bunks right here, and the rest of you can make yourselves at home on those bunks along the wall over there. Here is one blanket for each of you. Have a good day! Auf Wiedersehen!"

Dieter immediately climbed on one of the top bunks and staked his claim. Because Udo and Marlies were small, they had to share a bottom bunk. As I was perched atop my new bed, I could see row upon row of bunks. Some people were sitting and staring at others, some were sleeping, and some were crying. Everybody seemed bored to death. Some men were snoring, and babies were crying. Younger children were singing, playing, and crying. How could anyone sleep here with all of this noise?

"Welcome to our community," an old man greeted us. "It is a one-room community. This room is home to four hundred of us. We have everything in common here. We have all lost our homes, we all sleep on burlap sacks stuffed with straw, we all eat the same watery soup. Many of us have lost loved ones on the treks and from the bombs. Many of us are sick. Dead are carried out of this building daily because of starvation, and we are all afraid of the person next to us. That person might take our clothes if we leave them on our bed at night. So put your clothes under your straw at night," he rambled on. "And never leave any of your belongings alone. It is true what I tell you. Many of us have been here for a year. We have nothing to live for. We have turned into animals. Could you ever have imagined that Germans would stoop so low? The war has taken our homes, our families, and left us with nothing. And now the war has taught us to steal."

"No," Mutti said breathing deeply, "that is difficult for me to imagine. But do you know something? I have the feeling that the members of *this* family will survive this phase of their lives, too, because now we have freedom. Our freedom is worth more to us than the clothes on our backs and everything we had to leave behind."

The Family Tree
Top: Emil & Emmy Guddat,
Martha (Emil's sister), Fritz (Emil's twin)
Seated: Liane's grandparents –
August & Johanna Krüger, Henriette & Gustav Guddat
Front: Dieter and Liane

Emil Guddat married Emmy Krüger, December 26, 1932.

Although not a Nazi, Emil was commissioned as a supply officer in the German army – with Mutti, Liane, Dieter, and Marlies.

Beautiful Insterburg, East Prussia

As a result of WWII, childhood innocence was quickly lost for Dieter and Liane.

Emil Schmidtke
"Onkel Emil"
and wife, Amalie
"Tante Mally"

The Guddat family residence and leathergoods store were situated on the Hindenburgstraße where Hitler's motorcade passed through Insterburg.

Within a few months, Insterburg laid in ruins.

The quaint little town of Lippehne before the horrors of war invaded.
It is inconceivable to visualize dead bodies floating here.

Kätchen Mecklenburg
with Hanno and Vilmar

The Reverend Ernst Lehmann
"Onkel Lehmann"

The setting of *Refuge* and place of refuge for many –
Onkel Lehmann's "little farmhouse"
(picture taken in 1976, Poland)

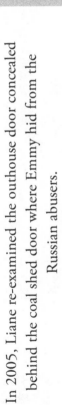

In 2005, Liane re-examined the outhouse door concealed behind the coal shed door where Emmy hid from the Russian abusers.

The simple things of life, like this handwagon and sewing machine, made the difference between life and death.

In 2005, Emmy's sewing machine was still in the farmhouse attic.

Imagine Emmy, Dieter, Liane, Udo, and Marlies fighting for survival in war-torn Germany.

Refugee camps were packed to overflowing. People lived in conditions like these for months and years. (US Army Photograph)

In spite of the difficult circumstances, the Guddats still celebrated Christmas in the refugee camp!

The MS *Berlin* took Liane to America amid stormy seas in January 1956.

Early on the morning of her 22nd birthday, Liane arrived in America and viewed the Statue of Liberty for the first time.

Luther Brown bought a German car, and a German girl came with it!

Liane's mother could not afford to travel to her daughter's wedding, but Emil's sister, Martha, stood in her stead.

Emmy, Udo, Dieter, Marlies, Emil (1957)

Udo, Marlies, Liane, and Dieter (2013)

William & Kätchen visited Emil & Emmy in Florida.

Emil & Emmy Guddat celebrated their 60th wedding anniversary, December 26, 1992.

Luther & Liane Brown celebrated their 60th wedding anniversary, October 19, 2017.

From Fear to Freedom

SUSTAINED BY FAITH—
AN EAST GERMAN FAMILY'S
STRUGGLE FOR SURVIVAL

From Fear to Freedom

SUSTAINED BY FAITH—
AN EAST GERMAN FAMILY'S
STRUGGLE FOR SURVIVAL

Liane I. Brown

REDEMPTION
PRESS

Published by Redemption Press, PO Box 427, Enumclaw, WA 98022

Toll Free (844) 2REDEEM (273-3336)

First published © 1993

Redemption Press is honored to present this title in partnership with the author. The views expressed or implied in this work are those of the author. Redemption Press provides our imprint seal representing design excellence, creative content, and high quality production.

All language translations are the author's.

All Scripture quotations are taken from the King James Version of the Bible (Public Domain).

James A. Brooks completed another original painting for the cover of *From Fear to Freedom,* depicting the reunited Guddat family and Liane as their "herald." For so many immigrants, the Statue of Liberty is a symbol of hope and freedom, but especially for Liane who viewed its splendor for the first time when she arrived in America on her twenty-second birthday.

ISBN 13: 978-1-68314-746-6 (Paperback)
978-1-68314-747-3 (ePub)
978-1-68314-748-0 (Mobi)

Library of Congress Catalog Card Number: 2019930065

Dedication

To the descendants of
Emil and Emmy Guddat
so they can know
our testimony of
God's sustaining faithfulness
and unending love.

He that dwelleth in the secret place of the most High
Shall abide under the shadow of the Almighty.
I will say of the Lord, He is my refuge and my fortress:
My God; in him will I trust.
(Psalm 91:1–2)

CONTENTS

Preface

Readers of my first book, *Refuge*, often ask, "How did you get to America?" For several years I offered a quick reply to that question and shrugged off the request for a sequel.

Viewing world events, however, especially those of Eastern Europe, I realized that the longings of hearts for freedom have not changed. World maps are continuously being redrawn, wars and regimes enslave millions, while the cries for freedom still echo on American shores. I have known the torment of oppression, fear, and lack of freedom. Therefore, I felt jolted into action to relate our story as refugees.

From Fear to Freedom is based on my mother's, father's, and Kätchen's written accounts, extensive interviews with our friend Edith, and my own experiences. Every incident is true.

I thank the Lord for having made it possible for my family and me to come to America. I thank America for having bestowed upon us the privilege to become her citizens. America, you have blessed us far beyond our expectations; you have given us a home and the freedom about which countless millions can only dream.

NORTH SEA

DENMARK

SV

NETHERLANDS

o Bremerhaven

Nienburg
o

o Hannover

⊕ Berli

BELGIUM

BRITISH ZONE

RUSSIAN ZONE

o Oberhausen

GERMANY

LUX.

o Frankfurt

AMERICAN ZONE

CZECH

FRANCE

o Stuttgart

FRENCH ZONE

o Munich

AMERICAN
ZONE

R

AUST

FRENCH ZONE

SWITZERLAND

BRITISH ZON

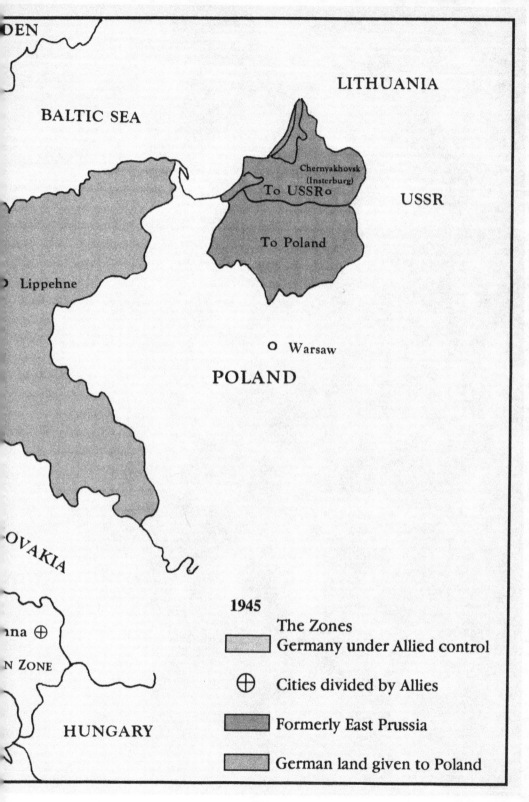

DEN

BALTIC SEA

LITHUANIA

Chernyakhovsk
(Insterburg)
To USSR o

USSR

To Poland

Lippehne

O Warsaw

POLAND

OVAKIA

na ⊕

N ZONE

HUNGARY

1945
The Zones
Germany under Allied control

⊕ Cities divided by Allies

Formerly East Prussia

German land given to Poland

German Words and Expressions

Vati – Daddy

Mutti – Mommy

Opi – Grandpa

Omi – Grandma

Uropi – Great-grandpa

Onkel – Uncle

Tante – Aunt

Herr – Mr.

Frau – Mrs.

Schäfle – little sheep

Pittimaus – Marlies's nickname

Uschi – name of endearment

Guten Tag! – Good day!

Gnädige Dame – madam

Ja – yes

1

Berlin Camp

"Fire! Fire! Help! Fire!" people shouted and cried in panic. "Help! Help!" Flashes of light zigzagged across the room. Four hundred refugees in one barracks building! Frightened beings jumped off bunk beds, children cried, flames shot into the air. "Help! We are going to die!" The smell of heavy smoke pierced my nose. The two exit doors remained locked from the outside as they had always been at night. "Hit harder! Faster!" someone yelled at those beating the flames with coats. Straw mattresses burning fast, the fire leaped from bed to bed. People stumbled over each other, beating on the doors. "We have to get out! Unlock the doors, someone! Unlock the doors!" they yelled, pounding at the wooden door. Did we gain our freedom from Communism just to die in a refugee camp in Berlin?

More straw sacks ignited. Brave people used precious clothing to beat at the tall flames. The inside of the barracks was lighter on this night than during the day. "My clothes! Someone, save my clothes!" a lady cried, but the flames devoured them. More and more flames leaped upward, shooting their crackling sound into our souls.

"Did we escape the enemy's bombs in East Prussia just to die here?" Mutti asked. "Lord, help us!"

Finally the room began to darken. "Beat faster, faster! We are almost done! The fire is almost out!" Mothers, clutching their children, became black silhouettes. Old people, huddling against the wall, frozen from fear, looked like stone carvings in free West Germany, the land in which they had hoped to find peace, food, shelter, and freedom from fear.

Because it was impossible to open the barred windows, heavy layers of smoke hovered over the room. Did the camp administration realize the dilemma in which their charges found themselves?

Choking and breathless, my heart continued to pound as I climbed on the top of the bunk, covered myself with my coat, and listened to children crying softly, people sobbing, praying, angry at the smoker who started the fire. God protected us again. He was good—I still had my sack filled with straw. Others in the room did not. I thought to myself, I would never again complain about bleeding scratches inflicted by sharp, tough straw.

After tucking everyone in again, Mutti reached up to touch me. My brother Udo, almost three years old, and my sister Marlies, six, would soon forget this night, but nine-year-old Dieter and I, twelve, would always remember.

"You children, stay here on your beds and guard your clothes carefully," Mutti instructed us the next morning. "I will go to the camp kitchen and pick up our bread and coffee. Onkel Emil will help watch our belongings. There are too many thieves in this room. Many have nothing and just take whatever they need."

I was fortunate to have worn two sets of socks, underwear, and dresses when we escaped from Lippehne, Poland. Most of our bundles of possessions were taken from us at the border, yet we considered ourselves blessed. A milk can filled with what looked like beet syrup had not been taken from us. Wise Mutti had filled it with lard and used the syrup as a

cover-up. How delicious that lard tasted now on our slices of camp bread. People watched us with envy as we tried to quietly eat our breakfast.

Udo carried a little potty in his rucksack during our escape. No one took it away either. What would we have done without that at the camp? It was forbidden to use the outdoor bathroom at night.

After breakfast Mutti, her friend Kätchen, a young preacher's wife, and Onkel Emil, a World War I invalid with an artificial leg, went into a huddle to discuss our future. For a year and a half, these single partners of three families had shared a lot of sorrows and some joy, supporting one another and bearing one another's heartaches. Kätchen and her two sons, nine and seven, knew that her husband and the father of her children was alive and a preacher in West Germany but had been unable to contact him. All of us had lived at her father's house in Lippehne, near Küstrin, when the Russians overran that town. Emil Schmidtke had made plans to meet his wife at that little farmhouse, but she never arrived. Mutti had not heard from Vati in two years.

It was impossible, the adults decided, to continue living in the crowded camp. This was April 1946. Germany had capitulated almost one year ago, yet there was no peace for the refugees. Some of our bed neighbors had lived in the camp for ten months. "We can't do that," Onkel Emil said. "Yesterday I heard someone say there is another camp on the other side of Berlin. That camp is not supposed to be as crowded as this one. Why don't we go there this afternoon?"

After our watery camp soup had been quickly devoured at lunchtime, we grabbed our belongings and started for the bus station. Mutti and Kätchen paid for the tickets with money the camp administration gave them. More than ever, the long bus ride exposed us to a Berlin lying in ashes. No beauty could be found on our route through the former capital of Germany—rubble, and nothing but rubble as far as one could see, with only a few buildings here and there of this once glorious city. People—young and old—sat among the ruins, beating mortar off

bricks and stacking them carefully: whole bricks, half bricks, pieces. They worked with their hearts and eyes toward the future of a new and beautiful Berlin.

Finally, we arrived at the new camp—a huge Quonset hut. Before registering at the administration office, we checked out the accommodations. Shocked, Onkel Emil declared, "No way are we going to stay here. Look at these poor people! They are sleeping on the bare cement floor, packed in like sardines. We will not live like this. At least we had wooden plank beds and straw at the other camp. Let's go back where we came from." We all agreed, trudging back to the bus station, tired and hungry. We had missed our bread ration that evening but were assigned beds upon arrival.

"It seems this will be our home until God decides to move us," Mutti remarked. Life wasn't easy for Mutti. Washing out clothes in a small bowl without soap presented as much of a problem as guarding the laundry while it was hung to dry. Honest Germans had become thieves during the struggle for survival. Much had changed in the lives of refugees. The last basic, private stronghold, modesty, had also been stripped off the four hundred people living in one large room. Little mattered anymore. Many had been chased like cattle for too long by enemies, bombs, tanks, rapists, and fear. Sitting or lying on their burlap straw sacks with blank, hollow, ashen faces was all they could do now. After close to one year without an improvement in their living standards, even the faintest hope for a better future had vanished. Almost daily, the death angel visited the camp, often bringing envy to the living.

Our little group, however, longed for a better future rather than mere survival. Mutti searched anew for more information about Vati, her husband and our dad. Two years had slipped into eternity since we last saw him at my grandfather's funeral. Did he have any knowledge of our whereabouts?

Onkel Emil learned that his oldest daughter, who had worked for the weather information service in the German Air Force, had survived and lived in Nienburg, a town at the navigable Weser River. "Please help us get permission to enter West Germany," he wired her. "Emmy and children are with me." Prayers ascended to God's throne daily that Edith would receive the message and be able to help us move to the West. The German communication system was in shambles. Only God could intervene and help the message arrive in Nienburg.

Kätchen, the young preacher's wife and our dear friend, at whose parents' house in Lippehne we had suffered many atrocities at the hands of the Russians, was waning fast. Gravely ill, she weighed only sixty-seven pounds. Her two sons, Hanno and Vilmar, also resembled little skeletons. Kätchen, even in her weakness, however, always had a smile on her face. "The Lord will reunite our family," she would insist. "He is our refuge. He has helped us thus far and will continue to do so."

Having learned that her brother lived in Berlin was like a potion of survival medicine for Kätchen. She suddenly seemed to be well; she became cheerful, bubbly, and happy. Her brother would come and take her and his nephews into his apartment, he told her. From there she could make plans to move to Bockum-Hövel where her husband was pastor of a church.

While Kätchen began packing, I tried to imagine living without her and her sons. We spent one-and-a-half years with them. They were part of our family. My heart was broken and grief-stricken. My soul could not have been in greater despair had she passed away. I just loved her so much. And now I had to live without her? Mutti's face was also moist with tears when saying goodbye to our precious friend. "God be with you till we meet again," we sang. But would we ever meet again?

Why did we always have to say goodbye? Goodbye to Vati. Goodbye to my sweet Omi and Vati's sister-in-law. Goodbye to Mutti's parents on

the farm. Goodbye to my Uropi . . . goodbye to Vati's twin brother . . . goodbye to our friends . . . goodbye to our home . . . goodbye, goodbye.

The next day, at the camp meeting for children, missionaries told Bible stories and taught the song:

Fairest Lord Jesus! Ruler of all nature!
O Thou of God and man the Son!
Thee will I cherish, Thee will I honor,
Thou my soul's glory, joy, and crown!

I loved the melody of that song. I enjoyed the words:

Fair are the meadows, fairer still the woodlands . . .
He makes the woeful heart to sing.
(Anonymous, "Fairest Lord Jesus, Ruler of All Nature")

The song momentarily helped take away the sadness of my heart about having lost Kätchen. At night though, while people snored, tossed, groaned on their bunks, and babies cried, my thoughts could not leave Kätchen's side. Would she ever get well? Would others appreciate her as much as I did? The night hours yielded no answer to my questions. By morning, the newly washed dress under my straw sack, which my body was to have ironed during the night, had a totally wrinkled appearance because of all my tossing and turning.

One week after another, then one month after another, passed into eternity; the refugee camp had become our home. There were only three ways of leaving the camp—by death, moving West, or just walking away. Those who could not find loved ones through the Red Cross just lay on the straw sacks in their bunks and seemed to waste away: hopeless, helpless beings, too weak to yearn or grope for a glimmer of hope.

People who were not yet despondent vented their anger by shouting at Hitler. "He got us into this life of misery. He promised us so many

things, and we believed him. He has killed our families, taken our homes. Where is he now—our Führer? We marched for him. We fought for him. We sacrificed for him. We bled for him. Where is he now? I want to kill him—kill him!" one man yelled.

"Sh . . . Sh . . . ! Calm down, friend," another old man interceded. "He is already dead, they say. He and Eva Braun committed suicide somewhere in Berlin."

"I want to kill him too," another deranged person added. "My wife is dead. My son is dead. I can't find my daughter. If I find Hitler, I'll kill him."

Witnessing the rage and anger of our roommates reminded me anew of my great excitement when marching with the Hitler Youth in our town of Insterburg, East Prussia. It was wonderfully exhilarating to march and sing:

Our leader, he is Adolf Hitler,
We do well to follow him.
We love him with all our hearts,
Because he loves us.

The sports competitions had also excited me. Our bodies and minds had to be fit to follow our great leader. Muscles were stretched in sports arenas, minds in school. We had to learn, learn, learn; excel in everything we did. With uniforms meticulously pressed, every German young person had to march in precision behind the Führer.

But what had happened now to our great example? He had not only ruined our nation but other nations as well. He had caused death to millions of innocent people, hardships to millions more. I sensed the turmoil and utter confusion in my soul; I wanted revenge too. Hitler should have been chopped into a thousand pieces. Suddenly my own thoughts began to scare me. Had I become so cruel? Was that I? Had the love I was forced to bestow on him turned to hate? It seemed that way.

Insterburg, East Prussia, my hometown with the man-made lakes, beautiful parks, and huge sports arenas, slumbered in my memory like a picture-page in a book. Almost two years ago, we had to leave our bomb-ravaged city. Now, after sixteen months of suffering under the oppressive Russian government, fear, starvation, the death of our friends, and two and a half months in a camp, we continued to sit on straw sacks. We had hoped our stomachs would be filled in the West. Would we ever again have enough to eat? Did the world know of our suffering? We were not Nazis, yet we had given everything. Famished and diseased people all around us were giving their very lives. Yes, I think I was beginning to hate, beginning to hate Hitler.

"Frau Guddat," a lady whispered, "please don't tell anyone. I may lose my life. Please come here, here to the corner. Is anyone watching us?"

"No," I heard Mutti answer, "only my daughter."

"She will not turn me in, will she?"

"No, definitely not."

"I have something for you, something *very* special." With that exciting statement, she partially pulled up her black gathered skirt with one hand and with the other reached into the leg part of her lacy bloomers. "Here it is! You and your children are so nice. I just had to give you one. I was helping a farmer today and just took these from the field."

"I thank you from the bottom of my heart for this wonderful gift. You are so kind! We will enjoy this potato immensely. It will remind us of what potatoes taste like and cause us to dream of a whole plateful someday."

"Frau Guddat! Where is Frau Guddat?" one of the camp officials suddenly called into the barracks.

"I am right here," Mutti answered, taking Udo off her lap. With bounce in her step, the blond camp staffer walked toward Mutti.

"Frau Guddat, I think today is your lucky day. We have just found a great place of accommodations for you and your four children."

"Oh yes?"

"Yes, Frau Guddat! We found a farmer who has agreed to take you all in. Living on a farm will be healthy for you and the children. I noticed you are all undernourished."

A farm? Visions of my grandparents' beautiful farm in East Prussia immediately danced before my eyes—food, potatoes, meat, milk, yeast cakes, animals, hay wagons, horse-drawn carriages, the river. How wonderful! We were going to a farm!

"That sounds absolutely wonderful! Thank you so much," Mutti said with her lovely face aglow, radiant with joy.

"You may leave here today yet, Frau Guddat."

"Will there be pussycats and dogs, Mutti?" Marlies asked while stretching her little body upward in anticipation of the answer.

"I think so, Pittimaus," Mutti replied. "Most farms have cats and dogs. I guess we will soon find out."

"I can't wait to leave," Dieter joined in.

I couldn't wait either to leave the crowded camp.

"Tell me, please, where is this farm located?" Mutti asked excitedly.

"Oh, it is not too far from Berlin. It is in the Russian zone."

I could sense Mutti's heart sink. "The Russian zone?"

"Yes, Frau Guddat. The farm happens to be in the Russian zone."

"Thank you for your help, but my children and I can't go there," Mutti sadly replied as tears began to well up in her eyes. "You have no idea what we have suffered at the hands of the Russians. There is no way we will go."

"But this is the Russian *zone* Frau Guddat. It is not Russia or Poland."

"I am sorry. I don't want to see another Russian soldier as long as I live. We will just have to stay here at the camp until God shows us another way."

"All right, Frau Guddat, if that is how you feel, I will ask another family. Someone will be glad to live out in the country. Guten Tag!"

When Onkel Emil came in, Mutti told him about the offer of moving to the farm. "You made the right decision, Emmy. We don't know too much about this zone system, but the Russian zone is a place to stay away from."

"What are zones, Mutti?" I asked.

"Well, let me try to explain how I understand it. Germany lost the war, and when the war ended over a year ago, all our enemies wanted a piece of our country. In Potsdam, not too far from here, the conquerors agreed that Germany was to be divided into four pieces, just like cutting an apple. Each conqueror then got one piece. These pieces are called zones. Germany now has an American, a British, a French, and a Russian zone. Each zone with the Germans in it is governed by the nation the zone belongs to. The city of Berlin is also divided into four zones called 'sectors.'"

"You explained that beautifully, Emmy," Onkel Emil commented. "That is how I understand the zone system too. What we don't know is the political system in each zone. We'll find that out someday, I am sure.

"I have to tell you, Emmy, that I just returned from the Red Cross. There is still no news of my wife and second daughter. Only the Lord knows if they are still alive. So until you are reunited with your husband or settled somewhere and I find my wife, I will continue to stand by your side."

"Well, thank you, Emil. I appreciate that."

One day we were all outside our barracks enjoying the warm sunshine. In spite of all the misery around us, it almost seemed good to be alive that day. I sensed that Mutti was speaking to her heavenly Father. She was probably thanking Him for freedom from the oppressive Communist regime and asking the Lord to reunite our family. While Marlies, Udo, and Dieter were playing with children from the camp, Mutti suddenly called out, "Pastor Sawadda!" Startled, the kind-looking gentleman visiting our camp turned in our direction.

"Emmy Guddat! What are you doing here? How long have you been here? How did you get here? When did you leave East Prussia?" After the barrage of questions, Mutti began to recount the bombing attacks of Insterburg. She told the pastor of our resettling in Lippehne, Neumark, before the Russians overran East Prussia, our attempted flight, and how the Lord had miraculously brought us to Berlin.

"Oh, my dear child," said the man who had for years pastored the country church my grandparents and family attended. "Where is your husband?"

"Somewhere in Africa, I was told. We haven't seen or heard from him in two years. During one of the most difficult times in my life, when we suffered in the clutches of Communism, our gracious Lord revealed to me in a dream that Emil was alive."

"What about your parents? Do you know anything about them?"

"No, I don't."

"And your sister's family and brother's?"

"I don't know their whereabouts either."

"I go to the refugee camps of Berlin often in hopes of finding some of my former church members. Usually I am unsuccessful, but I surely am glad to have found you today," the pastor continued.

"You have no idea how happy I am to see you too," Mutti said joyously. "In the past two years, I have not met anyone I knew, family or friends. So you don't know anything about my relatives either?"

"No, I don't. But we'll continue to pray for them and place them in God's care, Emmy. That is all we can do. There is too much turmoil in our land. Millions of Germans have been chased out of their cities and villages by the Russians. Perhaps your relatives will arrive here in the West someday soon.

"But now I must get to the matter at hand. You and the children have to leave this camp."

"But we have nowhere to go."

"Well, I work at the City Mission here in Berlin. Perhaps I can help you." After prayer and tearful goodbyes, Pastor Sawadda left.

"I will keep in touch and do my best to help you, Emmy," he said before leaving.

"Only the Lord knows if the pastor will be able to change our situation," Mutti told me. "We must be strong and continue to hope, Schäfle. As you can see, without hope people just die. Hope is like an invisible thread that connects the soul with a longing for a better life in the future."

One week after the pastor's visit, a message was delivered to Mutti, "Come and live at the Mission—you and the family."

Were we really going to leave the camp? It seemed that way. Mutti had already begun to pack our bundles. After having inquired about the way to the Mission, the six of us left the American refugee camp. Onkel Emil, of course, went along since he considered himself part of our family. My brothers and sister did not want to leave all their new friends behind—for them camp life was fun. Even Dieter, with the huge open sores on his legs, enjoyed himself. "Only vitamins and nutritious food will help him," the camp doctor had said, but we had neither. Perhaps things would improve at the Mission.

Life seemed heavenly in our new home. We had our own room and real beds. The Mission workers showered us with kindness and love. They even offered us children milk to drink with our two daily pieces of bread which was sliced thicker than that at the camp.

We sang in the evening chapel service.

A mighty fortress is our God, a bulwark never failing;
Our helper He, amid the flood of mortal ills prevailing. . . .
Let goods and kindred go, this mortal life also;
The body they may kill: God's truth abideth still,
His kingdom is forever.
(Luther, "A Mighty Fortress")

Several women in the room wept silently, unable to sing. Refugees had been forced to let go of goods. Many already knew their kindred were gone too. The pastor, visibly saddened, gazed upon his helpless flock, people from East Prussia, Silesia, Pomerania, and Poland.

"Friends," he said sympathetically, "God has neither forsaken nor forgotten us even though it may seem that way at times. He said in His Word, 'I will never leave thee, nor forsake thee.' We may feel forsaken and forgotten, but we aren't. Jesus knows what we are going through. He once asked His own Father when hanging on the cross, suffering there for our sins, 'My God, my God, why hast thou forsaken me?' Even He, the Son of God, felt forsaken. He understands our problems. He wants to help us if only we would trust in Him.

"Perhaps some of you here don't know what it means to trust in Jesus. Trusting in Jesus is a matter of the heart; it is believing that God died on the cross for sinners. The Bible very clearly states that since Adam we are all sinners, every human being is born a sinner. Therefore, God sent His Son to die for our sins, to be buried, and to rise from the dead on the third day. You may say now, 'Yes, Preacher, I know all that. I believe that.' But here now is the critical and life-changing question—Have you ever invited this Jesus to save you from your sins?"

"No," a weeping lady said out loud, "how do I do that?"

"Thank you for your question. You just say in childlike faith and really mean it, 'Lord Jesus, I am a sinner. I thank You for dying for me on the cross. I know You were buried and rose again. Please forgive me of all my sins. Come into my heart and save me and let me live for You from now on.' If you pray something like that, or exactly like that, the Holy Spirit will enter your heart, the angels in heaven will rejoice, and you will have become a heaven-bound child of God."

I could see the lady bowing her head. I think she must have invited Christ into her life. While the faces of some folks in the room radiated joy, others just stared at nothing. After the closing prayer, however,

the grave-like atmosphere had vanished. Folks eagerly walked to the pastor and told him their problems. With his head tilted sideways, the gray-haired compassionate man listened intently to each burdened soul.

"I know you children enjoy living here at the Mission," Mutti told us one day, "but this is not a permanent solution. We have to continue praying for the Lord to guide us to an apartment or home of our own.

"By the way, children, tonight we will again recite all the poems we have learned for Vati's homecoming, right? He could come any day now."

"Rejoice! Rejoice!" Onkel Emil bubbled one day, and, trying to run, almost fell over his prosthesis. "I received a letter from Edith in West Germany. Her British employers have permitted her to have us join her in Nienburg/Weser. This is a miracle! The miracle we have prayed for. Say something, Emmy! Say something!"

Mutti responded by crying. "Will our wanderings soon be over? The Russians, camps, and Mission behind us? We will have our own place?" Lovingly, she stroked Marlies's curly head and hugged Udo.

Most folks at the Mission genuinely rejoiced with us; others, however, seemed to avoid us. Were they jealous? The dream of everyone was to enter West Germany and get settled. "We wish we could go with you," several mothers said after our last chapel service. "We, too, want to go to a better life, to a land where our children can have more food and a future. God bless you! God bless you! Please don't forget us here! We want to be blessed of God too."

Slowly we trudged from the Mission to the bus station. On our trip to the railroad depot, we traveled past huge mountains of rubble. Often we saw people crawl out of rubble-like caves. "Those poor people must live there," Mutti said in shock. Elderly men and women, unkempt and bewildered, sat on charred cement blocks or slouched on scorched, stuffed chairs. They were too old to clean bricks and rebuild Berlin. Their generation had lived the good life. They had built for their children and grandchildren. Now all was gone.

2

Heading West

"**W**e are now traveling through the Russian zone of Germany," a wise-looking man on the train told us. "These fields are now feeding our conquerors. The forests, always so beautifully cared for by German foresters, are no longer ours to protect and tend. We Germans are but pawns on a chessboard, pushed about by our conquerors. You might also say we are cattle to be butchered when we are in the way. Ditches along the routes of the refugee treks are filled with bodies of our loved ones—prey to the elements even in death. Our homes have been plundered and destroyed. Many of our women and girls are vegetables, due to being raped by Russians; their minds are blown. Are they luckier than the dead? I don't think so. I was not a Nazi. You probably weren't either. We did not deserve this."

Deep in thought, our travel companion stared out of the window, causing everyone else to quietly contemplate his statements. Only the wheels of the train interrupted the silence by beating the metal tracks and tirelessly moving us toward a better life in West Germany.

"Mutti! Mutti! See the big animals! They are black and white. What are they?" Udo asked.

"They are cows, my son, cows. They give milk."

"Can we stop and get some milk?"

"Oh no, my son. We have to stay on this train and go where it takes us." Then turning to me, Mutti continued, "I guess Udo has never seen a cow. How would he have known what one looked like? The Russians had killed every animal in Lippehne."

Nature, dressed in her rich summer garb, beckoned the eye of the soul into a peaceful world. Green pastures, apples trees, wheat fields, meandering rivers, mountain ridges, and forests hid the suffering and agony prevailing in the cities. Some of the towns at which the train stopped had not been bombed; life seemed peaceful. But then—suddenly—my heart began to pound. On the country road, running parallel to our train, a caravan moved, a caravan of trucks and Russian soldiers. We were not yet free and out of danger; we were still in the Russian zone.

"We have just crossed the border," our wise travel companion announced. "We are now in the British zone."

"Free at last!" Mutti burst out. "Free at last! A new life is beginning this very moment, a better life for all of us. No more fear. No more camps. Thank You, Lord, for giving us this wonderful day."

Children, swimming in the river which our train had just crossed, reminded me of our summer vacations at my grandparents' in East Prussia. For hours we would swim in the shallow river and ride the wooden logs which the currents of the river freely transported from the logging sites to the mills downstream. Broad, heavy logs were easier to ride than thin lightweight ones, we had learned. Trying to hide a favorite log in the low-hanging bushes for next day's play usually backfired. Somehow our treasures freed themselves at night and vanished.

Gone in a moment were the peaceful landscape settings and my dreams of days past. I was pulled back to reality when the bomb-ravaged city of Hannover came into view. Charcoal and metal beams dangled from once majestic buildings; half rooms of homes exposed bathtubs,

stoves, and furniture. Below the dangerous relics, however, people sat and cleaned bricks.

"Nienburg is only fifty kilometers from here," the conductor told Mutti who had inquired about the distance. "We will be there in a short time."

Mutti's excitement was quite obvious, "Soon we will be home, children. Do you have your coats and rucksacks ready? Trains don't stop long. We have to get off quickly." At last, the train slowed down; its ear-piercing whistle caused Marlies to jump.

"Nienburg—Weser—next!" the conductor shouted as we gently rolled past beautiful homes and tree-lined streets. A mother pushed a baby carriage, two kittens played on a lawn; no signs of war in this town. "Nienburg! Nienburg!" The name rang out again. Mutti anxiously slid the train door open and jumped off the high steps. The four of us followed. Onkel Emil handed down the bundles and limped off himself.

"Here we are in West Germany, far away from the Russians," he sighed while looking all around. "In which direction do you think we should go, Emmy? Where do you think Edith might live?"

"That is a good question," Mutti replied while also glancing in every direction. "Why don't we ask this gentleman here?"

"Excuse me, please," Onkel Emil started timidly, "we are looking for the Dunsing family in the . . ."

"Yes, yes, yes, I know the Dunsing family quite well. Just follow me. I am going in the same direction."

"You know the Dunsings? Well, that is divine guidance."

"Divine what?"

"Divine guidance."

"Just follow me," the stranger continued.

"Thank you very much, but we are not able to walk as fast as you, with the children and our bundles. Would you be kind enough, though,

to tell my daughter Edith, who lives at the Dunsings, that her father and family have arrived in Nienburg and we are on our way to her house?"

"Be glad to do that, very glad. Guten Tag. Have a nice visit," he said after having given us directions.

With rucksacks on our backs and small bundles in our hands, we all excitedly set out for our new home. Onkel Emil seemed to have more bounce in his leg; even the prosthesis appeared to move along more smoothly. His cane beat out the rhythm—home!—home! We were going home!

Mutti couldn't figure out why passersby gave us strange looks. We were clean, yes, but we were poor, poor in belongings but rich in freedom and joyous in heart. Why then did everyone stare at us? Some even walked a half circle around us. Was it because we were refugees?

"Edith! Edith! My daughter!" Onkel Emil called to the person running toward us. Then they hugged and cried on the sidewalk in Nienburg. Later we all hugged Edith, a tall and slender lady. I called her my friend. The sixteen years difference in age had never mattered to her. She always made me feel special as a young person. I was even invited to her birthday parties in Insterburg. And now my friend had helped us enter West Germany.

"Any word yet from your mother, Edith?" Onkel Emil inquired as we started walking again.

"No, I have not heard from her."

"What about your sister?"

"I don't know where she is either."

Huge old shade trees along the street and sidewalks filtered the summer sun and gave us relief from the warmth. While an elderly man sat on a garden bench, a lady pulled weeds in her flower garden. Children played ball and hopscotch. Life was so beautiful and peaceful in Nienburg; no rubble, no devastation. The windows of the homes glistened and lacy curtains hung in perfect folds. Above the orange tile

roofs of the half-timbered homes towered the copper-green steeple of a huge church. Anyone would like this town, I thought, even though no town could ever compare to our once picturesque Insterburg. But this town—except for the people who still looked at us as if we had come from the moon—was nice, really nice.

Setting the pace for the rest of us, Edith and Onkel Emil walked and chatted. They talked about the years of struggle for survival and their home in Insterburg.

"This is the place I call home," Edith announced when stopping at a stucco house. "The Dunsings have become like my own family. I met one of the daughters in the Air Force. She told me to get in touch with her should I ever be in need and not able to return to East Prussia. They are lovely and kind people. The upstairs part of the building belongs to them. There are eight of us now living in a few small rooms. They dearly wish they could take all of you in, too, they told me. But there simply isn't enough room for six more people. Because of my job for the British, I managed to get these documents for you all so you can stay here in Nienburg," Edith said while pulling papers out of her coat pocket. "These entitle you to sleeping accommodations and meals at the Churchill Camp outside of town."

Upon hearing the word "camp," Mutti's face instantly turned pale. "Are we going to a camp, Mutti?" Dieter asked. Mutti was incapable of answering.

"Just go in that direction," Edith said, "and you eventually get to the camp. I have to go to work now. Goodbye. I'll come and visit you tomorrow."

Her face wet with tears, Mutti reached for the bundles and began to drag herself toward another camp. We all followed in silence.

A refugee camp! Two years ago we had left East Prussia. When would our vagabond life end? Would Mutti be able to carry on? She was not well. The boils on her body were not healing. Quietly Onkel Emil

shoved along. What would this Churchill Camp be like? Would we sleep on the floor or on straw? Would the daily soup still consist of mostly water? Dozens of questions flooded my mind. Neither the warmth of the sun nor the beauty of the town could comfort our hearts. With people staring at us, we continued to walk in silence. I liked the quaintness of the homes and the bright red geraniums in the flower boxes, but I felt hurt by the looks of some of the residents.

Suddenly we heard, "Father! Father! Stop!" It was Edith who came running after us. "Frau Dunsing saw you from the kitchen window and said to me, 'We can't let those poor people go to that crowded camp. Just run after them and bring them back here. We are crowded already, but that doesn't matter. We'll somehow find room for them.' So come on back with me."

At once Mutti seemed revived. "Thank You, Lord, for answering my prayer. The Lord is good, children, isn't He?"

Strangers took in strangers. This family accepted us as we were—poor, destitute, tired, and hungry. Their already meager dinner portions that evening were made smaller yet so that we could have something to eat. Herr Dunsing had passed away two weeks earlier, but the family reached out to comfort us. Rearranging the whole household to help us wasn't easy. People slept on the kitchen floor and in every corner of that tiny apartment. How wonderful, I thought, not to feel like a refugee but to be shown kindness. The Lord surely was good to us.

"Frau Guddat, you may use our bicycle." Frau Dunsing approached Mutti the next day. "The walk to the camp is rather long. You can pick up your meals by bike. I will also loan you one of my milk cans so you can get your soup at noon."

"Thank you very much, Frau Dunsing! You are so kind and helpful. You have no idea what your generosity means to me and all of us. I appreciate you and your family," Mutti said in a broken voice.

Meager or not, our camp soup tasted much better eaten from a plate than a metal tin. "What are these orange pieces in the soup, Mutti?" Dieter asked holding a chunk of something strange on his spoon.

"I don't know, Dieter. What can it be? It is not a carrot." No one else in the household had an explanation until Edith told us that those orange things were from America and called "sweet potatoes."

Onkel Emil trudged daily to the housing authorities in search of an apartment for us. "We have a long list, Herr Schmidtke. You are almost at the bottom of that list. There are many ahead of you. We just don't have much housing available here in Nienburg. But we'll do the best we can. You just have to be patient. We are busy searching for housing all over town. Perhaps someday soon we'll find something for you."

"Edith," Onkel Emil started one evening when all fourteen of us were crowded together in the small living room, "tell me a little bit about your experiences as a prisoner of war."

"Well," Edith began, "the Americans captured me near the Elbe River. And I surely was glad to have fallen into American hands. Nobody wanted to fall into the hands of the Russians. Everyone knew of their atrocities. I was held in a private house, whose owners had fled, under heavy guard with 140 women. Our house overlooked the beautiful Elbe river. One day a clerk of the commander's office searched for an interpreter. My English wasn't great, but I knew I could do it and offered my services. I started working in the commander's office and really enjoyed it. My language skills improved quickly. Our food rations were very meager. Many of the women became ill from eating the American white bread. We simply weren't used to it."

Mutti's lap cradled the little heads of both Marlies and Udo. War stories did not interest them; they fell asleep. It seemed their weak little bodies could find true nourishment only in sleep.

"One day," Edith continued, "the commander asked me to choose some women to harvest hay for a farmer. I immediately selected my six

roommates. The wages were to be food only. We were all hungry and the prospect of getting some farm cooking sounded great. Since I helped my friends, they often brought some food back for me. So we had a fairly decent life in our camp.

"Several weeks later, the women of our camp were handed over to the British. With shovels, and heavily guarded, we had to march daily into the old battlefields and level the ground. It was a back-breaking job to level the ruts made by tanks. Often at night, drunk guards tried to come into our rooms. But we barricaded our doors and nothing serious ever happened."

"I wonder, Edith," Onkel Emil interrupted, "why the Americans handed you to the British."

"I don't know. I never found out. After having slaved on the battlefields for a while, I was given the job of interpreter again. By the end of the fifth week in the British prisoner of war camp, I heard my superiors eagerly talking about Russians and women. I listened more closely and realized that our camp was to be handed over to the Russians. 'You can't do that,' I interrupted the conversation. 'You can't give us to the Russians. Do you have any idea what they do to women?'

"'Please, Edith, you were not supposed to listen to our conversation.'

"'But you can't do that. The Russians are animals; they murder, they rape.'

"'We told the Russians that we have 140 women here and the 140 will belong to them. So that is that.'

"'No, you must let us go! I have to escape. I heard what they did to everyone in Nemmersdorf in East Prussia, near my hometown. All the females of that village were first raped and then killed. Please let me go.'

"'Okay,' he whispered. 'You alone may go. And don't tell anyone! We have to figure out a way to explain the missing person to the Russians. But we like you, so go quickly! Hurry! They are almost here.'

"I dashed up to my room and grabbed my few belongings."

"Oh, Edith, my poor daughter," Onkel Emil sighed. "How did you get away?"

"I started racing downstairs. All six of my roommates followed. They knew something was wrong. 'Go back! Go back!' I shouted, but they kept racing after me through the brush down to the shore of the Elbe. I jumped into the wooden boat I had always seen there, grabbed the oars and started rowing. Everyone clambered into the boat. One of my roommates fell into the water, but the others pulled her back into the moving boat. Suddenly, a short distance away, we saw the Russians marching toward our camp. 'Faster,' I said, 'let's row faster.' Bullets started flying from the shore. We rowed. We tried to duck. Bullets, nothing but bullets.

"'I'd rather die from a bullet than be raped to death,' someone said. 'Let 'em just kill us.'

"'No,' I said, 'we won't give up. We are almost across.' On the other side, we jumped out of the boat and dove into bushes. We had made it. We were free. None of the bullets had hit us. It was a miracle only God could have performed to save us."

Many sighs of relief escaped into our little room. Had God not protected Edith, I thought, she would not be in Nienburg. We in turn would still live at the Mission in Berlin or at some camp. I had tried to picture her rowing across the Elbe and the Russians shooting. How horrible! My heart pounded as my mind added another life and death story to its files.

3

Golden Anchor

"Emmy," Onkel Emil burst out when hobbling into the house at the beginning of our third week at the Dunsings, "the authorities found a place for us to live."

"Where, Emil? Where?"

"It is in the Golden Anchor Hotel."

"What did you say? Hotel?"

"Well, they told me it used to be a hotel for several hundred years. It is a refugee camp now."

"Oh."

"It is not as we know a camp to be, they told me. We will have two rooms there, one medium-sized for you and the children, and a tiny one for me. That is all I know about it. We can move in immediately."

"That sounds great, Emil, just great. Thank you for searching for a place so diligently and bringing our plight before the authorities daily. Your persistence has really paid off." That same afternoon, we thanked our new friends and started the forty-five-minute walk to our new camp.

We marched in goose file toward the outskirts of Nienburg across the wobbly wooden bridge. Car passengers stared at us as they drove by. The

swiftly moving water under the bridge almost made me dizzy. Anything we might drop, I reasoned, would fall into the river through the open side rails and gaping bars. I was glad when we all had crossed safely.

Making a sharp left on the other side of the bridge, we followed the elm-lined street to the Golden Anchor. Children played in the street and courtyard of the once grand hotel, a lodging place for river navigators. Large beams gave the framework building a massive appearance. The deeply worn stone step at the entrance testified to much activity through the centuries. Cold and gray-looking, wide cement floors trailed through the downstairs hallways. Every door was closed. To the left, halfway down the building, an expansive and worn-out staircase curved upward. The second door on the left, No. 11, was to be the entrance to our new home.

When Onkel Emil opened the door, it fell ajar. A table and chairs stood in the middle of the room; beyond it, a window beckoned in the sunlight. Two roughly made bunk beds lined the two walls. One single cot stood on one side of the window and an old dresser on the other. Lumpy burlap sacks on the beds had the old familiar straw poking through. A narrow door on one of the walls opened into a tiny room furnished with one bed and a black iron stove.

"Welcome home!" Mutti said moving through the room with her face as bright as the day itself. "What do you children think about our new home?"

"We like it. We like it," everyone agreed.

"May I go and play now?" Dieter asked, visibly bored by everyone's admiring our new home for so long.

"Yes, Son, you may go, but stay close to the house. We don't know anything about the area, so don't leave the yard."

"I won't. I won't," he said while making a dash toward the door. Mutti unpacked some of the bundles before the rest of us also set out to explore our surroundings.

Straight across the hall from our rooms, we saw the public bathrooms: three flush toilets, five sinks with cold running water, no tubs or showers. Downstairs in the big, dingy communal kitchen stood a large, scrubbed metal coal- and woodstove. Pots and pans were nowhere in sight. In the sprawling yard, two huge walnut and linden trees offered a lot of shade. A row of small sheds bordered part of the backyard. "I think you will all be able to find playmates here," Mutti told us when glancing at the large group of playing and running children. "There are several little boys your age," she told Udo while pointing them out.

Yes, this seemed like quite a nice place, much better than Berlin. Our home did not look like our beautiful place in Insterburg with Persian carpets and custom-made furniture. It was still a camp, a holding place for refugees, but it was better than the Churchill Camp which teemed with people. Our meals had to be picked up from the soup kitchen at the main camp. None of us, however, seemed to mind that forty-five-minute walk along the river and through town.

"Now we can again peacefully have our devotions and song time," Mutti said in the evening. "Things have been so distracting lately."

"Please, Jesus, bring my Vati back home to me soon," Marlies prayed. "I just don't know him anymore." For years now, we had prayed for Vati and recited our poems. Would he ever come? When would God answer our prayers?

"Emmy," Onkel Emil said joyously on the first evening in the Anchor, "close your eyes and open both hands. I have something for you." With all of us watching closely, he placed something from his cupped hands into hers. "Here you are. We outsmarted the enemies and the camp thieves for one and a half years."

"My wedding band! My stone-set ring, my watch! Thank you, Emil! Thank you for having carried these for me in your leg, literally, each step of the way." And they both started laughing heartily as we children

admired Mutti's treasures. It was great to see Mutti's beauty magnified by a smile.

"And here are all the children's birth certificates and some of your other documents. My leg is so much lighter now. I might just fall over from the missing weight. Can you believe, Emmy, that no one ever considered my wooden leg a hiding place? I think the Lord robbed our enemies of their reasoning power."

"You are probably right, Emil," Mutti replied while excitedly slipping the rings on her fingers. "I think I know what I will do with this stone ring, Emil. I will trade it for some food for us. I don't know how I will go about that, but the Lord will show me."

The following day Mutti asked me to accompany her to get dishes. We had to have something from which to eat our soup after picking it up in the borrowed milk can. "Where are we going to get dishes, Mutti?" I asked.

"At the British garbage dump on the other side of town. I talked to some of the women here today and that is where they got theirs."

While Onkel Emil babysat, Mutti and I headed for the dump. Upon arriving there, we realized that we were not the only scavengers. Other women and children scrounged for treasures as well. "I don't see any dishes here, Mutti."

"Now, Schäfle, you didn't really think we would find china here at the dump, did you? We are looking for a few metal tin cans, one for each of us, and one big one to cook in."

As I saw Mutti reaching for a can with a half dangling pea soup label, my mind raced back to Insterburg and our gorgeous gold-rimmed Bavarian china. It sparkled in our china cabinet alongside crystal bowls and stemware. Mutti's table was always so elegantly set. Her hand-embroidered table linens—made by her as a young girl—always brought comments of admiration. And now we had to eat and drink

from a tin can? I wondered how Mutti really felt while stooping and poking through tons of trash to find enough cans for all of us.

"Oops, oh no!" she suddenly called out. "Come here, Schäfle, come. I lost my stone ring." Quickly I stumbled over garbage piles to reach her and help her find the ring, but it was lost—lost forever. Gone was also the extra food supply Mutti had dreamed about. "Let's go home," she announced disappointedly. "At least we found one can for each of us. Someday soon we will have to return and search for a cooking pot. I can't find one today."

Dieter's legs continued to bleed and seep. "Lack of vitamins," Mutti was again told at the camp's hospital. In spite of his suffering, Dieter and I daily made the trip to the Churchill Camp to get our rations. At first our long walk seemed exciting, but soon it became rather boring. By the time we returned home, the soup was always cold and had to be eaten cold. We had no way to warm it up. The small bread allotment we received was never enough to satisfy our hunger.

After several weeks of camp food, Mutti was able to get ration cards for us. She also received child support from the government with which to purchase food. Joyfully she set out for the first time in eighteen months to shop at a German bakery. "When I arrived at the first store," she told us in the evening, "they had no bread. The second store didn't either. I found nothing but empty bread shelves all over town."

"Did you get bread today, Mutti?" Udo asked when bursting into the room.

"No, Son, I didn't. From quite a distance," Mutti continued, "I saw a long queue at the bakery. I placed myself at the end of the line and waited for the store to open. Finally, I noticed that the human line was moving a little. The store must have opened, I figured. After about two and a half hours of waiting, I had at last entered the crowded shop. I could not wait to reach the counter and buy a loaf for you children. Suddenly shocking words rang out from behind the counter, 'We are all

out of bread for today! Come back tomorrow!' One lady who managed to get one of the last loaves whispered to me, 'You have to come earlier.' And this, children, is how my day went."

On the following morning, Mutti set out for the bakery at 5:30 a.m. and was successful in getting one ration of bread. The somewhat gritty and yellowish bread was something new to the German palate. It was wheat bread, the baker told Mutti, mixed with cornmeal, a gift from America.

America! America! Every time I heard the word it sounded like heaven, a far distant land across the ocean to which the average person could never go. People were different there and so was nature. Vati's sister had emigrated to America in 1921 and, before the war, visited Germany every few years. I considered her room at my grandparents' in Insterburg a shrine, which was always off limits for us children. We could play in every room of our grandparents' home but Tante Martha's. At times, however, my sweet Omi did give me a special tour of the "shrine." I gazed at all the quaint things: painted wooden boxes, a Japanese tea set, Persian carpet, fancy clothes in the armoire, lacy things, perfumes. The atmosphere in the room was definitely foreign. Tante Martha's style of clothing always differed from those in Germany whenever she visited. In her letters, she talked about a place called Florida, where it was warm year-round. Postcards depicted straight-growing palm trees, pink buildings, beaches, and oceans. America was a country inhabited by special people and visited only by the rich. Even though it was off limits for me, I often dreamed about that distant land and, along with Mutti, wondered why we had not heard from Tante Martha in more than two years.

Mutti often expressed her concern about the whereabouts of all our loved ones. Where was our sweet Omi? Did she and Vati's sister-in-law survive having been chased out of our town by the Russians? How was Onkel Emil's wife and daughter, Mutti's sister and family, her brother

and family, and most of all, Vati? We hadn't heard from anyone. Was that what war was all about—leaders fighting, families losing each other, sacrificing their homes, suffering and dying? Would it not have been easier to just kill all the leaders or let them fight among themselves? Many times my heart was silently bleeding when remembering all our wonderful relatives, but I could not express my thoughts to Mutti; she was bearing burdens much greater.

Mutti again returned from the Red Cross one day, but this time she could hardly contain herself. "I have Vati's address now!—Vati's address! Children, come and see!" We all looked at the small piece of paper in her hand. "We will all write to Vati. This afternoon I have to go and buy some paper."

"Will he tell us when he is coming?" Marlies asked. "I want to see him and hug him."

"I don't know what he will tell us, Pittimaus. But we can tell him that we are all alive and waiting for him. Oh, thank You, Lord, for answering our prayers.

"Tonight we will recite our poems, children. We have to be ready for his homecoming. How wonderful that will be. We will be a complete family again."

After our noon meal, Mutti left me in charge of my brothers and sister and started out for town to purchase stationery. Returning in tears several hours later, she was very quiet. "What is the matter, Emmy?" Onkel Emil asked.

"Nobody would sell me even one sheet of paper. I went to five different stores. Some sales clerks even laughed at me. 'Paper? She wants paper!'" Mutti continued to weep. "I finally have my husband's address but can't write to him; I do not have a piece of paper. Isn't that ironic?"

Our family devotions that night seemed sad. Mutti continued to weep. "Lord, please help Emmy find a piece of paper somewhere, so that she can write to her husband," Onkel Emil pleaded. "She has to let him

know where she and the children are." After reading again from Psalm 91:1, "He that dwelleth in the secret place of the most High shall abide under the shadow of the Almighty," Onkel Emil and Mutti sang the choir number of that passage. In Insterburg, a hush always fell upon the congregation when the sixty-member choir sang that powerful psalm. The vibrations and majestic sounds of the huge pipe organ—one of the largest in Europe—made me feel as if I were really in God's presence. This evening, singing the psalm had a calming effect on Mutti.

"We'll start with your homecoming poem tonight, my little daughter," Mutti said. "Place yourself there at the door. That is the same door Vati will come through someday very soon." Marlies slid from the wooden chair, planted herself in front of the door, and curtsied so fast that her blond curls bounced off her shoulders:

"Vati, O Vati, I love you today.
Will you stay home so that we can play?
I waited so-o-o-o long to see your face
And know that it is only God's grace
That we can all be together again
And with you love Jesus and not be afraid.
I am so glad you are at our house.
I love you, Vati. Your little Pittimaus."

With each additional poem from the four of us, Mutti grew more joyous. "Can you children imagine how wonderful it will be when Vati returns?"

"I hope it will be soon," Udo chimed, "soon, soon, soon. What does he look like, Mutti?"

"Well, Son, I think he looks a little bit like you."

"What do I look like?"

"Well, that is a very good question. Now, let me see. Your hair is blond and straight, you have a cute nose and hazel eyes. Someday when we have a mirror, I'll let you look at yourself."

Often during the past six months, I had wondered what I looked like. I had short blond braids that seemed to have stopped growing; I would be a teenager soon. Had I perhaps become a little better looking? In comparison to my brothers and sister, I always felt like an ugly duckling.

4

Survival Campaign

"I heard you folks are Christians," a gentleman approached us while holding on to the handlebar of his bicycle.

"Yes, we are," Mutti and Onkel Emil said almost in unison.

"I am Pastor Zinser. I am planning to start a church of true believers here in Nienburg."

"Glad to meet you. I am Emmy Guddat, and this is my daughter, Liane. My other three children are down there swimming in the river."

"And I am Emil Schmidtke, formerly of Insterburg, East Prussia. I have known Emmy and her husband for many years. We attended the same church in Insterburg. We live in the Golden Anchor now and are awaiting our life's partners soon, Lord willing."

Having chatted for some time about families, the war, and hopes for the future, the pastor continued, "You know that Nienburg has a very beautiful church, right over there, across the river; but, unfortunately, few people of that congregation are true believers in the Lord Jesus. Most of them just practice their religion without ever having experienced a personal relationship with Christ. Like most people who call themselves Christians, they think going to church and doing good deeds will get

them to heaven. They are not aware of the fact that forgiveness for sin and heaven are offered only through Christ's sacrifice on the cross.

"Those of that church, about eighty of them, who do believe the Bible, have their own little meeting hall because they are not allowed to worship in their church. The pastor of that group has been very cordial and he is willing to share his small meeting place with us."

"That sounds absolutely wonderful," Onkel Emil replied. "We have already searched for Bible-believing Christians but found none."

"This is the time when hearts are tender and searching for the meaning of life," the pastor continued. "As believers we have the answer, and we must give it to the lost."

"When will you have your first service?" Mutti inquired.

"We are planning to hold our first service at 9:30 a.m. this coming Sunday." After talking for some time about various topics, the pastor prayed and left.

On sunny, warm afternoons, we all went to our favorite spot at the Weser, a bend in the river with a white sand bar about twenty yards long. We enjoyed swimming, playing, and watching the barges pull their cargo either downstream or upstream. So heavily loaded were some of the vessels that only about a foot or two of the hulls were visible. Laundry often fluttered on clotheslines, while women and children scrubbed decks and dogs ran from one end of the boat to the other, barking at us on the shore.

High on the riverbank, opposite our swimming area, towered the beautiful Weser Castle, a hotel for British officers. The large bay windows offered guests a scenic view of the river and rolling pastures on the opposite side. To the right of the castle, we could see a small river spilling its water like a waterfall into the Weser; next to that, open fields sprawled as far as the eye could behold.

"Dieter and Liane," Mutti said one day, "your efforts in gathering firewood for our meals have been great. But now that cold weather is

beginning to set in, we need more wood than ever. What I am asking now is that you two get up earlier yet and comb through the neighborhood for fallen branches."

"But, Mutti," Dieter pleaded, "we can't ever get up early enough. There is always somebody from the camp here who beats us to the sticks."

"I know, Son, I know, but please try."

"We will."

Combing through the fields daily, Dieter and I crawled under hedgerows, into ditches, and under trees in search of firewood.

"Look what I found, Mutti, right here in the yard, under that large tree," Dieter said excitedly one morning. "I found nuts."

"These are walnuts, Dieter. How wonderful! Are there any more?"

"Yes, they are coming down today. It is very windy. And when you throw rocks at them on the tree, you can get some down too." Quickly we all dashed outside to gather walnuts—"a gift from God," as Mutti said. No one else from the camp must have known about the nuts that had begun to fall; we were the only ones gathering them. Later, in our room, we cracked them on the floor with the heels of our shoes and feasted on nuts we had not seen since East Prussia.

"Schäfle, you and I will go to the farmers in the next village today and buy food," Mutti announced one morning. "Now that we have some money, we will buy what we need."

"All right, Mutti." A short time later, we set out for the small village of Lemke. It was fall and the potato harvest had begun. What did potatoes really taste like, I wondered; we hadn't eaten any in such a long time. When walking briskly in step next to Mutti, singing and humming duets, the distant village almost seemed to move toward us. Soon we would be there.

Dotted with bright yellow trees, the village would have been an artist's delight on this sunny day. Neat and clean farmyards and sandy, raked paths spoke of the residents' pride in their livelihood and

community. Even the quietly waddling ducks and geese reflected the peaceful setting of the village.

Suddenly, as we passed a fence, a large dog appeared, jumping up and down and barking at us so viciously that Mutti and I jumped sideways in fear.

"Well," Mutti said stunned, "we surely can't enter this courtyard. That ferocious dog will mangle us. Let's go to the next farm." There we found a shepherd dog tied near the front gate and decided to pass too. The third farm looked picture-perfect—lace curtains hung behind sparkling windows while red and yellow dahlias added a splash of color to the stately linden trees in the yard. Since there was no dog in sight, we walked through the large gate toward the house.

Mutti knocked on the front door. A heavy-set lady opened it. "May we buy some potatoes from you?" Mutti asked.

"No! No potatoes here for refugees! We don't have enough to eat ourselves. Get off my property! Get off!"

Having wished her a good day, we left.

"How do you plan to pay for your potatoes?" another farmer's wife asked us. "We don't want money. Do you have silver, gold, or coffee?"

"No," Mutti replied. "We have nothing. We are refugees."

"Ja, ja. I hear that every day. We are refugees. We are refugees. Everybody says that. Why don't you just go back where you came from and leave us alone? All you do is bum around our village and beg. We just don't have peace here anymore. You refugees are a real pest—a real pest. Get out of here now! Go, go, go!"

Shocked and in tears, we left the yard. "Lord, help. I need some food for my children," Mutti said to her heavenly Father.

Another farmer's wife picked apples from a heavily laden tree. Her apron, gathered by the hem with one hand, was filled with the red-cheeked fruit. Nearby, pigs foraged under an apple tree, pushing rotten apples around with their snouts. "You can go and get some of

those apples there," she said pointing at the tree under which the pigs played and snorted.

Mutti suddenly raised her head a little higher. "What your pigs won't eat, we will not eat either," she said in disgust, taking me by the hand and walking off.

"Excuse me, please," Mutti said to the lady at another farm. "May we please buy something to eat from you?"

"No! I have nothing to sell. I can tell you are refugees. Look at you—begging for food. Is that all you can do? No, I have nothing to sell you. Nothing."

"I am not asking you to give us something. I will pay you. I have money."

"I don't need your money, and besides, we barely have enough to eat ourselves."

"But could you perhaps sell us some apples? I have four children—my husband is a prisoner of war. We don't have enough to eat. Please help us."

"Just get out of my sight, or—," the woman yelled and let out a whistle. Instantly a huge dog on a running chain started racing toward us. "I will teach you refugees not to come and beg!"

After several more attempts at buying something edible and getting a negative answer each time, Mutti and I began the long walk home in silence. None of the women we had met seemed undernourished. Their pantries and basements were probably filled with canned goods, smoked meats, and sausages just as those of my grandparents always were. Would my dear Omi and Opi have chased away hungry people? I didn't think so. Often, during harvest time, hungry prisoners worked on their farm and were always treated kindly. The prisoners ate the same food we ate and enjoyed the same privileges as the regular farm hands. Several prisoners returned to the farm after having been released from jail and begged to work for my grandparents.

My parents, I reasoned, would have shared food with others also. Mutti always did when we lived under the Russian occupation. But why did the West German farmers' wives hide their full basements behind vicious dogs? Was it because they had not experienced war the same way millions of other Germans had? Their farms continued to slumber among rolling hills and fertile fields as they always had, even at the time of their parents and grandparents. Bible verses carved into beams still graced most of the farmhouse entrances. The paint on "Anno Domini" (the year of our Lord) 1600 or 1700 and the verses usually gleamed in white. Had the present owners perhaps forgotten the Lord to whom their forefathers dedicated their lands and whose blessings they invoked?

"Mutti, look!" I called out while pointing at a huge horse-drawn wagon filled with potatoes just passing us as we walked home empty-handed.

"If only we could take a bag of those potatoes home," Mutti responded, "our stomachs would be filled." The team of white horses pulled the wagon past us rather quickly. But then we saw something only God could have done especially for us. One potato fell off the wagon and rolled into the road. I stooped, picked it up, and put it in our bag. "Thank You, Lord," Mutti said, continuing to walk briskly toward Nienburg. Several minutes later, another potato rolled off, then another, and another. Our bag began to feel heavy as we picked up every single potato until our bag was full. Suddenly the Lord closed the valve on the potato blessing; no more rolled into the road, and we had only about a mile of walking left before reaching our camp.

Joyfully we lugged the miracle gift upstairs and stepped into our room. Onkel Emil glanced at the potatoes and thundered, "Is that all you bought from the farmers? You didn't buy any bacon or sausage? What is the matter with you two? I was looking forward to some real food." While tears welled up in Mutti's eyes, she said nothing. Neither did I.

From a lady in our communal kitchen, we learned that the government had found a way to help supplement the meager food rations; one pound of margarine would be exchanged for ten pounds of beechnuts. "Beechnuts? Where can one find so many beechnuts?" Mutti asked.

"In the Crow Forest."

"I have no idea where that is."

"Well," the lady continued, "you cross the Weser, walk through town and out into the country until you see the woods called 'Crow.' It is only about one and a half hours from here. I was there yesterday and gathered about five pounds of beechnuts."

"But they are so small. It must take a long time to gather five pounds."

"It surely did. But we do a lot to get a little fat for our bodies, don't we, Frau Guddat?"

"That is right."

Early the next day, Mutti and I set out for the Crow Forest. A cold wind blew, pulling the last leaves off the elm trees along the river. Winter's chill was in the air. What would winter in West Germany be like? Would it be as cold as it was in East Prussia? Would there be much snow? I knew we wouldn't be traveling to town in a horse-drawn sleigh as we did at my grandparents' home. Would we be playing in huge snow drifts?

Mutti and I walked and walked, it seemed for hours, before finally reaching the forest. But where were the beechnut trees? Stomping around and ducking under evergreens and oaks on damp, slippery, decaying leaves, we finally spotted some slender trees. "Those, over there, are beechnut trees," Mutti said while walking toward them. "Look at this beechnut leaf, Schäfle. It is oval with almost straight veins and serrated edges. If you know leaves well, you can always identify a tree. Sometimes you can recognize a tree by its trunk and bark, but it is a good idea to study the shapes and sizes of leaves too."

Looking up into the tall trees, we saw prickly open capsules. The seeds had already been offered to the earth for seedlings, food for wildlife,

and now for humans. "This should be a good tree to start gathering our margarine," Mutti said. While squatting, we began to push aside the leaves with our bare hands to expose the forest floor and slimy earthworms. There, right from the start of our new venture, we found the little three-sided beechnuts. Wormy nuts, those which had a small hole and were lightweight, had to remain on the ground.

"How many, Mutti, do you think it will take to make up a pound?" I asked.

"I have no idea, Schäfle. Since they are only about the size of an adult's small fingernail, I think it'll take quite a few."

Dragging damp leaves along with the bottoms of our coats, we waddled and dropped the little nuts into our pea cans. It would take a long time to fill one can with nuts because our hands became clammy and stiff from the moisture and cold temperature. In order to forget all the obstacles we had to overcome, Mutti and I decided to race against each other in filling our cans. When we had finished gathering under one tree, we dashed to another. Other margarine gatherers were also rearranging the forest floor. After a while, we had worked our way up to a fence. Printed on a metal sign we read, Danger! Explosives!

"But, Mutti, look at this tree here and the fat beechnuts. Half of the tree is on the other side of the fence, though."

"Yes, Schäfle, do you remember the lady telling us that all the wartime barracks over there are surrounded by minefields? We can't go in there!" I obeyed Mutti even though I knew I could beat her at our game if only I could crawl under the fence.

By the end of a cold and long day, we arrived at home with what Mutti guessed to be about seven or eight pounds of nuts. With our fingernails, we shelled quite a few of the oily, hairy nuts and ate them. Their bitter taste reminded me of apple seeds.

As the days began to shorten, Mutti and I went to the woods almost daily while Onkel Emil babysat. More and more people had become

aware of the margarine program and headed to the forests to gather little seeds most of them couldn't even identify before the war. With the increase of gatherers, it became more difficult to find good trees under which to harvest beechnuts. Rummaging through wet and frosty leaves also presented a big problem. Mutti and I tried to get warm by doing jumping jacks every now and then, or tucking our hands behind our closed knee joints or under armpits. It was impossible to gather nuts with stiff and frozen fingers.

"I know how to get my hands warm," an old crouching nut-gathering woman nearby said as she detected our struggle to warm up. "Just let your warm urine run over your hands. That feels so-o-o good."

Mutti and I continued to blow on our hands, with neither one of us commenting about what we had just heard. For a long time, however, I could not get the old lady out of my mind, and I wondered about her background.

Only occasionally did we hear explosions in the woods, and with the increasing number of people searching for beechnuts, Mutti and I became continuously bolder. We both began to disregard the fences and posted danger signs and daily gathered nuts in the danger zones and close to the barracks. At the end of our beechnut campaign, we had gathered ninety-nine pounds of the little seeds and received a credit slip for almost ten pounds of margarine. All our friends in the camp heard about our harvest and were astonished. No one was able to match our accomplishment.

5

American Aid

In Mutti's absence, Onkel Emil often became ill-tempered and spanked my brothers and sister. Dieter, unfortunately, got most of the spankings. "Why did you bring so few cigarette butts home today?" he yelled at us. "Why? Why? I have to smoke. The weather is changing and my wounded leg hurts. I have to smoke. You kids go and find me something to smoke. The rose leaves are all gone."

Trembling, Dieter and I returned to town. Anytime we saw a British soldier smoking, we stayed close by or walked behind him until he threw his cigarette butt into the gutter. Sometimes several kids would watch the same soldier and fight for the same butt. Hour after hour we followed smoking soldiers. We knew their every hangout in town. But no matter how many of those ugly discards we brought home in the course of a day, it was never enough.

Recycling cigarette butts was a tedious job, yet one which Onkel Emil enjoyed. Sitting at the table, he carefully opened every butt and scraped out each tiny shred of tobacco. As soon as a small mound had accumulated on a strip of precious old newspaper, he built a little mountain range the length of the paper. With both thumbs and

forefingers, he then began to fold one long edge of the paper over the tobacco. After his moist tongue had slithered along the other edge of the paper, he folded it over, and his saliva seal was completed. While holding his cigarette with both thumbs and forefingers, Onkel Emil would smoke and feel content.

On our half-hour walk to church on Sundays, Onkel Emil was always in a good mood. Gone were the worries about his wife from whom he hadn't heard in two years. At church, his concert tenor voice joyfully sang praises to the Lord. Finally the church attendance had grown to the extent that enough believers could be recruited to start a choir. Onkel Emil, of course, became the choir director, a position he had held in our Insterburg church. Singing without music books, however, was not easy. Everything had to be sung from memory, but with much practice, our acapella choir blessed the hearts of the congregants and enhanced the worship services. Oftentimes our choir sang in the city park where people gathered to listen. After the concert, we told them about our church and invited them to the services.

Sunday school for children was always held after the morning service. Many songs were sung each Lord's Day and subconsciously committed to memory. A Bible story highlighted the hour. At the end of the meeting, our teacher always encouraged us to invite our friends for the following Sunday.

In our camp, I occasionally met a girl about my age with blond, braided hair. She seemed very shy and never played with the other children. Every time I saw her and attempted to invite her, she would slip into her room right next to the large front entrance and close the door. One day, however, I became bold and knocked on the door of her room. When she answered, I invited her to Sunday school. She told me she would have to ask her parents. They did not permit her, a Lutheran, to go to "this group." Some months later, after I had become better acquainted with her, her parents did allow Hildegard to go with

me. Our friendship grew quickly and I, for the first time in several years, had a girlfriend.

"Tante Martha Borrmann!" Mutti exclaimed one day in shock when opening our door. "Where did you come from? How did you find us? Come on in."

Nobody could believe that Tante Martha from Memel, the northernmost tip of East Prussia, at the Lithuanian border, was standing in our room. She was my grandmother's sister. Every year we had spent part of our summer vacation with her. We children loved her cozy home and the clean cobblestone courtyard. Daily Tante Martha took us by ferry across the bay to the Baltic Sea. There we walked across sand dunes and under tall pines toward the ocean. Sometimes we strung a hammock between two of the long-needled trees and played or rested before climbing down the huge white dunes to the water. Scanning the beach from the top of the dunes, we often saw moose bathing in the water of our favorite vacation spot. One time Tante Martha was awakened from her nap in the hammock by some kind of noise. When she opened her eyes, she saw a moose looking down on her. Petrified with fear, she couldn't move and was so glad that after a few moments the majestic animal turned and walked away.

At the Baltic Sea, Dieter and I always filled our buckets with amber pieces which had washed ashore or fallen through the huge nets used by the amber fishermen. We were never very interested in the seashells, but the amber stones fascinated us. In Tante Martha's courtyard, we emptied our buckets and played for hours with the golden yellow, light brown, dark brown, or marbleized pieces of amber. Some had been highly polished by the constant movement of the waves and sand; others had dull surfaces. Dieter and I always competed for the largest chunks of amber (petrified resin) brought to the shore by white-capped waves near the East Prussian amber mines.

"Well, Emmy," Mutti's aunt replied, "it is a long story as to how I got here. But I can tell you that I found you through the Red Cross. You and the children are the only relatives from East Prussia who are listed. Do you have any idea what happened to your parents and all the others?"

"No, Martha, I just know that your sister, Mietze, lives in Berlin."

"Oh, she does? How do you know that?"

"Well, we lived in a refugee camp in Berlin for three months, and it was from there we searched for her and found her. When we went to visit Mietze in her bomb-torn house, she told us that her husband was shot by Russian soldiers just one day before the war ended."

Tante Martha's face had changed terribly since we last saw her. All through the center of her forehead, she had a wide red scar. Her face had become slender and her hair gray.

"I left East Prussia across the Baltic Sea by ship," my aunt continued, "and landed in Denmark. Somewhere on the ship, I fell and broke my skull. The doctor said it is a miracle that I am alive. I still feel quite ill at times, but the Lord has been good to me and seen me through all my suffering. Perhaps He wants me to be alive at His coming rather than dead. I believe the Lord's coming is near, and I am anxiously awaiting the trumpet call. With all the suffering and starvation in our land, I wish He would come quickly and take us home. I am tired of all my wanderings."

"Yes," Mutti agreed, "I am also anxiously looking for His return. It is difficult for me to raise the children without Emil. One thing, however, I do know, God is in control of everything. If He wants to take us up in the air to be with Him, that will be fine; if He wants us to be reunited as a family, I will be happy also. In the meantime, I am praying that one or the other will happen soon."

Since Tante Martha had no place to live, she moved in with us and babysat when Mutti and I went on our begging trips. In the evenings, Mutti and her unmarried aunt spent many hours reminiscing. They

talked about Mutti's years of dressmaking and tailoring school. They chatted about relatives, weddings, funerals, and church activities. Their greatest concerns, however, were voiced about not knowing the fate of all the loved ones. Three months after Tante Martha had come to us, she moved into a small room in the center of town offered to her by the housing authorities.

One day, finally, Mutti managed to purchase a piece of paper on which to write a letter to Vati. Each one of us added a short message before the letter was sealed and sent on its way to Africa. With the unusual excitement brought on by a few prisoners returning home, our homecoming celebration practices increased drastically. "We have to be ready and pray for Vati's speedy return," Mutti instructed us almost daily.

Edith came to visit us at the camp one day and handed Mutti a brown blanket. "This is for your children, Emmy. I think Liane needs a warm winter coat."

"Thank you, Edith. I surely do appreciate your concern for us." Mutti borrowed scissors from someone and set out to make a hand-sewn coat for me.

Our straw sacks, infested with bed bugs since our arrival at the Anchor, continued to be breeding grounds for the small pests. Even though we searched for the hungry bugs daily, collected and killed them, they continued to multiply. Standing at our small washbowl for morning cleanup, without soap, of course, Mutti could always detect fresh red bites on our bodies.

One day it was announced that each burlap sack which was brought outside would be filled with new straw. We dragged all our "mattresses" outdoors and in the evening fell asleep instantly on the fresh-smelling straw.

"Here is an airmail letter for you from America," the mailman told Mutti.

"Airmail? From America?" Mutti questioned while hastily glancing at the envelope. "It is from Tante Martha in America," she announced. Those of us who were at home crowded around Mutti to see the first airmail letter we had received at the camp. The airplane on the green stamp made my spirits soar to that faraway land. America! Americans bombed us; now they were feeding us. They were our enemies; now they say they are our friends. It didn't make sense. Americans were kinder than the Russians, everyone said. They did not rape women, young and old, and little girls. What made these two conquerors so different?

After having opened the letter, Mutti learned that Tante Martha, Vati's sister, had found us through the Red Cross. Several food packages were on the way for us, she wrote, and should arrive in Germany within the next few weeks. About four weeks later, the mailman brought a white package receipt which he said we should present to the customs office in town in order to get our parcel.

With Mutti holding the oblong package tag, our whole family stood in line waiting for our turn at the customs office. All those ahead of us had to open their packages which were then carefully searched by customs agents. Receiving more than one pound of coffee per box was against the law and resulted in high duty payments. When the search of our large gift box began, we all watched curiously. There were noodles, flour, coffee, sugar, and some grainy white powder. Everyone anxiously offered to help carry the heavy package home. Before unpacking our treasures, however, Mutti told all of us to sing our song of thanksgiving:

Thank the Lord with joyful heart,
He is gracious, He is good.
His great grace does weaken never,
It endures forever and ever.
(Jorissen, "Dankt dem Herrn mit frohem Mut")

Mutti immediately took our ham can cooking pot and sticks to the kitchen and prepared the noodles for dinner. What a feast that was! The white grainy powder, however, was a food Mutti could not identify. Since it did taste sweet, she made a spread for our bread with it by stirring a little water into it. All of us loved the delicious miracle paste, and we could have eaten it every day. Unfortunately, Mutti saved it to be eaten only for Sunday-morning breakfasts.

"I don't think the farmers' wives will reject our offer today," Mutti smirked while gently swinging her bag. "I have the feeling we will be able to trade almost anything today for meat. Unfortunately, we don't know how much trading power this coffee has. But since all Germans are drinking toasted barley now and real coffee is only an aromatic memory of the past, we should have a good chance of getting enough food to fill all our stomachs."

Almost every farmhouse was guarded by vicious dogs now. "You refugees, leave us alone! Don't bother us! You are scum! You are pests!" one woman yelled.

"But I have American coffee," Mutti hollered across the leafless hedge at the woman feeding chickens.

"You have what?"

"I have coffee," Mutti shouted while beginning to walk away.

Suddenly the woman's face lit up. She quickly tried to calm her yelping dog. "Let me see that coffee!" she bellowed while trying to control her beast. Mutti raised the shiny can. "All right, I'll trade that for something. What do you want?"

"I would like potatoes and sausage," Mutti replied.

"I'll give you a bag of potatoes but no sausage."

"Sorry," Mutti said and started walking again.

"No, no, no! Come here. I'll give you what you want. You wait here," she said and bounced into the house. Within a few minutes, she

returned and grudgingly poured potatoes from a basket into Mutti's bag and gave us a large piece of sausage.

"I'll take coffee again anytime," she said hastily.

Joyous and thankful, we started our long walk home. Would Onkel Emil be happy today?

Several weeks after our first package from America, another one arrived. It contained all types of food, odds and ends of yarn, knitting needles, coffee, and the strange white powder. I immediately claimed the knitting needles and started knitting a brown pullover for Dieter with a white argyle sailboat border.

"Liane, just look at all the wood down there on the ice," Dieter said one day while pointing at chunks of new wood shavings on the river. "We should go and get that."

"But, Dieter, don't you see that huge, open water hole and the fast current? That is the middle of the river where the Weser is deepest and does not freeze. Why do you think that wood it still there when everyone needs firewood?"

"You mean it is too dangerous to go and get it?"

"Yes, of course! The wood fell down there when the huge icebreakers were repaired."

"What are icebreakers anyway?"

"Icebreakers, Mutti told me, protect a bridge from the immense chunks of ice that will float downstream in the spring. The thick metal caps that are facing upstream are to cut the ice into smaller pieces. Anyway, little brother, somebody would have already taken those beautiful chunks of firewood if it were not so dangerous. If we get too close to the open hole where the ice is thin, we could break in and slip under it, never to be seen again."

"But wouldn't Mutti be happy if we brought all that wood home?"

Dieter had said the magic words—Mutti's happiness. Instantly my resistance vanished. On the other side of the bridge, we skidded on the

snowy grass down the riverbank and carefully stepped onto the ice. Cars and trucks rumbled across the gently swaying bridge above us. One step at a time, we edged toward the hole and the swirling current. We were almost there, halfway across the river.

"No, Dieter, let's go back! It is too dangerous!"

"I already got a piece," Dieter rejoiced. I began reaching for one also, and another, and another.

"Dieter, be careful!" I called while my heart was racing. "You are too close. Don't get that large piece. You'll fall in and die."

"I have to get it," he said and reached for it, almost touching the water. "I got it! I got it!"

Looking at the swirling water and realizing the danger, I suddenly felt dizzy. "We have to go, Dieter. We have to go. If we slide under the ice, nobody will ever find us. Would Mutti be happy then?" Both of us cautiously moved back from the icy tomb. We filled our arms with the wood harvest and tiptoed off the ice. After slowly crawling up the embankment, we started for home.

"Where did you children get this beautiful firewood?" Mutti asked with a big smile and sparkling eyes.

"Oh, we got that at the bridge. They did some repair work there today," I quickly answered, hoping Dieter would not go into any details of our dangerous mission.

6

The Film

"Every German has to go and see this film," posters all over town suggested. "Germans have to know what really went on during the war." The message of the film seemed urgent, and most of our acquaintances made plans to see it. Even though Mutti was never a movie-goer, she felt that as a German citizen, she had to be informed.

After Mutti and a neighbor had left for the theater, my brothers, sister, and I walked from the Anchor past several farms to the river. From the huge stone base of the bridge, we always had a beautiful view upstream and downstream. "If only this bridge had not been destroyed," I told everyone, "we'd be in downtown Nienburg in two minutes. Now we have to walk about forty minutes across the new bridge and along the moat to reach the opposite base."

"Who destroyed this bridge?"

"I don't know, Dieter. It was probably one of our enemies. I am sure we'll find out someday."

Shortly after we had returned home from our outing, Mutti entered the room with her eyes red and face ashen. We all wanted to talk to her about the film she had just seen, but she seemed to be in another world,

a world for which she had shed tears. She avoided answering Onkel Emil's questions as well as ours. Mutti appeared lifeless, yet living; hurt, yet without visible wounds.

"Mutti, what is the matter?" Udo asked. She remained silent, and with tears gently dampening her beautiful face, hugged him. Everyone went quietly to bed that night.

Never had I seen Mutti in such despair. For days she somberly went about her business. What could have happened at the theater that crushed her spirit? Would we ever find out? Would she ever be herself again? I did not like the new dreary and sad Mutti.

Then finally, one day when the spring thaw set in and the ice on the river began to break up and move downstream, Mutti's cold and sad heart seemed to warm up a little. Her spirits began to unfold like a dainty, white snowdrop flower. She started sharing with us the sadness of her heart and the burden she had chosen silently to bear. She began talking about the film of the Holocaust. She talked about Hitler's atrocities, the gruesome pictures, starving people, gas chambers, experiments performed by Nazi doctors on God's chosen people. I listened in horror while my whole body seemed to turn to ice. My thoughts groped for some sense. Adolf Hitler, whom I had seen myself from our large living room window when he visited Insterburg? Hitler, to whom thousands of Germans, young and old, sang songs and gave allegiance, killed so many Jewish people? Hitler, who said he loved his people? Why did not decent Germans do something about it? "Only very few knew, those living close to the camps," Mutti said. "The SS carried out Hitler's orders. Some camps were on Polish soil. German pastors were also among the dead, gypsies, and those against the regime. We know now that one of our friends was shot because he refused to kill Jews."

As a youngster, I always saw Jewish people wearing the yellow star of David on their coats. "They are God's chosen people," my grandparents and parents always used to say. My grandfather purchased supplies for

his leather shop from his Jewish friends, and I often saw them chatting at the store.

"There were Germans against Hitler," Mutti continued, "who tried to assassinate him several times. Even in East Prussia an attempt was made on his life a few years ago. That also failed. Looking back today, it seems that the devil himself protected Adolf Hitler so that he could continue to carry out so many evil deeds."

"What about other countries?" I asked. "Could they not have rescued those people?"

"I don't know, Schäfle. There simply seems to be no answers."

One thing I knew, however, I was ashamed of what our leaders had done. I immediately began to feel burdened, burdened by something I did not do and could not explain. My free spirit suddenly became weighted down by lead. Daily, no matter where I went, I felt I was carrying a large package of guilt. My thought life became bewildered, unorganized, at times fearful. I had witnessed death, destruction, rape, and starvation under the Communist regime in Eastern Europe, but none of those seemed to place a load of guilt on my shoulders as the atrocities which I had not seen, events I did not even know had occurred until a short time ago. I did not like this burden. Would I ever in my life be free of it? Would I, a German, ever be able to look at a Jewish person? Or would I have to carry this burden to my grave?

By the time the schools reopened for all the children of Nienburg, Mutti had managed to enroll me in the Lyceum, a girls' school located in the center of town. Even though we had no proof of my having taken and passed the entrance examination for the Lyceum in Insterburg, I was allowed to start. Of the forty-nine girls in my class, many knew each other from elementary school. One group of eight girls were especially close friends. They partied together, discussed their birthday gifts, and always wore pretty dresses, barrettes, and hair ribbons. They carried fancy leather book bags and wrote in white notebooks. I, in turn, had

to write on the backs of used freight sheets which Edith gave me and wear the same two dresses.

Our professors made very certain that we learned what they taught. Tests were never announced ahead of time; daily we had to be prepared to take them. School started at 8:00 a.m. with short outdoor breaks every hour to "fill our lungs with fresh air." Each day at midmorning, every student was given a can of warm soup—a gift from our conquerors. At 1:00 p.m. daily, six days a week, I started my long walk back to the camp to begin many hours of homework.

After several weeks of school, I noticed a girl in my class who never acted silly or giggled like all the other girls. She was always serious, just the way I seemed to feel. In talking to her, I learned that she was also a refugee from East Prussia. She, her parents, and sister lived in a private home, about thirty kilometers from Nienburg. The fact that we both came from the same part of Germany and were refugees quickly bonded us as friends. She was the only student in my class who came to school by bus.

"Do you still remember your poem, my little son?" Mutti asked Udo one morning while we were all sitting at the breakfast table trying to get our oatmeal soup down.

"Yes, Mutti, I do."

"I have the strange feeling that Vati will be coming home this year, and we must be ready for his homecoming."

"I am ready, I am. But I don't like this soup, Mutti," he continued. "Can't I have some of that sweet white stuff on bread?"

"No, Udo, that is just for Sunday mornings. You know that."

"But that is too long to wait."

"Well, you'll just have to wait. Everyone else has to as well."

We all knew that we had to wait, but we all tried to avoid the crushed oat breakfast. That was what Opi fed his horses and chickens on the farm. The hulls scratched our throats. Crushed oat seeds boiled

in water, without sugar, tasted terrible. Sometimes I'd try to swallow the hulls rather than slowly letting my tongue separate them from the kernel and spitting them into the spoon. Finishing our oatmeal breakfast always seemed to take a long time; but since we had nothing else, Mutti insisted on us eating every spoonful.

Our dear Tante Martha in America must have spent countless hours meticulously sewing double layers of muslin around the packages she mailed to us. Apparently, packages wrapped in paper and string could not hold the heavy food items. All the boxes we received, several per week, were sewn into fabric which Mutti used to meet all types of needs, from clothing to towels and bed linens.

Each American package contained, among different kinds of foods and clothing, one pound of coffee. When Mutti and I took the coffee to the farming communities, the farmers' wives who used to chase us with dogs and foul language now welcomed us with open arms, always giving us what we asked for.

"We thank You again," Onkel Emil prayed during our devotions, "for having sent Emmy's sister-in-law to America so many years ago. You sent her there so that she can now feed us and keep us alive. Many Germans are suffering from malnutrition, many are sick and dying, but You, Father, are performing a miracle in front of our eyes every time a package arrives. You feed us heavenly manna. We thank You and thank You again."

In spite of Tante Martha's efforts, the sores on Dieter's legs were still open and seeping, his cheeks hollow, and eyes set back as were Marlies's and Udo's. Dieter's shoes also became too small, and he finally had to go barefoot everywhere, even to school. Mutti wrote to Tante Martha in America asking her to send Dieter a pair if she could. When a brand-new pair arrived two months later, they were too small.

One day Mutti was excited about an idea she had. "When Vati returns," she told us, "we are going to test him. Vati has seen all of you

children when you were bigger already, and he will recognize you. Udo, however, he has seen only as a nine-month-old baby, and now he is almost four years old. There are four other little boys here in the camp Udo's age. When Vati returns, we are going to line them all up and see if Vati can pick out his son. What do you think of that idea?"

"I like it," Dieter chimed. "I like it. But all the boys have blond hair, too. How can he figure out who Udo is?"

"Well, that'll be the fun part. That's what we want to find out." Mutti's planned game sounded exciting. I could hardly wait to see the outcome.

I wondered if Vati would really recognize the rest of us, as Mutti thought, and if we would recognize him. I really hadn't seen that much of him since he was drafted into the army. Would he recognize his thirteen-and-a-half-year-old? "Mutti," I inquired, "how long has Vati been in the army?"

"He was drafted, Schäfle, in September of 1939."

"That long ago?"

"Yes, that long ago. It all happened very fast. Vati and I were waiting on customers in our leather goods store in Insterburg when the Nazi official entered the store and gave him a letter stating that he was drafted into the army. Vati had to report for duty that same afternoon."

"He had to leave that fast?" I asked.

"Yes, that fast. There was time to pack only a few things, pray, and leave."

"But I thought Vati wasn't a Nazi."

"That's right, Schäfle. He still had to go. Vati was glad, though, that he never had to fight at the front. He is such a gentle man and could never have harmed anyone; he can't even kill a fly. Whenever he did catch a housefly, he took it to a window and set it free.

"In the beginning of his service, Vati had to guard prisoners which was emotionally very difficult for him. But when the army had to fill the position of a quartermaster, he volunteered and got the job."

"What did he have to do then?"

"Vati was in charge of supplying food and clothing for seven hundred men and paying their wages. As a businessman, he liked that assignment. 'It was so much better,' he always wrote, 'than confronting an enemy with a weapon in your hand.'

"Vati's position, however, did not keep him out of danger. As he was moving supplies toward the Russian front one day, Russian planes bombed the various supply positions. One bomb fell only about ten feet from the wooden house in which he had his office. Bombs continued to fall all around him, but the Lord protected him. You see, Schäfle, Vati trusted in the Almighty. One of Vati's favorite psalms always was, 'He that dwelleth in the secret place of the most High shall abide under the shadow of the Almighty' (Ps. 91:1). He always loved to sing that too."

"Do you remember, Mutti, how you and the church ladies in Insterburg were making warm clothes for the soldiers? Some of your friends knitted woolen socks for them while I sat and crocheted for my dolls."

"Yes, I remember those meetings very well. Everyone was supporting the soldiers and praying for peace. Unfortunately, the average German did not know what Hitler's plans were, how many nations he would attack, and how much suffering he'd bring upon the whole world."

One day I came home from school and saw someone sitting in our living room. "Tante Mally!" I called out in great surprise while dashing over to hug her. "How are you?"

"I am thankful to be in Germany," she replied somberly.

"My wife is not well, Liane," Onkel Emil said. He sat on a chair close to Tante Mally. "She was forced to work in Russian horse stables for over a year. Her attempt to come to Lippehne and meet me there failed. She

was stopped by the Russians in Pomerania. She had to do hard labor with very little to eat and became very sick. When she became gravely ill and useless to the Russians, they finally let her go. Here she is now," he continued, "her frail body ravished by disease. We had no idea that she was coming." I could tell that Tante Mally was physically broken. The smile I remembered was no longer brightening her slender face; it now looked bloated. Her upper back was stooped low. Her whole body reflected pain and suffering.

Suffering—suffering. My mind raced to Lippehne again to the mother who, in utter despair, pushed her oldest child into the lake first, then her younger ones, and committed suicide herself. I thought about the butcher's wife who hung her children in the smoke chamber and then herself. Communism gave these women no hope for the future. I thought about the year and four months we had suffered under that godless regime without food, news from the outside world, or word from our relatives. There was nothing but death, starvation, murder, and suicide. I thought about Mutti's horrible experiences in the Communist jail, our escape from that hopeless life to a free life in the Berlin refugee camp.

Now we lived where each one of the nine or more million refugees from the East dreamed to be—in West Germany, yet we still didn't seem to be free. No longer did we feel oppressed by the government, but we still felt plagued by hunger, seeping boils, and the camp existence. Except for nightmares, we slept undisturbed on our straw sacks. Our dreams revolved around a full plate of food, Vati's homecoming, and a better future. Mutti, however, always said that "true freedom can be found only in Christ. If one lives close to the Lord, He does not necessarily take away the suffering, but He makes it easier to bear."

People all around us were missing loved ones. The word *Siberia* detached everyone's emotions from anything good and focused thoughts on torture and labor until death. Countless East Prussian mothers, dragged away from their crying children, had been shipped to Siberia

along with young girls snatched away from their families. They were transported as prisoners to the harsh, frozen environment to work in coal mines with little food and inadequate clothing. Only about sixty to seventy percent of these women and girls ever reached Siberia alive, we read.

The few fortunate ones, who somehow managed to return to Germany, talked about the cattle trains on which they were pushed and transported without food or water. Every few days, the doors were opened and the dead thrown into ditches. The elements became the undertakers for someone's loved ones. There were no flowery graves, no marble tombstones with etched names, or bones of relatives resting together in the family plot. Countless Germans herded into destruction left no trail of their existence. Adults vanished, children, and names. Were the living more fortunate than the dead? Many said they were not. Those from the East were looking for fathers and mothers, sons and daughters, grandpas and grandmas, dead or alive.

Miracle stories of reunions caused some to rejoice, and others to become jealous. Why did your husband live and not mine? Why did my baby slip out of my arms and vanish into the icy waters when I fled across the bay toward the Baltic Sea and your children are alive? Why did whole families with horses and wagons crash through the ice into the sea when trying to escape the Russian hordes and bombs? Why did a friend's two-year-old daughter have to die of starvation in Berlin? Why did almost everyone from East Prussia lose homes and possessions while millions in West Germany continued to enjoy the fruits of their labor and their heritage? "Why was my father tortured to death in front of our family, his eyes plucked out, hands hacked off, and then shot?" a friend asked us. Hopelessly people searched for answers while sinking deeper into the pit of despair.

7

The Flood

During our first Christmas celebration in West Germany, we were thankful to God for being able to live in the British zone where we could freely move about and go to church and school. The oppression, however, experienced under the Communist regime, slumbered in our weakened beings as a nightmare. Oftentimes that ugly nightmare would raise its dragon-like head during the quiet and dark hours of the night to bathe my tossing and turning body in cold droplets of fear. The straw sack quickly lapped up the moisture, leaving me cold and shivering in a room in which water froze during the night. Would dreams of the past always torture my undernourished body? Would I have to continue expending energy and lose my emotional well-being to haunting dreams of the past? Why, in my dreams, did my legs always move so slowly when fleeing from the rapist? Why did I, even in broad daylight, still fear that the Polish mayor, whose grasp we escaped, might come and retrieve his escapees? Outwardly at times, I felt free, but inwardly I continued to be a slave to an oppressive government. Outwardly I wanted to giggle and act silly with my classmates, but inwardly I couldn't. Outwardly at age

thirteen, I looked like a child, but inwardly I felt burdened by so many things. "Your daughter is always so serious," people would tell Mutti.

"She has seen a lot," she'd answer, "and gone through a lot. She is too serious. I wish she would laugh sometimes."

While we lived at the Anchor, many tasks had to be performed in order for us to survive. Not only did we have to be concerned about keeping alive through nutrition, but in the winter it was difficult to keep our bodies warm. One way to really warm up was to split wood. The logs allotted to us were piled up in our small backyard shed. After dragging some outdoors, we split them. Onkel Emil did most of the wood splitting, but I worked at it as often as possible. I felt elated when the borrowed ax head yielded to my strength by crackling through the log and laying it open. The thought that the freshly exposed grains, knots, and sap had not ever been looked upon by a human excited me. Splitting kindling gave me an even greater thrill; I enjoyed doing the tedious precision job with the large ax.

When Edith came to visit us at the camp, we often laughed about a certain woodpile story. Logs had been delivered to several families at the camp, including ours. It was impossible, however, to move the heavy, wet logs without first splitting them. But what could be done to ward off thieves? Everyone needed firewood. Onkel Emil got a brilliant idea. "I am going to sleep right next to the pile outside and scare off the robbers." In the evening, he took his cot and bedded down next to our pile of logs.

Edith realized that this was quite a feat for her father who always slept soundly and in his deep slumber used his throat to imitate lumberjacks. "I feel adventurous tonight, Emmy," she said. "Let's go and steal something."

"Edith, I am shocked!" Mutti exclaimed. "We are not thieves."

"But we will be tonight! Come, let's have some fun. We are going to steal wood. We are going to steal from my father."

"Oh," Mutti said, "that is a great idea. I am all for that kind of thievery. Let's give your father a little more time, though, to be sound asleep."

In the darkness of the evening, the two women ventured into the courtyard. Groping their way through the yard, Edith and Mutti realized that their victim was totally surrounded by his own snoring. "This is going to be easy," Edith whispered. Quietly they tried to feel for a skinny log, lifted it, and dragged it upstairs. Then they returned several more times.

"Well, Emil," Mutti asked the next morning, "how was your night out there? Did anyone try to steal anything?"

"Now, Emmy, what kind of question is that? You hurt my feelings by even asking that. I went out there to protect our woodpile, and that I did. Not one piece is missing. All night long no one came to steal."

"Is that so?"

"Yes, that is the way it is. What kind of watchman do you think I am?"

"Well, look here, Emil," Mutti said pointing at the logs next to the stove. "I guess you are not infallible after all." Then she told him the story which was later related many times over, but one that Onkel Emil never liked to hear, the story of having been outsmarted by two women.

The severe winter weather, which gripped all of Germany, imposed great hardships on refugees. For us, however, the frozen river became a saver of time and body energy. We could walk downtown in two minutes by crossing the ice, and with Tante Martha's packages arriving weekly, it was much easier to carry the heavy loads of food home.

One day Mutti again asked Dieter and me to pick up a package from the customs office. On the way home, about halfway across the river, Dieter decided to drop his end of the heavy box and simply walk away. "Dieter, come back and help me!" I called as he continued walking and pretended not to hear me. "Come and help!" I left the box on the ice

and started chasing after him, but he kept running and quickly vanished out of my sight. Stopping in my tracks, I looked back and there on the ice, in the middle of the river, was our box from America. In anger I retraced my steps to reclaim Tante Martha's gift of love and drag it across the ice toward home.

Snow began to fall heavily one afternoon. By the next day, Nienburg was embedded in a thick blanket of glistening crystals. "The snow sticks!" Dieter and Marlies announced joyfully. "It is great for snowball battles." By afternoon, all the kids from the camp gave up their fierce battles and started rolling large balls to build igloos. Putting my knitting aside, I joined them outside, and after many hours of work, we had built two large igloos, one seating twelve children, and the other eight. With snow gently falling outside, children crouched in their warm "homes" while I was elected to read stories aloud from a book one of the camp children had brought. During the following night, Mr. Frost cemented the igloos so that they were strong enough to withstand rough play for several weeks.

With spring wedging into northern West Germany and the lengthening of days, the ice on the river began to pull away from its banks. Day and night, we could hear loud sounds of crackling along the Weser. It appeared as if the water were rising too. Eventually the spring thaw ripped the solid ice cover into huge chunks. Dieter considered the whole event exciting and with great exhilaration bounced like a rubber ball from floe to floe while Udo, Marlies, and I stood in fear on the river bank watching our family acrobat. "Dieter come back!" Marlies hollered. "You are going to slip and fall into the water." But he continued to bound from one ice block across the open water to another, causing my heart to almost stop. We decided to tell Mutti about Dieter's dangerous folly. She gave him a grave warning the first time but reinforced it with a spanking the second time.

One night we were all jolted out of sleep. Something was beating against the walls of the Anchor. Was someone hurling logs at the building? The dark hours of the night yielded no explanation of this unique sound. As soon as daylight broke, and we all looked out of the window, the cause of the unusual noises and strange vibrations became apparent. The river had jumped its banks, bringing with it large ice chunks and debris, which pushed through the courtyard and slammed into the house. A neighbor of the camp paddled his boat through the hallway of the Anchor to rescue people and belongings. The evacuation caused great commotion, because the folks from downstairs had to move upstairs. Several could not be taken into already crowded rooms and had to sleep in the hallway. With the central kitchen under about eighteen inches of water, only those who had ready-to-eat food could sustain themselves. On the second day of the flood, the neighboring farmer rode up to our camp and, with his horse belly-deep in ice water, delivered milk for all the children.

One of the favorite "flood games" for the camp children was to take two chairs, step on one, with both hands swing the other ahead of them, step on that one and repeat that pattern along the whole length of the hallway. Nobody ever fell into the ice-cold, murky floodwater.

One week after flooding had begun, the water slowly receded, leaving behind fertilized fields and meadows. The flood also became a blessing in disguise to the refugees because of the abundant yield of firewood. By the end of the second week, the downstairs cleanup was completed and our visitors could return to their own rooms.

Huge ice floes continued to move swiftly downstream. At the bridge, the river at times was completely jammed by huge ice boulders. People stood on the shore watching nature's spectacle and the pilings of often house-high chunks into which more and more ice rammed. One day the icebreakers, which were supposed to cut the floating ice into smaller pieces, could no longer withstand the blockade and broke. With the

bridge itself now exposed to the wildly racing waters and ice, it lost its protection and collapsed. Several hundred residents from our side of the river were now completely isolated from town and stores. After the water had receded, several weeks later, and the ice had passed Nienburg, a hastily built pontoon bridge was the only means by which we could cross the Weser. A strong metal and cement bridge was later constructed.

"You must remember, students," our professor injected into his lesson one day, "I am teaching you to speak the royal English—the Queen's English. It is somewhat different from the English language spoken in America. The most important advice I have given you, and will continue to impress upon you, is that you have to learn every single vocabulary word of the lesson. Not only will you receive poor grades if you don't, but the foundation of this language you are learning will crumble. If you miss any of the assigned work, you probably will not be able to catch up. And as you already know, in this girls' school, you have to progress to the teacher's satisfaction or you leave the school. In the Lyceum you must perform.

"Today," our teacher continued, "we will set our vocabulary words aside and study some of the great British landmarks. We will start with Stonehenge."

Most of my classmates felt the way I did; they did not like English. The class seemed boring. I did not foresee going to England to view the Changing of the Guard or visit the Royal Family, but I nevertheless had to study and do well. Two years later, we would have to start studying French, besides continuing German and English, and perhaps Latin. It would be best to have a firm grip on English before diving into another language. One thing, however, I could not figure out—why most of my forty-nine classmates had already mastered the unnatural twisting of their German tongues to produce an English "r" sound while I continued struggling with "Robert Rowly rolled a round roll around." Would I

ever learn that pronunciation? I did not have that much trouble to stick out my tongue and model the strange "th" sound.

Looking at the beautifully lined white paper my classmates used oftentimes made me jealous. I still had to continue writing on the backs of old, used, dingy, gray-yellow freight sheets. I felt embarrassed; no one else wrote on freight statements. But I was glad that Edith did get them for me somehow from the British. Without her, I would have had nothing on which to write. Since only the teacher owned a school textbook, we had to do a lot of writing in class which was easy for me because of the beautiful fountain pen Tante Martha had sent from America.

It was impossible not to notice that something unusual had happened. Mutti's face literally glowed when I came home from school. Dieter and Marlies were already at home. "Children, come here, please, all of you. I have the most exciting news for you. Do you see this postcard here in my hand?"

"Yes, Mutti, I see it," Udo answered while trying to push his straight blond hair off his forehead.

"This card has made a very long trip. It came all the way from Africa. It is the first true sign in over three years that Vati is really alive."

"What does he write?" Marlies questioned excitedly. "What does he say?"

"Well, let me read it to you. It is Vati's own handwriting, 'Dear Uschi and Children, Thank you heartily for your letter. I am so thankful that God has protected you all. I will be home soon. God be with you, signed Emil and Vati.'"

Mutti had accentuated every single word while reading the card with moist, yet gleaming eyes. Beautiful Mutti with dark wavy hair—a tower of strength. No wonder Vati had married her. Unfortunately, he did not know that they would be separated for almost eight years of their fifteen years of married life. Did Mutti ever envision that kind of life on their wedding day? She had married a man who was well established in his

own business. There was no need of anything. Custom-made furniture graced the beautiful home, the finest china was hers, a car, vacations. Emil was not only a good businessman but a born-again Christian, one living out the teachings of the Bible as Mutti aimed to. She would be true to him amidst the storms of life, and surely he would not forget his vows to her.

Barely had Mutti finished reading the card when we began bombarding her with questions. "When is Vati coming home?"

"He wrote that it would be soon."

"Will he come by train?"

"I don't know."

"Can we go and meet him?"

"We wouldn't know where to meet him."

"How much longer will we have to wait?" Marlies asked.

"I don't know. Only the Lord knows."

"What if he comes when we are at school?" Dieter questioned.

"Then, Son, you'll see him when you come home."

"But I can't wait that long," Marlies admitted.

"If you don't know that Vati is here," Dieter pointed out, "it makes no difference."

"All right, children!" Mutti said trying to bring the question-and-answer session to an end. "There is no use speculating. Vati's homecoming is almost like the Lord's return; we know Jesus is coming back to take us to be with Him, but we don't know when. The Bible says we have to be ready at all times, and the same way we have to be ready for Vati's return. We know it will be soon, but we don't know when; it could be tomorrow, in a few weeks, or months."

"Oh no, not that long." Marlies began to pout and plopped herself on a chair.

"What is all the commotion about, Emmy?" Onkel Emil puffed when limping into the room. "I could hear the noise in here even when climbing up the steps."

"Vati is coming home soon. It can be any day now," Marlies rattled on. "We got a card from Africa. He is coming soon. We don't know when, but it will be soon."

"Is that true, Emmy?"

"Yes, Emil, it is. Here is the card. You may read it."

"That is wonderful news, Emmy," Onkel Emil said. "I am so glad for you and the children. It's what we have been praying for. Did you tell my wife yet?"

"No, I didn't. I think she is sleeping."

Ever since Tante Mally's return from Pomerania a few weeks earlier, she had not been feeling well. Having to slave in Russian horse stables had left her frail body weak and sick. Her doctor had prescribed rest for her.

"Tonight we will have our dress rehearsal," Mutti said.

"What is that?" Udo asked.

"That means we will recite all our poems and sing all our songs, pretending that Vati is right here in this room."

"I am ready," Udo said excitedly and carried that excitement all through the rehearsal.

The next day, very deliberate preparations were made for Vati's homecoming. Even though it was only the middle of the week, after school, I was again assigned the job of washing the window and floor. The straw sacks had already been "fluffed up," causing the dust to land everywhere, especially on the floor. After filling the washbowl with water, I took our flimsy rag and started "scrubbing" the boards. Since the whole room tilted toward the window in this ancient building, I started as usual, near the door. The minute the wet rag touched the old rough floor boards, little beads of water scattered like mercury from a broken thermometer. Some of the water rolled into the wide cracks between

the boards to moisten the accumulated dust, other droplets formed and quickly rolled toward the window. Lifting the dust off the splintery floor with a rag was a lengthy process. But when I was done, about an hour and several trips to the public wash basins later, the room smelled fresh and clean with only a hint of must penetrating the scent of straw.

"Now remember, children," Mutti reiterated at bedtime, "when Vati comes, you all help me line up the little boys from the camp. We'll see if Vati can figure out what his youngest son looks like."

Our pastor continued to pedal his old bike through towns and villages in search of displaced believers who needed help. Most of our new church members were refugees, others expellees—people from Eastern Germany chased from their homes and lands in order to free them for the takeover by Russia and Poland. Materially, these people had been stripped of everything, yet their faith in the Lord remained strong. Many testified they lived closer to Him in their destitute state than they ever had in their abundance.

Onkel Emil not only directed the church choir but was the Sunday school teacher for the children, a very strict teacher. Because of his great love for music, he taught us many songs. Edith also sang well and often enhanced the worship services by singing solos. She also played the church's pump organ.

With the budding trees and lengthening days, summer was only a short time away. The second anniversary of the end of World War II had passed without fanfare as had Dieter's tenth birthday; there were no elaborate birthday presents, big parties, or fancy birthday cakes. Even with the supplemental packages from America, Mutti never managed to fill Dieter's stomach. In spite of all the hunger pangs, though, Dieter was always creative at play. "Look at this, Liane," he said one day when we were on our way home from the milk store, "nothing can spill out of the can if you swing it fast enough." He had taught me to swing the camp soup in a circular motion close to the body and over our heads

without spilling a drop, but we had never before tried it with milk. "See, it works just the same. You just have to do it fast."

The sunny days seemed to warm up the water at the gravel pit more quickly than at the river. Soon we could again work on improving our swimming skills. On the way to the pit, we often stopped to gather and eat sour grass. Lush green pastures yielded a lot of that nutritious weed which Mutti used to cook soup. Some of the plants we were accustomed to gathering for food in East Prussia could not be found in Nienburg. The forests around our new town, however, yielded many types of mushrooms. Sometimes we returned home with as many as four or five different kinds of delicious gifts of the wild in our bags.

Dieter, the most athletic one of our family, always knew how to distinguish himself from the rest of us. He could skip rocks better, throw pebbles farther, run faster, dive longer, jump farther, and climb trees higher. One day, while taking a walk in the field, he tried to convince all of us that he had truly mastered riding a cow. With one leap—like jumping a high bar—he landed on the back of a peacefully grazing beast.

"Dieter," Mutti called in shock, "that is dangerous."

"Oh no, Mutti, I have done that many times before. See! Nothing to it," he said while raising his arms and holding on to the animal with his legs. As soon as the cow, however, realized that something was on her back, she gave a rodeo performance which caused all of us to hold our breath while Dieter rode the wildly twisting Jersey. Suddenly the cow reared and my brother landed bottom first in a fresh, steaming manure pile. Dieter's audience could hardly stop laughing while he quickly scrambled out of the mess, dashed down to the river, and dunked continuously in hopes of freeing himself of the odorous riding bonus.

Several days later Mutti again went to the Weser with us. "We have to take advantage of this beautiful weather," she said. "You children can have fun while soaking up sunshine vitamins."

Dieter's swimming skills improved the fastest, but for some strange reason, he swam mostly underwater. While Mutti sat on the blanket daydreaming, Dieter apparently had a plan. He jumped into the water and swam toward the huge barge that was about to pass us. "Dieter, come back!" Mutti called at the top of her lungs. "Come back!" But he didn't hear her and suddenly vanished under the vessel. We all looked toward the moving barge in shock. My mind began to work overtime. Dieter was dead. Why did he get so close? The propeller was cutting him into pieces. A small dog raced along the deck yelping at us; the lady on the barge took time from hanging her laundry to wave.

"Dieter!" we all called. "Dieter!" as the long barge slowly moved downstream with the small lifeboat behind it rippling through the water. Suddenly, after the barge had passed, we saw someone standing on the opposite bank of the river waving at us. It was Dieter.

"Hi, Mutti!" he yelled with his hands cupped over his mouth.

Mutti was still trembling and angry when Dieter, totally oblivious to the dangers to which he had exposed himself, swam back. The punishment was to cure him of ever attempting such stunts, but it was difficult for him to fend off the temptation.

At school one day, the girls in my class encircled our beautiful blond classmate. "You are really going to America?"

"Yes, I am planning to go to New York."

"Where are you going to live?" someone inquired.

"I will be living with relatives."

"Will you ever come back to Germany?"

"I'll probably come back for a visit."

America! I could hardly believe it. Someone I knew was going to America. The more mail and packages we received from America, the more in awe I was of the country where no one went to bed hungry, and nobody slept on straw but in nice soft beds as we used to. America, where no bombs had ripped homes and families apart, where the Statue

of Liberty was located, where ships took rich people on vacation, and where refugees were unknown. America, from where letters arrived in only two weeks, where everyone was happy—except those whose relatives were killed fighting against Hitler—and where many went to church. America, where people had so many clothes that they could send some to refugees in Germany, where women's feet were narrow so that the shoes didn't fit the broad feet of refugees, and where people evidently collected buttons because they cut them all off the clothes before sending them to the poor. America! It was easier for me to believe that someone was going to heaven than to America.

8

Family Reunion

For our morning devotions, Onkel Emil read Bible verses from
Proverbs 3:5–6.

"Trust in the Lord with all thine heart;
 And lean not unto thine own understanding.
In all thy ways acknowledge him,
 And he shall direct thy paths."

"These verses are wonderful instructions for all of us whether we go
to school or stay here at home awaiting God's direction for the future," he
said. After we had sung a song, he closed our devotional time with prayer.

"You children have a nice day at school and be careful on the long
walk," Mutti advised us lovingly. "Remember to be kind to each other."
Then she kissed the three of us goodbye.

Even though Onkel Emil sometimes yelled at us children, he seemed
more subdued and at peace since his reunion with his wife. Tante Mally,
a tall lady with her black hair pulled into a bun close to the neck, was
somewhat stooped. Due to edema, her normally slender face was now

swollen, as were her legs. She tired very easily and never said much, yet I loved to be in her presence because of her gentle spirit and kindness. Boisterous and quite loud at times, Onkel Emil was just the opposite of his wife.

In the afternoon, Udo dashed into the room from outside calling, "Mutti, I lost my button. My pants' button came off."

"Well, Son," Mutti said calmly to her youngest son, "that is just too bad. I don't have another button to sew on your pants."

"But I have it, Mutti. I have it. Here it is—in my pocket," and he dug deep for the button.

"I am so glad you have not lost the button because I simply don't have one, and it is impossible to buy one at the stores." While Mutti sat down on a chair near the window, Udo leaned against her knees. He continued to chatter about the games he and his friends had been playing and watched Mutti sew the button to the waistband of his pants. I sat at the wooden table and continued doing my homework. Suddenly we heard someone knocking on the door.

"That must be Hildegard," I said. "She and I are going to pick daisies in the fields today and sell them in town."

"Come in!" Mutti and I answered almost in unison. When the rickety door fell open, she looked up and cried out,

"Emil! Emil! You are here!" and rushed to embrace her husband. Both of them stood weeping for a long time while his small bag of belongings dangled from his arm. When Vati closed the door and put down his sack, I dashed toward him. We kissed and hugged. I cried. I had missed him so much. Udo still stood at the window next to the chair with a somber look on his face.

"And this is Udo?" Vati asked while looking at his son, but Udo did not move. He seemed glued to the wooden floor planks, staring at the stranger who had just entered our lives.

"Yes, Emil, this is your youngest son."

Vati, in tears, moved closer to Udo. "You are my son? You are Udo? How you have grown! The last time I saw you, you were just a little baby. Come here, let me look at you more closely!" Slowly Udo edged toward his dad who stooped and hugged him. My youngest brother, however, remained rigid, quiet, and unemotional.

"And you, Liane, are no longer the little girl I remembered. You are almost a young lady," Vati said and hugged me again. "Where are Dieter and Marlies?"

"They are outside playing with their friends," Mutti answered. "Why don't you, Schäfle, go and ask them to come upstairs."

When the three of us entered the room, Vati and Mutti again were embracing and crying. "Dieter! My son! You look like a young man!" Vati exclaimed. "I can't believe how you have grown in the past three years." Then Vati hugged and kissed him.

"And Pittimaus! Come here! Let me hug you! How you have changed!" Marlies threw her little arms around her dad's neck, squeezing and kissing him. "Seeing you all is the greatest moment of my life. Each and every day, through all these years, I prayed for your safety. Each and every day I prayed for our reunion. And our heavenly Father has answered my prayer. You are all here. We are all alive. We are all together. I don't really know what is going on in today's Germany, but from what little I have heard, not every family from the East is as blessed as we are today."

"You are right, Emil," Mutti agreed. "You have no idea of the heartaches that have befallen millions of Germans."

Marlies would not let go of Vati. She hugged him over and over again while Udo continued to watch the reunion from the sidelines.

Suddenly the side door of our room opened and Onkel Emil and Tante Mally appeared. "We heard all the noise and commotion and knew what had happened, but we did not want to interrupt the family celebration," Onkel Emil said stretching his hand toward Vati. "Welcome home, Emil! Welcome home!"

"Yes, Emil," Tante Mally added, "welcome home."

"'This is the day which the LORD hath made; we will rejoice and be glad in it'" (Ps. 118:24), my Sunday school teacher continued. "This is the day of yet another great miracle. Your family has been reunited. A few months ago, my wife returned from Pomerania. The Lord surely is good to us." Then suddenly Onkel Emil started singing Psalm 91, "'He that dwelleth in the secret place of the most High shall abide under the shadow of the Almighty'" (Ps. 91:1) and with everyone except my brothers and sister joining in, we continued, "'I will say of the LORD, He is my refuge and my fortress: my God; in him will I trust'" (Ps. 91:2). When we had finished, many tears of rejoicing and thanksgiving to God for His marvelous blessings continued to flow.

"Can I say my poem now?" Marlies pleadingly asked Mutti.

"Well, Pittimaus, I think we will start our 'Vati-homecoming program' the way we have practiced it, which means we start with Udo. But first, we all have to find a seat somewhere. Some of you children can sit on my cot so that Onkel Emil and Tante Mally can have these chairs."

Excitement mounted in the room. Vati, the one we had been praying for, the one whose looks and manners I had often tried to envision, was in our very room. Vati, to whose invisible bond Mutti was always clinging, stared lovingly at her. Vati, whose kindness and Christian values Mutti would not let us forget, had suddenly reentered our lives. Vati, whose honesty and obedience to authority during the war set him apart from many in the eyes of his superiors, stood before us. Vati, whose children hardly knew him, was in our midst, and we were about to honor him. He had not changed much; he looked almost the way I remembered him. His forehead was still high and his hairline recessed—just like mine. He and I also had hazel eyes and long noses in common.

"Emil," Mutti started, only with difficulty pronouncing the name of her loved one, "for over three years we have prepared for this homecoming

celebration. And here you are—at last. The Lord truly performed a great miracle by returning you to us. We thank Him for His goodness and kindness. Your youngest son will now open our festivities."

Udo, my little brother, pudgy-looking yet undernourished, slowly meandered toward the door, turned, bowed, and recited the poem Mutti had written for him years before. With his eyes fixed on Vati, he neither cracked a smile nor walked over to his dad when he had finished. He simply would have marched straight back to the cot had Vati not caught and hugged him.

With lightning speed my blond, curly-headed sister dashed to the "stage," curtsied, flooded her face with a smile, and joyously delivered her poem. Then she stretched out her little arms and flew toward Vati who hugged and kissed her. Dieter's and my lengthy poems also seemed to please Vati. After another welcome message, Onkel Emil suggested we sing a favorite song:

"As long as Jesus lives
And His strength upholds me,
Sorrow and worry must flee,
And my heart truly glow for Him.

"He is a good Shepherd
Who faithfully guides His sheep;
He leads me to green pastures
And quenches my thirst with morning's dew.

"That's why I look steadfastly upon Him.
Oh, what blessed assurance!
My Jesus loves me, that is certain;
He is my eternal hope."
(Gebhardt, "So lang mein Jesus lebt")

We all continued to sing one song after another as we have always done during our devotion time. It was great, though, to have a bass voice added to our choir. With Onkel Emil singing tenor, Mutti alto, and the rest of us soprano, we had a complete choir.

"Now it is my turn to say something," Vati started. "First of all, my thanks goes to our Lord who has so graciously reunited us. He has answered our prayers. He has made it possible for all of us to be together again. He has protected and given strength. We just sang the song 'God is love—He saves us.' The Lord has not only saved spiritually those of us who have believed, but He has saved us physically. Now I have absolutely no idea what happened to all of you during the past years. What I do know, however, is that the Lord has literally snatched us from the clutches of the enemy. I was a prisoner in Africa and told you in my forty letters and cards how I was doing. So you know all about me, but only recently did I receive mail from you. I am completely in the dark in regard to what happened to all of you."

"Emil, what did you say?" Mutti wondered. "You wrote to us? We have not once heard from you. To which town did you send your mail?"

"To Insterburg."

"Well, that explains it! We left Insterburg three years ago, in August of 1944, during the height of all the bombing attacks. Your mother, the children, and I took a train from Insterburg to Lippehne, near Berlin, just about two weeks before Udo's first birthday."

"Udo's birthday? That was the exact day I was taken captive by the Americans in Marseille and thrown into prison."

"So that is what happened to you that day! Your mother told me as we were celebrating our son's birthday that she couldn't stop thinking about you, and that she was praying for you that whole afternoon."

Reflecting on everything that had just been said, Vati slowly—as if fearing the answer—asked, "Where is my mother now, Emmy?"

"I don't know, Emil. She lived with us for a while, and when your sister-in-law came, she moved in with her until they, and many others, were chased out of town by the Russians."

Everyone in the room quietly pondered what had just been said. Vati bowed his head. "No one has heard from my mother and sister-in-law? What about my twin brother? Perhaps he is with the women."

Mutti gently placed her hand in Vati's. "Your brother was killed defending Pillau."

Poor Vati! Why couldn't the news about his family be better? He dearly loved his brother, sister-in-law, and mother as we all did. They were devout Christians. I never saw them do or say anything that was not right. God in His great wisdom had taken Opi to heaven just before our whole family was ripped apart. He escaped all the heartaches that befell the rest of us.

Opi, the patriarch of our family, looked as I pictured the prophets, with his white beard. He was the only dead person I had ever seen by the time I was ten years old. Opi truly loved the Lord and people of all ages. I wondered about our sweet Omi, his wife. Was she still alive? My heart seemed to twist in agony as I again remembered that wonderful lady. Finally, I could no longer suppress my tears. This was such a joyous day, yet such a sad one; one in which to feel blessed, yet one in which to mourn.

The sadness in our room reminded me of the atmosphere in my grandparents' living room the day of Opi's burial. Vati, home on a two-day leave from the army, had sat at the pump organ playing in a truly solemn manner. We often used to sit around the table while Opi read the Bible to us and prayed. That day his chair was empty. His body rested on his bed in the next room. He was in heaven, the adults said and seemed to rejoice. I, however, could not rejoice. To me he was gone forever. No longer would I spend time with him in his leather-scented saddle shop. No longer would I watch him sit on his cobbler's bench

repairing saddles and bridles for his farmer customers and friends. No longer would we stroll together through the garden, admiring his unique fruit trees and berry bushes. I had to learn living without him. Would I have to live without Omi, also? Suddenly I was pulled back to reality when Vati sadly asked, "What about your parents, Emmy? Where are they? And Opi?"

"I have no idea where they are or if they are alive."

"And your sister and family, Emmy, and your brother? Have you heard from them?"

"I don't know their whereabouts either. Only the Lord knows," was Mutti's somber reply.

"But the war ended over two years ago and so many people are still missing? I had no idea that this was happening in Germany."

"Millions upon millions, Emil, have been killed," Onkel Emil added, "not only by the Nazi regime, but by Germany's enemies. Apparently, you have not had much contact with the outside world. We were in the same predicament for sixteen months. We knew nothing about what was going on elsewhere."

"Yes, Emil," Mutti said, "I can see that we will be talking for a long, long time to fill you in about what happened to the children and me during the past years and to our homeland; and all of us have to learn what you have experienced."

"I think we should all pray now," Vati suggested, "and thank the Lord for His goodness to us and especially pray for all our relatives whose whereabouts we don't know. We have to ask the Lord's protection on all of them, and ask Him to let us find them all soon."

Many tears were shed on the afternoon of our special day, the day we all had been awaiting so anxiously—Vati's homecoming day.

9

Family Life

Vati appeared tired on his first morning as a civilian in Germany. "It was too noisy out there in the hallway," he said. "All night long someone was going to the bathroom, and of course they all had to walk past my cot." Vati had to sleep outside our door in the public hallway because there was no space large enough for another cot in either our room or Onkel Emil's. "But I don't feel sorry for myself. Just think, I am home—in Germany—with my family. Nothing is more important than that."

Mutti just beamed. Everyone else appeared to be livelier and more chipper than usual. Vati was home!

"Today I have to go to the doctor for a checkup," he announced. "All prisoners of war are required to do that. Then I will go and look for work, get my food ration card, and check on housing for us."

Mutti continued to exude happiness. Perhaps she was so joyful because she realized the burden of responsibility for the family had been taken off her shoulders.

In the afternoon, while I was trying to concentrate on my homework, Vati began to relate some of the experiences of the day. "'Herr Guddat,'

the doctor told me, 'I wish all German prisoners would return from the prison camps in such excellent physical condition as I find you to be. Aside from the rash on your arms and legs, you are in great shape. You have no idea what the few prisoners who came from Russia look like. They are just skeletons—skin draped over bones—hardly able to function. Thousands are literally being worked to death in the coal mines of Siberia, I am told. Only a few have somehow managed to return to the West. The few women I have seen in my office who came from Siberia are racked by sexual diseases. You are very fortunate, Herr Guddat, very fortunate. I have not seen one refugee in such good physical shape.'"

"Yes, Emil, I also think that you look great," Mutti stated. "Did you have good food at the camp?"

"The food was wonderful. We were given six hundred grams of bread per day, had good meals, and could buy a lot of fruit at the camp store."

"You got six hundred grams of bread?" Mutti asked quite surprised. "We get only 125 grams per person now. The children are always hungry. But we are thankful for what we have now. There was a time when we could not buy any bread. For two-and-a-half years now, Emil, our children have gone to bed hungry. If it weren't for the Lord and your sister sustaining today, I don't know what would happen to us."

"Do you mean Martha is helping us, Emmy?"

"Yes, she is."

"And she hasn't heard from our mother either?"

"No, Emil. She is still waiting and hoping for a word from her too."

"Now tell me, how is my sister helping feed our children?"

"She is sending us about one food package per week, sometimes two. Now and then she puts in a piece of clothing for the children. Her acts of kindness have been keeping us alive here in the West. You probably noticed Dieter walking around barefoot. That is because he has no shoes. Martha sent him a pair, but they were too small."

Vati's eyes began to fill with tears. "I also noticed his bandaged legs."

"Yes, he has open sores on both legs, Emil, because of malnutrition—'lack of vitamins,' the doctor told us."

"Oh, Uschi, what you must have gone through. Isn't it amazing, though, to think that God sent my sister to America in the 1920s so that she can be an encouragement and a help to us a quarter of a century later? God surely is good! He had everything planned, and He knows what we are going through now. He knows about our future."

"Yes, Emil, that is what kept me going; He was in control of everything. In Him alone did we trust. Nazism has failed us and so has Communism. Whatever we are experiencing now appears to fail. Hopeless people sit in camps and die either of heartache or starvation. You should just see the camps in Berlin. Millions of refugees and expellees were heading toward Berlin and the West in hopes of a better life."

"What do you mean by 'expellees,' Emmy?"

"These are Germans, mostly from East Prussia, Pomerania, and Selisia who were simply chased out of their homes by the Russians and told to go West. That is how Omi and your sister-in-law had to leave. Many were forced to leave during the winter months. They left on foot and pulled their children and loved ones in hand-wagons. Many froze or starved to death on the treks. Eyewitnesses told us they saw hundreds dead or dying, especially children, the old, and the sick. Their bodies were just pushed into ditches to 'make room for those who could still walk.' Children froze to death in the arms of their mothers in the minus ten- to twenty-degree temperatures. Someone reported seeing countless children dead in the snow."

"What time of year did Omi leave?" Vati asked with deep concern in his voice.

"She and your sister left in the spring."

Bursting into the room, Dieter called, "Vati, I would like to show you the Anchor. Did you know that this was a hotel for sailors years

ago? I want to show you the river, the gravel pit, the fields, the barges, and our beach at the Weser."

"All right, Dieter. I'll let you give me a tour. You seem to know this place rather well."

"Yes, I do. We have lived here for one year already."

"But instead of just you and I going, why don't we all go together as a family? You can be our tour guide."

Stepping out of our room, Dieter led us to the right. Along the lengthy hallway we walked on wooden floors past dingy and dark doors. One family or more lived behind each door. Children's cries penetrated our ears as we meandered to the end of the hallway, made a U-turn, and walked to the staircase.

"The river water came up to this step here," my brother explained, "during the spring flood. Some of the ice chunks were beating on the walls outside. Everybody from our camp down here had to move upstairs. Some people stayed with us, and some lived in the hallway."

"Ja, Vati," Marlies joined in excitedly. "All our igloos melted. They were in the backyard. We built them and . . ."

"She means the children from the camp built them," Dieter interrupted.

"There was deep water down here," Marlies continued. "The water came in very fast. One man was paddling a boat here in the house."

"Yes, we couldn't use the kitchen either," Dieter explained. "Then a farmer came on horseback and brought milk for all the children. The water right outside this door touched the horse's stomach."

"How long did the flood last?" Vati asked.

"It lasted for a long time," Marlies answered. "The huge ice floes on the river broke the bridge too. Nobody could go to town."

"What you children are telling me is very difficult to imagine on this warm and sunny day," Vati admitted. "I have been in very hot weather in Africa for three years. I can remember the cold East Prussian winters,

but I didn't know that it got so cold here in West Germany. Right now, I can't even imagine thick ice on the river."

"Yes," Mutti said, "it was very cold here in the house too. The water in our washbowl was frozen many mornings."

"Did you know, Vati, that this building is hundreds of years old?" our tour guide asked.

"No, I didn't."

"When we walk around this corner here, we come to the backyard. There are our walnut trees. We got quite a few nuts last year."

Our stroll took us to the river and along the hedgerow path to the gravel pit—a large man-made lake with a small island. Vati obviously enjoyed the family tour and country setting of his new home.

Ready to doze off on Mutti's lap after our evening devotions, Udo suddenly appeared wide awake again when he heard Vati say, "Now I will tell you children a horse story."

"What color was the horse?" Marlies inquired.

"It was a bay-colored horse, Pittimaus."

"Oh."

"When I was in Russia to help feed the German soldiers, we had a few calm days; no Russian bombers were flying above us and dropping bombs. An attack would have to come soon, everyone thought. 'Emil Guddat,' an officer said, 'since you are going to be transferred to Holland anyway, it would be best for you to leave today yet. There might be heavy fighting tomorrow which would prevent you from leaving. I am going to send a corporal with a horse and wagon to pick you up and take you to the train station. So you hurry and get ready.' I quickly gathered my belongings, climbed up into the wagon, and sat down next to the corporal. He held the reins and the whip.

"It was a cloudy and dreary day as we rode through huge forests. We saw no villages or houses, only woods. In the afternoon, it got darker

and darker and darker. I almost became afraid. Finally we couldn't see anything."

"Did you hear any wolves howling?" Dieter asked.

"No, Dieter, not that night. But I often heard wolves in Russia."

"So back to my story. 'Do you know the right way to the train station?' I asked the corporal. 'No,' he said. 'I don't know the way, but the horse does. The horse has come this way often.' Now let me tell you, children. That answer really made me restless as the horse pulled us through the darkness. We still didn't see any villages; no lights anywhere. I prayed for the Lord to help us. The corporal was quiet, and so was I. Suddenly the horse stopped. What happened? I wondered. 'This is the station,' the corporal said. 'We are here.' I couldn't believe it, but it was true. We were at the station—the horse did know the way."

"I didn't know horses were that smart," I confessed.

"I didn't either, Liane. But when I at last sat on that German train, I was very happy and thanked the Lord for His guidance and the wisdom He had given that horse. I am sure you can tell me countless stories of how the Lord protected you and helped you, right?"

"Yes, Vati, we can," Dieter said in a reflecting tone. "We have been protected many times when Liane and I went on our begging trips in Lippehne. The Russians could have shot us. They killed many people. But they did not kill us. Sometimes they even gave us pieces of bread."

"You poor children . . . and I could not be there to help you. War is terrible. The Russian children were hungry, too, and suffering. I tried to help them and give them something to eat whenever I had a chance."

"When the Russian hospital moved out of Lippehne," Dieter continued, "we found some bread crusts under the beds and in the garbage. We took them home and Mutti cooked bread soup for us. One time, a soldier gave me a little roasted pig's head. Mutti fixed a big pot of soup from that."

"Why did the children have to go begging, Emmy? Didn't you have any money to buy things?"

"Oh, Emil, I don't think we will ever be able to help you understand what the conditions were like those sixteen months under Communism.

"When the troops first came to our town, they killed, raped women and girls, shot people at random, and plundered. There was chaos, total chaos. They burned homes, looted, ransacked, and devastated everything in sight, including all the stores. Hungry Germans went from one abandoned store or house to another in search of food. You could not buy anything in all that turmoil, which started three and a half months before World War II ended. And after the war, things continued that way for almost one year before Polish settlers opened the first store. The Polish people had been taken out of their homes in Poland and were brought in by the Russians to claim and settle the land for them. By that time, all the Germans, except our group, had been forced to leave as I mentioned to you earlier."

"Why was an exception made for you? Why did you stay that long?" Vati tried to find out. "You probably would have been better off in the West."

"We were not able to leave," Onkel Emil replied, "because of my work for the Polish government. I was the head tailor in the Polish tailor shop and had twenty-eight women working under me. I was too valuable to the government. We tried to leave several times but did not get permission. And since I always claimed Emmy and the children as my family who had to take care of me, the invalid, none of us, including Kätchen Mecklenburg and her sons, were allowed to go West. We were the last Germans left of a town of about five thousand inhabitants."

"All this is very difficult for me to understand."

"Yes, Emil," our quiet and sad-looking Tante Mally added. "It is difficult for me too."

Vati continued on his job hunt. One day, finally, the employment office had a work assignment for him.

"I am going to be a night watchman," Vati informed us. "Making sure that no one breaks into businesses, such as banks and stores, is what I'll start doing tonight. So when all of you are asleep, I will patrol the streets of Nienburg, and when you are awake, I will have to sleep. I am sure the Lord had all this planned. Now I no longer have to sleep in the hallway," and with a chuckle he added, "now I can sleep in one of our nice soft beds."

Our church group was growing in number, and the Sunday school attendance, with Vati as the new teacher, soared. The children liked Vati because he truly knew how to make Bible stories come alive. In preparation for Thanksgiving, on the first Sunday of October, we began practicing new songs and memorizing Bible verses as well as poems. I was proud to have my father as head of the Sunday school and felt flattered by how sharp he looked in the second-hand suit the church had provided for him.

One day news spread with lightning speed that the farmer across the river was harvesting his rye.

"We must go and glean there," Mutti told me. "We can take the grain to the mill and have some extra bread to add to our meager rations. The problem is that it will take us at least an hour to walk to that field. By that time, others will already be there."

"There is no other way to get there faster, Mutti," I reasoned.

"Oh yes, there is."

"But how?"

"Swim. We must swim to get there faster."

"That is too dangerous, Mutti. The river flows very swiftly there. I have seen that when we picked blackberries in that area."

"Well, Schäfle, we are good swimmers, aren't we? We'll ask Onkel Emil to walk to the field and we'll swim."

"But we can't swim straight across. And what about the barges?"

"We just have to make sure before we jump in that no barges are in sight."

"We'll also have to walk upstream," I added, "to allow for the fast current that is going to pull us downstream."

Standing at the riverbank and contemplating our dangerous mission, just to gather ears of grain, made me fearful. The water seemed predictable at our regular swimming area. At this location, however, the swirls of water were tighter and faster. What if we didn't make it across? What would happen if I didn't have enough breath and drowned? Eerie thoughts flooded my whole being. My heart began to race. Was I really a good swimmer?

"Let's go, Schäfle!" With our bags tied to our backs, we jumped in and started swimming. Toward the middle of the river, the current became overpowering and pulled us downstream fast. "Don't struggle!" Mutti called. "Aim for the shore, but let the current carry you."

Relax, I thought. *This is unfamiliar territory. Just a little bit farther.* With the shore in reach, the pull did not seem quite as strong, and we finally reached the bank bordering the rye field.

"We made it, Mutti," I said while climbing up the bank.

"If we see the farmer, we will ask permission to glean in his field," Mutti suggested, but there was no one in sight. Peacefully Mutti and I began gleaning at the edge of the field. The bright sun quickly dried our bathing suits and warmed us. Here and there green frogs were leaping among the rows of stubble. Many, however, did not escape the stately stork that also visited the freshly harvested field to find and gulp down his favorite food.

Moving along in a squatting position caused our backs to ache. My feet were scratched and bloody from the sharp stubble even though I knew how to walk barefoot in a field without getting seriously hurt. "In a stubble field," my grandmother in East Prussia had taught me, "you

place your feet on the ground and slide them along—like skating—rather than lifting them up and bringing them to the ground from the top. That way you don't cut your soles." I thought about the lesson and the wonderful time we always had at her farm playing among the sheaves. Suddenly I was awakened out of my daydream. A short distance from us, a whip cracked once—twice—three times. We turned around, and racing toward us, we saw a farmer sitting on a rake pulled by a team of angry horses.

"Off my field, you thieves!" he yelled. "Off my field!"

"We were going to ask you . . ." Mutti tried to say as we scrambled down the river bank, but he whisked by. My heart was about to escape my body; Mutti was shaken too. Breathlessly we later peeked up into the fields to see what was happening to the gleaners we had seen on the other side of the huge field. They had all been chased off too. Even the stork had left.

"Mutti, are we thieves?" I wondered.

"I don't think so, Schäfle. None of the farmers I have ever known from East Prussia gathered ears of grain. My parents never did. Whatever fell onto the ground during the harvest was left as food for the animals. Right now there isn't even enough food for people. Everyone is trying to survive. I don't think it is stealing."

"I think this is just a mean farmer, the kind we have met on our begging trips."

"You are probably right, Schäfle. You know in Bible times people gleaned in the fields. The Bible talks about gleaning grapes, wheat, and barley. Ruth, the daughter-in-law of Naomi, gleaned wheat and barley."

Standing up again to see what was going on in the field, we noticed that nobody was left. Only the stork had returned for his frog dinner. On the northern end of the field, we suddenly detected Onkel Emil hobbling along.

"Let's finish filling our bags really quick and give them to him. Then we'll swim back." Mutti said. "We'll have to come back tomorrow. There is so much more left."

Swimming back was considerably more enjoyable. I relaxed and gave myself totally to the current which carried us almost to our regular swimming area. Mutti and I gleaned in the same field one more time. But the news of extra food through gleaning had brought out many eager gatherers. Quickly the field was freed of all the ears of grain so that I didn't think a field mouse could survive the winter.

When we had returned home, Mutti asked all of us to go outside, roll the ears of grain in our hands until the kernels fell out, blow the chaff away, and eat the seeds. "Fresh kernels are full of living vitamins," she said. "Eat lots of them, children, lots of them."

Working on only several ears at a time seemed enjoyable, but when we started on our full bags, all of us would have probably preferred hunger to the headaches we got from constantly blowing away the chaff. Headaches or not, we all had to help with the rest of our harvest. Instead of blowing away the chaff, however, Mutti offered that job to the gently blowing breeze by holding the bowl with the mixture high and slowly pouring it into the ham can on her lap.

"What are you going to do with the kernels, Mutti?" Udo asked.

"I will take them to the mill and ask the miller to grind them into flour."

"And then Mutti is going to bake delicious bread," Marlies injected.

"You are right, Pittimaus."

The "splinters" we ground into our hands from the "hair" of the ears of grain were just as difficult to remove as tiny prickles from a fuzzy cactus. All pain, however, was quickly forgotten a few weeks later when each of us received a few extra slices of bread for our morning and evening meals.

Harassment

Silently, in great anticipation, all six of us stood at the door to our new home while Vati rang the doorbell. On the street and in the neighboring yards, everything was quiet. Only birds chirped joyously, and barn swallows dipped from the sky in large loops and flew back into the clouds. What would life outside a camp be like? All the homes in this street were well taken care of with fences painted and hedges trimmed. Dahlias and geraniums added splashes of color to the neighborhood. Everything depicted an owner's pride. What a change from Berlin and the Anchor!

Suddenly we heard rustling on the inside of the door and the sound of a turning key. The door opened and a short, stocky lady in dark clothing appeared, her hair loosely pulled back. "Guten Tag, Gnädige Dame! We are the Guddat family," Vati introduced us. "The housing authority informed us that we would be living here at this address."

"Ja," she said roughly, "I don't know what I have done to deserve this. Four children in my home! There will be rules here to be observed, Herr Guddat, rules. Rules for you and your family! Just remember that," she continued while turning and leading us through an oversized glass

door. "We have to share this hallway. This is just for passing through, nothing else. Your two rooms are here on the right. Those rooms over there are mine. I do not want any loud noises coming from your rooms. From 1:00 to 3:00 o'clock in the afternoon, I want total silence. That is my nap time. Here is your house key," she said while handing it to Vati. Then she turned and went into one of her rooms.

I tried to forget the harshness of our landlady and anxiously inspected our home. A small room at the corner of the house had two windows but no heat. A chaise lounge filled a short wall near the window. A tiny cabinet stood at the opposite wall. The second room resembled our place at the Anchor except that this was furnished with an additional wood stove and armoire. Looking out of the large window across a hedge, we saw lush vegetable gardens separating our house from a two-story apartment building.

"Let's sing the song 'Thank the Lord with Joyful Heart,' children," Vati announced, "as an opening for our evening devotions. But we must sing softly. We do not want to antagonize our landlady." Sitting around the table we sang the praise song to God in a hushed tone.

"Thump . . . thump . . ." we heard and were quickly rushed from our heavenly thoughts back to earth. An object was being beaten against our wall. "Quiet! Quiet!" Frau Boden yelled as we all sat in shock.

"How will we be able to live here," Mutti asked, "when we can't even whisper?"

"Heavenly Father," Vati began to pray, "You have given us this home. We thank You for Your goodness and kindness of delivering us from the camp. We thank You that You died for us and rose and have shown us so much love and compassion. Let us do the same now for our landlady. She must not know You. You have brought us here to her home for a reason. Let us be a light shining for You, and let Your light shine into the heart of this unhappy person. Lord, we have not experienced what

she is experiencing right now. She has strangers living in her home. She was forced to take us in, she is angry. Let us repay her in kindness.

"And, Lord, You know about my job situation. I don't make enough money as a night guard to provide for us. Please help us to get a store again. We don't have money, but with You all things are possible. Food is scarce, and the children are always hungry. Thank You for my sister who is sending us food packages and clothing. Lord, shower many blessings upon her for her kindness."

Vati continued praying for us children and all our relatives from whom we still hadn't had any news.

In our new home, we all learned to talk in whispered tones. The only time we used our voices without restraint was when Frau Boden went to town. Clothed in a dark coat, with a large fox slung around her neck, a cane, and a large black purse, she slowly made her way down the street. Each time we saw her leave, we felt a heavy burden lifted off our souls until she returned several hours later.

On a Saturday afternoon, Mutti knocked on Frau Boden's door to make a request. When the door opened a crack, Mutti said, "As you noticed, Frau Boden, we have been observing all your rules in regard to the use of the toilet. You know we have used it only at the times you specified. But now I would like to ask your permission for us to take baths in the tub."

"What? What do you want, you refugees?" she railed. "You want to use my bathtub? Why didn't you bring yours along? Wh-y-y? My sister would turn over in her grave if she knew that refugees were bathing in her tub. You can continue using the washtub in the basement."

"No, thank you," Mutti replied kindly. "It is getting too cold down there for us and the children."

"All right," she yelled, her face still bright red with anger. "You use it . . . on Saturdays between 4:00 and 6:00 o'clock. At no other time. I

permit you to fill the tub only once. You will, of course, scrub the tub and the whole bathroom."

"That is a matter of course, Frau Boden," Mutti replied. "Refugees know how to clean. They all, at one time, took pride in their homes as you do. But now they don't have homes. They have lost everything, including loved ones, hope, and health. But, Frau Boden, we are still people; we still have dignity. You might want to remember that." With that comment Mutti stepped back into our room.

"She acts like a dragon," Mutti whispered to herself. "How will we be able to continue living here?"

"We want to go back to the Anchor," my brothers and sister pleaded through Dieter, their chosen spokesman. "We can't live here. We are not even allowed to talk."

"We have no other place in which to live," Mutti explained. "Since Edith moved from the Dunsings to be with her parents at the Anchor, there is absolutely no room for us there."

"We can't even play outside here," Marlies added. "Frau Boden hollered at us because we made footprints on the sand she had raked. We were just getting my friend's ball."

"There is nothing, children, we can do, nothing. We have to learn to live with all these rules and regulations."

It was no longer restful and peaceful at home. My soul seemed to be bobbing on a treadmill. Don't talk out loud, whisper. Don't walk, tread lightly. Don't sing. Were we to weep? Don't let the closing door make a noise. Don't use the bathroom between 1:00 and 3:00 o'clock. Don't go in the backyard. Don't step on the raked sand. Don't bring a grain of sand into the house on our shoes. Wipe your feet over and over and over again. Turmoil, nothing but turmoil in my soul. That things had improved for us from the conditions of the camp was a farce. We lived in a real prison now. Only outside our two rooms could we experience inner cleansing and revival. There, we could speak like normal beings

and were not treated like scum. At school I wanted to laugh with my classmates but couldn't. Life had sentenced me to being serious.

Dieter's and my newly acquired hobby, stamp collecting, grew through trading some of the many American stamps we soaked off Tante Martha's packages. Our most common stamp, the purple three-cent Thomas Jefferson stamp, gave us dozens of trading opportunities. Half a sheet was pasted on a package one day. The purple three-cent, Win the War stamp, twenty-cent Garfield stamp, and nine-cent Harrison stamp were scarcer in our collection. My favorites, however, remained the large airmail stamps, and especially the green fifteen-cent stamp which depicted New York City, the Statue of Liberty, and an airplane. The colored stamps seemed to be brightening up our dreary lives.

"Those are beautiful stamps, Liane," Vati told me. "When I was in France during the war, I, along with several other men, stayed in an abandoned house. One room had shelving filled with countless boxes of unusual postage stamps. How I wish you could have seen them and owned some of them!"

"Well, look at this stamp, Vati," I said one evening. "Do people really live in all those skyscrapers? Are there really no trees? How can anyone exist like that?"

"I don't know. Maybe the stamp artist just didn't paint the trees."

"Do you think you would ever want to go to America, Vati?"

"Well, there was a time I wanted to go. My sister always told me so much about it."

"When was it you wanted to go?"

"It was right after I was taken from the French prisoner of war camp in Marseille to an American ship, a Liberty ship. A Liberty ship is a ship that delivers food to the hungry. I watched pontoon boats traveling to the shore continuously with supplies. The American relief operation was quite an undertaking. When I was on that ship, we were served decent food for the first time in three weeks. In the French prison, I received

only a little bread each day and watery soup. On the Liberty ship, we literally devoured the white bread, butter, corned beef, cheese, and hot chocolate we were given for lunch, with meat, potatoes, and vegetables for dinner. I was so thankful and felt like a king.

"When we prisoners were told that we would be taken to America, I was somewhat excited. America, I thought, land of the free. I didn't know where all of you were; as a prisoner I had no way of searching for you. Somehow, though, I expected to find you after I had arrived in the United States.

"From Marseille the ship went to Toulon, laid in the harbor for two days, and then started on a very stormy voyage in the Mediterranean for Oran in North Africa."

"Did you get seasick?"

"No, Liane, I didn't, but more than half of the prisoners did. Those of us who were well enjoyed the wonderful food more than anything else. It was just like being on a vacation cruise. To make things better yet, the captain of the ship gave all of us the liberty to walk around freely.

"But when we were to disembark in Africa, instead of America, a friend of mine and I wanted to hide on the ship. We heard that the ship indeed was going to America over Gibraltar. We had checked out several hiding places and didn't think anyone would miss the two of us from a total of eight hundred prisoners. But when we began to consider the dangers, the mines, and the U-boats that were possibly still hiding in the Atlantic, we decided not to become stowaways.

"But can you imagine what happened after we disembarked?"

"No, what?"

"After having disembarked, we all had to line up to be counted; instead of eight hundred prisoners there were 802. No one knew how that had happened. My friend and I easily could have remained on the ship without anyone missing us. So you see, Liane, I was once tempted to go to America. After I had found you and was released, perhaps you

could have joined me there. People say it is quite easy to make a new beginning in the 'land of golden opportunity.' But just think of how much we would have to give up if we went to America."

"I don't think we have anything left to give up, Vati."

"Oh yes, we do. We would have to give up our homeland, devastated as it is, and our hope of ever returning to East Prussia. We would also have to give up our mother tongue. Would you be willing to change everything you have ever known?"

"I don't know, Vati. I don't know much about that faraway land. All I know is that her people fought to be free from England in Boston Harbor, and that the country is very rich and very beautiful. Look at these stamps here with pictures of Colorado, Utah, and Vermont."

"That is beautiful scenery—truly beautiful. But Europe is beautiful, too, the Alps in Switzerland and Bavaria, the Riviera, the Baltic Sea, the North Sea. I wouldn't want to give up all that."

11

Christmas in Africa

"**O** come all ye children, O come one and all, O come to the cradle in Bethlehem's stall," our church children's choir sang for the Christmas celebration. With Vati in charge of all the Christmas festivities, children recited poems, interspersed with testimonies and songs from the adult and children's choirs. The story of the birth of Jesus was read from Luke 2 in the Bible. Many of our refugee friends still did not own Bibles, but with lips and jaws moving, it was apparent they could quote the whole chapter. A Christmas tree in front of the church decorated with real candles added to the warmth of the celebration. Not all adults participated in the celebration with sparkling eyes and glowing faces as did the children. The tragedy of lost and missing loved ones had moistened the eyes of some believers even on the day of miracles.

"Heavenly thought does lighten the burden," someone said, "but we can't stop wondering about our relatives. We still have no word from them. Jesus helps us to live one day at a time."

"Here is my story about a special Christmas celebration away from home," Vati said standing next to the tree during the church Christmas observance. "I was a prisoner of war in an African camp with eight

hundred captured German officers. The fenced-in camp was located near the Sahara Desert, and situated within the compound stood a large horse barn. With the approach of the first Christmas, the prisoners acquired permission to use the barn for the Christmas festivities. Eagerly they worked to give the barn the atmosphere of a church. Sconces were made and hung on the walls, a primitive altar crafted, and a large needled pine tree decorated with wax candles.

"The celebration started with a string quartet playing many of the beautiful German Christmas songs such as, 'Lo How a Rose E'er Blooming,' 'O Tannenbaum,' and many more. A forty-voice men's prison choir added to the festive spirit of the celebration. When the electric lights were turned off and the candles lit on the tree, the Lord suddenly began to add His special decorations. One little colorful bird started circling the tree, then another, and another. Several different kinds of God's feathered creatures came to celebrate His Son's birth. The number continued to increase, all of them fluttering around the tree—close to the candles—chirping and twittering praises to God. It was the most unusual and beautiful sight. I don't think too many prisoners listened to the minister because everyone's eyes were fixed on God's creation, His miracle for that night.

"There we were, celebrating the miracle of Jesus's birth, God's Son, and before our very eyes another show of His love for us was unfolding. I wish all of you could have seen the little colorful birds; they were much more beautiful than the glass birds which decorated my parents' tree when I was a boy.

"So, today again, we celebrate His birth. Jesus was born of a virgin. What a miracle! He could have remained in his beautiful home in heaven, but He came to be born in a manger. His earthly parents were as poor as most of us in this room. Jesus grew up in poverty. He and His family were refugees. They fled from King Herod who wanted to kill the young child. Jesus knew what it meant to be hungry and thirsty. He came to

earth to feel everything we are feeling. Everything we are experiencing our Savior has experienced. That is why we can go to Him knowing He'll understand us.

"Today we echo the question asked over nineteen hundred years ago—Have you any room for Jesus? Do you have room in your heart for Him? Did you ever invite the Son of God into your heart? If not, just ask Him for forgiveness of your sins knowing that He died and rose from the dead for you. He'll forgive you and save you from an everlasting hell.

"Many of us had been in bondage to earthly possessions. We didn't have time for the Prince of Peace. Perhaps we had to come to this refugee stage in life so that God could get our attention. Just reach out and accept God's Christmas gift—His Son—today.

"Now let us sing 'Silent Night,'" Vati continued, "the song that is sung all over the world. The French sang it with us in Africa. My sister said it is sung in America. Wherever the birth of Christ is celebrated, this song is touching hearts. God gave this beautiful song to the world through Franz Gruber as we all know."

January 1, 1948! "What will this year bring?" Vati asked at the breakfast table. "Will we find our loved ones? Will we be able to return to East Prussia? The future doesn't look very bright right now. In fact, it looks bleak, very bleak. Only the Lord knows what will happen. Isn't it wonderful that we can trust in Him?"

"Yes," Mutti agreed, "only the Lord knows. Just think of last year and the miracle He performed. He gave Vati a rash which could not be cured in Africa, only to get him back to us in Germany. 'He needed a change of climate,' the camp doctor had told him. And now Vati is here with us." Lovingly she looked at her husband. "His friends are still in Africa. We surely have a wonderful God. We truly are a blessed family."

"Thump . . . thump . . ." was the old familiar sound on the wall again. "Quiet!—Quiet!" Frau Boden yelled.

"But we are quiet," Udo whispered angrily. "I don't like it here."

"None of us do," Marlies agreed, "but we can't go anywhere else. We have no place to go."

"Will we ever be able to eat as much as we want, Mutti? As much as we had in Insterburg?" Dieter asked. "I am always hungry."

"Only the Lord has the answer to that question too," Vati answered. "But since we are talking about eating, let me tell you some African food stories, all right?"

"I don't want to hear about food," Dieter said.

"These stories might not make you hungry, Dieter. They are a little different."

"All right then, Vati."

"On a sunny day in Africa, we were walking on the sandy roads of the camp compound. Some prisoners of war sat outside their barracks playing chess, some practiced their musical instruments which the Red Cross had given us, and some were studying and doing homework. I already told you that we had quite a few teachers among our prisoners. Some of the men wanted to continue their education in specialized fields and attended our camp school."

"I'll be glad when I am finished going to school," Dieter interrupted. "Why would anyone want to go to school?"

"It gave the men something to do since we were not allowed to work. If you have nothing to do, Dieter, school can be exciting. But you are too young to understand that. I took some astronomy courses at the camp.

"Back to my story now. As I said, it was a sunny day. Suddenly we heard something. It sounded like wind. But there was no wind. It also sounded like rain hitting a roof somewhere far away, but there was no rain. Then we looked and far beyond the camp we saw a dark cloud. That was strange, too, because there was no other cloud in the sky. The sound, like a huge buzzing bumblebee, got louder and louder and continued to come closer. The cloud was so thick that it got dark when it moved

in front of the sun. Closer and closer this cloud came. Everybody was looking skyward. What could this be?"

With some of his blond hair hanging straight over his forehead, Udo was spellbound.

"'What could this be?' everyone asked. Suddenly this noisy cloud began to look lacy when it moved over one corner of our camp. 'These are locusts!' someone said. 'Millions and millions of locusts.' And then we saw some fall to the ground—the tired ones—as all the other countless insects buzzed over our heads. As quickly as this cloud came, it was gone again. The sound became weaker and weaker and moved continuously farther away. Everyone was glad the locusts didn't land at the camp because they would have eaten everything, not only grass, bushes, and leaves, but also wood.

"Now I told you this story had something to do with food, right?"

"You didn't eat those locusts, Vati, did you?" Marlies asked.

"Yes, we did. One officer in our camp had eaten them before. He made a fire and roasted them until they were nice and crisp, and then those who wanted to ate some."

"You really did eat them?" Mutti asked.

"Yes, I did. I simply had to try them because it says in the Bible that John ate locusts and honey. The locusts were quite big, but there was only a little meat on the hind legs that was edible and really quite delicious."

Eating locusts was something I would prefer not doing, I reasoned. But that still sounded better to me than eating cats and dogs. One day a relative of ours sat at dinner with a friend. The meat was prepared in a delicious manner and tasted wonderful until the host said that he had jars and jars of cat and dog meat buried in his yard. During this time of starvation, very few animals were seen roaming the streets of postwar Germany.

"Do you have another food story?" Udo inquired.

"Yes, Son, I do. Eight hundred men ate a lot of food and the African farmers around our camp were always thrilled to sell their products to the camp. Usually they brought the food to the camp ready to prepare and eat. One day, however, they did not bring in ready-to-cook meat but brought us meat that was still alive. They walked in with a camel."

"Did it have one hump or two humps?" Dieter wondered.

"It had one hump, Dieter. An animal with two humps is a dromedary."

"Did you like eating camel meat?" I asked.

"Yes, Liane, it was delicious. It tasted very much like beef."

Udo wondered if Vati had another food story.

"Yes," Vati said, "I can tell you something about dates. I don't think you little ones know what dates are. Dates are the fruit of a palm tree, the date nut palm. Each fruit is almost the size of a thumb. Some kinds are smaller than a thumb, some larger. When the dates are picked off the tree—they grow in clusters—they don't have a very good taste. They are not very sweet. So the African farmer digs a deep, large hole, lines it with burlap, and fills the hole with freshly picked dates. Then he covers the top of the dates with burlap and puts a thick layer of soil over everything. For two to three years he leaves the dates in the ground. And do you know what happens to the dates in the dark earth? They get sweeter and sweeter and sweeter. Somehow they make their own sugar, and when the farmer opens up the hole two or three years later, he takes out large chunks of sweet, brown dates."

Udo asked, "What does he do with all those dates?"

"He takes them to the market to sell. I am sure he also keeps some for his family. The prisoners could always buy them at the camp store. Someday perhaps we will be able to buy dates so that you children can try them. So that is the end of our food-story time for today. Did you children learn anything from these stories?"

"Yes, I did," Marlies said. "When you see a cloud of locusts coming, run into the house. If you don't, dead locusts will fall on your head."

Vati's search for a new job continued. The night watchman job was "better than nothing," he said, but it neither brought in enough money to feed the six of us nor was it satisfying or challenging. If only there were an opportunity to have a leather goods store again! We'd probably make more money that way and start saving to eventually build a house. Our living conditions, all six of us eating, sleeping, cooking, living, doing homework in one room—the small room could not be heated during the endless winter season—were deplorable. The abusive landlady had all of us constantly on edge. No one knew what she would yell about next. One day it might be that we were opening our window to air out our room and bedding, the next she might be upset about a footprint on the freshly raked walk which had to be used by everyone to get to the house. "Lord, You see our predicament here. You are in control. Show us which way to move," Vati would pray. "Living here is worse than living at a camp, but You have placed us here for a reason. Show us what that is. Please help me to find employment that is more challenging."

"Guten Tag, Tante Martha Borrmann," Mutti said while hugging her aunt who was about to enter the room. "What brings you to Nienburg today?"

"First, I came to see all of you and your new home—"

"I am sorry, Tante Martha," Mutti interrupted, "please whisper while you are visiting with us. We are not allowed to talk out loud."

"What do you mean, Emmy?"

"Our landlady wants things quiet here. It is difficult with the children, but we are trying our best.

"And what is the other reason you came to see us today?"

"I came to celebrate. Celebrate the fact that God's chosen people have been regathered, and as of yesterday, there is a nation again in the world called 'Israel.' It has happened just as God said it would. Rejoice,

Emmy! Rejoice, children! The Lord's return is near!" she continued. "I am so glad the Lord allowed me to be alive to witness this great event."

"Yesterday Israel gained its statehood?"

"Yes, Emmy, yesterday. Bible prophecy is being fulfilled before our very eyes. Thousands of Jewish people from all over the world are expected to return to their own land just as the Bible said. God is gathering His people and readying them for His coming. For years I have longed for the day when I could see this. No matter what the heathen have done in their quest of trying to eliminate the Jewish race from the earth, they have failed because the Jews are special people—God's chosen people."

"That is true, Tante Martha," Mutti said, "but why did they have to endure so much? Germany's crimes, exposed to the world at the Nuremberg trials, have shocked humanity. Why did God not intervene? The film I saw still gives me nightmares. It simply can't be described what these people endured. Why?"

"I don't have the answer, Emmy. Someday, in heaven, many will be asking God about the Holocaust, and why He appeared to be silent when His chosen ones were suffering. Germany will be judged for its deeds. Any nation of the world that persecutes Jews will be judged. But until that horrible judgment falls, we must love God's people and never forget that our dear Savior was a Jew. How can we love Christ without loving a Jewish person? It is impossible, absolutely impossible."

Centered in the old part of the city of Nienburg, the Lutherkirche was of Gothic design unlike the older, ornate German cathedrals of Cologne, Nürnberg, Regensburg, or others known for their Baroque splendor. During the summer months, farmers set up their produce tables on the broad cobblestone courtyard surrounding the base of the church. Every Saturday, they sold anything their land and labor produced, from delicate raspberries to hard turnips.

Copper-clad, the church steeple towered high above all the town's buildings. The large bells beckoned the faithful to the Sunday services or

reminded citizens below of human mortality by announcing someone's departure for the life beyond. The bells also announced the passing of time or rang for weddings.

Inside, the church evoked a reverent spirit of the visitor when viewing the altar and many Gothic arches. Outside, the massive-looking building, faced in red brick, gave a solid portrayal of Martin Luther, the founder of the Reformation and Protestant movement. Most of Nienburg's citizens attested to being members of the Lutherkirche, yet showed their support by attending services only at Christmas or Easter. Perhaps they considered "church taxes," taken out of every member's paycheck by the government, an absolution of obligation. The church was there; everyone was used to it. It was a building every town had—except those destroyed by the enemy. One could hear the bells, yet shut out their pleading. The church was a place to get married, baptize children, be confirmed in the faith, and have one's eulogy read; a place to appease one's conscience. How else would one fulfill the laws of Christ?

It was easy to be faithful. After confirmation, only a few days of one's life were needed to prepare for the heavenlies. Religious instructions leading to the festive confirmation Sunday had been endured, the meaning of church ordinances rehearsed, and Scripture verses committed to memory. Striding through town in white dresses and handsome suits, fourteen-year-old boys and girls garnered the admiration of the townspeople. In class, God was even asked to forgive everyone's sins. It was routine, mechanical, beautiful. Everyone was praying the same prayer; they were asked to. Did God forgive sins collectively, or did one have to make it personal? "We all prayed the same prayer," my friend told me.

"Did you believe everything you prayed?"

"No, I didn't think much about it. We were supposed to say that or we wouldn't get confirmed and become a member of the church."

"Did you mean it when you asked Christ into your heart?" I wondered.

"I don't know. It was just something we had to do."

Asking my friend these questions probably would not have concerned me a few months earlier, but as a new babe in Christ for just a few weeks, I became more spiritually aware of things around me. I knew my life had changed in that tent meeting. "I am a sinner," I had prayed. "Please, Lord, forgive me of my sins. Come into my heart and save me." I meant what I prayed and was absolutely certain that Christ answered my prayer by giving me eternal life. Through the preaching, I learned that I would be eternally separated from God if I did not decide right then to whom I would yield my life, the Creator of the universe or Satan, the deceiver.

Why did only some members of the Lutherkirche think a personal commitment was necessary? And why were they ostracized from their congregation? Why were they not permitted to worship in their sanctuary and often came to fellowship with our group of Bible believers? I could not find the answers to these questions.

On July 18, 1948, dressed in long white gowns, twenty-one people, men, women, and teenagers, stood in the sandy area along the Weser river to be baptized. Many curious townspeople, families, friends, and reporters had gathered to witness this first event ever in the city's history—a baptismal service as it was performed in Bible times. Folks even watched from the other side of the river. Standing there with twenty others, knowing that I was about to take another step of obedience as a young Christian, filled my soul with love for the One who died for me on Calvary.

With the sun shining down on the born-again ones that warm summer day, suddenly Satan began to rob me of my joy. "You are different, very different from your classmates," he whispered. "Are you sure you want to be that way? They will laugh at you when they see your picture

in the paper. You are the only one of fifty students in your class. Look at yourself! You don't really want to be baptized today by immersion and become a laughingstock. You are just fine without all this. There is still time for you to change your mind."

With the onslaught of the devil continuing, I suddenly heard the choir sing:

"Who are these all dressed in white?
They are those—they are those who are washed clean in the blood of the Lamb."
(Palmer, "Wer sind diese, weiß geschmückt?")

"Thank You, Lord," I said. "I am on Your side. Help me to be faithful to You."

"We welcome all of you here today," Pastor Zinser started, "to witness the baptism of these twenty-one folks. They have done what Jesus said; they have confessed their sins and asked Christ to come into their lives. They were tired of playing church and carrying their burdens alone. They learned that Christ died for their sins, was buried, and rose again. And now they are standing here as a testimony of their love for and obedience to Christ. These twenty-one are not being saved today. That has already taken place in their hearts. Today they are identifying with Christ. Jesus Himself was baptized by John in the River Jordan. You are going to witness a biblical baptismal service today. We believe in everything the Bible tells us to do, and baptism is one of the ordinances for the believers."

The baptismal service had its impact on our town; the church increased in number. Some of our Lutheran friends wanted to be baptized and join our church. My girlfriend from the camp later also accepted Christ as her Savior and was baptized in the Weser.

12

The Miracle Business

It was Monday morning, June 20, 1948. Shoppers returned from town with strange news. Advertisement pillars around town bore the same messages, "Currency reform begins today in the three Western zones, the American, British, and French. All old money is without value. Go to the bank with documents and receive forty Deutsche Mark per person, including children." The Russians refused the currency reform in their zone, the posted newspapers stated; they refused to cooperate with the other Big Three. Instead they continued their efforts to take over all of Berlin by stopping the inter-zonal traffic of the Western forces to bring supplies to their various sectors. To keep the people in the Western sectors of Berlin alive, the West responded to the Russians' harassment by airlifting everything from food to coal in order to retain their claim on their share of the city.

Vati returned from the bank with 240 Deutsche Mark. Along with everyone else, he questioned the buying power of the new money. Was that money sufficient to start building a new life, or was it just enough to keep people alive? Not until after Mutti had gone to town with the new money did we get an idea of the purchasing power of the Deutsche

Mark. Within a few weeks, the shelves of dry goods stores were stocked with all types of merchandise. Grocery stores eventually also began to fill up with various edibles the populace had not seen in years. Were the "hunger years," as Mutti called them, over? Would refugees be able to live like the natives someday?

"Perhaps we can return to East Prussia before too long," Vati said. "Things are changing so quickly. The borders have been redrawn, if only we knew how. It would be easier to restart a business back home than in a new town. Perhaps our home and store in Insterburg were not destroyed."

"We don't know, Emil, about that situation. One thing, however, you can't imagine," Mutti continued, "you can't imagine the destruction of Insterburg. So much of it was in ruins when we left. You remember Insterburg as it once was, and you are longing for that. But our hometown will never again be the same. Even if we can return, it will take years and years to rebuild. Many were killed there too. Who of the survivors would even want to return and rebuild? And who would want to again live so close to the Russian border? I wouldn't. We have suffered too much under that regime."

"All the news from that part of the country is still blacked out," Vati continued, "except for the few lines we surprisingly received from your mother; and they don't say anything about the political aspect. If only we knew what is going on there. Perhaps the conquerors and the world will take pity on the millions of German refugees who are still wandering about aimlessly—living and dying in camps, forests, and ruins—and return their lands to them. Are they not seeing our plight?"

"Yes, there is much to wonder about. If only Hitler would have been eliminated from the political arena long before he did begin his devilish reign! He must have been possessed of the devil and protected by Satan himself. Some of his inner circle," Mutti continued, "tried to

assassinate him a number of times, but he always escaped unharmed. Every assassination attempt failed."

"Is it true, Emmy, that someone planned to kill Hitler in East Prussia while he was in a conference at the Wolfsschanze?"

"That is what I heard, Emil. He appeared to be immune to anything plotted against him. The bomb, they say, was planted right under his conference table."

"Well," Vati reasoned, "we can only speculate now in retrospect as to what would have happened if things had been different. We just know that for some reason God permitted all the events that have shaken Europe, and especially Germany, and we as Germans collectively will probably have to suffer for years to come because of Hitler's treatment of the Jewish people. And in the final end, God Himself will judge our whole nation. That is what will happen according to the Book of Revelation in the Bible."

I tried to do my homework but couldn't concentrate. Things seemed hopeless. God Himself would judge Germany for something Hitler and his SS did? When would that happen? Next week? Next year? Tante Martha Borrmann always talked about the Antichrist and the number 666 on people's foreheads. I believed the Bible and knew God's plan would be carried out, but the future surely didn't seem very bright. At times I felt burdened and without joy when thinking about things to come. Perhaps it would be best for the Lord to come quickly as so many were praying in our prayer meetings. Three years and several months after war's end, we still didn't have enough to eat. We were still living in one room. We still couldn't rise up and start a new life.

"Tonight," Vati announced, "we have to earnestly pray about something. As you all know, my night watchman job doesn't pay very much, and the employment agency still hasn't found another job for me. So, during the past few days, I have gone to several storekeepers in

town to see if they can help me. I thought if perhaps I can buy a store, we can again open up a leather goods business."

"Do you mean we are going to be rich again, Vati?" Dieter asked.

"No, Son, if we have a store, we won't be rich, but perhaps you can have a few extra slices of bread to eat, maybe even with butter and honey."

"I can't wait for that day, Vati."

"Now let me get back to what I was trying to say. I stopped at a tobacco store. The lady didn't have any customers because all the allocated cigarettes had already been sold, so we just talked. The unique thing was that her husband had just received work in Hannover and they were trying to sell the store in order to move. I told her about our predicament. 'Well,' she said, 'since you are trying to start a business, I will be very generous. I will sell you the store and all the furnishings for one thousand Mark.'"

"Emil," Mutti said in shock, "where are we going to get that kind of money?"

"I don't know. But that is not the only question to be addressed. The other question is how we as Christians can sell cigarettes. We believe smoking is not good for the body. We believe in keeping our bodies clean, inwardly and outwardly. How then can we justify selling cigarettes to others? Now, we wouldn't be in the tobacco business long . . . just long enough to get on our feet, make some money, and then change over to leather goods."

"Well," Mutti sighed, "that sounds like a nice dream, but I think that is all it is. When do you have to give the lady your answer, Emil?"

"One week from today. We have one week to come up with the money. If it is the Lord's will that we start a business in such a strange way, He'll help us. If the door closes, we will consider it of Him also. In the meantime, we'll all pray for His will to be done."

Vati spent the next few days talking to bankers about a loan for starting a business. "If you don't have any collateral, Herr Guddat, we

are sorry, but we can't help you," he was told by several bankers. None of our refugee church friends could help us, yet Vati continued to pray for a miracle—but none came.

Disappointed, Vati set out for the store one week from the day he received the purchase offer to inform the store owner that it was impossible for him to come up with one thousand Mark. After he returned home in the afternoon, Vati gathered all five of us around himself to tell us what had transpired that day. "We all prayed about our future and the store," he opened the conversation. "You all know that this was the day the store owner needed an answer from me in regard to the purchase. This morning on my way to tell her that we could not buy the business, I prayed as I walked. Suddenly a friend called 'Hello, Emil, how are you today?'

"'Oh,' I said, 'I am not doing too well today.'

"'Why not?' he asked.

"'You see, I am just on my way to turn down a business opportunity because I don't have one thousand Mark to buy a store.'

"'Is that all that makes you so sad?' my friend asked. 'You just come on down to the bank with me. They know me and my business there. I'll cosign a loan for you.' So my friend and I went to the bank, and an hour later, I handed the store owner one thousand Mark. We are owners of a new store today. A miracle has happened today. It must have been the Lord's will."

Vati traveled to Hannover by train—about thirty miles away—to purchase cigarettes directly from the manufacturer. Each business was allotted only a certain number of packages per week. Vati, however, presented his plight to the manufacturer and was told that he could purchase as much as he wanted from then on—on a cash basis only. With his first merchandise, an order of eighty packages of cigarettes, he returned to Nienburg to prepare for opening day, October 1, Mutti's birthday. Vati's sister from America had sent a coffee can filled with flints

for the new business. They would be sold for twenty pfennig, one-fifth of a Mark, apiece and were an item the competition on the other end of town did not have.

Early on the morning of October 1, Vati and Mutti made the fifteen-minute walk to town. There were a few more things to ready in the store before opening the door to the public. From quite a distance, however, my parents noticed a long queue already near their store. That was probably the line of people waiting to get to the bakery around the corner of the building, they thought. But, coming closer, they realized that all those people waited for the opening of Emil Guddat's store. Since the business had no back door, Vati and Mutti had to enter through the front door with customers pushing into the store right after them. In one hour every package of cigarettes was sold even though the last packages were broken up to sell only three cigarettes to each customer. With the money and a cardboard suitcase in hand, Vati immediately walked to the train station and boarded a train to Hannover again. The next morning, the scene repeated itself.

News of cigarettes being available at the store on the northern end of town daily—rather than weekly—quickly spread among all the smokers. There was a long line at the store before opening hour every morning, and the Sold Out sign usually went up within one to two hours. Vati purchased another inexpensive suitcase and began traveling to a second manufacturer in Bremen. The refugee's business was flourishing even though the profit was considerably smaller than in leather goods. Vati increased Mutti's food allowance, and once every few weeks, on Sundays, we got a small taste of meat. One day Vati surprised us with a package of dates and figs, delicacies that had been so plentiful at his African camp. Our favorite meal continued to be potatoes with eggs in mustard sauce and browned cauliflower, or potato pancakes.

At Christmastime we each received a small present. The prayer for the New Year was to be able to change the store into a leather goods store.

"When that is well established," Vati announced one day, "perhaps the Lord will let us build a little house somewhere." In the meantime, we all had to sacrifice privacy, continue to whisper, never put our weight down when walking, and endure all types of insults from our landlady.

One Sunday after church, Mutti was preparing dinner and needed something from the basement where everything that required cold storage was kept on the cement floor. When she returned upstairs, Frau Boden had slammed the door shut. Mutti knocked on the door—and with us still not home from Sunday school—no one but Frau Boden could open the door. Mutti knew the dinner was burning on the stove. The lady from upstairs also smelled it and came down to help Mutti break the window and lift her into our room while our landlady pretended not to hear or smell anything.

One day Vati decided to purchase a lady's used bicycle from one of his customers. No longer did we have to carry potatoes, carrots, and five-pound loaves of bread home from town until our arms seemed to be pulled out of their sockets. Our "new" mode of transportation was to be used only for business rather than pleasure and had to be chained to a bicycle stand every time it was parked somewhere. On Saturday afternoons we all pitched in polishing and sanding the rust off our family treasure in order to ready it for the following week.

"Look at this, Emil," Mutti said one evening while handing Vati a letter from the Red Cross. Vati unfolded it and read out loud, "Honorable Frau Guddat! We are very happy to inform you that we have learned of your husband's whereabouts. Emil Guddat is a prisoner of war in Africa. You may contact him at the following address."

Vati and Mutti embraced and laughed. "We have had you home for over one year already. And we are so thankful." Mutti beamed. "But just think of all the work the Red Cross has to accomplish to aid millions of refugees and prisoners. It must be a difficult task."

13

Saved Again

As our church youth group increased in number, finding a place in which to meet was not easy. None of our parents had spacious homes; all refugees seemed to be living in cramped quarters. When Paul, our young people's leader and a refugee from Ukraine, began to work for a British Salvation Army major, our problems were solved temporarily. Not only did the major permit us to hold meetings in his home—the house of a former Nazi—but often he also treated us to hot chocolate and cookies. The major spoke only in English, and I quickly realized that my school English was quite limited. I understood very little. When he talked fast, I understood nothing.

During the summer months, our group conducted the young people's meetings in fields, forests, or along the riverbank. Our meetings were solely dedicated to Bible study, singing, and prayer. On Sunday afternoons we visited elderly church members who could not walk to the services and held our meetings in their homes. Our song time—without hymn books of course, since we had none—usually lasted forty-five minutes because everyone loved to sing. The elderly often invited their friends and neighbors to our meetings.

Mutti traded one of her dresses for a used guitar and started a guitar choir in our church. Since music was a vital and effective tool to invite non-churchgoers to the services, revival meetings always started with a half-hour of guitar music. Visitors came just to hear the music but then decided to stay for the service and, oftentimes, accepted Christ. All the music had to be reconstructed from memory by the choir members and then written on pieces of scrap paper.

During West Germany's short summers, everyone had to work hard in order to prepare for winter. The small coal allotments every household received were not enough to carry a whole family through the winter. The government, therefore, offered citizens certain sections of land on which to cut peat. Early one summer morning, Vati and Mutti set out for the peat bog on their bicycles.

"Children," Vati announced upon their return in the evening, "you almost became orphans today."

"What does that mean, Vati?" Marlies asked.

"That means that we were almost killed today and you children would have been left alone—without parents."

"What happened?"

"Well, I will tell the four of you exactly what happened," Vati said in a somber tone. "You already knew that several days ago some of our friends had cut peat for us in the peat bog. Peat is not very good for heating our room—coal or wood are better, but peat is all we can get right now in preparation for the winter months.

"Mutti and I traveled by bike for almost forty-five minutes to the swampland. It was such a beautiful ride in God's sunshine, past lush forests and fields. We saw cattle grazing peacefully, swallows diving from the sky and swooping past us, bright red patches of poppies in the fields, and not a cloud in the sky."

"Did you have a picnic?" Udo inquired.

"No," Mutti answered, "we planned to do that after our work."

"We had to take all the chunks of peat that were stacked and restack them," Vati continued. "Peat is a product of the swamp, and it is dripping wet. In order for us to use it, it has to be dry. Like wooden play blocks, the chunks were piled in a circular tower; a real wide base at the bottom and then higher and higher with space in between so that the air could get in and dry it. The outside had dried beautifully. What we had to do today was to turn the whole tower inside out because inside, the peat was still quite wet.

"We parked our bikes on one of the little swamp islands and started restacking. There were a few gray puffy clouds in the sky, but later we noticed black threatening clouds every time we looked up. All of a sudden, it seemed the sky turned pitch black, and thunder began to roll closer and closer. We saw lightning a short distance away. Quickly, we threw our blanket over the bikes and searched for a small island where we would be safe."

"Why didn't you jump on the bikes and take off?" Udo wondered.

"Metal draws lightning. We would have been killed instantly," Mutti replied.

Marlies was curious as to why our parents did not hide under trees. "Trees draw lightning too," Vati said. "There was no place for us to find safety. We were far away from a town or village. Lightning bolts began to hit the water to our right, then to our left. The huge black clouds began to dump all their water on us. We held each other very tightly while ducking there on our island. Lightning, thunder, torrents of rain. Our ears seemed to explode. Crashes and more crashes all around us. 'Lord, who will take care of our children,' we asked, 'if You take us to heaven today?' We heard no answer to our question. Blinding bolts ripped through the musty swamp air and zapped into the water all around us."

"We knew we were going to die," Mutti continued, "and we were prepared to die. Anyone who has Jesus in his heart is going to heaven. We were not afraid to go to be with Jesus. We were ready." With tears

gently rolling down her cheeks, she said, "But we just didn't want you children to remain alone here on earth. You would have been orphans."

"But," Vati continued the near-death story, "with electric bolts driving into everything around us, we could do nothing but rest in the Lord. Life or death—we were in His hands. He decided, however, to let us live and sent us home to all of you."

"That is a miracle. We must thank the Lord for again making us a family," Mutti said while drawing Udo still closer to herself, "a true miracle."

My greatest desire was to own a watch. In order to get one, I had to earn money, and with the forests always yielding an abundance of edibles, my small enterprise began. The biggest money-makers were blueberries. After picking the low-growing berries in the woods and meeting Mutti's needs first, I sold the rest by the roadside. In the fields, my girlfriend and I picked daisies and blackberries and sold them at a street corner downtown. By summer's end, I estimated that it would take me only about two or three more years before I had saved enough money to buy an inexpensive watch.

Udo's happiness could hardly be measured when he received a ball for his sixth birthday. "Play with the ball only in front of the house," Vati told him. "It would be too bad if you lost your birthday present." For a time my little brother heeded his dad's warning, but since most of his friends played in a field at the edge of our development, he decided to take his ball there also. When he, Marlies, and Dieter returned from play sad-looking and quiet, Mutti surmised that something had gone wrong. "Why are you so sad, Udo?" she asked. He did not answer, neither did his brother nor sister. All of them stared at the freshly scrubbed wooden floor. "Tell me, Udo—What happened?"

"I lost my ball," he confessed and started sobbing.

"You lost your birthday gift? Where?"

"At the fox farm."

"You took your ball all the way over there?"

"Ja, Mutti. Dieter and I were playing catch on the way to the field, and it went over the fence."

"Now wasn't there some way for you to retrieve it?"

"No," Marlies added, "it rolled into a foxhole real fast. Dieter climbed over the fence and stuck his arm deep into the hole, but he couldn't reach it."

Whenever I wasn't chained to my homework, I helped with the household or laundry. No one realized, however, how difficult it was to miss a day of school, something I had to do every few weeks in order to help Mutti on the scrub board. I did not mind helping, but missing vocabulary words and expressions, which the professors expected us to know the next day, was difficult.

French had become my favorite language; English I endured, French I loved. The nasal sounds gave me a special thrill. I worked diligently at French because I had found something that really captured my interest. Our professor made French come alive by traveling to France or the French part of Switzerland and returning with new stories and expressions. "You were speaking French again in your sleep last night," Vati or Mutti would often tell me in the morning. For some strange reason, they never heard me practicing English in my sleep. Was that because the professor was more intent on grammar than the practical, conversational English? He had never visited Great Britain or the United States. His teaching methods seemed dull and boring. The black-haired, bespectacled, short professor at times was unaware of the fact that all fifty of us girls really didn't care to learn English. Instead of listening and learning, we sometimes caused him to blush and squirm by—on someone's command—staring at his crooked tie or a missing galosh.

At the Lyceum, however, we did have to learn, whether we felt like it or not. We had to study English as well as French, German, physics, chemistry, history, mathematics, geography, art, and religion, and

participate in sports activities, or leave the school. There were others waiting to get in. A few unsatisfactory grades could cause dismissal; no second chances were given. Often I'd fall asleep with my head on the dinner table while studying into the late evening hours. On Saturdays the teachers would always pile an extra load of homework on us to be sure we had something to do on Sundays.

"This afternoon, we are going to see our forester friend," Vati announced. "Mutti will be at the store, Liane has to do homework, and the rest of us will go to the Crow Forest."

Everyone was excited about the outing with Vati and again seeing the quaint home of the forester located at the edge of the woods. How I wished I could have gone along! The forester—in charge of keeping the forest floor free of debris, branches, dead trees; transplanting; and planting—had studied the art of forestry for years. He was helping oversee one of the most revered German treasures, the forest, which always resembled a park; it was neat and clean. Countless townspeople were lured into this majestic cathedral of nature to move about in awe and wonder, inhale and smell the potpourri fragrance, and find spiritual and physical renewal. Sandy paths, often winding, led the wanderer past patches of lush green or brown spindly grasses. At times a whole patch of mouse barley would sway in the breeze, giving the appearance of yards and yards of fluttering silk fabric.

The warm summer sun squeezed all the scents out of the pine needles which mulched the forest floor. Berry patches invited the wanderer to stop for a tasty treat. Many kinds of mushrooms were pulled from the black forest earth by the knowledgeable delicacy hunter. Hundreds of acres, a short distance from town, belonged to everyone to enjoy and cherish. Picnic blankets could be spread anywhere. Different types of mosses and flowers drew all stops of admiration out of the organ of life; music of the soul harmonized with the bird's chirping. Even the homely crow with its shrill song joined in the chorus of life. Hares zigzagged

through the forest carpet, their long ears flapping while playing havoc with the eyes of a city resident. Gentle breezes caressed pines, maples, majestic oaks, and beechnut trees.

In the midst of a clearing towered a tall, wooden tree stand. The skill of a hunter or forester, armed with a rifle, helped protect the balance of nature. Nothing was useless in the cathedral of life; the very air purified and healed diseased lungs. Sticks, branches, and dead trees provided firewood for the poor. Food, tended by the Creator Himself, yielded nutrients to sustain human and animal life. Visitors to the cathedral of nature always appeared reverent; they meandered, cycled, meditated, enjoyed. Never did they act loud and boisterous. They always talked in hushed manners.

In the evening Vati, my brothers, and sister returned from their outing excited and bubbling. They talked about the forester, his kindness to them, his little courtyard, but most of all his wonderful dog. The dachshund was always at his master's side. He was the forester's companion. "Someone to talk to," he'd say, "since the death of my wife." The kind dog also loved children, and they in turn loved him.

"I wish I could have a dog like that," Dieter said with his brother and sister in agreement. "Wouldn't it be fun to have him and always play with him the way we did today?"

"Frau Boden would never allow us to have a dog here. Can you imagine what she'd do if he would ever bark?" Marlies asked, thereby closing the discussion for the evening.

Upon his return from the store the next day, Vati said, "I have something very sad to tell all of you. Our forester friend came into the store today."

"Did he bring his dachshund along?" Udo asked.

"No, he didn't. He couldn't. And that is why he was so sad. You knew that the little dog was his best friend, didn't you? He kept the forester company when he worked and made him happy. Those two were always together; they were inseparable.

"Well, today the forester was doing some kind of work in front of his house. The little brown dachshund, of course, was there too. Suddenly—it sounded like a storm—the little dog began to yelp and yelp. The forester turned around and in shock saw an eagle dig his claws into the sides of the dog. Quickly the forester grabbed his gun and aimed for the eagle, but the powerful bird carried his little friend high into the air, holding him tightly in his claws. The forester shot again and again while the scared dog just yelped and yelped. Every shot missed the powerful bird. 'Why did I have to miss that bird?' the forester asked me. 'What am I going to do without my wonderful companion? First, I lost my wife and now my faithful little friend.'"

Shocked, we all listened to the sad story. Marlies cried. I cried while picturing that horrible scene. Udo and Dieter sat on their bunks, serious and visibly shaken.

14

Sad News

By age sixteen, I considered myself old enough to have my braids cut off and get a permanent, but Vati and Mutti disagreed. I wanted to change, be beautiful, yet everything worked against me. The old brown coat, made of an army blanket, was one of my greatest obstacles. I was tired of it. *If I have a choice someday,* I thought, *I'll never again choose anything brown.* Wearing the same two dresses year in and year out, while most of my classmates wore many beautiful clothes, also hindered my dream of improving my looks. Vanity really showed itself in my pride of owning my first pair of stockings. I cared for them as if they were a treasure. One day, however, I somehow got runs in my hose and had to take them to the repair shop in town. That was the first and last time they were repaired professionally. "Those prices are exorbitant," Mutti said and purchased a tiny crochet hook for me. "I'll teach you how to pick up the cross threads of your runs and repair them yourself." I learned quickly and never again spent one pfennig on my precious hose.

Even though at times I resented the fact that I could not improve my looks outwardly, I felt at peace most of the time. Jesus loved me; I was His, and I loved the One who had done so much for me. He had

died for me. I was sure that I was bound for heaven. My baptismal verse, Romans 12:2, "And be not conformed to this world: but be ye transformed by the renewing of your mind," told me how I should live. I loved to read my Bible and enjoyed the heated competition in the young people's group of memorizing the whole eighth chapter of Romans. My girlfriend, Hildegard, at times was ahead of me in committing the chapter to memory, which caused me to work extra hard to meet the deadline. Only a few of our young people memorized the whole chapter.

My greatest desire, since we left Berlin, was to see Kätchen again. I often wondered about her and missed her. Would we ever again meet on earth? Were she and her family living in cramped quarters as we were? What would she have done to survive at Frau Boden's? Would her frail body have been able to take all the mental abuse? Would she have laughed at the landlady who forced her maid to whistle the whole time she picked cherries, or would she have told the maid to go ahead and eat some cherries?

Would Kätchen's husband, also a former prisoner of war, have been as angry as Vati was when Frau Boden put up a barbwire fence to keep his children from side-stepping on the path? I think so. Finally, after having reasoned in vain with the landlady, Vati went to the housing authority to file a complaint against her. "A high barbwire fence," he stated, "kept me from the very things the human soul needs most. For three years, I daily looked at the obstacle to freedom which separated me from my family. Now that I am finally living with my loved ones, do I have to feel again the incarceration of soul? Daily my landlady's action reminds me of the torture and agony of soul I have endured. My daughter, whose wardrobe is small, also tore her dress on that fence when she passed by on a windy day. I request your seeing to it that Frau Boden remove the fence leading from the front door to the street."

The efforts of the housing authority to have our landlady remove the fence failed and the matter was handed over to a judge. He ruled against Frau Boden who stood in his presence irate, fuming, and defiant.

"Lord, we praise and thank You for all Your kindness and mercies to us," Vati prayed during our devotion time. "You have brought us together again. We are a complete family. But, Lord, we continue to be concerned about our loved ones, Uropi, my sister-in-law, and my mother. Are they still on earth, perhaps suffering somewhere, or are they with You? We have Your peace, yet we are concerned and burdened without knowing about them. Please show us somehow soon.

"We also pray for the Schiller Omi. Only You know how much she is suffering with her open cancer sores. Please ease her pain.

"And, Lord, You see our terrible housing situation. Frau Boden is wearing us down. She wants to get rid of us so she can have her rooms back. Please help us. You are blessing the business so abundantly. Are we to continue in it and build a small house or shall we take the savings and start a leather goods store? Please show us the way.

"Thank You for our church and all the folks who have found their way to the cross recently. Help them to grow in You. Thank You for Calvary and our wonderful salvation. Protect us all tonight. Help the children in school tomorrow. Let them be good students and good examples to everyone. In Jesus's name. Amen."

"Isn't it wonderful, children," Mutti asked the next morning, "that we no longer have to sleep on straw mattresses? We can get up in the morning without red bites and scratch marks all over our bodies."

"And I no longer have to drag my mattress out of the house every morning," Vati added, "the way I used to in Africa."

"Why did you do that, Vati?" Dieter wondered.

"I'll tell you why. Our mattresses were always full of pesky bugs which multiplied very fast. Since the walls of our camp huts were built

of clay, they just teemed with ants. Every morning the ants would come out of the cracks and go into the mattresses for their breakfast."

Marlies thoughtfully and disgustingly asked, "What kind of breakfast?"

"The bedbug breakfast. The ants just loved to eat those tasty morsels. So when the prisoners noticed how the chain of life was working, some started pulling their mattresses out into the camp street every morning until at last, every man was doing it. Outside, the ants came from everywhere and ate the bugs. So our pests vanished every morning, but new ones appeared again during the night. In the summer, we even slept in the camp streets where it was cooler."

"That makes me shudder," Marlies admitted, and I agreed.

Vati continued his travels to the cigarette manufacturers by rail while Mutti spent most of her time at the store. Our meals were plain and simple with meat on the menu perhaps once every seven to ten days. The arrival of a package from America became a rare event. Tante Martha had sacrificed much in time and money from her very meager income at the Mission Home in New Jersey to help us stay alive. We still laughed sometimes about the powdery stuff she sent which we mixed with water to make into a Sunday breakfast spread, and which we later learned was powdered milk. We also laughed about the gray, hard chunk we thought was lard but turned out to be homemade soap.

Stories about the "land of golden opportunity" circulated throughout Germany; more and more people planned to emigrate to America. German girls and women who had married American soldiers, the so-called "war brides," left the country by the hundreds. "That is the quickest avenue for women to leave war-ravaged Germany," someone said.

Refugees who had relatives in the United States or Canada tried with all their might to leave Germany. Building a new life from scratch was difficult for many, if not impossible. Those who had already crossed

the Atlantic sent glowing reports of instant job opportunities, owning cars, and building homes. Sometimes American or Canadian church organizations sponsored the emigration of whole families. A large group of families from our church started their paperwork to leave for Winnipeg, Canada; one family planned to go first and then help the others across the ocean.

"You should join us too," the pastor told Vati and Mutti. "We will need you as an organist and choir leader in our church over there, Emil."

"I don't speak English," Vati said, "and we don't know anything about Canada and the conditions there. I think my family and I, with the Lord's help, will continue to try building a new life here in Germany. I really don't have any desire to leave my homeland and become a foreigner."

With the excitement mounting in our church, so many learning English and planning to leave for the "promised land," I thought more and more about what it would be like to leave Germany. Every time, however, that my heart strayed halfway across the ocean, it quickly returned to my family and homeland. Perhaps the Russians would give up the German states they confiscated and let us return to East Prussia.

We learned much about the difficult and tiring steps that had to be taken toward emigration. On both sides of the Atlantic, health reports, police reports, financial soundness of the sponsor, and other facts had to be checked to satisfy both governments. Since many refugees were sick from malnutrition and exposure to the elements, they often received disappointing reports. Even with all paperwork completed, some were held back and sent to sanatoriums for the healing of their tuberculosis infected lungs. Only healthy people were worthy of settling or homesteading in Canada or America.

Our pastor and his wife were among the first to leave Germany. The church was literally in mourning when those planters of His vineyard left. Would a new pastor be willing to take the flock under his wings, visit his members in rain or sunshine by pedaling a bike countless miles

every week? Would he be willing to bicycle every Sunday after the service to the new sister church that had been started? Would he be willing to pedal mile upon mile to wipe the tears of someone whose loved one had just gone to heaven? Pastor Zinser had sacrificed over and over again, only the Lord knew how much. And now we were to say goodbye to him? What would our young people's group do without all those who were planning to leave? "There will be others who'll join the ranks and take our places," they would humbly and hastily say.

Refugees, fumbling through life without hope and purpose, plagued by concerns for loved ones, often searched for spiritual answers by attending revival meetings. The tent meetings, less formal and inhibiting than the majestic cathedrals, always drew many visitors. The evangelistic meetings, which our church sponsored for several weeks during the summer months, were attended by several hundred visitors. Curiosity seekers often left the services as born-again Christians.

Whether refugees were children of the Most High or children of the devil, the gnawing questions remained the same in regard to unaccounted-for relatives and friends. Were they dead in some ditch, buried in a ship at sea, in Siberia, or were they being tortured in some faraway jail? Would children find their parents, and would parents find their children? Would the minds and bodies of women savagely raped by the Russians ever be whole again, or would they remain in their vegetative state? Would the refugee camps ever be closed because everyone lived in a home or apartment? Would Germany ever be able to face the world again, or would Hitler's evil deeds haunt its citizens for generations to come? No one had answers to these questions. No one could project into the future. Germans walked through time like somber silhouettes—shadows in the darkness of night groping for yet not finding answers.

Feverishly the Red Cross continued to collect names and addresses with the goal of uniting families. Occasionally a family reunion took

place. More and more prisoners of war of the Western forces gained release from camps. Only a few, however, returned from Russia. Horror stories about death and life in the Siberian camps infrequently filtered into the hearts of Germans. Skeletons, we heard, worked in the mines. They were hungry and cold. Those too sick to march or work greeted the slave master's rifle bullet with a sigh of relief. Herds of humanity—men, women, children—had to produce for the conqueror on the road to death. Life was cheap. There were thousands who would be happy to reach for a slice of bread in exchange for mining tons of coal. The Red Cross could not reunite dead bodies frozen in the tundra with searching family members. East Prussian, Selisian, or Pomeranian meetings were arranged in West Germany to help in the search or to gather information, but few accomplished more than exchanging woes and sad tales about their homeland.

"Tante Martha Borrmann," Mutti joyously whispered, leading her into our room, "how good to see you again!"

Tante Martha, with the vertical scar on her forehead, bright red from the hairline to her nose, did not smile as she always did. "I have sad news today," she started immediately. "I have heard from my sister Emma, who in turn heard from Emil's sister-in-law."

"That is wonderful news. Praise the Lord! She is alive . . . and my mother-in-law?"

Tante Martha, with a look of sorrow on her face, answered, "She is in a better place, Emmy."

My heart broke when I learned that I would never again see my sweet grandmother on earth. She loved me so much, and I loved her dearly. Udo was not that touched by the sad news. He was only eighteen months old when the Russians chased our grandmother and Mutti's sister-in-law out of Lippehne, the town northeast of Berlin, where all of us had sought refuge.

"Do you know, Tante Martha, how she died?" Mutti asked with a tear-stained face.

"Yes, I know the whole story, but it is too horrible to repeat."

When Vati returned from the store, we all learned of the savage circumstances that led to his dear Christian mother's death.

After his sister-in-law and Omi left our town on foot to head west with the treks of homeless, they came to a small village somewhere and searched for a place to rest. The Russian hordes had noticed Vati's young sister-in-law and rushed into the house in which they stayed. The sister-in-law, having been raped by a soldier in Lippehne, climbed onto the roof of the house and raced from housetop to housetop to escape her pursuers. She was successful in outrunning them. In their anger at having lost the trail of their prey, however, the hordes returned to the first house in search of more young women but found none, only a room full of elderly people. Spewing revenge and madness, the beasts had grabbed my seventy-eight-year-old grandmother, and with everyone in the room watching, took turns raping Omi. She died an agonizing death a short time later.

15

Home at Last

"'Herr Guddat,' the bank president told me today, 'your business must be going well. I have been watching your account, as I said I would, and have concluded that you are a worthy candidate for a loan. How much money do you want to borrow to build your house?' he then asked."

"Do you mean, Vati, we can leave this terrible place?" Dieter interrupted. "We are going to have our own house?"

"Yes, Dieter. But it will take quite a while before the house is finished and we can move in."

Everyone was rejoicing. Did that mean we could talk like normal people and also not have to sneak out of the house in hopes of avoiding Frau Boden's verbal attacks? Would we really someday be free of this person whose only mission in life, so it seemed, was to harm us?

"We are going to build?" I asked.

"Yes, Liane, in the Rösler Street, just at the border of the next village," Vati continued. "The town of Nienburg has given us a land lease because we are refugees. That means we don't have to buy the land. For just twenty Mark per year we are entitled to live on that lot."

On the following Sunday afternoon, we took a walk to our lot. "But somebody is already living on our land," Dieter pointed out. "Who is living in that shack?"

"A man wanted to buy this land," Vati explained, "and started building the little house you call a 'shack.' Unfortunately, he ran out of money and now has been told to vacate the property."

All six of us were excited about the prospect of having our own home. Our future neighbors on either side owned nice little houses with small neatly kept yards. Two boys played in the backyard of one of the homes. Our house would be the second from the end of the street, bordering a cemetery. The broad cemetery entrance was located just around the corner.

On Sunday afternoons, German cemeteries drew many citizens to the resting place of loved ones. Even those not having anyone laid to rest in that particular cemetery strolled through the beautiful park-like settings to admire the lovingly tended graves and enjoy the peaceful atmosphere. The splendor of dozens of different types of flowers planted on gravesites almost took the sting out of the thought of death. Each grave had been meticulously cared for during the week by a relative or caretaker. There were no overgrown sites. With all the relatives we had lost during the war, however, our family was left without one grave to tend.

In preparation for the building of our house, Vati bicycled to our lot every night after work and started excavating the basement by hand. Sometimes one of our customers helped him with the digging. It would take quite a while to dig a hole large enough for a bicycle garage, laundry room, cold storage room, and a room for coal or firewood. On the first floor, Vati and Mutti planned a living room, an eat-in kitchen, a bedroom, and bath. Upstairs, under the peaked roof, were to be two bedrooms, one for the boys and one for the girls, with slanted walls on one side. A small storage room and a bathroom with toilet and sink were also planned for upstairs.

"Will I be able to invite my French pen pal to come and visit us when our house is finished?" I asked Mutti.

"Yes, Schäfle, you will. At this time, as you realize, it is absolutely impossible to have guests."

All of us were excited about moving the following year. But I knew for certain that Dieter, Marlies, and Udo would miss their many friends. Dieter, our athlete, had directed many sporting events for the neighborhood kids in the fields at the edge of our development. Parents were thrilled about their active and sports-minded children with whom Dieter routinely arranged "Olympic" games. He would definitely be missed in our old neighborhood. Our house, separated from Frau Boden's by a fifteen-minute walk, was too far to keep up with the sports practice sessions.

Construction of our house moved along according to schedule. "No, we can't move in yet," Mutti told us. "The house is still too damp inside and unhealthy to live in. In this cold weather, the plaster isn't drying very fast. So we have to be patient a little longer. We have now waited seven years for our own home, and I am sure we can wait another few weeks. Don't you agree?" We simply had to agree; we had no choice.

Vati and Mutti purchased several pieces of basic, used furniture for our dream home. On moving day, we took our few belongings to the new home. Mutti, an immaculate housekeeper, had cleaned our rooms before we left, but decided to go back to Frau Boden's just to assure herself that everything was spotless. Arriving at the house, Mutti was met by Frau Boden with a broom in her hand hollering and yelling at her about things not meeting her approval. Mutti rechecked everything again, found things in perfect order, returned the key, and left.

"I am so glad we are finally free of that . . . dragon," she confessed at night. "I am sorry, I am sorry. I shouldn't have said that. It is not nice. I have to learn to . . . control my tongue. Life will be so wonderful here. No longer will we be harassed, demeaned, and emotionally tormented.

The Lord was gracious in giving us strength to endure five years of harassment."

Praises and thanksgiving ascended to the throne of God daily for His goodness. We had a new home—our own! We could sing, talk, play games, and enjoy family life without fear. We could invite friends, have choir parties, guitar choir practice, and young people's meetings in our home. Evangelists now had a place to stay. The Guddat house became a favorite place for all types of church activities.

Dieter quickly made friends with the neighbor boys. But why was the grass between the house next door and ours dug up one day? Mutti simply couldn't figure it out. She later heard Dieter talking in his room, but knew he was alone up there. To whom might he be talking? Himself? Upon investigating, she learned that Dieter had built a primitive telephone system between his room and the neighbor's house so he could talk to his friend.

Dieter was the only one not able to rid himself of the effects of malnutrition. Daily he still had to sit in his room and bandage his legs. His open sores had begun to heal somewhat, but the new skin formed only very slowly. Faithfully he struggled to wash the pus and blood out of his bandages. I felt so sorry for him every time I saw him wrapping his legs. His quest for adventure, however, and teasing his younger sister were not hampered by his bandaged legs.

Marlies became quite annoyed with Dieter at times. "Why does he have to tease me all the time, Mutti?" she asked in despair. "Today he took the doll Tante Martha sent from America, wrapped a string around her neck, and dangled her out of the window. I thought he was going to drop her and quickly ran outside to try to catch her. But when Dieter saw me, he quickly pulled her back up again. Why does he have to do such awful things to me, Mutti?"

"He is a typical boy, Pittimaus. Boys are always into something."

"He almost killed me one time, remember? When we lived in the Anchor? That wasn't funny."

"Of course, I remember, and I know that wasn't funny. You ran into the path of a flying pebble. That, of course, was destined for the other side of the river and not for your temples. He didn't do that on purpose."

"I know that."

"We almost lost you, though, to that flying stone. Had we not had help from the Lord, you would have bled to death."

Udo's new friend was the younger brother of Dieter's friend. Playing ball was their passion. Every day after school, they could be found in the sandy street chasing a ball or teasing the neighbor's shepherd dog which, fortunately, was fenced in. Otherwise, the dog probably would have attacked the boys.

After the man behind our house had torn down his "shack," Vati and Mutti began to landscape, plant young trees, start flower beds, and build a patio. This was our home; it would be that until we died. Our place was small but cozy and well cared for. A young blue spruce tree was the centerpiece of the backyard.

Upon returning home from school one day, I noticed that something must have happened. Mutti's eyes were red, her cheerful spirit was gone. "Children," she said when all of us were at home, "I have something to tell you." My brothers, sister, and I stood quietly in the living room waiting for her to continue. With tears moistening her cheeks, she said, "I received a letter from Lithuania today. It was mailed five months ago. The Schiller Omi is dead. She went to heaven."

"No, it can't be!" I said and began to weep bitterly. "Not your mom too. She can't be dead." I wanted to see her again. I couldn't wait to return to East Prussia and to the beautiful farm, sit in her cozy living room, or watch her work in the kitchen. Never—never would life be the same without her. Dieter was also saddened by the news, yet Marlies and Udo could not fathom our loss. They were too young to remember, too young

to remember Omi's love for her grandchildren, her cuddly lap, warm hugs, and special treats. Too young to remember her beautiful garden, the river, the animals, sitting next to her in the coach, and holding on to the horses' reins on the way to town. Too young to remember being bundled up under heavy blankets in a horse-drawn sleigh. But I remembered—unfortunately.

Mutti walked toward me and embraced me warmly. We both sobbed. My whole body was racked with pain yet filled with love for my grandmother whom I could never again see on earth. I became numb to pain. All our close relatives were dead now. Despair and disbelief began to zigzag through my body. I knew she was dead. I glanced at the picture her Christian Lithuanian friends had sent Mutti. I recognized my wonderful Omi in that casket. She died of cancer, an agonizing death, they wrote. For weeks she screamed in agony and pain. They had taken her into their home because she had no one. At life's end she had no one, no relatives, no children, or grandchildren. Strangers, God's children, had taken her in, given her a home, and cared for her.

War! War! War! War was horrible. It not only destroyed dwellings but also relationships—relationships lovingly built over the course of generations and wiped out through forced separation and death. Had life been worth living for Omi? Did she work all her life on the farm and raise children just to suffer in the arms of strangers? Her husband died while fleeing from the enemy, heartbroken over the loss of his farm. And our dear great-grandfather, at age ninety-three, had been found murdered in a snowbank. Vati's twin brother was killed while defending Pillau.

My emotions simply couldn't wade through any more dark valleys. I became paralyzed in my grief, numb to everything around me except the heartaches which filled the whole room. I was alone in our new living room, yet I wasn't. At one moment warm thoughts of my loved ones caressed me, the next I was filled with anger—anger at Hitler who had devastated my life. He had devastated the lives of millions of

others. Silently—alone in my world of grief—I mourned, sobbed, and reminisced. I couldn't pray. I didn't know what to say to God. Was all this grief in His plan?

I continued to mourn silently for days, then for weeks, for months, and for seasons. Earth continued to turn on its axis. Some days the sun did shine, and then it rained. The year slipped into eternity, just as all our born-again relatives had slipped into God's presence. But my heart would not ever again be the same.

Dream Come True

"**Y**our daughter has a unique talent for the French language," the French professor told my parents after she had made a special trip to our store. "Please let her continue with her studies."

"Liane plans to go to a business school, and we can no longer afford to pay her school bill," Vati told my kind teacher.

I was quite touched by my teacher's concern for me. That I was good at something other than needlework gave me the desire to perhaps someday become a teacher of languages and needle art. If only I could enjoy the English language! Delving into the world of business in the meantime, and making some money, had to be my first priority. All around town small cigarette stores were popping up; Vati no longer had the edge on the market. I had to help with the finances.

Because of its excellent location, the leather goods store on Main Street, in the center of town, did very well as I always heard from the owner's daughter, my classmate. Our store, however, on the outskirts of town, did not have the proper location, Vati and Mutti reasoned, to support another leather goods business. With only a slight increase of population on our side of town, a second store was hardly justifiable.

My parents did not often voice their concern, but when they did, I had the feeling that Vati's dream would not come true in Nienburg.

Our French professor planned a trip to Switzerland for our graduation. My girlfriend and I were the only students who received an invitation to stay with our pen pals. This cut the cost of the trip substantially; the school administration paid for most of my remaining expenses.

Viewing the majestic Alps, climbing mountains, rolling in snow, and getting severe sunburns in April were unique experiences for all of us. After our first day on the slopes and our red faces swollen, all of us were required to wear a see-through scarf over our faces. Our tender classroom skin could no longer be exposed to high altitude sun rays. At the museum of natural history in Lausanne, we shuddered at the sight of jars in which human fetuses at various stages of development were displayed. At the United Nations palace in Geneva, we were told while walking the marble halls and viewing huge conference rooms, that the world's problems could indeed be solved by representatives and heads of governments.

My French girlfriend's family treated me with much kindness. Being able to converse with them in French, learning new phrases and expressions, gave me great impetus and the desire to continue studying that beautiful language, even if I had to do so on my own.

At the end of the one-year course at business school, those with top grades had a job waiting for them. As a nineteen-year-old, I then began working as an accountant for a transport company. Balancing real books and tracking a company's flow of money, rather than working with fictitious textbook accounts, was very exciting to me. In fact, I considered that almost as exciting as the realization that the building, in which my office was located on Main Street, dated back to 1634. During my lunch hour, I often looked at the carved date and the house blessing on the huge beam above the entrance door.

Dieter furthered his great interest and love for electronics by starting a two-year apprenticeship in a private firm. Vati and Mutti were told that their son had great talent for his chosen field; he would someday excel in that type of business.

One day, when all of us sat around the table, Vati read a letter Tante Martha from America had written. "You should see if somehow you can come to America," she wrote. "Unfortunately, I can't be your sponsor. I am working here at the Mission Home for very little pay. Last winter I worked in Palm Beach, Florida, however, and saved enough money to come and visit you next year."

With the last sentence barely spoken, great jubilation began to flood our room.

"We are going to America," Marlies half sang, "going to America, going to America."

"But, Pittimaus," Mutti said, "where did you get that idea?"

"Tante Martha said she is coming next year, didn't she?"

"Yes, she wrote that."

"She is probably coming to see us first and then take us with her."

Vati read the letter again so that there would be no misunderstanding. Tante Martha could *not* sponsor our family. She would have to own a home, have money, and possibly a job lined up for those of us who could work, Vati explained. If something should happen to any of us while we were in America, Tante Martha would have to be fully responsible for us financially until we could take care of our own medical bills. The purpose of a sponsor was to free the government of undue burdens.

"Do you think you would go to America," Dieter asked, "if you had a sponsor?"

"No," Vati answered quickly, yet with sadness in his voice. "This is my homeland. I don't speak English, and I am too old."

In spite of everything my parents had experienced in life, neither one looked their age, forty-seven years. In fact, Mutti and I were occasionally

addressed as sisters. Vati didn't have a wrinkle in his face. How could he talk about being old? Twenty-one of our church friends had already left for Canada; more were planning to leave. It was much easier to start a new life in the new land than in Germany, they wrote. Why didn't Vati want to go too?

"Perhaps you can talk things over with your sister when she comes," Mutti suggested.

"No, my dear wife, I will not go to America. It is difficult enough to make a living in Germany, but here at least we speak the same language as those around us. Overseas we would be foreigners, and that is probably worse than being a refugee. My true dream and desire is to return to Insterburg and start there again in that beautiful city."

"East Prussia may not ever again become a part of Germany," Mutti reasoned sadly. "It is too firmly placed in Russian hands. Why, I wonder, did the Western forces deal so much land to the Russians?"

"We don't know the details of the deals made at Potsdam, Emmy, and why. But for some reason the Russians have for centuries attempted to devour our beloved East Prussia. The city of Insterburg itself is about 370 years old now. During every century, the Russians attempted to take and keep our hometown. In 1655, they took over Insterburg. In 1757, they again forced their way in, plundering and burning much of the city. About one hundred and fifty years later, in 1914, during the First World War, they again stormed into the city. Each time, we managed to take it back."

"This time, Emil, I don't think we'll be able to get it back. From what people say now, the town has been annexed to Russia. It even has a Russian name. Westerners are not allowed to visit it. So I think, Emil, we have to give up our dream and forget about ever returning to Insterburg. We can continue struggling in West Germany or go to America."

"We have only one option as I see it—stay here and pray for the Lord to lead us in the way He has chosen for us."

"Yes, Emil, I know He will lead us as He has in the past. He alone knows about the future. Oftentimes I still wonder what the children and I would have done had I been able to foresee the future. When the first Russian tanks rolled into Lippehne, soldiers raced into our house looting, threatening to kill, raping, and killing in the streets. Every ray of hope would have been gone without the Lord on my side. I believe I already told you how many mothers, driven by utter despair, decided upon death as the only option for them and their children. I am glad I didn't know the future. The Lord alone saw us through those horrible years. I praise Him for His goodness and protection, and I am thankful that we are a complete family again . . . only through His grace."

"And we know, my brave and courageous wife, that the Lord will see us through our present need also."

In a leather goods paper, Vati read the following ad, "Ideal location for leather goods store. Prosperous area of Oberhausen/Rhineland." The Christian business man who had placed the ad predicted a great financial future for a business at that location. Vati and Mutti traveled to that industrial area of Germany by train, evaluated the store site and concluded that the area, indeed, appeared to be very prosperous. After deliberations and prayer, they signed a contract.

While shelves were being built for the new store, Vati ordered suitcases, purses, shopping bags, wallets, manicure sets, and briefcases. The store opened on December 1, 1953, with great sales on opening day and throughout the Christmas season. Mutti and a female employee managed the Oberhausen store, while Vati in Nienburg, three hours away by train, continued with the cigarette store. I was busy with our household and my job. Until the new store could carry the family financially, the two stores would have to be managed simultaneously.

The thought of having to leave our cozy home, however, was difficult for all of us to bear. My greatest personal loss would be our church and the young people's group. I'd miss the fellowship of my peers, the

Sunday afternoon bicycle trips, and the excitement of helping with church services in the outlying villages. Even though Vati told us about a good church in Oberhausen, not too far from the store, I could not get excited about moving.

"Where will we live when we leave here, Vati?" Udo asked one evening with concern in his little voice.

"We will have to live in an apartment. We'll have to sell this house, pay off the mortgage, and put the rest of the money into supplies for the new store."

"But I will miss my friends here," Udo continued.

Both Dieter and Marlies appeared to agree, and Vati sensed that. "We probably won't be leaving here for another year or so, Udo. So you'll have a while yet to be with your friends."

"Does that mean Mutti is going to be away for one whole year?"

"No, Marlies, only about three weeks. Mutti and I will be taking turns living in Oberhausen."

"Where does she live now?"

"Mutti sleeps on the couch in the store. A curtain makes one end of the store into a small bedroom during the night."

"Poor Mutti," Marlies compassionately said, "she has such a nice bedroom here."

"Yes, children, it is very difficult for us to get started again. We all have to make sacrifices. Mutti is always willing to do that for the sake of the family. She doesn't grumble or complain about inconveniences she has been forced to endure. You children have just the most wonderful mother.

"In fact, I have to admit that all of you have been very understanding during this transitional period, too. I appreciate that. We will all have to pull together even more now, be kind to each other, helpful, and work together. Working together for a common goal will help all of us become stronger as individuals. It will also build a strong family. Most

of all, however, we have to be strong in the Lord, live close to Him, read His Word, and pray. If we do that, the Lord will continue to guide us through these struggles."

"Why couldn't we stay right here in Nienburg?" Marlies wondered again.

"Because it seems the Lord has closed the door here for a leather goods store. He is faithful, however, in keeping His promises if we do what He asks us to do. Mutti and I had chosen a Bible verse as our life's verse when we got married."

"Yes," I interrupted, "I know that verse.

"Delight thyself also in the LORD;
And he shall give thee the desires of thine heart." (Ps. 37:4)

"You are right, Liane. And I believe that verse. If we live for the Lord daily, walk with Him, talk with Him, and shine for Him, He will give us the desires of our heart. Unfortunately, the road to the beautiful city of fulfilled desires isn't always easy. There may be detours due to road repairs; sometimes the road may become washed out due to flooding. A big storm may have caused a tree to block passage. There may be all types of obstacles, but if we are faithful to the Lord, He'll help us overcome and reward us with countless blessings."

17

American Visitor

Beautifying our little yard was Mutti's favorite pastime; she spent every free minute doing so. The sour cherry trees promised a good crop, and the crimson roses in front of the house had begun to ramble upward on their white trellises. The rock garden that surrounded the flagstone terrace, which Mutti and Vati had built so painstakingly, was planted with different types of flowers. If only we would not have to leave our new home!

Since my company moved out of town and I lost my job, I began taking turns with Mutti running the store and caring for the home. "Go to town, Schäfle," Mutti said before dashing to the store, "and buy five pounds of sauerkraut. It is time for us to freshen our scatter rugs."

Scattering the damp sauerkraut on a rug, brushing it back and forth until every little speck of dust and sand clung to it like a magnet, was a job I enjoyed. The kraut deodorized, cleaned, and freshened the rug all at the same time. It was easier, too, than beating the floor coverings outdoors with a rug beater. The purchase of an expensive vacuum cleaner had never even been discussed.

"I don't think you should have him sit on the broom, Marlies. That isn't good for the bristles," I said.

"But I put a thick rag under it, and it shines the floor so much better with Udo sitting on it." During their daily chores, and especially since Mutti was in Oberhausen again, my brothers and sister always searched for shortcuts with chores—and often found them.

"Do we have everything ready for Tante Martha's arrival tomorrow?"

"Yes, Vati," I answered. "We are all set for our visitor from America. Unfortunately, Mutti can't be here for the big day."

"Yes, it is unfortunate, but there is nothing we can change. Mutti has to be in Oberhausen."

While I was at the store, and my brothers and sister at school, Vati went to pick up Tante Martha from the railroad station.

"You children have changed so much since last year's picture," Tante Martha remarked when she saw us. "All of you have grown quite a bit. The last time I visited Germany and saw Liane, she was just five years old; now she is twenty. And Dieter was a little two-year-old. Marlies and Udo I am seeing for the first time. Come here, you two, let me hug you," she said while reaching for both at the same time and hugging them.

"It is good to be on German soil again," she continued, "and see the only blood relatives I have left on this earth." Turning to Vati she continued, "We came from such a large family, Emil, and here we are, just the two of us and your family. War is terrible." That last statement later appeared to hover above the dinner table for the duration of our meal. At times everyone ate silently; only the knives' clanking on the cheap dishes could be heard as they were guided in pushing potatoes, peas, or meat onto the fork.

"Did you have good food on the ship, Tante Martha?" Marlies broke the silence.

"Yes, I surely did. The food was excellent, and it was so relaxing for me to sit and enjoy a meal that I hadn't cooked. At the Mission Home, I prepare the meals every day."

"How many people do you feed?" Dieter wondered.

"I cook for about forty people every day, Dieter, but I do have help in the kitchen. I cook for the farmer and his family, the office workers, the gardeners, maids, several elderly guests, and of course, the kitchen help. When we have missionaries home on furlough or retreats at the home, there may be a hundred or more people at the table. I also bake all the bread for the Mission Home family—I have done that for years."

"You must work very hard," Dieter judged, "but you don't get much money?"

"No, Dieter, I get very little money. I consider my work here on earth work for the Lord. I am giving my time and energy so that missionaries who are sent out by the mission board and supported by Christian friends can go to foreign lands and preach the salvation message. I receive just enough money to buy the most basic things such as soap, toothpaste, and so on."

Dieter isn't usually that inquisitive, I thought. *He must be checking out the possibility of Tante Martha sponsoring us to go to America.*

Tante Martha enjoyed our quaint little town of Nienburg. We showed her all the sights, the river, the farmers market, and took her to the Anchor. She loved our church and relayed greetings from her friends at the Mission Home to everyone. Our friends loved her friendly and warm spirit. Several times during the week, she would visit the cemetery and admire the beautifully kept graves. She also admired our stamp collections.

Tante Martha, for some reason, spoke more openly about her faith and Savior than German Christians did. She passed out hundreds of tracts which she had brought from America; everyone she met in Germany was offered a printed salvation message. When walking to

church, she openly carried her Bible. I felt uncomfortable just carrying a song book and warding off the stares of passersby; no one ever carried a Bible. Only the preacher and Sunday school teacher used a Bible at church. Did all Americans display their beliefs so openly?

Germany must be different from America, it seemed. Here during tent revival meetings, believers were open and bold in their witness. Was that due to the persecution our group sporadically experienced from the citizens of Nienburg to whom the gospel was foreign? Jehovah's Witnesses were allowed to march through town to their baptismal service at the public swimming pool while our group of believers was called all kinds of names and forbidden to baptize in that very pool.

"Emil," Tante Martha requested as we sat on the patio to enjoy a balmy summer evening, "I have never heard how it came about that you were captured in France. How did you get from Russia to France?"

"Just before a big offensive was expected in Russia, I was transferred to Holland where I spent two months. From there, I had to go to Marseille, France. There, as elsewhere, my duty was to supply the troops with their daily food rations. We had eighteen hundred soldiers stationed along the Riviera, about fifteen to twenty men to one bunker."

"How did you get so much food to the soldiers?"

"The food ration canisters were transported and delivered by truck, the water in bottles. Every week I traveled a fifteen-mile stretch along the beach by motorcycle and delivered paychecks to the soldiers.

"For a year and a half, several other officers and I lived in a suburb of Marseille. We stayed in a house that had been abandoned by its former residents. Then, one day in August of 1944, the British, French, and Americans began shooting at the coast. When we heard that American tanks had moved toward our position, we quickly took all our files and money—anything that could help the enemy—and burned them. Then the command came to surrender. There was no use fighting; we were outnumbered and surrounded.

"When I saw the first American tanks in the distance, a friend of mine and I decided to run to the small field hospital set up at a farm. Through the woods we ran, ducking, watching, and trying to sneak quietly along the forest floor which was littered with dry timber. Our place of refuge was only about a mile away. A short time after arriving at the hospital, a French soldier came in, saw my boots, liked them, and told me to take them off, which I did. After he gave me his worn-out boots, he took mine and left. Two days later, however, all of us at the hospital were taken captive by the Americans and thrown into a French jail.

"At the jail we spent three weeks with very little food; we could hardly walk because of weakness. The Americans then took all the prisoners and moved them onto a Liberty ship. America was to be our destination, and I became quite excited. I was looking forward to seeing you. Somehow, though, they changed their minds and transported us to Africa. So that is how I ended up in Africa, Martha."

"You were captured on Udo's birthday, right, Emil?"

"Yes, on Udo's first birthday."

I heard Vati and his sister talking outside, below my window, long after the rest of us had gone to bed.

Tante Martha helped me with my daily household chores. Often, she would talk about Insterburg, the first time she saw me, my first tooth which she had detected, and my first word. "I can't believe that you are a young lady now. I wish I could have watched you grow up and been a part of your life. You, Liane, have always occupied a special place in my heart," she told me one day.

"Well, Tante Martha, you did have a great part in my life. When I was hungry, your packages helped ease the gnawing hunger pains in my stomach. When we were cold, you sent yarn and knitting needles so that I could knit sweaters, pullovers, and socks for the family. When I returned to school and didn't have a fountain pen, it was you who sent me one.

"For some reason, I also believe that you prayed for me to become a believer in the Lord Jesus."

"You are right, Liane, that I did. Nothing is more important in life than being a child of God."

"So you see, you have influenced my life greatly, Tante Martha, and I thank you for that. For one needlework project, I received the best grade in the whole class. Had you not sent me the fabric, I could not have made anything."

"I'd like to see that project, Liane. Do you still have it?"

"Yes, I do." Quickly I rushed into the bedroom and lifted the white lace-edged runner off the old nightstand. "Here it is! It is the first piece of drawn work I have ever done. For some reason, the threads had different thicknesses and were difficult to pull, but somehow I did manage to finish it."

"It is beautiful, Liane, simply beautiful. Your drawn work blocks in the corners are done with so much detail. I am absolutely amazed to see you turn an old diaper into something so lovely."

"A diaper?" I asked in shock. "I spent months doing drawn work and embroidery on a diaper?"

Tante Martha, with her wrinkle-free face and perpetual smile, seemed to enjoy life. Reading the Bible and sharing thoughts and statements of her former pastor, Dr. Haldeman of New York City, with others excited her greatly. Underlined passages in her Bible gave evidence of a studious person. "Living for the Lord is all that matters in life," she always said. Sermons heard years earlier, and entrenched in her mind, were brought to the surface routinely to encourage and strengthen others. The Lord's coming in the Rapture was a favorite topic of hers. During her visit, she daily tried to guide our thoughts toward her wonderful Savior.

Tante Martha spent hours sitting at our old secondhand piano, playing and singing hymns. "Come and sing with me," she would often

say when our housework was done. "I really like this song," she remarked while flipping through her American songbook. "Do you know it?"

"No, Tante Martha, I don't. I have never even seen a songbook written in English."

"Since you can read music, Liane, just sing along with me."

"I would love to tell you what I think of Jesus,
Since I found in Him a friend so strong and true;
I would tell you how He changed my life completely,
He did something that no other friend could do.

"No one ever cared for me like Jesus,
There's no other friend so kind as He;
No one else could take the sin and darkness from me,
O how much He cared for me.

"Ev'ry day He comes to me with new assurance,
More and more I understand His words of love;
But I'll never know just why He came to save me,
Till someday I see His blessed face above.
(Weigle, "No One Ever Cared for Me Like Jesus")

"This song is my testimony, Liane. No one ever cared for me like Jesus. People around us may fail, but He never does."

Again I began to wonder why Tante Martha had never married. She loved family life and children. Why did she leave Germany to go to America all by herself in 1921? There were family rumors about a broken engagement and her having left for the land across the ocean because of a broken heart. But no one ever said much more, and I felt too timid to ask. In retrospect, however, whatever caused her to make the long, lonely journey, it must have been in God's plan. Who but Tante Martha could have helped us survive the "hunger years"?

After having sung "How Great Thou Art" in English, I began to realize that the English language was really being spoken in other parts of the world. In English class, I had often doubted it. Grammar, the story of Stonehenge, Big Ben, and the Thames always seemed boring and archaic. Speaking and singing with my aunt, however, gave English a new perspective. My "r" sound began to roll more freely, and as I watched Tante Martha, it became apparent that the tongue did not have to be extended as long as a lizard's when pronouncing the "th" sound. I became glad that I did have to learn English in school if only to sing hymns with my aunt.

After our simple evening meal consisting of a slice of dark bread with a little butter and cheese or liverwurst, and peppermint tea, Tante Martha suddenly announced, "I would like Liane to come to America. I notice that all of you are struggling to start a new life. Perhaps she could help you better from America."

My heart instantly began to pound and ready itself to jump out of my chest. Then my whole body became numb from shock. Did I hear her correctly? I was to go to America? Everyone sat in silence staring at me. Why was I to be the chosen one? There were six of us; why not Vati, Mutti, or Dieter? He was seventeen years old.

"Unfortunately, I can't help you to emigrate as a family. My financial status prohibits me from becoming a sponsor."

"That is all right," Vati said. "I don't want to go to America anyway. With the Lord's help, the Oberhausen store will succeed and we'll be on our feet again."

"Why don't you want to go?" Dieter asked again, probably hoping for a different answer from the usual.

"You know the answer, Dieter. But I shall repeat it for all of you once more. I am too old—I'll be fifty years old next year—and I can't speak English."

"But you can learn, Vati," Marlies added encouragingly.

"Even if by some miracle we could go to America, I don't think anyone would hire someone my age."

"How would Emmy feel about the topic we are discussing, Emil?"

"She would go immediately," Vati answered. "But as I told you before, Martha, I am still hoping that the Russians will return East Prussia to the Germans so that we can return to Insterburg and start there."

"Well," Tante Martha stated, "right now I really don't see that your dream may become reality. If Chancellor Konrad Adenauer, your excellent German statesman, was not able to regain control of the former German states, I don't think anyone else will be either. He had America's support in everything he attempted to restructure Germany and your economy. Yet in spite of all the support, the super powers could not see eye to eye in regard to the states which Russia, without anyone's approval, annexed."

"I would simply love to return to Insterburg, Emil. Eyewitnesses reported that our parents' new house has not been destroyed. That was to be our inheritance."

"Yes, Martha, yet you feel that we should just let the Russians have everything? How can we let them have our father's store, my store, and the house?"

"At this time we cannot claim it, Emil."

The moment I stopped listening to the conversation, Tante Martha's statement rang in my ears, "I would like Liane to come to America." If the rest of the family had no intentions of going, why then should I go? I loved my family. The war had kept us apart from Vati and struggling for too long. I could not leave now—definitely not. I wanted to go into my room and be by myself.

"How would Liane get to America, Martha?" I suddenly heard Vati ask. Quickly I tuned in again. She probably did not have an answer to that question—I hoped—and I would be able to push thoughts about America out of my mind.

"We have a relative, Emil, the daughter of Charles Ley from St. Louis. She, her husband, and three sons live on Long Island, outside of New York City. They would like Liane to come and work for them as a governess."

"What is a governess?" I casually asked.

"It is someone who takes care of children and also does some housework," my aunt replied. "The children are all boys, two, five, and seven years old. They live in a neighborhood of wealthy people. I think Liane would like it there."

"But I don't have money for a voyage."

"That is taken care of too, Liane. They have decided to purchase your ticket."

My heart was no longer pounding; it was beginning to ache. *Lord*, I said deep inside, *is any of this of You? My thinking is in turmoil, my heart yearns to know Your will, but my body wants to remain in Germany. Life is great for me. I have friends, a loving family, a church, and young people's group in which to serve You. Are You asking me to leave all this behind? Lord, please help my troubled mind.*

"How far does this family live from you, Martha?" Vati asked.

"About two hours by car."

"Does that mean you could see Liane often?"

"Well, we should be able to see one another about once a month."

"How do you feel about this offer, Liane?" Vati asked, putting me on the spot.

"I feel *very* confused. There are pros and cons to such an offer. The thought I dislike is, that, should I go, I'd have to leave all of you."

"We'll have to see what Mutti has to say when she hears about this next week. I am sure she will express my thoughts by saying, 'It is your life, Schäfle, and you do as you think the Lord leads you.'"

Confused, bewildered, and in tears, I went to my room. Marlies already slept soundly and probably enjoyed some happy dream while I

felt like Job in the Bible. My body was not plagued by diseases as was Job's, but my innermost being had lost its robust outlook on life. The emotional pendulum swung from despair to bewilderment, back and forth—all night.

Vati and Mutti had traded stores again to give Mutti a chance to visit with her sister-in-law. The reunion was a very happy one. Joyously the two women worked side by side and chatted for hours.

"If only I knew what to cook for dinner today," Mutti said after I had returned from the store for the two-hour break. "Yesterday we had potatoes, eggs, and spinach, the day before potato pancakes, the day before that rice with sugar and cinnamon, and today . . . ? I simply don't know what to feed everyone."

"How about buying a couple of pounds of meat, Emmy," Tante Martha suggested, "and we'll fix a delicious vegetable soup."

Mutti, without speaking, just looked at me. I interpreted her facial expression as saying, "Martha, do you have any idea how much a couple of pounds of meat cost?" Instead she said, "That is a good idea, Martha, but perhaps we should have fried cauliflower and potatoes instead.

"Do you do any butchering at the Mission Home?" Mutti asked.

"Yes, Emmy. The farmer does the actual slaughtering, and we cut up the meat and freeze it. In the main kitchen, we make several different types of sausages. It usually takes us several days to process one cow. Since we eat meat almost every day, one animal doesn't last very long with so many people at the table. The fat is used to make soap. I believe I sent you some of that."

"Yes, Martha, you did. Unfortunately, we had no idea what that was. We had taken it to be lard and tried to use it for frying potatoes."

"Yes," Tante Martha chuckled, "we at the Mission Home laughed about that for some time. But do you know, Emmy, as insignificant as it may seem, the fact that I did make soap for years helped me out of serious trouble one time."

"What do you mean by that, Martha?" I asked as we all stood in the kitchen working on our dinner.

"During the war, things were not easy for the German population in America either. All those of German descent could be made suspect of any crime against the American government. Germans and even I, a citizen of the United States at that time, were closely watched by the government and our daily lives scrutinized. Since America was at war with Germany, no German could be trusted in our country, it was reasoned. Many of my friends had to go before an inquisition board.

"One day I was summoned to appear before a former Polish man in our town. It was a long interrogation process, and I had no trouble answering all the questions because I was not guilty of any crime against my adopted nation's government. I neither worked as a spy nor participated in antiwar activities.

"Then the official asked to what radio station I listened, and I answered. The final question almost stumped me, 'Miss Guddat, what are you doing to help the American war effort?' I thought and thought, and answered, 'I make soap from old discarded fat to help the Mission Home and our country.' When the grim-looking inquisitor heard that, he dismissed me, and I was never questioned again."

"That was interesting, Martha. I never really thought about you in regard to living in a country that was at war with us."

"Yes," Tante Martha continued, "because of our war with Germany, Americans also had to sacrifice. Certain food items were even rationed. But the greatest sacrifices were made by those who lost husbands, fathers, brothers, and sons in the war against Germany."

18

No Roadblocks

"The Lord is really blessing our Christmas business," Mutti told me after we both returned to our small rented room tired and worn out.

"Yes," I said, "sales have been very good. Only a few more days till Christmas Eve."

"We should be packing our suitcases tomorrow and have them ready for our trip the next day," Mutti suggested. "There may not be much time to pack after the store closes at 2:00 p.m."

We did not expect to be too busy on Christmas Eve, yet the opposite was true. "Why do men wait until the last day to shop for their wives?" Mutti asked after a barrage of male customers. Feverishly we put the items they did not select back in boxes and on the shelves. Barely had we made a path behind the counters when the store again began to fill with shoppers. Most of them did not know what they wanted, and giving advice was time consuming.

I glanced at my watch; it was 1:45 p.m. Customers were still milling around the store trying to decide what to purchase. The next time I checked, it was 3:00 p.m. "Do you know what time it is?" I whispered.

"It is 3:00 p.m. We have to close up or we'll miss our train and will have to spend Christmas Eve in our small room here in Oberhausen."

After the last shopper left at 3:30 p.m., I practically fell over boxes while rushing to the door to lock it. "We can't clean up," Mutti hurriedly announced. "Let's take the money, the record books, and run to get our suitcases." Mutti, who had not been feeling well due to what the doctor called iron depletion, ran to the station so fast that I could barely keep up. The moment we stepped onto the train, it started moving. Neither Mutti nor I talked for some time; we were simply out of breath, yet happy to be able to spend Christmas Eve in our cozy home in Nienburg.

"Children, I want you to know that the Lord has sent us a buyer for our house," Vati announced one evening, "and Lord willing, we will leave Nienburg after Marlies's graduation in March." With the huge tile oven radiating warmth on that cold winter day, we all sat quietly. We knew that the move was forthcoming but still hoped it could somehow be avoided.

"Where will we live, Vati?" Marlies asked, sobbing.

"We will be living in an apartment. I think I have already found a nice place for us. It is on the second floor of an apartment building."

"Will we have to live with a landlady again?"

"No, Udo," Vati answered, "we'll have our own entrance. Our apartment has two bedrooms, a living room, kitchen, and bath. There is also a cold storage room in the basement."

"It sounds as if we are going to be packed in there again."

"Yes, Son, it is going to be different from this house. I surely wish we could stay here, but we simply can't. The house has to be sold to pay off the mortgage and build up our inventory in Oberhausen."

"What am I going to do about my apprenticeship, Vati?" Dieter asked.

"I am sure, Dieter, you will be able to finish it there. Oberhausen is a large coal mining town with a lot of businesses. You'll have no problem finding something very quickly."

While everyone around me talked about the move to Oberhausen, the new store, city, church, and life, my soul was still rent in two: *America, Germany, America, Germany, what shall I do? Can my thinking continue to be suspended between two continents only to be caught like a fish on the crest of a powerful wave?*

Vati had planned for the annual church-choir party at our house to fall on my twenty-first birthday. Not everyone knew it was my birthday, but they quickly found out when I was asked to request a special choir number which everyone would sing for me. This was done for every member celebrating a birthday.

One of our choir members, a young man, stared at me all evening. He must have noticed the light blue taffeta blouse I had made with black velvet bows and the black skirt. It was a new outfit in which I felt good. Or was he staring because of my transparency and lack of party spirit? No, that could not have been it. He did not know that I had begun the emigration process.

Rather than going to America as a visitor and not being able to earn money, it was better, I was advised, to emigrate. It would take up to one year to have all the paperwork completed such as police checks, health checks, and family records. The question of the emigration quota could present a problem. If that was already filled for the year of 1955, I couldn't go anyway. The emigration process, however, had begun with the option for me to withdraw the request anytime.

I still did not know if I wanted to go to America. I searched the Bible for comfort of soul. "Please, Lord, give me one verse to calm the turbulence of my innermost being. You know my future. I want to be in Your will." Every time I prayed, however, the answer came in a song our guitar choir had sung several times:

Even though I don't know the way, You know it well.
That calms my soul and makes it peaceful.
It is in vain for me to be woefully troubled
And letting my heart beat anxiously from morning till night.
(Redern, "Weiß ich den Weg auch nicht")

Only the Lord and the old piano, where I often sat and played the song, have recorded the tears my body spent in agony over the decision I was not able to make. Yet one day the burden was lightened when I said to my heavenly Father, "If You want me to go to America, Lord, let everything run smoothly. If things move along without roadblocks, I shall consider it Your will that I leave Germany. If, however, problems arise, You are telling me to stay here." Placing my future completely in the Lord's hands helped me to begin living again.

After we had moved to Oberhausen, I immediately started working as a bookkeeper in a large appliance firm, Dieter continued his apprenticeship in an electronics firm, and Marlies was hired by Vati to work at the store and run errands. Udo continued attending school.

"Let me see—let me see!" Marlies said impatiently, trying to pull the green passport booklet out of Dieter's hand.

"So that is what a passport looks like," he said. "You are really going to America, Sis, huh?"

"I don't know yet. I have no idea if I am going. Only the Lord knows. I don't really want to go."

"But why do you have a passport then?" Dieter asked.

"I am going to get my paperwork done and wait on the Lord."

"If I ever had a chance like that," Dieter added, "I'd surely go."

"You would leave the family?" Marlies wondered.

"Yes, I would."

Our church in Oberhausen, a large, dark-red brick structure, must have been at least a century old. The angles at which it was built gave it a rustic and cold appearance. Inside, however, one's spirits felt light. The

pastor and his family were friendly, but the members seemed reserved. It would probably take some time for us to feel at home. Even though Vati, Mutti, and I joined the choir, we could not feel a kinship with the choir members. They, too, kept to themselves and did not reach out to newcomers.

Dieter, however, quickly became friendly with a young man his age whose name was also Dieter. The two friends became inseparable. They both played the piano and at times delighted the whole congregation through their four-handed selections.

"Please pray for my husband," a lady requested one night at prayer meeting. "There was a cave-in at his mine today. He is still down there with twenty others. No one knows whether they are dead or alive."

In shock, my heart took in the request. Could that perhaps be the reason Christians appeared more lifeless at this church? Many from the congregation worked in the mining industry. "When he leaves in the morning," one lady told us, "we never know if we'll see each other again."

I wondered how families could live like that. *Lord, please, don't ever ask me to marry a coal miner.*

The city of Essen—known for its Krupp metalworks, a munitions manufacturer during the war—and the towns of Oberhausen and Duisburg seemed to be melded into one huge city, yet were governed by separate city councils. It was difficult for us to distinguish the borders which surrounded hundreds of thousands of people. This area, also known as the industrial area of West Germany, or the coal pot, was the dirtiest in which we had ever lived. Our white window sills had to be freed of black soot daily. On the way to work, white blouses or shirts became flecked with black ashes.

Sales of leather goods rose before Easter and plunged immediately thereafter. "Come by the store during your lunch hour, Liane," Mutti

said one day. "We need groceries, but have to sell some things first so that I can give you grocery money."

Upon my arrival at the store, Mutti greeted me with a look of concern on her face. "We have sold only one wallet all morning," she said. "That gives us just enough money for you to buy bread today." She gave me the money and I left. On the way to town, my mind raced back to Nienburg and the slow sales during our last year there.

"The newly opened department store downtown," Vati said in the evening, "has a large leather goods section. Their prices are lower than ours because as a chain store they do quantity-buying at great discounts. I am afraid we will not be able to compete with that store."

"Now, Emil," Mutti tried to encourage her husband, "perhaps our business has to become better known first. If we had the money, we could advertise more."

"We have been at this location now for one year and nine months. I think people know that we are here.

"At the civil defense office, I was told today that my volunteer job may become a paying job before too long. 'At this time, however,' my boss told me, 'there is peace in Germany. But since the Russians cannot be trusted, we have to prepare for any eventuality. You are helping us in that effort. I presume you are willing, Herr Guddat, to continue working for the defense of our country, am I right?'

"'Yes, I am willing to defend my country. I have done that before. But I also need money to feed my family.' I told him. Those here in the West who haven't lost anything don't seem to be able to understand that."

"You are right, Emil."

"Yes, some of the Westerners even act as if they are ashamed of us. Every now and then, I think of the reaction I got from the businessman who owns the clothing store next door. When I placed the very first ad, I wrote, 'Businessman—formerly Insterburg, East Prussia—is opening

a leather goods store.' 'You shouldn't let anyone know,' he scolded me literally, 'that you are a *refugee*. That is very poor business sense.'"

"You never told me that before, Emil. That is terrible. And he calls himself a Christian?"

It would be shameful if I were to go to America without knowing anything about West Germany. That thought and not being able to pay an expensive train fare, gave me the impetus to take a bicycle tour with my sister. Thousands of young people traveled in safety on the many bicycle roads. With the daily necessities strapped to our bike racks, Marlies and I set out to see the country. At times we met young people and chatted with them for a while before one or the other fell back to take in the sights or stop for the day. Most cyclers fell into their beds at youth hostels, which charged only half a Mark, exhausted after a day of traveling, while others sat around playing guitars and enjoying folk song sing-alongs. Great camaraderie existed among the wanderers. One never needed to be concerned about a broken-down bike; someone would always come to the aid of another.

"To Wander Is a Miller's Joy" and "High on the Yellow Wagon" were some of the folk songs Marlies and I sang while pedaling through West Germany. At times I felt like a bird let out of a cage; I felt free, alive, and energetic during my one-week vacation. Forgotten was the dirt of cities. We sisters enjoyed lush fields, tall, shady trees, open country roads, hills, valleys, and clean, fresh air.

Touring along the Rhine River with its vineyards trailing up huge banks were sights we would never forget. Castles, centuries old, towered high above the river. Looking down, we saw barges that resembled charcoal beams floating slowly up- or downstream. The meandering Rhine had set the direction for the road engineers. If roads trailed upward, we often walked; if they sloped downhill, we cut through air and wind at high speed. We sounded like huge, buzzing bumblebees.

"Tomorrow we should be in Andernach, Marlies," I said. "I'd like to get at least that far before returning. Then we'll pedal home on the other side of the Rhine."

"But how are we going to get across the river?"

"There'll probably be a ferry which can drop us off."

The town of Andernach had been in the news frequently during the past months. It was there that the first German army of one thousand soldiers had been assembled after World War II. After an almost ten-year occupation of Germany, the allied forces decided that Germans themselves had to have a part in the defense of their country against the Russians. With the continuation of the Cold War, Germany would become a battlefield, it was reasoned, and Germans had to help.

Marlies and I did not quite reach Andernach because we came upon a ferry whose captain offered to take us across the Rhine free of charge. On the way home, we visited the beautiful city of Bonn, capital of West Germany; bypassed Cologne because of lack of time, and also Düsseldorf. Upon arriving in Duisburg, near Oberhausen, neither Marlies nor I were able to sit on our hard seats, so we began walking. In the evening of the sixth day, two hungry bicyclers arrived in Oberhausen tired, yet refreshed; weary, yet uplifted. Best of all, however, was the fact that two sisters had a chance to get to know one another better. It might have been the last time for us to be together. Only the Lord knew. Many times on our tour, He used the summer breeze to quietly dry my tears.

"Here is some mail for you, Schäfle," Mutti said smiling while handing me a letter. Glancing at the return address, I sensed the need to be alone, but I wasn't. Mutti stood next to me. With trembling hands and a racing heart, a cold chill encased my body. This could be the roadblock I had hoped for. Less than nine months had passed since I requested the emigration permit. It always took one year, I was told. So it was true, I was not going to America. Those horrible months of despair had ended; I could be free of the burden of an uncertain future.

Trembling, I opened the envelope. "Your request to emigrate to the United States of America has been granted." Tears flooded my eyes. I could not speak. Mutti read the letter and hugged me. How I would miss her, her warmth and love. She had endured so much under the Communist regime and sacrificed so much for me. Every morning, she'd still tiptoe into the living room, where I slept on the couch, to awaken me with a kiss. Her love for me and the rest of the family was boundless. Soft, naturally curly hair framed her wrinkle-free face. She always looked the same, young and beautiful, even at almost fifty years of age. Vati not only found in Mutti a great wife but also a wonderful mother who truly loved and cared for her children. In her Christian walk, she never wavered from the straight and narrow path.

Hundreds of thoughts bombarded my mind while Mutti tried to comfort me, "You still don't have to go to America, Schäfle. You don't have to leave Germany."

"But the roadblocks," I admitted, "they are all gone. Everything has gone so smoothly and so fast. It must be the Lord's will."

"You don't have the money for your voyage yet. That could present a problem," Mutti said, searching for another angle. She could be right, but my innermost being began to see God's hand.

During the next few months, I faithfully worked for my employer while also beginning to prepare to leave Germany. A new dress and a bathrobe were added to my small wardrobe. The song of my heart remained the same, "Even though I don't know the way, You know it well."

My sponsors did send the necessary funds, $190 for my one-way ticket which was postmarked December 5, 1955. The MS *Berlin* was scheduled to leave Bremerhaven on January 4, 1956. No longer could I doubt that the Lord had prepared the way to America.

Farewell

I n December, during the festive Advent season, I began to pack my belongings. "Why are you packing your towels and collectors' cups?" Marlies asked. "Aren't you coming back to Germany?"

"I plan to return when my year as governess is up, but perhaps I can use these things while I am in America."

"Are you taking your old school books too?"

"No, all those stay here. I don't think I'll need the story of Alice in Wonderland in America, or any of my other books," I chuckled. "I'll just take my French and English New Testaments, towels, and a few special birthday gifts."

While celebrating around the Advent wreath every Sunday afternoon with my parents, brothers, and sister, I tried to firmly impress their images upon my mind. Dieter, with his curly hair and manly cut, still did not get enough to eat. Mutti and I found him early one morning—while he expected everyone to still be sleeping—in his bed with a tray of six open-faced sandwiches, munching away.

Marlies, my sister, with blond braids, was especially close to Dieter. He teased her often but always defended her and even battled others in her defense.

Udo, my youngest brother, with a slender face and blond, straight hair, studious and athletic, never made too many waves. He could fight the kitchen-towel battles during kitchen cleanups as well as the rest of us.

Vati and Mutti never seemed to change—I would definitely remember what they looked like. On that fourth Sunday of Advent, their eyes were sparkling, as were those of my brothers and sister, from the reflections of the four candles on the Advent wreath. While the brown-tiled oil heater in the corner of the living room gave off the warmth needed to feel comfortable on that cold dreary day, I felt warm and cozy in the family circle.

The volume of leather goods sales at Christmas did not come up to the previous year. Without a doubt, the department store downtown was to blame for that. The owner of the clothing store, a few steps from our business, also voiced his concern; business for everyone on our street seemed to go downhill.

On Christmas Eve, however, Vati and Mutti appeared to have forgotten about the floundering business. After having lit all the candles on the spruce tree, Vati sat at the piano playing, "Ihr Kinderlein Kommet."

O come, little children, O come one and all,
O come to the cradle in Bethlehem's stall . . .
(Schmid, "Ihr Kinderlein Kommet")

This was the signal for all of us to enter the living room and, for the first time, view the beautifully decorated tree. We were all dressed in our best clothes to give the evening a "festive flair," as Mutti would say.

After having sung many Christmas songs, Dieter and I played the "Petersburger Schlittenfahrt," one of Vati's favorite piano pieces. It felt good sitting next to my handsome brother and playing for the rest of

the family. We all enjoyed performing for our small audience. It would probably be quite a while before we'd play another piano duet. When Vati read the biblical account of the birth of Jesus from the book of Luke, my tongue silently mumbled along. Most of us knew the story word for word.

"Christ was born in Bethlehem," Vati explained. "He was the son of the Virgin Mary, yet the Son of God. His parents were poor in earthly possessions but had great spiritual wealth. You see, the Bible tells us that the angel Gabriel appeared to Mary and told her that she would bring a very special baby into the world. The angel even told her the name of the baby; He would be called Jesus. What does Jesus mean?"

"Jesus means Savior," Marlies answered.

"That is correct."

"Do you know any other names for Jesus?" Vati wondered while looking at all of us.

"Christ."

"That is a good answer, Udo. Christ also means 'The Anointed One.' Do you know another name?"

"Emmanuel," I added.

"Emmanuel means 'God with us.'"

"Lord and Master," Marlies said.

"That is right."

"In Isaiah," Mutti said, "Jesus is called 'Wonderful, Counsellor, The mighty God, The everlasting Father, The Prince of Peace.'"

"That is a very good answer, my dear wife."

"I know that verse," Udo shared. "It is Isaiah nine, verse six.

'For unto us a child is born, unto us a son is given:
And the government shall be upon his shoulder:
And his name shall be called Wonderful . . .'

and all the things Mutti said."

"Can you think of any other names that are given to Jesus?" Vati asked. "There are many more in the Bible, but I am thinking of a very special one. It is a name that describes why Jesus came to earth." Since no one came up with the answer, Vati said, "What about 'Lamb of God, which taketh away the sin of the world'?" (John 1:29).

Oh yes, I thought. *How could we have overlooked that?*

"When we think of a lamb—you all know that from our Sunday school," Vati added, "we think of the countless sacrifices that we are told about in the Old Testament. Innocent animals had to die for the sins of people. I think that one day God was simply tired of the blood that was continually being spilled. 'I am going to send my Son as a final sacrifice,' He said. 'Anyone looking at His horrible death on the cross and confessing their sins will be saved.' People who want to go to heaven must believe that Jesus died for their sins, that He was buried and rose again. There is no other way. Some people think they can get to heaven by being a good person, doing good deeds, helping others, or going to church. All these are good. But the Bible does not say anything about that being the road to heaven. What does it say in John three and verse sixteen, Marlies?"

"For God so loved the world, that he gave his only begotten Son, that whosoever believeth in him should not perish, but have everlasting life."

"This is right," Vati said. "In the Book of Acts we have the verse, 'Believe on the Lord Jesus Christ, and thou shalt be saved'" (Acts 16:31).

"Yes," Mutti agreed, "only through the Lamb of God can we be heaven-bound."

After Vati prayed, we continued singing all the Christmas songs we knew. Our Sunday school hymnal contained 309 songs of which forty-three were Christmas songs. All of us had committed most of them, with all the stanzas, to memory. We rejoiced in the few gifts we received, but the highlight of Christmas Eve was always the celebration of the birth of Christ.

When the large church organ thundered on Christmas morning, "Lo, How a Rose E'er Blooming," I thought of the prophets and how they were guided by God Himself to foretell and record for us the miraculous birth of Christ. Then I heard the two Dieters enhance the service with a piano duet. This was followed by the choir singing elaborate selections in praise of God's gift to men.

After dinner in the afternoon, we all sat around the table playing board games and Bible riddle games which Vati made up. Winners were always rewarded with a few raisins, a nut, or a piece of hard candy.

"My friend and I are planning to go to Canada," Dieter told me as I finished packing my suitcases. "He has relatives there, and they invited him and me to come."

"You are going to Canada and your friend is going with you? Are you serious?"

"Yes, he and I plan to go. We want to escape being drafted into the new German army. We have seen enough war, don't you think, Sis? I want to get away from here."

"Did you start on your paperwork yet?"

"No, I haven't, but I think it'll probably go as fast as it went for you."

"So you are going to leave home too? How do Vati and Mutti feel about that?"

"I just told them today, and they don't have anything against it. I am finished with my apprenticeship and should be able to do rather well in Canada. Electronics is the field of the future, and, from what I hear, the Canadians like specialists. I'll probably work for someone first, learn English, and then start my own business."

"That would be great, Dieter. We can perhaps see each other now and then too. Now I won't feel so alone. Just the thought of being so far away from the family depresses me sometimes."

"Well, I don't feel quite the way you do, Sis. That's probably because I am a man."

A man? My brother was a man? I had never looked at him that way. He was my brother, the one who often got me into trouble when we were little. He was also the one who wouldn't give one inch during the heat of the latest kitchen-towel battles. The "wars" ended only when someone else gave in, but never Dieter. I guess he just grew up alongside of me without my taking notice. And since the army didn't draft children, I presumed he really was a man.

During my personal prayer time on New Year's Eve, my soul cried out to God, "Why do I have to go to America? You see the future, Lord. You have the answers. I know it is Your will, but I still don't want to leave my family. You just have to help me and give me Your joy to live the life You are setting before me. I place myself into Your hands. I am Yours for whatever Your eternal purpose might be. Just guide me—don't leave me alone . . ."

On the evening of January 3, my packed suitcases stood in the hallway. At 6:00 o'clock the next morning, Mutti and I would leave by train for the German port of Bremerhaven. How I wished all of the family could have seen me off. But there were several obstacles, the greatest being the travel expenses.

Our last devotional time that evening was very sad. I would miss the singing and family circle. What would it be like in America? No matter how many questions I had asked myself, I never found a single answer. "You will be our herald," Vati said to me that night as spokesman for the rest of the family. "You will be our herald." What did that statement mean? My mind searched in vain for the meaning of it.

After tearful goodbyes early the next morning, Mutti and I left Oberhausen, the city in which I had lived for only nine months. With the metal wheels of the train beating the tracks in a monotone rhythm, Mutti and I sat on the wooden slat seats staring out of the window. It was a cold January morning, outside and inside the train, yet my heart radiated warmth of love for my mother. She had suffered in a Communist

jail for me and given herself sacrificially in order to find the father of her children. For too many years she lived without her mate. She suffered the mental anguish of having known that her grandfather had been killed by the Russians; her dad had died while fleeing from his farm to escape the enemy that ravaged East Prussia. Her mother had died in the arms of strangers instead of her own. She had lost her mother-in-law, brother-in-law, and an uncle. Yet she'd say, "He doeth all things well."

Now her firstborn was about to leave the nest. Would we ever see each other again on earth? The mighty Atlantic Ocean was about to separate us. Oh yes, I planned to return to Germany, but would I? And when would that be? "No, I will not marry a foreigner," I had said many times. "I will be back."

Cold, damp air awaited us when we got off the train directly at the pier. The clammy January air forced people to keep their hands warm by blowing on them—one's own breath was the only available warmth. While the gray haze hovering over the North Sea chilled my face, the cold even dug through my heavy gray winter coat to find my bones.

After checking in my belongings, I was told to board the ship. With the massive MS *Berlin* solidly resting on the water, Mutti and I walked up the plank to the deck. There was plenty of time for us to find cabin #419, four stories below the upper deck of the ocean liner. Mutti and I walked and walked while following all the signs which finally led us to a porthole. To the right was my room. The porthole in my cabin let in just enough daylight to see the small room, dresser, and bunk bed. My bed was to be the one on top; my co-voyager had not yet arrived.

Mutti and I then toured the ship, locating the ornate dining room, dance hall, smoking room, and an indoor swimming pool. The latter tempted me greatly. "I will go swimming often during the next twelve days, Mutti. Wouldn't it be great if you could come along with me?"

When visitors were asked to leave the ship, I accompanied Mutti to the main deck. We embraced and kissed. "The Lord bless you, Schäfle. Stay close to Him," she said in tears. "We will always be praying for you."

"I will be praying for you too."

As she turned, I knew I would be separated from my best friend for a long time. Slowly she walked down the planks to the gray cement dock. From there she looked up to search out her daughter. In a cold drizzling mist, I looked down, waved, and tried to smile through my tears. Mutti waved back, sadly.

Finally the MS *Berlin* slowly pulled away from the dock. My life as a refugee had ended. What would I be called in America? Immigrant? With my eyes fastened on Mutti, her stature became smaller and smaller and then vanished in the mist.

20

Stormy Voyage

"**I** would like to welcome you on board the MS *Berlin*," a gentleman dressed in a white coat and black trousers greeted the seven of us at our assigned table. "I will be your waiter at every meal for the duration of your voyage. If you have any special dietary needs, please let me know. I am here to serve you and make this trip an enjoyable one for you."

Being seated at an elaborate feast with six strangers was a challenging experience, but we did not remain strangers for long. After the initial, formal introductions, everyone freely shared dreams and hopes for their future in America. All of us were Germans, three men, three women, and I. The three women were war brides whose husbands, American soldiers, had married them in Germany, returned to the States, and then called for them. "That is the only way to get to America," one of the young ladies told us. I, of course, had to disagree.

After having eaten through all the courses of the first delicious meal, I went to my cabin. On the way, I passed the pool and decided to change and go swimming. My roommate, an elderly lady from Boston, immediately gave me cause to rejoice for having buckled down and learned English because she did not speak German.

Spending the afternoon at the pool with only a few other people and exercising was exciting. After a fantastic evening meal, I went to the upper deck for fresh air and noticed that the ship no longer moved through calm waters. The sea had begun to form small waves. Climbing onto my top bunk at night, I snuggled into bed, listening to the sound of the mighty engines which helped carry me to the land of milk and honey. With a prayer on my lips, I fell asleep on my way to America.

Going to the dining room the next morning, I found it difficult to walk normally and not bump into a wall every now and then. The water in the pool, I noticed, slopped back and forth as one big wave. After breakfast, a sign posted on the glass door of the pool read, "No swimming due to sea conditions." Sadly I went to the upper deck.

How would my body utilize all the new food I was pumping into it? What would it do with Holstein calf roast, gold perch with mushrooms and wine sauce, creamed broccoli, Portuguese salmon filet, barbecued rib steak, tomato salad, custard? It was all new yet so delicious, and I ate everything I possibly could. Gone were the days of leaving the table hungry, the days of begging for a crust of bread from the Russian troops, digging through slimy, rotten, and stinking potatoes at some abandoned farm in hopes of finding some that had been overlooked by the decay. Gone were the days of begging from farmers and being chased by vicious dogs and people. The refugee now lived like a queen. The Lord had truly prepared a table before me. If only my family could experience this with me!

Because of seasickness, my cabin partner was no longer capable of leaving her bed. With the cabin air unpleasant, I began staying out of the room all day. On the upper deck, I met an elderly gentleman, captain of the Salvation Army, who was returning from a visit with relatives in Sweden. I told him about the generosity of a British Salvation Army man and the kindnesses he had shown my young people's group in Nienburg. We talked about stamp collecting, also a hobby of his, and he taught me new English words and expressions. He also told me about Long Island,

my destination. "The island is about 150 miles in length and stretches east from New York City into the Atlantic Ocean."

A young man, member of the German Seventh Day Adventist church, and I discussed Christianity, and I told him about my life as a refugee. His goal was to evangelize America.

As the MS *Berlin* neared the halfway mark of the voyage, the mighty Atlantic increased its fury with every passing day. Winter winds built their intensity and whipped the waters continuously higher. House-high waves became common. My stomach began to churn. Walking was difficult, climbing steps almost impossible. With the ship's stern dipping forward, one would fall forward on the staircases; and when it rolled back, one would fall backward. In order not to give in to "feeding the fish," I remained outside, all bundled up, most of the day. Everywhere I looked, passengers carried and used their little bags while looking pale and sick. The rails were littered with purging voyagers. I would not think about my stomach, I decided; I would be positive and inhale the fresh, cold winter air instead.

"I have to strap you into your bunk tonight, Miss Guddat," the cabin steward said. "This is going to be a *very* rough night, and being strapped in is the only way for you to stay in your bed."

"Do you know that I always feel like a mummy after you have tied me up?"

"That may be so, but I am paid to take care of my passengers and that I will do. I cannot have you fall out and kill yourself. Besides, this is the roughest the sea has been in the past five years."

Lying on my bunk, mummified, my stomach seemed to follow the roll of the ship; once it leaped to my feet, then to my throat, then from the right to the left. It sloshed around within me with every movement of the ship.

Could a heavy ocean liner like the MS *Berlin* sink? I wondered. Of course it could. What a strange thought! Suddenly, deep within

my soul, I heard myself listening to and singing one of my favorite guitar songs:

Master, the tempest is raging!
The billows are tossing high!
The sky is o'ershadowed with blackness,
No shelter or help is nigh.
Carest thou not that we perish?
How canst thou lie asleep
When each moment so madly is threat'ning
A grave in the angry deep?
The winds and the waves shall obey thy will:
Peace, be still.

Whether the wrath of the storm-tossed sea
Or demons or men or whatever it be,
No water can swallow the ship where lies
The Master of ocean and earth and skies.
They all shall sweetly obey thy will:
Peace, be still; peace, be still.
They all shall sweetly obey thy will;
Peace, peace, be still.

Linger, O blessed Redeemer!
Leave me alone no more,
And with joy I shall make the blest harbor
And rest on the blissful shore.
(Baker, "Master, the Tempest Is Raging")

"Thank You, Lord, for this song. You are at the helm of this ship and at the helm of my life. And should this be the end of my life, I will be with You in heaven because of Your sacrifice on Calvary!"

No longer could I hear the engines of the ship; the maddening waters won the noise battle. Even with my arms tied up, the hands automatically searched for something to grasp and cling to. Finally my thoughts drifted further and further away until the body succumbed to its need for sleep. "Peace, be still . . . Peace, be still. . . ."

Several times during the night, I was awakened by the pounding of the surf, but in my semiconscious state, the same words continued to ring in my heart, "Peace, be still . . . Peace, be still. . . ."

In the morning the steward came to loosen my fetters and help me out of bed. "Good morning!" I said to my roommate, but she didn't answer. Pale and yellow, she lay in her bed. Was she dying? She had vomited and not eaten since we left Germany.

Quickly I went through my morning ritual and dashed to the upper deck for fresh air. Arriving on the top deck, I found all the exit doors locked. No one was allowed to go outside, the sign said. During the night, most of the windows on the upper deck were smashed by the sea. *How will I survive without fresh air?* I thought. That alone had helped me stay well.

Walking into the dining hall for my breakfast shift, I was shocked to see only seven people of two hundred in the whole room. "Where are all the others?" I asked the waiter.

"I guess they are all sick. Most of our 450 passengers are sick today. I have worked on this ship for quite a few years but have never experienced a storm of this magnitude. You are one of the few lucky ones, Miss Guddat. You must have a strong stomach."

"I felt queasy at times," I replied, "and I probably could have joined the rest of the crowd, but I refuse to give in. One of my professors at school had drummed into the heads of us students for years that 'a lot of sickness is in your head.' Well, I thought of that often on this voyage and decided not to give in."

"That is a good theory, Miss Guddat," the waiter agreed, "and I am glad it worked for you so far."

"I surely don't know how it will work without fresh air. I know that helped a lot."

"Yes," he said, "I heard that the upper deck was hit hard during the night. But now, tell me, what would you like for breakfast this morning? Our kitchen is filled with food today—and you have to share it with only a few other folks. So what would you like to eat?" I hardly knew what to ask for. Was I already in heaven?

On day ten of our voyage, my Salvation Army friend finally appeared on deck to admire a more peaceful ocean. "Have you been sick too?" I asked. "I haven't seen you for days."

"Oh yes," he admitted. "I have been quite ill. But, thanks to the Lord, He has brought us through the wildest voyage I have ever experienced. And I travel frequently.

"We should be docking in Halifax, Canada, before too long. From there it is just a short trip to the New York Harbor."

"What do you mean by short trip?"

"Less than a day, I'd say. I would like to ask a favor of you, Miss Guddat, since you can write in German."

"Surely, what is it?"

"I would like you to translate and write these two 'thank-you' letters for me, one for my steward, and one for the waiter. They both have done such a good job. I want to thank them and give a little money gift."

"Oh," I said, "is one supposed to pay them? I have only six dollars to my name."

"No, you don't really have to, but it would be nice."

After having written the notes, I decided that I would simply thank my waiter and give the steward one dollar. That was quite a bit of money—over four German Mark.

Slowly the continent of North America came into view. Halifax itself laid shrouded in a mist. After a few passengers had disembarked and several boarded, our ship began to steam in a southwesterly direction toward New York. Most of the passengers had recuperated from their seasickness and again appeared in the dining room.

"Tomorrow we will be in the land almost everyone in the world is dreaming about, but few ever get to see," the elderly gentleman at our table said. "It is the only country in which true freedom can be found. Thousands have left everything to acquire that freedom. Thousands more have been killed for just dreaming about America, whispering the word, trying to crash through borders, or floating on rafts while praying for winds to take them to America. America!—America!—It echoes from the heart of freedom-loving people. Thousands more, in Communist lands, find the strength to live only through holding on to a dream that might someday lead them to America."

"Yes," I said, "we are truly blessed. We have been chosen to experience the land of golden opportunity while others can but dream." My doubts about America almost totally melted in the bright sunlight of the freedom aspect. Returning to my room to pack my little suitcase, I continued to reflect upon that dinner conversation. *I am truly blessed,* I thought.

When I arrived on deck at 6:00 o'clock the next morning, my Salvation Army friend quickly found me. "Happy Birthday, Miss Guddat," he said. "May God richly bless you in this new land that we see stretched out before us. What a special day this is for you; January 16, your birthday, and a new life in America. Here is a little present for you."

"Thank you so much, but that was not necessary."

"Oh yes, it was."

Upon opening the box, I was shocked to see a large silver collector's spoon from Sweden. In an envelope, he handed me Swedish postage stamps.

"That is New York City," he said pointing at the skyline. "And do you see that statue over there?"

"Yes, I see it."

"That is the Statue of Liberty, America's symbol of freedom."

"I know the statue from postage stamps. I had no idea, however, that it was so majestic. The stamps surely don't do it justice. Never would I have imagined it being that tall."

Suddenly several boats appeared near the MS *Berlin*. "Those are the pilot ships," my friend said. "It is their duty to safely guide our ship into the harbor."

"They surely do look small in comparison to our gigantic ocean liner," I added.

"That is true, but they do have a very big job to perform."

As the ship began to align itself to the pier, I tried in vain to search for Tante Martha's face in the crowd below. On the ship, new friends said goodbye and wished each other good luck. "I'll keep in touch," passengers promised each other, but would they? Friendships formed during the twelve-day voyage were probably more prone to fade than the memory of the violent voyage to the land of the free.

21

Promised Land

The dock that stretched alongside the MS *Berlin* in York Harbor was almost empty. I stood alone on my twenty-second birthday. Everyone knew what to do when leaving the ship. They had loved ones meet them, embrace and kiss them, and then whisk them away; others seemed to know about connections to their destinations. I didn't. Tante Martha hadn't come to meet me as she wrote she would. How could I possibly get to Long Island? Would five dollars cover the trip? My heart fluttered as I contemplated my predicament. "Are you lost, Miss?" a gentleman asked.

"I am waiting for someone to pick me up."

"Oh, that is good. You are almost the last one here."

That was quite obvious, I thought. So here I was in America, land of the free. I surely was free. But for some reason I didn't feel free; I felt bound by the unknown. New country, new language, everyone a stranger, and I was free? Free to do what? Die of despair?

"Lord, I don't know the way, but You know it." I could call the Mission Home in New Jersey and check on Tante Martha's whereabouts if I knew how to use the American telephone. I could go by subway to Long Island if I knew how to use the transit system and had an idea what

to do when I got there. I could probably get a taxi to Manhasset on the island if my five dollars were sufficient. Or I could just stay there and die of despair or the cold. Four options—which one would I choose?

"This is a special day for you, Miss Guddat," my Salvation Army friend had said earlier. And he was right. I had never felt so lost. We had lived in many towns without my ever having lost my way, but here, in New York City, I was lost just standing at the harbor. How could anyone find her way here? From the MS *Berlin*, I saw nothing but skyscrapers.

"You are the only One, Lord, who can help me out of this dilemma. Please don't let me freeze here any longer. Show me what to do."

I looked down at my dark green suitcases next to me. They had left Germany brand new. Now the man-made molded pieces of luggage were old and beat-up looking. Our customers in Germany traveled with leather luggage, but this was all Vati could afford to give me.

How much more time should I allow myself to get out of this dilemma? Waiting seemed to get me nowhere. The excitement and rejoicing that had flooded my soul when the ship docked had vanished with the passengers. I felt bewildered, lifeless, numb, alone. Was I really supposed to be in America? I listened to the ship's engines which were still churning. I wondered where the ship that brought me to this dismal point in my life would cruise to next? I should have asked the waiter or the steward. But then, why did I care about that now? I was standing at the crossroads of my life—in New York Harbor.

Suddenly I heard, "Lia! "Lia!" Only one person called me that. I turned toward the sound and there she was—finally—Tante Martha!

"Am I ever glad to see you," I said sighing with relief while hugging Vati's sister.

"Are you the only one left here? I am sorry. I didn't have the right time for the ship's arrival. Happy birthday to you, my niece! I can't believe you are really here in America! My little one whose first tooth I detected, and whom I used to push through Insterburg in a baby carriage

when I visited East Prussia. She is here now in America, a young lady twenty-two years old. I can't believe it."

"Well, Tante Martha, it is true. And you had everything to do with it. And the Lord, of course."

"So this is all the luggage you have?"

"Yes, Tante Martha, that's all. The contents of these few suitcases represent everything I own."

"We are going to take a taxi to Long Island. That is the best way to travel with suitcases. Usually I take the subways when I am in New York. You know I lived here for a number of years, and my church, which was pastored by Dr. Haldeman, is right in Manhattan. I know the city about as well as I know my room at the Mission."

Sitting in the taxi, Tante Martha tried to point out various landmarks; the Empire State building, layout of streets, entrances to subways, streets that didn't have names, just numbers, and bridges.

"I'll never be able to learn all that," I said, totally overwhelmed by the magnitude of the gray-looking city. "How can anyone live in this town?"

"Well," she said, "it is not so bad if you are used to it. Millions of people live here and like it."

"I don't think I could ever like this. I need nature, trees, forests."

"Someday I'll give you a tour of the city. I'll take you to Macy's, Grand Central Station, the Empire State building, and we'll eat at a German restaurant on Forty-Second Street. I'll also take you to my former church."

New York City would not be a place for me. I knew that from the start. I could not believe how horrible an American cemetery looked. There seemed to be one tombstone on top of another. I wouldn't even want to die in New York.

Long Island, in contrast, was more to my liking. We passed lovely homes, bays, country roads, evergreen trees, and open fields. Everything I saw appealed to me. Turning from Southern Boulevard in Manhasset

into a development, I could scarcely trust my eyes. There were mansions, huge lots, little hills, trees. Even on that January day, everything looked green.

"How many people live in each home?" I asked.

"These are all one-family homes," Tante Martha answered.

"What would one family do with so much space?"

"Well, the rich need a lot of room for entertaining, the maid lives there, the butler, and, of course, each child has his own room." Each child a room? I could not fathom that.

The taxi driver played havoc with my eyes while flying through the winding roads toward our destination. The minute my eyes had fastened themselves on a Tudor style home, we passed one even more beautiful. No two houses were alike in that neighborhood.

"Here we are," Tante Martha joyously said. "This is going to be your home for the next year."

Passing between two tall evergreen shrubs framing the large front door of the brick home, Tante Martha rang the doorbell. A young boy opened the door.

"Come on in," he said. "My mom had to go to the store. She'll be right back. We have been expecting you."

"Something is burning," Tante Martha said the moment we set foot in the house. "Let me go to your kitchen, Son. Is there something on the stove?"

As soon as Tante Martha began stirring the burning sauerkraut in the large aluminum pot, the lady of the house stepped in. "Welcome!" she said. "I am sorry I wasn't here to greet you. I just had to make a quick trip to town.

"So this is Liane! Welcome to America and our family! I hope you'll like it here with us."

"Thank you."

"These are our three sons. They are four, seven, and nine years old. And there, under the table, is our Spitz. I am sure she greeted you when you came in."

Americans spoke very fast, I noticed. How would I ever be able to understand what they said? My mind simply wasn't able to translate that fast. I decided to "tune out" while the two ladies were discussing what to do with the scorched sauerkraut. Instead, I looked at the large dining room and the floor-to-ceiling mirrored wall behind the buffet. There wasn't one fingerprint on the mirror. The long brass planter on the buffet, overflowing with trailing ivy, sparkled even in its reflection. Eight high-backed chairs with striped upholstered seats surrounded the massive, oblong antique table, which was highly polished.

To the right of the hallway entrance spread the large living room, furnished with a brown couch, matching arm chairs, leather-inlaid end tables, several table lamps, and a television. Crystal chandeliers decorated the wall on both sides of the mirror above the fireplace. Sheer curtains hung over blinds topped by satin drapes which fell in perfect folds from below the tasseled canopy. All types of figurines rested on the various tabletops and the mantel. Only in museums had I seen such riches.

"Liane," Mrs. Weaver approached me, "let me take your suitcases upstairs to your room."

"Suitcases? What is that?"

Tante Martha quickly translated, and we all started walking up the carpeted, winding staircase to the second floor.

"To the right here is the bedroom of the two older boys, and this is the bedroom of the youngest." We walked past the crib to a door and a small step down when Mrs. Weaver continued, "And this is your room. We added this to the house for you. Below this room is the garage. Now, how do you like your room?"

"It is beautiful, just beautiful."

217

Three of the walls of my own room consisted of mostly windows from which I could touch trees and see the steep backyard and outdoor fireplace. I felt as if I was in the middle of a forest. Green draw drapes hugged the narrow stretches of paneled walls between the windows. The back of the green couch, with wooden arms, folded down into a bed. A chair, small table, and lamp gave the room a cozy look.

"While I go and finish dinner, you and your aunt take time to visit and unpack. I'll call you when I am ready."

"This is absolutely wonderful, Tante Martha. I have my own room. What a birthday present!"

Lying on my couch at night, I took out my calendar booklet and started writing and memorizing the words I had learned that afternoon: suitcase, drapes, drip coffee, foam, pleasure, wipe up, and immune. *I will have to do that every day,* I told myself, *write down new words and expressions and learn them at night.*

"Thank You for America, Lord! You have brought me here safely. Thank You for Your protection on the dangerous voyage. Bless Vati and Mutti, Dieter, Marlies, and Udo. How I wish they could experience all of this with me. You are so good."

During the night, I tossed and turned. My feet were cold; I missed the featherbed into which I could snuggle them. How could one get warm with a tightly tucked-in sheet and blanket? That was the American way, and I wanted to learn, but I surely didn't sleep well under a thin blanket in a cold room.

The next morning I felt tired but ready for my devotions. "Lord, I need an extra special verse for my year in America. Please give me one. Flipping the Bible and pointing at a verse is not how You work in a Christian's life, but could You, today, please make an exception? I need Your help and guidance." With that earnest prayer, my Bible opened to the first chapter of Joshua and my eye fell on verse nine, "Have not I commanded thee? Be strong and of a good courage; be not afraid, neither

be thou dismayed: for the LORD thy God *is* with thee whithersoever thou goest."

"Thank You, Lord! I need nothing more than Your precious promise that You are with me even in America." After my room was in tiptop shape, my blankets and sheets folded and put in the closet, I went downstairs.

Mr. Weaver had already left for his office in New York City. I was asked to prepare waffles for breakfast for the rest of the family and sprinkle them with powdered sugar. When the two oldest came to the eat-in kitchen table with their dark slacks, white shirts, and slicked-down hair, I set the waffles before them. Instead of eating, they just drank the orange juice and picked at the food. "Hurry up!" their mother called from the hallway. "The school bus will be here any minute!"

"I am done, Mommy," the oldest one answered and jumped up from the cushioned bench. After putting on bow ties, jackets, and top coats, both boys took their book bags and dashed out of the house while their mother held on to the door.

I looked at the delicious waffles—which I had not eaten since our days in East Prussia—that had hardly been touched. *I'll save them for tomorrow's breakfast,* I thought. But before I had figured out how to save them, their mother came and threw them into the garbage. I couldn't believe it. Food was garbage in America? The four-year-old ate a little more than his brothers, but his leftovers were also tossed away. When I started eating my waffles, I savored every delicious bite. I could have eaten them all day long but was embarrassed to act like a hungry lion.

Throughout the morning, I learned what my duties would be. After cleaning the kitchen, I had to change the wet bedding of the four-year-old, clean and dust his room, change the bedding of the other boys, do the laundry in a machine in the basement, and dry it in a dryer. I had to clean and tidy up the rest of the house, except the master bedroom and bathroom upstairs, which, I was told, Mrs. Weaver liked to clean herself.

For lunch I was offered a sandwich made of toasted white bread, butter, liverwurst, and a gherkin. It was delicious, and I could have eaten two, three, or perhaps four such sandwiches but had to hold back. The youngest boy nibbled at the center of a peanut butter and jelly sandwich. The rest was also thrown into the garbage. All the while, the built-in kitchen radio played, "Love and marriage, love and marriage, they go together like a horse and carriage."

On the evening of my first full day in America, I again studied the vocabulary words which I had written into the calendar book throughout the day. My new words for the day were: lunch, sled, sleigh-riding, garbage, dust pan, vacuum sweeper, dust rag, hanger, junky, satisfied, and increase vocabulary. By the end of the first week, my vocabulary had indeed increased.

When Mrs. Weaver left me alone with the boys, they tried to test my authority but quickly learned that with Mom away, Liane was in charge. The food I was to discard I always ate when no one was looking; I simply could not throw out food.

On Sunday morning, after my employers had returned from mass, they drove me to church. I presumed Tante Martha had searched out the small group of Bible-believing Christians and asked the Weavers to take me there.

In my letter to Germany, I tried to tell my family about America, the many big cars on the roads—nobody seemed to ride a bike—milk being delivered to the front door, and the tasteless, white fluffy bread that I could get down only after it had been popped in a special appliance called a toaster. I told them about a supermarket stuffed with food. I told them that no one in our neighborhood knew about clotheslines; everything had to be dried in a tumbling machine. There was also no scrubbing board in the house; a machine did all the washing. The laundry was done every single day, even on Sundays. Not one armoire was in the whole house; everything went into built-in closets.

I told my parents about my employers' drinking a cocktail every night before dinner, and that a bar in the basement was filled with countless bottles of alcoholic drinks. I told them about the children's spending most of their time on their own; they even ate by themselves.

Seven days after my arrival in America, Mrs. Weaver said, "We like your work. You have done a good job. Things are going to work out really well for all of us. My husband and I will pay you twenty-five dollars per week."

Twenty-five dollars? I thought, that is almost 110 Mark. That is fantastic.

Then she continued, "Of course you have to pay off your voyage. How will it be if we deduct ten dollars every week until the $190 are paid up?"

"That will be fine," I said but was inwardly very disappointed. I had no idea the voyage had to be repaid. That didn't leave much to send to Vati and Mutti. Several weeks later I decided I would not accept any payment until I was free of debt, a goal I finally reached in April. In April, I also noticed that my maroon-colored suit no longer fit because I had gained thirty pounds.

"What are you doing on your days off?" a pretty blond lady asked me after church one Sunday.

"I don't have a day off," I answered. "I work seven days a week."

"That can't be," she said surprised. "And it isn't healthy for you either. You have to have some time for yourself."

"I do write letters after all the children are in bed at night."

"But that is not enough," she insisted. "Why don't you see if you can get next Sunday off. We'll take you home with us for dinner after the service."

"Thank you very much," I said.

At the Ekstroms' I immediately felt at home. Their small one-bedroom apartment was lovingly furnished with pieces from the past.

Frilly white curtains covered the windows. "What do you call this piece of furniture?" I asked Shirley.

"That is a dry sink," she said and explained its use in early America.

"And what do you call these pieces?"

"That is milk glass," she told me. "I love milk glass."

Shirley's husband, Marvin, a tall and blond bank teller, seemed to adore his wife and three-year-old son. At the dinner table, we tried to get to know one another, and by the time they took me home in their huge car, after the evening service, I felt refreshed and ready to face another week.

The letters I received from Germany conveyed very little. "We are doing fine" was a sure phrase in every piece of correspondence, but were they? Since living and eating was totally related to the success of the store, how was it really going? Was the big competition continuing to squeeze the life out of the fledgling leather goods business? Would my parents ever tell me, or would they purposely keep me from knowing the truth?

In another letter, I told my parents about my new gray uniform with a lace collar, cuffs, and apron which I had to wear for parties. I was proud of that uniform until I learned that only maids wore them, and that it was a status symbol of the rich to have a maid. No one in America, I wrote, called me "refugee." I was now called "maid."

First Disappointment

"I heard you are German," a young man with blond hair and wearing a blue suit approached me after the Sunday morning church service.

"Yes, I am."

"I bought a German car," he continued, "and it has German writing on the motor. Do you think you could come and translate that for me?"

"I can try," I said, "but I really don't know technical American words."

As we left the private home in which the believers met and went to the parking lot, he said, "By the way, I am Luther Brown."

"And I am Liane Guddat."

Luther then opened the back of the blue Volkswagen, and I began to translate as best I could while ancient trees hovered above us filtering the strong spring sun.

"Thank you so much," he said. "I guess I can get the gist of what it says. Now, let me ask you another question. Do you think you would like to go out with me sometime?"

"Sometime perhaps."

After I told Marvin and Shirley about Luther, they said, "He seems to be a nice young man," and gave me their approval.

Visiting Long Island one Sunday, Tante Martha was glad, I thought, to see her niece adjusting to America and even singing in the six-member choir. "Who is that fine-looking young man over there?" she asked me after the service.

"That is Luther Brown. He moved here from Pennsylvania a few weeks ago," I answered.

"Does he have a girlfriend?"

"But Tante Martha, why are you asking all these questions? I am going back to Germany next year." She just grinned and winked at me.

The Ekstrom family had become my new American family—their home was also my home. They were the kind of Christians who seemed to thrive on helping others. Shirley's parents had to leave their apartment and temporarily made their daughter's living room their home. Whenever I was invited to stay overnight at the Ekstroms, Marvin, Shirley, their young son, and I slept in one bedroom.

"We'll go to Jones Beach someday," Mrs. Weaver had always told me, but as the summer began to heat up, she neither took her sons nor me. Instead Mrs. Weaver and her husband spent continuously more time at their country club or traveling to Bermuda and Europe. The small praying Hummel figurine they brought me as a gift from Germany, I was told, reminded them of me. One day I noticed a bill from the country club lying open on the buffet. The charge for one month's drinks was four hundred dollars.

"Mrs. Weaver," I asked one day, "is it all right with you if, when you are out of town next week, the boys and I go to see Tante Martha at the Mission Home in New Jersey? I would like your sons to see a farm since they have never seen one. Luther said he'd be glad to take all of us up there for the day."

"That will be fine, Liane. Luther is a fine young man, and I am sure the two of you will take good care of my boys."

My charges behaved beautifully, even the middle one whom I previously had to show who was boss after he had thrown himself on the floor, kicking and screaming for half an hour. A little spanking, with his mother's approval, had paved the way for good future behavior.

At the farm, the boys stood and stared at the different kinds of animals they had only heard about. Tante Martha showed us the cows in the barn and demonstrated that milk really came from a cow's udder and not a milkman's bottle. In the chicken coop, the boys gathered eggs. Geese and ducks in the pond seemed interesting to them. But when Tante Martha took us all to see the pigpen, the oldest grabbed his nose, turned, and ran a hundred-yard dash in the opposite direction.

In June I was asked to speak to a high school class about our experiences under the Communist regime. From the moment the history teacher and I entered the classroom, I noticed the very relaxed attitude of the students. When I spoke, some would get up and walk around the room, write notes, or even leave the room. To me, the students' behavior was shocking, but the teacher must have been accustomed to it because she did nothing to stop all the confusion. I was, of course, taken back to my school years and the strict attention and respect we paid to anyone in a higher position than ourselves. How could students learn anything in such an unruly setting? I wondered.

Luther, an engineer at the Sperry Gyroscope Company on Long Island, seemed to like me. "I'd like you to meet my parents someday," he said. "How do you feel about that?"

"I guess that is fine with me."

After we had driven toward Pennsylvania for several hours, I began to see the predicament in which I found myself; the seriousness of the situation suddenly hit me. *I am to meet his parents?* It seemed like a natural suggestion at first, but to drive for so many miles to accomplish that caused me to see that this was no ordinary meeting of people; I was being taken there for an inspection. What did this man, next to

whom I was sitting in a German car, have in mind? I sensed he liked me, and I liked him too. Meeting his parents, however, denoted something serious . . . on his part.

Suddenly Luther stopped the car at the edge of a mountainous road. "I just wanted you to see the view from up here. Do you see that church down there on the right? That is the village of Carrolltown." Then he began to look at my face and hair. "I guess you'll pass," he declared.

Pass what? I thought. I was right—pass inspection.

Luther's father, a supervising principal, asked me to play his favorite Christmas song, "Silent Night," on the piano. "I have never played 'Silent Night' in July," I admitted. "It just doesn't seem to fit into summer." After I had finished playing the most beautiful Christmas carol, though, he seemed pleased and took me outside to show me his well taken care of vegetable garden and flower beds. Mr. Brown's one thousand or more Christmas trees had been sheared and basked in the summer sun.

When the time had come to return to Long Island, Luther's father said to me, "Our son, I presume, mentioned to you how he asked our permission to bring you home."

"No, he didn't," I replied.

"Well, he told us in one of his recent letters—and he writes to us weekly—'I bought a German car and a German girl came with it. When may I come and show them to you?'"

"That was quite original," I chuckled.

"Goodbye, Son," both his parents said, hugging him. Then, turning to me, they said, "Goodbye. Come again," and hugged me, also.

All the way back to Long Island, the two words "come again" rang in my ear. "Come again." I must have passed inspection, but why was I being inspected?

When Luther spent his one-week vacation in Pennsylvania with his parents, and I did not see him at church, I realized that I missed him. How was that possible? I wasn't falling in love, was I?

Three months later, one Sunday afternoon, Luther and I drove to the northern shore of the island. At Sunken Meadows State Park, he nervously stopped the car away from the main parking area. When we started to get out, a member of the beach patrol came to inform us that we could not leave the car there.

"Why don't we go down to the beach?" I asked. Leading me by the hand, he said nothing and started walking. Finally he asked me to sit down in the sand and there made small talk for a while.

"Do you think I'll be a good father?" he finally asked while holding my hands.

"Well, I don't know, Luther, I guess so. Why do you ask that?"

Then in an almost trembling voice he asked, "Will you marry me?"

I? Marry an American? I had vowed not to marry a foreigner. I planned to go back to Germany. This couldn't be true. Was he serious? My heart raced. My plans for the future became entangled with the question of the present. There was a young lady at church chasing after him; why was he asking me? My head not only throbbed, it pounded. We had known each other for only seven months. My thoughts tumbled over each other, forward and backward, somersaulting from one corner of confusion and shock to another. "I can't give you an answer today. I have to think."

"Think about what?"

"Think about the answer. There have been too many changes too quickly for me this year. I can hardly comprehend it all, and this would be the most important decision of my life."

"Do you love me?"

"Yes, I do."

"So then, what is so difficult? I feel it is the Lord's will for us to get married. How much time do you think you'll need?"

"I think probably a week."

For the next day, my day off, I had signed up to polish the newly delivered pews at our new church. "Lord," I prayed, "did You plan for me to be away from the noisy family today just so I can concentrate on You and Your future plans for me? It is so quiet here in Your sanctuary. We are alone here, Lord, You and I. You see my heart; it is rent, trying to know Your will. Do You want me to marry Luther and live in America forever?

"You see, Lord, I can no longer think clearly. I can't reason. I am confused," I continued while waxing and buffing the new wood. "You have said You will never leave me nor forsake me. All year long, to this twenty-second day in October, You have kept Your promise. And I know You are not going to leave me at this crossroad of my life. Help, Lord! Help me with the answer. Dry my tears. Don't let them continue to fall on this new wood and bury themselves in the pews forever. Thank You that I can be here alone before You and that I can talk to You."

On our trip to Tante Martha's the following Sunday with the Ekstroms and another friend in the car, Luther was very quiet. There was not one moment during the whole morning, before or after church, nor after dinner when we could be alone to talk.

In the afternoon, our whole group decided to take a walk on a picturesque country road. The Lord must have used His mighty palette to meticulously paint the leaves in the most vivid colors. Germans delighted in seeing yellow and brown leaves in the fall, but here in America the splendor of the various types of maple trees was indescribable. We stooped to pick up leaves and admired them—veins outlined in red, the leaf red, yellow, and green, color combinations only the Lord could devise. I noticed that this beauty of God's handiwork also excited all my friends. Bright green stately evergreens, intermingled with maples, set off the colorful trees even more. At the pond of the Mission Home, only a few wild ducks marred the colored reflections in the water.

While we all walked downhill and chatted, Luther and I began to lag behind. "I have thought about the answer to your question and prayed about it a lot," I started with a pounding heart.

"Yes . . . ?" he asked, stretching the word.

"The answer is 'Yes, I will marry you.'" I was as shocked as he was. He took my hand, squeezed it, and gave me a peck on the cheek just as Shirley turned around to find out what had become of us.

"I still don't know," Luther said somewhat hurt, "why it took you so long to give me an answer."

"I had a lot to think about and sort out," I said.

Marvin, Shirley, and Tante Martha were very excited when we whispered to them about our engagement. They all gave us their blessing.

For their anniversary on Sunday, November 18, Marvin and Shirley had invited the whole young adult Sunday school class of sixteen to their home. Everyone sat around chatting and playing games. "We'll play another game now," Shirley announced. "For that we have to turn off all the lights. I will then walk from person to person and hand you something."

The moment the lights went off, Luther who sat next to me, slipped the engagement ring on my finger—as prearranged.

"Turn on the light, Honey, please," Shirley said to Marvin. As soon as everyone focused their eyes on the pink sweetheart rose in their hands and the little tag on which Shirley had written, "Engagement of Luther and Liane," various comments of surprise and shock were uttered. Then congratulations began and continued for some time. Only the person sitting opposite me couldn't rejoice. With her eyes fastened to her skirt, she didn't say one word. I felt badly for her because Luther had chosen me over her.

My parents knew about my dating Luther, his work, and his hobby of flying. One letter, however, in which I had enclosed money and told them about the engagement, they never received. When the following

letter arrived in Germany and mentioned wedding plans, their reaction was total shock.

December days on Long Island resembled those of West Germany—cold, dark, and dreary. Neither at home nor at church was anything mentioned about Advent. Inwardly I longed for the warmth of the candles of the Advent wreath and the singing of Christmas carols. How else would one prepare the heart for the Lord's coming? Stores at shopping centers blasted Christmas songs that didn't have much to do with Christ's birth. Brightly colored glass balls and thick golden garlands were haphazardly slung around the trees. Most Germans would have described the store trees as "gaudy." This was America, however, I had to remind myself—a new land with new customs.

On Christmas Eve, Luther and I were invited to the home of a young couple from church along with all the other young adults. Anxiously I awaited the celebrations of the evening. It would be my first Christmas Eve in America and that at the side of my future husband. For several hours, everyone sat or stood and enjoyed eating many delicacies from the smorgasbord while telling jokes and laughing. The spinning record on the turntable played Christmas music to which no one listened. Impatiently, I began looking at my watch. When would the Christmas celebration begin, the singing and Scripture reading? It was almost 11:00 p.m.

Shortly after 11:00 o'clock, everyone exchanged gifts. I still looked at my watch. The best was yet to come—the celebration of the meaning of the season. Suddenly, at almost midnight, the party broke up and everyone left, including Luther and I.

In my room—all alone—for the first time I realized that I missed Germany. I sobbed myself to sleep. Tomorrow, Christmas day, would be celebrated differently, I hoped.

Walking downstairs on Christmas morning, I heard a lot of ruckus coming from the living room. The boys, all in their pajamas, had already ripped open the packages that just a day ago laid neatly under the tree.

Pretty wrapping paper, wadded up, and ribbon littered the whole room, interspersed with toys and clothing.

"Give me this," one yelled, tugging at a toy.

"No, that's mine. You can't have it," the other hollered.

"Were you boys supposed to open all these presents before your parents get up and before the Christmas celebration?"

"Oh yes," the oldest one answered. "We do that every year."

As I stood in shock, Mrs. Weaver entered the room. "Merry Christmas, Liane," she said. "Here is a present for you."

"Thank you so very much," I said. "Shall I open it now?"

"Yes, you may do it now."

As I admired the beautiful towels, Mrs. Weaver said, "You can put them in your hope chest."

"Hope chest? What is a hope chest?" Kindly, this lady who had taught me how to make stuffing for a Thanksgiving turkey, spread peanut butter and cream cheese into celery to make hors d'oeuvres, and make a wrinkle-free bed with neatly folded corners, now explained "hope chest." I had learned so much about American customs and life. But I think perhaps the Weaver family had also learned some things from me.

After the Christmas brunch, I continued to eagerly await the Christmas celebration—but my waiting was in vain. The kitchen radio played, "O Come All Ye Faithful," "O Tannenbaum," "Silent Night," and "God Rest Ye Merry Gentlemen." Somehow I did not feel rested. I felt churned up, longing for something spiritual. In my innermost being, I quoted the second chapter of Luke, "Glory to God in the highest."

"Yes, Lord, I give You the glory," I said lying on my couch at night and thinking about my first disappointment in America—the American Christmas.

23

Wedding Bells

"Loving family looking for governess," the newspaper ad read which led to my second place of employment. "As a governess you just have to take care of children," everyone told me. "That is easier than what you have been doing."

After an interview with the couple, I met the three young children. They looked like very nice children. I knew I would get along with them really well and accepted the offer. The next day, Marvin and Shirley helped move my belongings into my small but comfortable new room.

On the second day of my new job, I realized that not only did I have to care for the children, but I was asked to do the cooking, washing, and cleaning of the huge home as well. Late in the evening, I fell into bed exhausted. On the first Sunday, I could not tear myself away from all the work to go to church. There was no time to see my fiancé either. I slaved from early morning till late at night. How was I going to do this for six months? I asked myself but was too shy to speak up. If they threw me out, where would I live? On the street?

Determined not to tell anyone about how difficult life was, I tried to keep up with all the jobs that were piled on me; I had to. There were

no choices. Somehow I would endure. When Marvin and Shirley picked me up for church on the second Sunday, I did not tell them anything.

Several weeks into my contract, as I was busy scrubbing floors, the doorbell rang and the lady of the house answered. I heard voices but continued working. Suddenly I looked up to see Marvin, Shirley, and Luther.

"What are you doing here?" I asked surprised.

"We came to move you out of here."

"But you can't do that, I have to stay. I have no place to go to; I am obligated," I stammered.

"You can't argue with us," Marvin said sternly. "We have already talked to your employer. Please take us to your room so we can help you pack. You are going to come and live with us."

A short time later, in the Ekstroms' car, I could no longer control myself; tears flowed freely. "You are close to having a nervous breakdown, Liane," Shirley said. "We had to come and rescue you."

"Do you have any idea how glad I am you did?" I asked. "But how did you know what I was going through?"

"We could read you like a book," Shirley answered.

"What does that mean?"

"Well, we'll let Luther explain that to you."

While staying at the Ekstroms, I checked out a babysitting agency. After an interview, my name was added to their file. I would be called every time they had an assignment for me, which happened quite often. I later rented a small room for fifteen dollars per week in a quaint Cape Cod-style housing development. Transportation was my greatest problem. If I was not able to walk to my employer's home, get a ride from them, or take a bus, Luther or the Ekstroms had to take me to work. Several weeks into my independent life, bigger jobs were offered. One family with four children, including a newborn, employed me for four weeks with a daily payment of sixteen dollars.

On affluent Long Island, parents traveled frequently and needed reliable child care. After my reputation had spread among customers, I decided to break away from the agency and strike out on my own. My opportunities increased as families began to schedule their vacations according to my availability. Even the Weavers asked me to take care of the boys for several weeks and paid, as did everyone else, ten dollars per day. I enjoyed living like a queen in beautiful homes, eating the finest food, entertaining children, and just washing dishes. Most of my employers had cleaning ladies.

On the rare days I was home, I had begun sewing my wedding gown on a machine I purchased for sixty dollars. The cost of the satin and French lace was thirty dollars. Saturday, October 19, was to be our wedding day.

After the service one Sunday morning, a lady approached me in the church aisle and said, "You looked so sad today, Liane, up there in the choir loft. What is the matter?"

"Oh," I said, "I guess I was thinking of home. Today is communion Sunday in Germany too."

"Why don't your parents come to America?"

"Well, it isn't that easy," I confessed. "They would have to have sponsors, and who would sponsor a whole family?"

"We'll sponsor them," she immediately said.

I must have been dreaming. Someone wanted to pave the way for my parents to come to America? I continued talking to this lady and, indeed, she was serious about sponsorship. Quickly I mailed off a letter to Germany and began to await a reply.

"Mutti is excited about the prospect of going to America," Vati wrote, "but my objections remain the same. I am still doing volunteer work for the civil defense department in hopes that this will lead to a paid job. Our future is wholly in the Lord's hands. We will continue to trust Him."

Luther and I decided to help Vati come to America for the wedding by paying for part of his voyage. Here, we would go job hunting with him and find reactions of prospective employers toward older immigrants. Vati accepted the offer, and Mutti added that with her having to remain in Germany, October 19 would be one of the saddest days of her life. "When you are a mother someday, Schäfle, you'll understand. But I wish you and Luther the Lord's blessing as you start walking together. Lord willing, we'll see each other again here on earth."

Since I had never witnessed an American wedding but knew it was different from a German ceremony, Luther and I planned to attend the wedding of friends of some church members, people we had never met before. Unfortunately, the distance to that town in New Jersey was much farther than we had anticipated, and we got there just as the ceremony had ended. "No problem," Shirley and my bridesmaids said. "We know all about weddings."

In September our pastor wrote a letter asking me to meet him at his church office on the twenty-seventh and return the books I had borrowed. After Luther and I had chatted with him in his office for a short time, the pastor said, "I think we should go downstairs to the fellowship hall." Presuming it was to discuss the reception which was to be held there, all three of us started down the steps with me leading the way.

"Why is it so dark down here?" I asked the pastor as my feet groped for the steps that led into utter darkness. When I opened the door, suddenly cameras flashed and voices yelled, "Surprise!" "What is everyone doing here in the darkness?" I stammered.

"We are here to give you a bridal shower," Shirley answered while someone turned on the lights, and she led the shaking honored guest to a chair.

"A what?" I asked.

"A shower."

I knew only three definitions for showers—rain showers, taking a shower, and showers of blessings. This was a totally new one to me. After I had received a drink of water and had somewhat recovered, I began to identify all the ladies who had come to honor me. There was Mrs. Weaver, her elderly neighbor who helped me pin my wedding gown, the lady who offered to sponsor my family, Shirley's mom, my three bridesmaids, and thirty-five other ladies. My future would be filled with the most wonderful gifts from so many ladies—silver of all kinds, bed linens, table linens, kitchen supplies, towels, and much more. To think that my husband-to-be had helped plot this wonderful surprise! I surely was glad that I had just a few days earlier moved into our one-bedroom apartment. There would not have been space in my little room for all of the beautiful gifts.

When I answered the phone a few days after the shower, one of the elderly church ladies angrily said, "Now, Liane, you told me that I could decorate the arbor with ivy for your wedding, didn't you?"

"Yes, that is what we talked about."

"But now Mrs. Ex said she is going to decorate it. She says, she knows how to do it better." On and on she complained and told me about the war that had broken out because of our wedding.

"If I had known that our wedding would cause so much trouble," I said crying, "we probably would have eloped. I would never have thought that Christians fight over something like that. You two ladies have to work that problem out yourselves. I wanted this wedding, the first in our new church, to be a special occasion for everyone. I am a lover of peace, not war."

When Vati arrived from Germany, all the preparations for the wedding had been made—the gown was done, the seven fancy organdy aprons for the serving girls finished—and I had time to spend with him. One lady who wanted me to care for her children begged and begged

for us to postpone the wedding so that she and her husband could go to Europe.

"What will you do when we are on our honeymoon?" Luther asked Vati one evening at the dinner table.

"I plan to borrow someone's bicycle and go to my sister in New Jersey."

"By bike?"

"Yes," he said. "I like to bicycle. It'll probably take me awhile, but I'll get there—eventually."

Both Luther and I looked at each other. How could Vati know? He had never seen congested New York City and the polluted Lincoln Tunnel. After explaining things to him, Luther said, "We'll have to find someone to take you to your sister. It is impossible to go there by bike."

While Luther worked, Vati and I took a train or bus and started job hunting during the few days before the wedding. Everywhere we went the comments were the same, "He is fifty-one years old and doesn't speak English? Sorry, we have nothing for him."

"But he will learn English," I said.

"Sorry."

Disappointed, we gave up our search. "We'll try again after the wedding, Vati," I said. "In the meantime, however, I will have to teach you a few English phrases so that you can talk to our wedding guests. You already know 'Thank you' and . . ."

"Please," he finished.

"Yes, Vati, I used to say 'please' for a long time, but the correct phrase is 'you are welcome.' 'Please' is usually just used in a sentence; it is a request."

"You are welcome—that sounds funny."

"I know, Vati, I felt the same way. But that is correct. 'Please' is used in connection with a request such as 'pass the butter, please.'"

"The phrase you absolutely have to master before the wedding is, 'I am very glad to meet you.'" We practiced and practiced that sentence. At the reception of our wedding, I was quite proud of Vati when folks made it a special point to tell me how beautifully my father spoke English. All he said was "I am very glad to meet you." No one seemed to realize that this was almost the extent of his knowledge of English.

One day after the wedding, on our way to Florida in the little blue Volkswagen, I got sick and later learned that I had the Asian flu. In a small cabin outside of Washington, DC, I laid with a high fever while my husband and a nurse saw me suffer through the entire honeymoon. After returning home we found out that our best man and Tante Martha, who had taken Mutti's place, also had become ill the day after the wedding. The Lord was gracious in holding the disease back until after the ceremony and letting us live, while hundreds of people died during the 1957 flu epidemic.

By the time Vati's departure date for Germany had arrived, we had unsuccessfully checked into many job possibilities for him in New Jersey and New York. Not even a leather tannery, nor the M&M Company in Hackettstown, New Jersey, would hire him.

Sitting next to my husband and Vati at church on his last Sunday in America was a happy yet sad day for me. "This do in remembrance of me," the pastor read from the Bible during the communion service.

"Yes, Lord, I do remember Your suffering on the cross for me. Thank You for Your sacrifice. And now I look forward to Your coming again, just as I had looked forward to Vati's coming. But now he is leaving again. Lord, why can't Vati and Mutti come to America?"

"You see, child," the Lord seemed to say, "your Dad isn't willing yet."

After the service, Vati was again assured that he had a sponsor in America for the whole family, and with Dieter emigrating to Canada the following April, there were only four to be sponsored.

"What about you now, Vati, where do you stand in regard to America?" I asked.

"I do like what little I have seen of your vast country, but I also realize that learning a language at my age isn't easy. And, of course, the job situation is very sad for someone like me as we have seen."

"But the leather goods business isn't improving."

"You are right. It is on a continuously faster decline. But I am still counting on the civil defense job. The Lord knows about our future, Liane.

"Trust in the LORD with all thine heart;
And lean not unto thine own understanding.
In all thy ways acknowledge him,
And he shall direct thy paths. (Prov. 3:5–6)

"That is my verse.

"America, and all those I have had the privilege of meeting, have been wonderful to me as well as to you. But only the Lord knows if this will be our homeland someday. I surely don't.

"I am so glad that you have such a nice Christian husband. The Lord is surely blessing you. Who would have ever thought that you'd stay in America? You were so adamant about returning to Germany. Your in-laws are wonderful people too."

"They surely are. I could have looked everywhere and probably not found any as kind and wonderful as they are."

"Your father-in-law and I were trying to make each other understood on the day of the wedding. He had a tiny English-German dictionary and while with one hand pointing at you, he pointed at the word *beautiful* with the other."

"That is funny, Vati, talking about me behind my back. I am glad my friends made a movie and tape of the wedding. When we send it to

you, you can all look at an America wedding with its uniquely different customs."

Vati's departure saddened my heart, but I rejoiced in the fact of being married. Shopping for drapery, bedspread, and upholstery fabric gave me great joy. The 1890-bedroom furniture, which was given to us, looked great with the blue satin bedspread, daisy print dust ruffle, and matching curtains. Our circle of friends increased along with visitors to our home.

Shortly before Christmas, a letter arrived from Germany saying, "Our business is continuing on a downward slide. We were forced to start bankruptcy procedures. A few weeks ago, we began taking steps toward emigrating to America. Only the Lord knows our future. He is in control. He knows why He is forcing us to total financial ruin. We may not ever learn the reason we have to go through this. We are praying for you and Luther. Please pray for us that we may remain in His will. If it is God's will, we may see you next year."

Free at Last

"**W**elcome to America!" the four of us said almost in unison when Vati, Mutti, Marlies, and Udo set foot on American soil at New York Harbor. The sun, warming a cool day in May, testified to all the hugging, warmth, and love in our hearts for one another. Two years and four months had slipped into eternity since I last saw Mutti as well as my brother and sister. Marlies looked so grown-up with her permanent, and my little brother was no longer little.

When I tried to introduce everyone, Mutti said through me, her interpreter, "We already know Luther, Marvin, and Shirley from the wedding movie. I am so glad to meet you all in person. So you came to pick us up; that is kind of you."

"How was your voyage?" Luther asked.

"It was wonderful, absolutely wonderful. The food was unbelievable," everyone except Mutti agreed. She was seasick throughout most of the journey.

"Schäfle," Mutti whispered, "are you by any chance expecting a baby?"

"Yes, Mutti. Lord willing, you are going to become grandparents in October." Mutti's eyes filled with tears as she hugged me.

"You don't have much luggage," I said.

"No," Vati replied, "we had to sell all but these few personal belongings in order to pay for our voyage. We do, however, have a knitting machine. We figured if I don't get a job, Mutti and I will knit socks and sell them."

Quickly everything was loaded into the Ekstroms' car and ours. Then we all headed toward Sea Cliff where America's newest immigrants would start a new life.

"That is your new home down there on the cliffs," I said. "It is the guesthouse of the folks who live up there on the hill. All those steep steps lead to the house of your sponsors." Slowly, and almost reverently, we all walked down the stone steps toward the cottage, as Luther opened the door to my parents' first home in the land of the free. After all of us filed in, I apologized. "I am sorry, it still smells smoky in here. But it is a miracle that this house didn't burn down last night. The Lord had His hand in preserving it.

"Last night, after 11:00 o'clock, something began to trouble me. 'Let's go and see if everything is perfect for Vati and Mutti's arrival tomorrow,' I said to Luther. 'How about stopping at the house again to make sure?'

"'Everything was fine earlier this evening,' Luther said. 'What could have changed by now?' He decided, however, that we'd go again. On the walk down the steps to the house, we already smelled smoke. After Luther unlocked and opened the door, billows of smoke rolled over us. 'Oh no!' I said aghast. 'Fire! Where is the fire?' We searched for quite a while before Luther finally found the cause, the burning refrigerator.

"So, my dear ones, you see, the Lord saved this little home for you."

Hanging over a steep cliff, the back porch overlooked a bay on the northern shore of Long Island. Large maple trees spread their canopies

over the immigrants' home and the rocky shore. Sea Cliff, an old, quaint village prided itself in the Bohack supermarket, just a few minutes from my folks, a few shops, and winding, narrow roads leading past Victorian-style homes nestled on uneven lots.

Work at the Sperry Gyroscope Company continued for Luther as usual, while I spent my days introducing Vati, Mutti, and Marlies to the American way of life and helping them in their search for employment. Mutti was hired immediately as an assembly-line seamstress in a dingy Glen Cove garment factory. As a meticulous seamstress and tailor, however, she was not satisfied with doing piecework. Her nerves became raw in just one week on the job. At night her sleep was disturbed by the sound of countless noisy machines buzzing in her head. "We'll look for another job," I tried to comfort her after the sixth workday. The following morning our search began again.

Marlies started working in a household for thirty-five dollars per week. My father-in-law, an educator all his life, suggested that Udo should start school at the German grade level. "He'll learn English quickly," Dad Brown told me, "and will fall right into the academic life. It sounds to me as if he is quite a smart young man."

After hunting down various job leads for Vati without success, we returned to an employment agency. They offered him a position in New York City cleaning office buildings. In order for Vati to arrive in the city by subway at 6:00 a.m., he had to get up at 4:00 a.m. Patiently he worked there in spite of all the obstacles thrown in his way. "Emil, we are telling you for the last time . . . you are working too much," his coworkers scolded him again. "Take it easy like we do. You are making us look bad, and we are not going to stand for that. Just work a little and then rest like we do. You Germans are working too hard."

"But I get paid," Vati told them. "I have to work."

"No, you don't. We won't let you."

In June our whole family took a trip to Niagara Falls to meet Dieter, who, as an immigrant to Canada, was not permitted to cross the border. While Luther was driving through upstate New York, Mutti suddenly said, "I guess we are in the Quaker state now."

"Where do you get that idea, Mutti?" I asked.

"It says that right there on the red barn," she replied, pointing at the large sign.

"We do have to learn a lot, Mutti," I admitted while trying not to burst out loud with laughter. "That is not a state, Mutti. That is a motor oil company." We all laughed then.

Overlooking the Falls from the Canadian side and watching it spill thousands of gallons of water into the small Niagara River was breathtaking. *How great Thou art,* I thought. *How marvelous Your creation, how powerful, how unique! No human could conceive such wonder. And no human mind could have ever predicted that six refugees from East Prussia and one new family member, an American, would admire Your handiwork on the border of the "land of the free."* All of us were caught up by the emotional drama of a family reunion set and directed by God Himself at the stage of Niagara Falls.

Dieter, we learned, had labored as a carpenter for three months in Toronto and was about to start working as an electronics technician. "In one year," he told us, "I expect to have built up enough capital to start my own business." Dieter's friend had married and stayed in Germany.

The joyous Niagara Falls reunion quickly came to an end. It was a wonderful day, and Vati thanked the Lord unashamedly for it.

While I was babysitting for a Jewish family one evening, the lady inquired about my family, their job situations, and language problems. I told her about Vati, his long train and subway rides, the harassment at work, and his willingness to take almost any job closer to Sea Cliff. She listened intently and then said, "I know of a German import-export

company right here on the island. Why don't you take your dad there for an interview?"

When Vati and I went to that company, he was hired on the spot. He gave up his cleaning job in New York City and started working for a company whose owner was German as were most of the twenty-one employees. The language spoken at the workplace—German!

Mutti, in the meantime, settled into a sewing job at a sweater shop in Locust Valley. Every morning she and I took the train from right below our apartment and traveled to the store where we spent the day in a backroom, hand-decorating cashmere sweaters with velvet, satin, or grosgrain ribbon or appliquéing antique embroidery. Finally, with the increase of Mutti's vocabulary, she no longer needed an interpreter, and I began staying at home. Mutti's excellent workmanship and speed with which she finished a project brought high praises from her boss and customers but envy from the other seamstress.

Members of our church responded very kindly to my parents. For my folks, however, attending an American church where they understood little was difficult. "The moment you forget about translating everything you hear, and start thinking in English, you'll begin learning very quickly," I told them. "It took me about six months to come to that point. By Christmas, you should be able to begin learning English more rapidly."

"That will be great," Mutti said. "What we learned from records in Germany surely did not help us very much when we arrived here. But we'll find our way into the language quickly, Schäfle, you just wait and see."

At my folks' apartment in Sea Cliff, plans were made for the future. Purchasing a television set so that learning English would progress at a faster pace seemed to be a luxury, yet a priority item. Next on the list was the purchase of a car so that Luther could get out of the taxi business. In the meantime, the knitting machine remained solidly packed in the

shipping box while Vati and Mutti were earning and saving highly-prized dollars.

Vati, not only a businessman but one who believed in biblical business principles, did not, however, put all the incoming funds into a savings account. Some of the money he sent to his former creditors in Germany. "They lost money because of our bankruptcy," he said. "I'll acknowledge my regrets and send them whatever I possibly can."

Marvin and Shirley continued to play a great part in all our lives. My folks' first beach party in America was arranged by my friends. Unfortunately, the day was unusually cool and the wind seemed to enjoy whipping sand into all our food; even the hot dogs Vati cooked in a small pot crunched when we bit into them.

On a September day, we were all invited to the Ekstroms' home. I told Shirley I'd bring a marble cake. As I walked into their apartment with that in hand, voices yelled "Surprise!" so loud that I began to feel faint from shock. This was a baby shower—the first I had ever attended—for the Brown baby. How exciting to have Mutti share in this special event with me and help me later figure out what to do with seventeen uniquely beautiful blankets and so many other gifts. Only in America, I was sure, would folks do such touching things for an immigrant.

On the evening of October 4, 1958, Luther and I drove my folks from store to store in search of the best television bargain. After returning to their place, I baked a cake, and we chatted before finally calling it a day at 11:00 p.m. "We'll pick you up for church at the regular time tomorrow morning," Luther said.

Instead of picking my family up for church, however, Luther called them to say, "Sorry you have to miss church today. I know you are waiting for me, but I can't pick you up this morning."

"Why not? What is the matter?" Mutti asked.

"Just a few minutes ago," Luther told her, "you became grandparents. You have a grandson. His name is Carey Vaughn."

What a time of rejoicing and thanksgiving that was in the North Shore Hospital of Manhasset later in the afternoon! Not only did my family begin a new life in America, but another branch was added to the family tree, a branch that, like a banyan tree, would eventually plunge its roots deeply into American soil.

After Vati and Mutti gained their independence from us by having purchased and paid cash for their first car, a Chevrolet, they checked out a German church in Woodside someone had told them about. "It was just like being in Germany," they bubbled after their first attendance there. "We like your church," Mutti said, "but we just don't understand enough to feel at home." With sad hearts, Luther and I saw them leave and drive thirty miles to a church in which they felt "at home." Faithfully they attended all the weekly services.

One day Luther and I visited my parents' church. We slid into the pew where Mutti, Marlies, and Udo were already seated; I sat between Mutti and Luther. As the service opened, I began to weep, seeing Vati at the organ playing with all the stops pulled and his feet dashing across the pedals.

A mighty fortress is our God, a bulwark never failing;
Our helper He, amid the flood of mortal ills prevailing.
(Luther, "A Mighty Fortress Is Our God")

While the large organ pipes and the walls of the sanctuary vibrated, people sat like statues listening to the powerful piece that was followed by a Bach rendition.

America—how great thou art! My innermost being sighed while my body trembled with joy. I felt as if I had been touched by God Himself. I told myself, *I will never take this land for granted. I will not be ashamed of my tears when I view your flag. Your stars and stripes will continue to remind me of the fear and oppression we had to endure in order to better appreciate you. America—your citizens suffered so that I can enjoy your*

freedom this very day. Someday soon, I want to become your citizen. I hope you will count me worthy. America—no longer do I think about you and view you from afar; you are mine now—my homeland—your people are my people. Your freedom is my freedom to enjoy and defend.

How good You are to us, Lord! my soul whispered. *Lord, I will never be able to comprehend Your blessings. I am offering these tears as a thank You for Your goodness and grace to me . . . and my family!*

After Vati was asked to take over the church choir, it began growing rapidly. With only forty seats in the loft, there was always a waiting list for prospective choir members. "Your dad," Vati's pastor told me one day, "was the answer to our prayers. For seven years this church had been praying for a German organist and choir director."

Epilogue

Emil and Emmy prospered in America. Through determination and hard work, they quickly purchased their first car and a home. Emil worked for the German Brinkmann company until his retirement. Emmy thrilled her upper-class clientele with hand-decorated cashmere sweaters in Locust Valley, New York. After retirement Emil and Emmy moved to Florida to fulfill her dream of "walking under palms." Their four married children, grandchildren, and great-grandchildren celebrated Emil and Emmy's sixtieth wedding anniversary at their home in Paradise Palms, Boca Raton, Florida.

Throughout the years, both Emmy and Liane crafted exquisite Christmas décor to raise funds for their Russian missionary efforts. Emmy's husband wondered why she always had to keep so busy. "I have finally forgiven the Russians," she replied. They purchased and distributed hundreds of Russian Bibles, donated funds to build a Ukrainian church, and helped support several Russian families.

Emil and Emmy never stopped singing the praises of America and the freedom God allowed them to experience. Emil was promoted to join the heavenly choir at the age of eighty-nine—but we wouldn't be

surprised if he directs the choir! Almost completing her ninety-seventh year on this earth, Emmy joined her husband in heaven.

Luther and Liane Brown moved from Long Island to upstate New York. Upon Luther's retirement from IBM, they moved closer to the Guddats in Florida. Thirty years later, they celebrated their sixtieth wedding anniversary in their new hometown of Chattanooga, Tennessee. They have three children, nine grandchildren, and an ever-increasing number of great-grandchildren.

Liane receives many invitations to speak at churches, schools, colleges, ladies' retreats, and civic organizations. "Whenever I am asked to speak somewhere," Liane says, "I am excited about telling what God has done in our lives. I am also happy to be able to thank the American people for having helped the Germans after WWII by sending clothing and food. As a speaker, I am thankful for the opportunity to share my joy of being a citizen of the United States and to convey my appreciation for the true freedom our family has found in this great land."

Order Information

REDEMPTION
P R E S S

To order additional copies of this book, please visit
www.redemption-press.com.
Also available on Amazon.com and BarnesandNoble.com
or by calling toll-free 1-844-2REDEEM.

ORDER INFORMATION

REDEMPTION PRESS

To order additional copies of this book, please visit
www.redemption-press.com.
Also available on Amazon.com and BarnesandNoble.com
or by calling toll-free 1-844-2REDEEM.